IRISH ART

&

MODERNISM

1 8 8 0 - 1 9 5 0

S . B . K E N N E D Y

Published for

The Hugh Lane Municipal Gallery of Modern Art, Dublin

by

The Institute of Irish Studies at

The Queen's University of Belfast

Published 1991
The Institute of Irish Studies
The Queen's University of Belfast

British Library Cataloguing in Publication Data
Kennedy, S.B.
    Irish art and modernism 1880–1950
    I. Title
    709.415

Exhibition:
Hugh Lane Municipal Gallery of Modern Art, Dublin, 20 September–10 November 1991; Ulster Museum, Belfast, 22 November 1991–26 January 1992.

ISBN 0 85389 402 7

Printed by W. & G. Baird Ltd., Greystone Press, Antrim

Louis le Brocquy, *The Spanish Shawl*

IRISH ART AND MODERNISM
1880 – 1950

FOREWORD

The contribution being made by Irish artists to the development of Modern Art was first brought to public attention by Sir Hugh Lane in 1904, with an exhibition he mounted at the Guildhall, London. This exhibition identified as Irish, many leading artists who were then working in Britain and on the continent. The exhibition was a great success with eighty thousand visitors paying admission and it further strengthened Sir Hugh's argument for the establishment in Dublin of a Municipal Gallery of Modern Art where Modern Classics could be viewed by all. The Municipal Gallery first opened its doors in 1908, at Clonmell House, Harcourt Street. In 1933 it moved to its present residence, Charlemont House, where it continues to house an exciting and representative collection of Modern Art.

Now, in 1991, with this exhibition Irish Art and Modernism, the Hugh Lane Gallery of Modern Art presents an opportunity to review the work of and role played by Irish artists in a European context, between the 1880s and 1950, and to contemplate the effects the revolutionary movements had on the development of an Irish School of Painting. In his excellent scholarly book S.B. Kennedy charts the development and influence of the Modern Movement on Irish Art. This publication, which is the culmination of many years of research promises to be an important source of reference for the period.

Dublin Corporation joins me in congratulating Dr. Kennedy on his excellent work and was delighted to publish it in conjunction with the Institute of Irish Studies. Credit for initiating this exhibition must go to Miss Ethna Waldron, former Curator of the Gallery. We are most grateful to her for her foresightedness. I would also like to thank Christina Kennedy who skillfully co-ordinated the entire exhibition; Patricia Flavin whose quiet efficiency proved invaluable, Caitriona Smyth and Anne Stewart, Exhibitions Officer at the Ulster Museum who was always at hand to help. I would also like to thank our sponsors; Bulmers for their generous financial assistance towards mounting the exhibition in Dublin, Dublin '91 for assistance and Aer Lingus for sponsorship of transatlantic transport.

We are most grateful to those lenders who have generously provided us with works for the exhibition.

Barbara Dawson
Director
Hugh Lane Municipal Gallery of Modern Art

To

DOREEN AND ALISON

PREFACE AND ACKNOWLEDGEMENTS

THIS book was originally written in a different form as a doctoral dissertation at Trinity College, Dublin. Later I began to re-work it for publication and shortly afterwards Miss Ethna Waldron, formerly Curator of the Hugh Lane Municipal Gallery of Modern Art, asked me to continue the text as planned but to append a catalogue section and to arrange an exhibition based on the text. Thereafter, our common aim was that the work might, to some extent, have a use after the exhibition as a source of reference.

My reasons for writing the book were two-fold. Firstly, there seems to be a need for a comprehensive one-volume history of Irish art of the period which I have addressed, and in that period, it seems to me, the advance of what is generally termed 'Modernism' dominated all other developments in Irish art. Secondly, at our present remove in time from the events, political and otherwise, of the early years of this century it is possible to discern a distinct Irish 'school' of art and to define its characteristics in a manner which has hitherto proved illusive.

The structure of the book falls into two broad sections: namely, those chapters which form the bulk of the text and which discuss the development of Modernism in Ireland; and what I have called the 'Academic Tradition', that is, the tradition which, to a large extent, Modernism cast aside in its advance. Each of these lines of development acts as a rod by which we can measure the progress or retreat of the other.

In preparing both the main text and the catalogue section I owe a great debt to innumerable people and institutions for their help and although I should like to thank everyone, they are far more than I can mention. My greatest debt, however, is to Professor Anne Crookshank of Trinity College for initially suggesting that I should embark upon this research. She supervised my original dissertation and kindly agreed to read several chapters from the present work. Her comments have always been perspicacious and greatly valued by me. I am much indebted, too, to Ethna Waldron for her role in this and for giving the whole a clear purpose and direction. As the text developed it has been read at different stages by Bruce Arnold and Ted Hickey and I am grateful to them for their comments and suggestions which, in terms of both accuracy and style, have saved me from a number of possible embarrassments. All remaining errors are my own.

I must also acknowledge the staff and members of the following institutions who helped me in various ways: Armagh County Museum; Irish and Local Studies Department, Central Library, Belfast; Public Records Office of Northern Ireland,

Belfast; Trustees and Director of the Ulster Museum, Belfast, and my colleagues in the Art Department there, in particular Ann Stewart; Servite Priory, Benburb; Vincentian Fathers, Celbridge; Clonmel Art Gallery; Crawford Art Gallery, Cork; University College, Cork; Drogheda Public Library; Aras An Uachartain, Dublin; Archbishop's House, Dublin; Blackrock College, Dublin; Hugh Lane Municipal Gallery of Modern Art, Dublin; National Archives, Dublin; National Gallery of Ireland, Dublin; National Library of Ireland, Dublin; National Maternity Hospital, Dublin; Public Record Office, Dublin; Rotunda Hospital, Dublin; Royal Hibernian Academy of Arts, Dublin; Royal Dublin Society; The Board of Trinity College, Dublin; University College, Dublin; Medical Missionaries of Mary, Dundalk; Limerick Art Gallery; New York Public Library; Jesuit Retreat House, Tullamore; Garter Lane Arts Centre, Waterford.

Apart from others listed in the bibliography, the following individuals all answered my letters of enquiry, showed me their collections and freely gave their hospitality and kindness, and a number of them have given permission to quote from copyright and archival material in their care (every effort has been made to trace copyright holders, and I should be grateful to hear from any who have escaped my notice): Vaughan Biscoe, Michael Bowles, the late Thea Boyd, the late Edwin Bryson, H. Bryson, Tom Carr, Rhoda Coghill, George Connell, Dr. H.E. Counihan, Elizabeth Harry Crooke, Igor Cusack, Roy Cusack, Jennifer Davidson, Myles Digby, Oliver Dowling, Lord Dunraven, Vera Exley, Mrs. Eyre-Maunsell, Sir John Esmond, Denise Ferran, R.R. Figgis, Carmel Flynn, Anny Lewinter Frankl, Rowel Friers, Muriel Gahan, Brigid Ganly, Liam Gaynor, Raymond Gilmore, John Griffith, Richard Guy, Noel Gwozdz, Stanley Halliday, Mons. John Hanly, Jenni Haughton, the late Henry Healy, W. Heaney, Lord Hemphill, Kathleen Henry, Dorothy Herdman, Patrick Hickey, David Hone, Mrs. R. Hughes, Diane Hunter, Elizabeth Hunter, R.B. Jackson, the late John Jordan, Dr. J.B. Kearney, Michael Keating, Peter Lamb, the late W.A.N. MacGeough Bond, Gladys McCabe, Peggy McDonnell, J.L. McQuitty QC, John Madden, Annette Meenan, Noel Moffett, Kevin Murnaghan, James Myler, the late Jim Nawn, Lady Catherine Nelson, Tom Nisbet, James Nolan, P. O'Boyle, Sheila O'Clery, Dr. H. O'Connor, N. O'Donoghue, E. O'Driscoll, the late Seán O'Faolain, John O'Gorman, Joan O'Mara, Stephen O'Mara, Elizabeth Ormsby, Donnchadh O'Suilleabáin, W. O'Sullivan, Victor Ouimette, Scarlett Pfau, Sheila Pim, Hilary Pyle, Fr. Sean Quigley, Christopher Rakoczi, Dr. A. Reford, J.P. Reihill, Toni del Renzio, the late Miss Shelah Richards, Thomas Ryan PRHA, Anita Shelbourne, Elizabeth Solterer, Beatrice Somerville-Large, Ralph Spence, T.E. Spence, W.G. Spencer, the late Patric Stevenson, Ann M. Stewart, John Taylor, Nesbit Waddington, the late Victor Waddington, Mervyn Wall, George Walsh, Barbara Warren, Ruth Whitaker, Terence de Vere White. To this list I should like to add the late Cecil King, who first recalled in outline the rich texture of the period to me.

Throughout the greater part of this project I have had the confidence and encouragement of Ms. Barbara Dawson, Director of the Hugh Lane Gallery, and I am grateful to her and her staff, notably Ms. Christina Kennedy, for seeing the whole thing come to fruition. Bryan Rutledge of the Ulster Museum produced the excellent photographs which illustrate much of the book and my thanks are due, too, to those other photographers who are acknowledged elsewhere. In the actual publishing of the book I have been guided by Dr. Brian Walker of the Institute of Irish Studies at The Queen's Univeristy, Belfast, and by Mr. Bryan McCabe of W. & G. Baird Ltd.

and I am indebted to them for their forbearance in the face of my constant queries and for seeing to the appearance of the final publication. Finally, I owe a special debt to my wife and daughter who have borne with me patiently during the long gestation of the book, and to whom I dedicate it with love.

S.B.K.

Seaforde, Co. Down
April 27, 1991

CONTENTS

ABBREVIATIONS

ARHA	Associate of the Royal Hibernian Academy of Arts
b.l.	bottom left
BMAG	Belfast Museum & Art Gallery (now Ulster Museum)
b.r.	bottom right
c.	*circa*
cata. no.	Catalogue number
CEMA	Council for the Encouragement of Music and the Arts (later the Arts Council of Northern Ireland)
Coll.	Collection
Exh.	Exhibited
HLMG	Hugh Lane Municipal Gallery of Modern Art, Dublin (formerly the Municipal Gallery of Modern Art)
IELA	Irish Exhibition of Living Art (all exhibitions held in Dublin)
Inscr.	Inscribed
Lit.	Literature
MGMA	Municipal Gallery of Modern Art, Dublin (now the Hugh Lane Municipal Gallery of Modern Art)
n.d.	not dated
NGI	National Gallery of Ireland
NLI	National Library of Ireland
n.p.	not paginated
Prov.	Provenance
Repr.	Reproduced
RDS	Royal Dublin Society
RHA	Royal Hibernian Academy of Arts, Dublin/Academician of the Royal Hibernian Academy
TCD	Trinity College, Dublin
t.r.	top right
UCD	University College, Dublin
UM	Ulster Museum

All references to the *Irish Times* are to its Northern edition. Unless stated otherwise, all works of art referred to are in private collections.

INTRODUCTION

THE popular view of the development of Irish art in the first half of the twentieth century is that it was little touched by the theories and ideas of the Modern Movement save for the efforts of one or two individuals, principally Evie Hone and Mainie Jellett, who are usually portrayed as valiant souls working amid a sea of apathy and hostility. Even Jack B. Yeats' familiarity with Modernism has been denied. This view, as is often the case with widely held generalities, includes enough elements of truth to have remained hitherto unchallenged. However, as soon as one begins to examine specific details of the period and the work of a number of artists it becomes clear that there was in Ireland a substantial knowledge and understanding of Modernism in many quarters. The primary purpose, therefore, of this study is to uncover the historical facts that have been buried beneath the popular view.

The rise of the Modern Movement in Ireland in the 1880s co-incided almost exactly with the beginnings of the Literary Revival. Like that Revival, it was rooted in the Protestant middle classes who had both the leisure and sufficient money to travel abroad and were thus able to absorb avant-garde ideas. But whereas the Literary Revival was closely associated with the separatist revolutionary politics of the time, the Modern Movement in art ignored these and derived sustenance from innovative trends elsewhere. Thus by 1922, after the achievement of political independence, when the Literary Revival had largely run its course and the Nationalist movement sought to consolidate its position by looking inwards, above all to the traditional culture of the west, the more progressive artists had forged a broader and less isolationist philosophy.

The Literary Revival, and indeed Celtic revivalism in general in the second half of the nineteenth century, had little impact on the visual arts—that is, excepting the decorative arts—in Ireland. That the revivalists, J.M. Synge, W.B. Yeats and Lady Gregory in particular, unlike their painter-contemporaries, could look to a *tradition* of literature and folklore, especially that of the west, largely explains this. Nevertheless, none of the painters such as Walter Osborne, Nathaniel Hone, Sir John Lavery or Sir William Orpen took much interest in politics and even Jack B. Yeats, who is often cast as the painter of revolutionary Ireland, was really an observer, there was nothing prescriptive in his work.

The period from the 1880s until the 1950s in Ireland was greatly coloured by ideas of national identity. Those who embraced Modernism, in so far as they thought about such things at all, felt that the new art, which was internationalist in outlook, best expressed the spirit of the age and the opportunities created by political independence; but their more nationalist minded contemporaries felt that the only appropriate themes for a country seeking self-sufficiency were those drawn from its own traditions. It is the pull between these two sides that accounts for many of the tensions of the period, but the overall thrust in the visual arts, unlike the literary arts, was, nevertheless, inspired by the international Modern Movement.

Arguably too much effort during the period was wasted by artists and critics alike on pondering how to create a distinct Irish school of art. Instead they should have concentrated their energies on their work and drawn inspiration from the world around them in a manner which might have allowed a distinct school to emerge of its own accord. Yet in a real sense a distinct Irish school *did* exist as, hopefully, this study will show; but it was not the quasi-sentimental, nationalist offering which, at heart, many longed for.

Essentially the closing years of the nineteenth century saw the Modern Movement in Ireland in embryonic form and its early development, as we have said, paralleled that of the Literary Revival, although it was more exoteric than the latter. The first decade of the twentieth century, stimulated by the work of Sir Hugh Lane, saw growing interest in what was regarded as a need to establish a distinct Irish school of art concomitant with that of the Literary Revival. But Lane's efforts, which brought about the Dublin Municipal Gallery of Modern Art, paradoxically emphasized the divergence of opinion between the Modernist viewpoint and that of the more nationalist elements in the community. It was only after the outbreak of the Second World War that Modernism may be said to represent the dominant way ahead. In a sense the whole essence of this era in Ireland was swept aside and forgotten by the radical changes which, from the mid-1950s onwards, affected all aspects of post-war society in the countries of the Western world. Much of the rhetoric of those later years now appears less convincing than it did at the time and so we are now well placed to reassess the rich texture of the earlier period.

Our starting date, the 1880s, coincides too with the beginning of one of the most momentous periods in Irish history which culminated in the Anglo-Irish Treaty of 1921 and political independence in 1922. Yet, surprisingly, those events had little or no influence on the art scene. Until the late 1930s the country was inward-looking in all its affairs and it was not until the outbreak of the Second World War—or the 'Emergency' as it was termed in neutral parlance—that it began, psychologically at least, to jettison many of the dreams and much of the romance of its early years and to face the world in a more pragmatic manner. That the academic tradition, which trod a path between the two extremes of Modernism and Nationalism in art, survived throughout these years and the period which followed—in part simply by ignoring the tide of events—is, contrary to what one might expect, fortuitous; for not only did it provide at the time a yardstick by which to measure the progress of the new movement, but now that Modernism can be judged as a historical style free from polemics we can see afresh the richness of that alternative tradition. Our terminal date, 1950, has been chosen for convenience because it marks the half century and is close to the publication of Thomas Bodkin's *Report on the Arts in Ireland* which, with the subsequent advent of *An Chomhairle Ealaíon*/The Arts Council of Ireland (1951) and the economic expansion of the 1950s, greatly changed the art scene in Ireland as elsewhere.

The use and meaning of the terms 'Modernism' and the 'Modern Movement' herein are as generally understood, that is, the tenets of the mainstream of art since the time of Manet. Yet we must be careful in assigning such terms to a given period, for periods, as G.M. Trevelyan reminds us, are not historical facts and we must therefore not expect too much rigour from the application of such terms. Nevertheless they have sufficient stability and common currency to be evocative of the essential nature of the period. Modernism was international in character and affected all the arts. For the first time since the Renaissance it represented an abrupt break with tradition and saw the forging of a new set of values and critical criteria. In the visual arts it contained the basis of many sub-movements, of which Impressionism, Post-Impressionism, Symbolism, Fauvism, Cubism, Futurism, Surrealism and Constructivism were the most influential in our period. The Irish Modernists drew their inspiration almost exclusively from Fauvism and Cubism, as those movements had evolved in France. They turned hardly at all to Post-Impressionism or Symbolism; only towards the end of our period did they take any notice of Surrealism and they almost totally ignored contemporary developments in Germany and elsewhere. In Ireland Modernism was not associated with the Arts and Crafts Movement of the late nineteenth century as was the case in England. The Irish Arts and Crafts Movement of the time rather concerned itself with the wider Celtic revival crusade. Consequently early Modernism in Ireland did not have the benefit of an existing critical apparatus, nor was it evangelistic in character, as it was in England. The Irish painters rather *adopted* the new ideas, they did not *question* them. In essence, Modernism was pluralistic and was the antithesis of nineteenth century Naturalism and, by acknowledging the inherent properties of their materials—the flatness of the picture plane, properties of pigments, media, shape and support—and by ceasing to use them descriptively after nature, the artists who embraced it greatly enriched our understanding of the artistic process. That Modernism did not have a more immediate appeal in Ireland is surprising for it was the art of a rapidly changing world which saw many of the social characteristics of the preceeding age disappear and one would imagine that this momentum might have been seized upon by the architects of revolutionary Ireland. But perhaps the ambiguity inherent in its pluralism was too unsettling for them. Significantly, too, for a revolutionary time, no Constructivist art was produced in Ireland until a decade or so after the end of our period. Also, unlike their English and Continental colleagues, none of the Irish Modernists wrote a manifesto or other declaration of policy and Mainie Jellett's writings are the nearest thing we have to such statements which elsewhere figure so prominently in the history of the Modern Movement. Moreover, and again surprisingly for the times, unlike their contemporaries elsewhere, Irish artists never saw Modernism as an expression of a socialist utopia; in Ireland the debate surrounding it was smothered by the quest for national identity.

CHAPTER ONE

AN IRISH SCHOOL OF PAINTING

'I am trying to wake up
these sleepy Irish painters
to do great things . . . '

Hugh Lane in Lady Gregory, *Hugh Lane's life and achievement*
(London, 1921), p. 44.

1884–1901

THE origins of Modernism in the visual arts in Ireland can be traced back to the annual exhibition of the Dublin Sketching Club held in December 1884. That year was the tenth anniversary of the founding of the Club and the members decided, probably in an attempt to raise the standard of their exhibitions by making them less parochial, to invite James McNeill Whistler, John Singer Sargent and two other American painters—Julian Story and Ralph Curtis—to exhibit with them. Their reasons for selecting these particular guests are unknown to us but the sculptor Frederick Lawless, who was a member of the Club, had known Whistler in London a year or so earlier and Walter Osborne, another member, had admired Whistler's work at the Grosvenor Gallery earlier in 1884 and probably they suggested bringing them to Dublin. John Butler Yeats, too, was almost certainly involved in the arrangements.[1] Of these artists Whistler was the most avant-garde. He was one of the most controversial artists of his time and his notorious 'Nocturnes' and other atmospheric compositions of the period were a continual irritation to many critics who held the celebrated Ruskin affair of 1877 still fresh in mind. Whistler had been involved from the beginning in the Modern Movement in painting; he had exhibited in the *Salon des Refusés* in 1863 and numbered Degas, Manet, Monet and Toulouse-Lautrec amongst his friends. Like them, he showed a contempt for the sentimental and anecdotal painting then popular and proclaimed instead that what mattered in painting was not the subject but the colours and other formal structures and patterns in the composition. Since shortly after his move to London in 1863 he had fought the battle for modern art almost single-handedly. That such a controversial figure should have been invited to exhibit at the annual exhibition of an otherwise conservative club is surprising; however, the exhibition brought to Dublin for the first time some of the latest ideas in contemporary painting.

Whistler showed no less than twenty-six paintings—including his subsequently famous *Arrangement in Grey and Black: Portrait of the Painter's Mother* of 1871, the *Arrangement in Grey and Black, No.2: Portrait of Thomas Carlyle*, 1872–3 (cata. no. 1),[2] and *Harmony in Pink and Grey: Portrait of Lady Meux*, 1881–2 (Frick Collection, New York)—more than had hitherto been seen anywhere outside of London. Critical reaction to these works came swiftly and, of the guest exhibitors, Whistler was almost alone in being singled out for discussion. Generally one senses a reluctance on the part of the critics to be specific in their support or condemnation of his work and this, no doubt, stemmed from a lack of understanding of it and a fear of possibly making a *faux pas*. Both the *Irish Times* and the *Freeman's Journal* dismissed his small sketches as being 'mere blotches of colour' but agreed that the larger works, especially the *Mother*, *Carlyle* and *Lady Meux*, were masterly. However, the nub of their criticism was that so many pictures on loan, hung as a group and seperated from the other works in the exhibition, constituted a rebuke of the more amateurish work of the Club members and were therefore inappropriate in the context. 'The exhibition ought to be one thing or the other,' said the *Irish Times*. 'It ought to be a loan exhibition pure and simple, or an exhibition of the year's club work.'[3] But such criticism was never convincingly argued and one senses the writers' uncertainty about their ground. Perhaps a more accurate account of the stir caused by the exhibition was that given some years later by Booth Pearsall, one of the organizers of the exhibition, to Whistler's biographers: 'The whole of Dublin was convulsed,' he said, 'and many went . . . to see the exhibition who rarely went to see any thing of the kind.'[4] Opposition to the exhibition was strong within the Club and some members even drew up a resolution that never again should such pictures be exhibited, but they were out-manoeuvred and Whistler was, in fact, elected an honorary member of the Club. Moreover, he was invited to Dublin to deliver what would have been the first hearing of his Ten O'Clock lecture[5] but the visit did not materialize.

This exhibition had no obvious lasting effect on the Dublin art scene, but it was the first of a number of exhibitions to be held there during the ensuing thirty years which stimulated an awareness of modern painting. But most importantly for the future, it implanted the idea that the best way to raise the standard of Irish art was to expose it to external influences and not to insulate it against them. There was in Ireland, as in Great Britain generally, no tradition of painting to which the more progressive artists could look for stimulus. The academic art promulgated by the Royal Hibernian Academy (RHA) had long degenerated to a form of stasis and most academicians ignored the growing awareness of cultural heritage brought about by the Literary Revival. In the same period, and earlier, many Irish artists had veered away from England to study on the Continent, particularly in France, where they found a stable aesthetic tradition from which to draw on, but when they returned home they frequently experienced great difficulty in having their work accepted for exhibition in the annual Academy and other salons because of the elements of modernity which they had assumed. George Russell, better known by his pseudonym 'AE', a prominent influence on the Literary Revival and himself a painter, later reiterated the need to expose Irish artists to the best of contemporary art from abroad and lamented the fact that no distinct Irish school of painting existed to complement that of the writers. In an open letter, dated 10 September 1898, to the editor of the Dublin *Daily Express* he noted that no Irish artist (he did not mention his own work) had found inspiration in traditional Celtic sources as had the writers. This lack of what he called a 'national' art he blamed on the fact that few great paintings found their way into Irish exhibitions. Consequently there was little to awaken public interest in art and even the Royal Hibernian Academy, he said, suffered from the same malady because there was no appreciation of good art. To remedy this situation he suggested holding an exhibition of paintings representative of recent developments in contemporary art and invited financial and practical support for the project.

The eventual outcome of Russell's letter was the exhibition, *Modern Paintings*, held in Dublin in April 1899.[6] In all eighty-eight works were shown by French, Dutch and English painters of whom the best remembered are Corot, Millet and Daubigny, representing the French landscapists; Courbet and Clausen for Realism; Leighton, Millais, Orchardson and Watts for the Pre-Raphaelite influence; and Degas, Manet, Monet, Wilson Steer and Whistler for Impressionism. From these names it is clear that the exhibition indeed represented the main developments which had taken place in painting in the previous fifty years or so, but for the course of Modernism it was the inclusion of a number of pictures by the French Impressionists that was important. This was the first time paintings by the better known Impressionists were shown in Ireland and the public and press delighted in them.[7] The *Irish Times* praised their sense of freedom, vigour and agility, and thought Whistler's *Miss Alexander*—which had been seen at the Dublin Sketching Club in 1884—'would seize and compel attention in any company.' Generally, it concluded, 'There is not a work of the entire 88 which is not fully deserving of attention'[8] and it hoped for similar exhibitions in the future. Dublin was fortunate to have had such paintings and, by comparison, London, apart from two small exhibitions—twenty 'Impressions' by Claude Monet, shown at the Goupil Gallery in 1889, and paintings by Toulouse-Lautrec shown at the same venue in 1898—saw no such works in quantity until Durand-Ruel organized a comprehensive show of French painting covering the period from Boudin to Cézanne in 1905.

While Russell (AE) ultimately was disappointed in his hopes that the exhibition would kindle a distinct Irish school of painting, it nevertheless emphasized the poverty of the local art scene. Moreover, there was a lack amongst all the critics of any in-depth discussion or analysis of the works on show and this highlights the absence of a critical apparatus. Such criticism as did appear was always couched in terms of generalities, although in this the Irish critics were by no means unique, as is witnessed by the outrage evoked by the London critics some years later at Roger Fry's Post-Impressionist exhibitions of 1910–11 and 1912. But the exhibition represented a further step on the path to public awareness in Ireland of modern painting.

The next step along that path was an exhibition of paintings by Nathaniel Hone and John Butler Yeats held in Dublin during October–November 1901. This was an event of the greatest importance. Indeed, writing about it half a century later, the critic Thomas MacGreevy felt that for him it was 'the inevitable point of departure of the modern Irish School of painting'.[9] The Hone-Yeats exhibition came about through Sarah Purser's exasperation at the hostility of the Royal Hibernian Academy towards all but the most strictly academic art and its persistent neglect of two of its most able members, Nathaniel Hone (1831–1917) and John Butler Yeats (1839–1922).[10] Sarah Purser (1848–1943) had been one of the most prominent portrait painters in Ireland during the late nineteenth century. She studied art in Paris and continued to make regular visits there until late in life. She knew Degas and was thoroughly familiar with the work of the Impressionists, and her own modernity and vigour were widely acknowledged in Dublin. Like AE, she hoped to see the emergence of a distinct Irish school of painting and felt that it might even find its source in the work of Nathaniel Hone and John Butler Yeats. Miss Purser's intervention in the careers of Nathaniel Hone and John B. Yeats was timely. By 1901 Hone had virtually ceased painting and never exhibited, and, in recent years, Yeats' work had been accepted by the Academy largely as a matter of expediency. For some time past the RHA had petitioned for an increase in its annual grant from the government[11] and for new premises near the other art institutions in Kildare Street and Merrion Square, Dublin. In 1900 its newly elected President, Sir Thomas Drew, in an attempt to invigorate the institution and to encourage public support for its claims, wrote to all the Irish artists he knew, including Yeats, urging them to submit works for the annual exhibition.[12] Yeats complied with this request and submitted portraits which were accepted. The following year, at Miss Purser's suggestion, he again submitted portraits but they were all rejected peremptorily and it was this action which spurred his friend to arrange, at her own expense, his exhibition with Nathaniel Hone, held from 21 October–3 November 1901 in the rooms of the Royal Society of Antiquaries at number six St. Stephen's Green, next door to Yeats' old studio.[13]

This exhibition was a seminal event in the advance of Modernism in Ireland. For Yeats it was a turning point in his career and, more generally, it marked the introduction of Hugh Lane to Irish art. In all, twenty-eight landscapes by Hone and forty-four works, mainly portraits, by Yeats were shown. The press, generally, were appreciative, the *Irish Times* praising the integrity evident in the work of both men. Hone's strength, it thought, lay in his simplicity of manner, his broad view of nature and omission of irrelevant detail; while Yeats, everyone agreed, was at his best when depicting character and personality. The *Daily Express* even compared Yeats to Rembrandt and thought his study of John O'Leary (National Gallery of Ireland) to be 'a great portrait', possibly the finest painted by an Irish artist in recent years.[14] To Sarah Purser, who wrote the introduction to the catalogue, the exhibition provided clear evidence of the existence of an embryonic Irish school of painting and George Russell, writing in the *Irish Statesman*, hoped it would attract 'in a mood of true understanding, those who would like to believe in the existence in Ireland of a genuine art.'[15] However, the most consequential thing about the exhibition was its outcome.

Hugh Lane and Irish Art 1902–1926

Principally, two things resulted from the Hone-Yeats exhibition. Firstly, Hugh Lane, on his way back to London from a visit to his aunt, Lady Gregory, at Coole, chanced upon it and was so impressed by Yeats' portraits that, virtually on the spot, he conceived the idea of commissioning him to paint a series of portraits of distinguished contemporaries to be the basis of an Irish national portrait gallery. Secondly, Lane acquired what was to be an abiding interest in Irish art in particular and, later, modern art in general and dedicated himself to establishing a gallery of modern art in Dublin. Thus began a course of events centered on Lane who, more than anyone else, introduced modern painting to Ireland. These years also coincided with the residence in Dublin of George Moore who was then at the height of his powers as a novelist and critic. Moore had known several of the French Impressionists when he was a young man in Paris in the 1870s. However, apart from delivering occasional lectures during his years in Ireland (1901–11), he took little to do with the visual arts although he was at the time active in the Dublin literary and theatrical worlds. He was, however, a close friend and patron of William Orpen and it was through him that Orpen became involved in the Irish cultural revival. But Moore was always keen to acknowledge his contact with the Impressionists and had written about a number of them in his book *Modern Painting*;[16] so that his presence in the city gave added stimulus to the growing interest in avant-garde art.

Hugh Percy Lane was born in Co. Cork in 1875 the son of a Church of Ireland rector and his wife Adelaide, an elder sister of Augusta, Lady Gregory. He spent his boyhood travelling on the Continent with his mother but in 1893 began his career as an art dealer, with Colnaghi's in London. After a few years he set-up as a dealer on his own, specializing in old masters. Of the portraits which Lane commissioned from Yeats only five—those of Edward Dowden, W.G. Fay, Sir Horace Plunkett, J.M. Synge and W.B. Yeats—were completed, Yeats disliking the discipline of a commission and feeling more at ease when painting what he called 'friendship portraits'. However, after some manoeuvring by Lane, Orpen completed the projected series with portraits of Augustine Birrell, Michael Davitt, Timothy Healy, Nathaniel Hone, Sir Anthony MacDonnell, William O'Brien and T.W. Russell.[17] But aside from Lane's activities the exhibition with Hone heralded another change of fortune for Yeats. John Quinn, a New York lawyer, read reviews of it in the press and wrote to Yeats asking if he could buy a number of the pictures, thus offering patronage on a scale hitherto unimagined by the impecunious painter and beginning a friendship which lasted for more than twenty years. A year later, in 1902, Quinn, who at this time was just beginning to take an interest in both the visual and the literary arts—he later became an important patron not only of Irish art, but of Modernism in general, supporting such figures as James Joyce, Joseph Conrad, T.S. Eliot, Picasso, Matisse and Gauguin long before they made their reputations—visited Ireland for the first time, met John B. Yeats and his two sons, as well as AE, Douglas Hyde, George Moore, Edward Martyn, Lady Gregory and other literary figures and thus began what was to be a life-long association with Ireland. Moreover, in the years both before and after Yeats moved to New York in 1907, Quinn, Lady Gregory and Lane persuaded him, despite his reluctance, to make portraits and sketches of virtually all the leaders of the Irish Renaissance. Thus the closing years of Yeats' career were fruitful ones and we have from his hand a portrait of many of the influential figures of his day.[18] Finally, being virtually a retrospective exhibition of the work of the two men, the Hone-Yeats show was one of the first of its kind ever to be held in Ireland.

Hugh Lane's involvement with the Dublin Municipal Gallery of Modern Art (now the Hugh Lane Municipal Gallery of Modern Art) is well known and has been widely documented so that here we need only recall the main points of the affair. Principally these concern two distinct phases: firstly, the period leading up to the opening of the Gallery in temporary premises in Harcourt Street in 1908 and, secondly, the period from 1912 until 1926. The events of the latter period are the most important and centre on Lane's offer to present thirty-nine important French pictures to the gallery if certain conditions were met by Dublin corporation; the celebrated issue of his will with its unwitnessed codicil; his death in 1915 and the subsequent report of the British Government Committee of Inquiry regarding his intentions in the codicil to his will.

Lane's preoccupation with Irish art had the often familiar characteristics of a sudden romance, namely infatuation and a disregard for practical considerations. That his intentions were sincere is beyond doubt, but one cannot help thinking that, by his impetuousness, he brought many of his difficulties upon himself. As a picture dealer his motives were always questioned by a suspicious public, although his actions were philanthropic. Even his munificent offer of the thirty-nine works—which included such well-known masterpieces as Degas' *Sur la Plage* (cata. no.3), Manet's *Concert aux Tuileries* and *Éva Gonzalès* (cata. no.4), Monet's *Vétheuil: Sunshine and Snow* (cata. no.5), Pissarro's *Printemps, vue de Louveciennes* and Renoir's *Les Parapluies*—comprising his 'Conditional Gift'[19] to the Dublin Gallery was, perhaps paradoxically, fated because of those conditions, and yet without the leverage which they exerted one wonders if Dublin Corporation would ever have created a suitable gallery in which to house the pictures.

Before 1908 Lane's whole attention was focused on establishing a gallery of modern art in Dublin. His principal aim in the project, as he wrote in the catalogue of the exhibition of Irish painting which he arranged for the Guildhall, London, in May 1904, was to foster an Irish school of painting and this he felt could best be done by exhibiting contemporary works by Irish and non-Irish artists side by side in a permanent gallery. At first he thought such a gallery might be associated with the Royal Hibernian Academy but later decided to pursue his own course in the matter. In the spring of 1904, on hearing that the collection of the recently deceased James Staats Forbes was to be offered for sale, with favourable terms to any public gallery interested in purchasing either all or part of the collection, Lane, with the projected gallery in mind, negotiated the loan of a group of the works for exhibition in Dublin. Staats Forbes had been a railway manager and art connoisseur. He amassed a large collection of nineteenth century French and Dutch paintings, the former mainly of the Barbizon School of which he had numerous Corots. Indeed it was Forbes' Corots and other contemporary French paintings, seen at this time, that awoke Lane's enthusiasm for modern painting and, as a result, in mid-September 1904 he travelled with William Orpen to Paris and Madrid in search of modern works. By the time of his return a fortnight later he had not only both purchased and borrowed numerous paintings but espoused French Impressionism. To the works thus assembled he added others which he and his friends offered to present to Dublin. Thus when his *Exhibition of Pictures presented to the City of Dublin to form the nucleus of a Gallery of Modern Art, also pictures lent by the executors of the late Mr. J. Staats Forbes and others* opened in November 1904 it included works by, amongst others, Emile Blanche, Boudin, Corot, Courbet, Daubigny, Daumier, Degas (*A Peasant Woman*, now Lane Gallery), Fantin-Latour, Nathaniel Hone, Augustus John, Lavery, Mancini, Manet (*Éva Gonzalès*; *The Strolling Musician*; *Concert aux Tuileries*), Monet (*Waterloo Bridge*, now Lane Gallery; *Vétheuil, Sunshine and Snow*), Monticelli, Dermod O'Brien, Roderic O'Conor, William Orpen, Walter Osborne, Pissarro (*Printemps, Vue de Louveciennes*), Puvis de Chavannes, Renoir (*Les Parapluies*), Sisley, Steer, Whistler and John B. Yeats. This was by far the most comprehensive exhibition of modern painting yet seen in Ireland, or for that matter in the British Isles.

Lane, naturally, wanted to purchase from the exhibition as many works as possible for his proposed gallery. But once again controversy arose as to his intentions. In particular Sir Thomas Drew, president of the Academy, opposed Lane's scheme, suggesting ostensibly that public money which might otherwise go to Irish artists would merely find its way into the hands of picture dealers. But more plausibly, however, Drew probably saw the proposed gallery as a threat to the Academy's claim for a better endowment. However Lane and his supporters triumphed, notably after the Prince and Princess of Wales, who were then passing through Dublin, donated pictures for the new gallery, and other support came even from President Roosevelt[20] in America. Finally, in March 1905, Dublin Corporation voted to erect and to maintain a gallery in which to house the collection of pictures. But the Corporation was tardy in proceeding with the matter and it was not until September 1907 that they acquired Clonmel House in Harcourt Street as temporary premises for the gallery, which eventually opened to the public in January 1908 with Hugh Lane as its honorary director and Ellen Duncan as its first curator.

For the opening of the new Dublin Municipal Gallery an illustrated catalogue of the collection was prepared. The preface was by Hugh Lane and there he summarised the history of the gallery, noted the works which he had unreservedly presented to it and stated that he would similarly present his thirty-nine Continental pictures—his so-called 'conditional gift'—then on loan to the gallery, if Dublin Corporation kept its promise to erect a suitable building on an appropriate site 'within the next few years.' He also expressed the hope that the gallery would eventually cede to the National Gallery of Ireland those works which, 'having stood the test of time', are no longer considered to be modern. Thus the collection should always represent contemporary trends although the mechanicism as to how all this was to be done was unspecified.

The Harcourt Street premises were always considered to be temporary until such times as a permanent gallery should be erected. But after a few years Lane began to feel that the Corporation was procrastinating over its commitment to a new building, all efforts to find a suitable site for it having come to nothing. In November 1912, he decided to take a firm stand on the matter and wrote to the Town Clerk reminding him of the terms of his conditional gift. Henceforth dates his disenchantment with the Dublin authorities. The following January, however, the Corporation decided to go ahead with a new building, but the problem of a site was still unresolved. Lane had his scheme for a gallery, designed by Sir Edwin Lutyens, to span the river Liffey; the Corporation had theirs (other considerations apart, they wanted an Irish architect to design the new gallery), and a compromise proved impossible. Thus, in September 1913, the Corporation decided that they alone should select both the site and the architect. Meanwhile Lane, piqued at the whole issue, had removed his 'thirty-nine pictures' from the gallery and lent them to the National Gallery, London. In October 1913 he made a will bequeathing these works to London. Later however, in February 1915, before sailing to America, he wrote a codicil to this will leaving the thirty-nine works to Dublin, provided that a suitable building was found for them within five years of his death. But the codicil was not witnessed and was therefore invalid when Lane drowned in the 'Lusitania' in May 1915.

Thus began what became a contentious issue between the Irish and the British over the ownership of the thirty-nine pictures which remained in the National Gallery, London. Despite well substantiated protestations from Lane's executor, Lady Gregory, and others arguing for the return of the pictures to Dublin, the Irish case devolved only upon the moral aspect of the issue, the legal facts never being in doubt. Finally, after much wrangling on both sides, the British Government in 1924 appointed a Committee of Inquiry to examine the issue and to determine whether Lane, when he signed the codicil, thought it to have legal force and, if so, to recommend if the legal defect should be remedied by legislation. The findings of this

Committee were published, after much delay, in June 1926, and it decided in favour of the Dublin argument, but also resolved that, had Lane known of recent developments at the National Gallery's Millbank site (now the Tate Gallery), he would have destroyed the codicil. Therefore it recommended that the thirty-nine pictures should remain in London. The British Government accepted these recommendations and thus effectively settled the legal side of the issue but the moral aspect went unresolved. The matter has never been finally settled. In 1959 a compromise agreement was reached whereby the collection was divided into two parts which were alternated between Dublin and London every five years;[21] but in 1979, in recognition of the undesirability of moving such important paintings so frequently, a new agreement, lasting fourteen years, was concluded whereby thirty of the pictures remained in Dublin and eight others in London. Renoir's *Les Parapluies* was to alternate between the two cities every seven years.

Other events 1906–1922

Another important, although little remembered, event in the early march of Modernism in Ireland was the *Exhibition of Modern Paintings* held at the Municipal Art Gallery, Belfast, during April–May 1906. Referring to the exhibition of works from the Staats Forbes collection, Belfast's *Northern Whig* in an editorial suggested that Belfast, like Dublin, ought to have a gallery of modern art, although perhaps on a smaller scale.[22] The paper suggested that the best way to initiate such a project would be to arrange an exhibition of good modern paintings which would serve both to stimulate interest in art and to improve public taste. The *Whig*, however, was not alone in its thoughts. The Ulster Arts Club, too, had for some time been concerned about the lack of public support for the arts in Belfast. As far back as February 1903 Mr. Shannon Millin, a local barrister, had read a paper to the Club entitled 'The Past and Present Aspects of Art in Belfast'. In his paper Millin reproached the city for its lack of support for the arts, noting in particular the inadequacy of the art gallery, then accomodated in a room in the Central Library. Other cities of at least comparable size and wealth to Belfast, said Millin—and he named Liverpool, Manchester, Birmingham, Leeds and Glasgow—made provision for the arts from public funds and it was time, he said, that Belfast did the same. Finally, he called upon the various cultural organizations in the city to press the Corporation to erect a new museum building in which pictures 'of worth' could be fittingly displayed. Leading articles applauding Millin's lecture appeared in the local press and the *Whig* published his text as a booklet.[23] The Arts Club endorsed his views and invited interested parties to join with it in pressing for action by the Corporation, but this was to no avail.

In December 1904 another Belfastman, Maurice Joy, published an article entitled 'Art in Ireland' in the *Whig*. Joy bemoaned the absence of a tradition in Irish painting and lamented the fact that in the visual arts there was no equivalent to the contemporary Literary Revival. He went on to praise Hugh Lane's determination to establish a gallery of modern art in Dublin, saying that 'the progress, almost the existence, of art in Ireland depends upon . . . it'.[24] Joy then argued that Belfast, too, should play its part in stimulating a native identity for which, he said, a 'respectable art gallery' was essential. To remedy the defects of the present gallery, with its poor collections, he suggested holding a loan exhibition of pictures 'of the first order', which Hugh Lane might be invited to organize as he had recently done in Dublin. From such an exhibition, he said, works could be purchased to form the nucleus of a good municipal collection. At this point in the debate the *Whig* took up the issue and in a series of editorials urged the Corporation to discharge properly its duties in the matter. By January 1905 the paper announced that Lane was willing to arrange a loan exhibition 'if the city were in earnest' about the matter. Progress, however, was slow and it was not until the following November that a Joint Committee of representatives from the Ulster Arts Club, the Ulster Society of Architects and the Belfast Art Society was established to arrange an exhibition such as Joy had suggested.[25] Hugh Lane was elected honorary director of the project and he agreed to include a number of the Staats Forbes pictures along with others from Messrs Durand Ruel in Paris and from his own collection.

The exhibition eventually opened on 20 April 1906 and comprised 143 works by, amongst others, Burne-Jones, Constable, Corot, Courbet, Daubigny, Degas, Fantin-Latour, Lavery, Leighton, Manet, Millet, Monet, Morisot, Orchardson, Orpen, Pissarro, Puvis de Chavannes, Renoir, Rossetti, Sargent, Sisley, Vuillard, Watts and Whistler. It was, in Lane's words the most representative exhibition of modern painting yet seen in Ireland,[26] surpassing in scope even the Staats Forbes exhibition. The press were delighted with it, the *Northern Whig*, for example, commenting:

> As one climbed the staircase of the Free Library . . . past the familiar row of specimens of Irish marbles, the sets of photographs in frames, and the cast of Michel Angelo's Madonna it seemed for a moment too good to be true [that] one would find in the art gallery . . . a collection of acknowledged masterpieces. Manet, Monet, Whistler and Rossetti in Belfast—the idea appeared little short of preposterous. But when one had passed through the green baize curtains that veiled the glass door the first glance round was sufficient to assure one of its truth. . . . [Here] Mr. Lane has achieved an even greater triumph than in Dublin last year, for this collection is better selected, more compact, and more strikingly representative of the different tendencies of modern painting.'[27]

Of the various schools of painting represented in the exhibition the *Whig* most admired the French school. 'From Monticelli to Corot to Renoir and Vuillard,' it said, 'one can trace step by step the evolution of the school whose achievements are the glory of modern art'. And of the French Impressionists in particular it commented: 'Impressionism, after almost half a century of storm and stress has come into its own at last. . . . For these pictures express the very spirit of modern life . . . they have succeeded in destroying the age-old conventions, and . . . have taught men to paint, "not sentiments, but sunlight". They have given the death-blow to the subject-picture . . . and have extended and strengthened the range of pictorial vision.'[28] From the point of view of Modernism the Impressionist pictures were, indeed, the most compelling works in the exhibition. They included Manet's *Éva Gonzalès* and *Concert aux Tuileries*, Monet's *Vétheuil*, Pissarro's *Vue de Louveciennes* and Vuillard's *La Cheminée*, all of which belonged to Lane, and a group of works, some of which cannot now be identified with certainty, including Monet's *Waterloo Bridge*, Renoir's *Child in Blue*, Sisley's *Paysage-Environs de Moret* and Berthe Morisot's *Sur La Plage*.

The day following the opening of the exhibition the *Whig* in an editorial reminded its readers that the real purpose of the exhibition was to stimulate interest and to collect funds in the hope of acquiring a number of the paintings for the municipal collection. It called for a degree of philanthropy from the more wealthy members of the community and reminded them of the recent gift of pictures and money made to the Museum and Art Gallery by the recently deceased Sir Robert Lloyd Patterson.[29] In conclusion, the paper called upon the Corporation 'to look to the honour of the city' that Belfast might not lag behind Dublin in such matters. Lane, too, was keen to have a gallery of modern art in Belfast and during the exhibition he wrote to the local press offering help to establish it. Of the works then exhibited, he said, about twenty would ideally form the nucleus of a modern collection. Those which he had in mind included George Clausen's *The Stone-pickers*, a Corot, *View of Italy*, John Lavery's *The Pink Lady*, Courbet's *The Snowstorm*, Berthe Morisot, *Sur La Plage*, Fantin-Latour, *Roses in a Glass*, a Vuillard, *La Cheminée* and Puvis de Chavannes' *The Toilet*. Many of these pictures belonged to Staats Forbes' executors and, at prices ranging from £150 (Corot) to £800 (Courbet), they were offered for sale at considerably less than their full market value. Futhermore, Lane said that if the Belfast Corporation purchased some of them he would donate a number of others from his own collection. His object in this, he said, was to make accessible to the people of Ireland 'examples of the finest modern art, in the belief that by so doing [their] latent gifts ... may be developed and an Irish school of painting arise.'[30] However, even this generous proposal brought no response whatsoever from the Corporation and, despite the fact that the exhibition was well supported with more than one thousand visitors attending it on some evenings,[31] the matter was allowed to lapse.

While the exhibition, naturally, had its share of those who disapproved of much of the new art, the letters columns in the local press reveal both considerable and consistent support for it. Indeed, that a provincial newspaper like the *Northern Whig* should have promoted such avant-garde art is surprising and illustrates that many people in Belfast, as in Dublin, were remarkably well informed about contemporary developments in painting. Moreover, these people clearly looked abroad for their inspiration and in matters of art were not subservient to London as they were in so many other ways. Generally speaking, too, the Belfast press at the time displayed a liberal attitude towards the new art to a degree that was hardly matched by the British national press some years later when Roger Fry arranged his celebrated exhibitions, *Manet and the Post-Impressionists* and the *Second Post-Impressionist Exhibition*, at the Grafton Galleries, London, in 1910–11 and 1912 respectively.[32] Fry's exhibitions, of course, are generally regarded as marking the onset of the Modern Movement in England. Finally, we can share Patrick Shea's speculation when, writing his history of the Ulster Arts Club in 1971, he reflected briefly on the 1906 exhibition and on Hugh Lane's offer of help to lay the foundations of a collection of modern pictures for Belfast. If Lane's offer had been taken up, asked Shea, would the infamous story of the Lane pictures be as it is to-day?[33] For when Dublin, too, finally spurned him and when London was only luke-warm, might not he have offered his thirty-nine Continental pictures to Belfast?

* * *

As is evident from the artists and the pictures which we have mentioned Hugh Lane's interest in modern art was restricted almost entirely to French Impressionist painting. Yet by the early 1900s Impressionism, in European terms, was no longer an innovative movement. Lane was uneasy with later developments in French painting, with Fauvism, for example, and he ignored completely Cubism, which he must have seen in Paris, and the German Expressionists such as the Brücke painters in Dresden or the Blaue Reiter artists in Munich, all of whom were well established in his time and whom one would expect a connoisseur of modern painting to have been aware of. He also ignored the Vorticists in England whose work he must certainly have seen. Thus one is led to question the rigour of Lane's understanding of modern painting and, indeed, of Modernism as a movement which was well established before the outbreak of the First World War. While Lane unquestionably had a shrewd eye for a good painting that is not to say that he greatly understood the aesthetic underlying its creation; and it was an emphasis on the latter which so distinguishes Modernism from the art which preceded it. But Lane's interest in French painting extended the tradition introduced into Ireland by George Moore and Edward Martyn so that the Irish Modernists in the early twentieth century, building upon the foundations and example laid for them by the previous gereration of more Realist painters—artists like Nathaniel Hone, John Lavery or Walter Osborne, all of whom worked for a time in France—looked from the beginning almost solely to the example of French art. Indeed before the beginning of the twentieth century Roderic O'Conor was the only Irish artist to take any interest in a more avant-garde art than Impressionism but he did not work in Ireland.

Looking back at the *fin de siècle* and the first decade or so of the twentieth century, that is, to the years of the Literary Revival, it is clear that the most tangible contribution in the visual arts to the spirit of the Revival was not a work of art at all but, rather, the Dublin Municipal Gallery of Modern Art. Yet, paradoxically, as we shall see later, after Hugh Lane's death the authorities responsible for the Gallery turned their backs on almost any form of Modernism, a stance which they maintained until the 1960s.

* * *

The interest in modern painting stimulated by the events which we have discussed led to other important exhibitions of avant-garde art in Dublin and Belfast. From 25 January until 14 February 1911 Ellen Duncan, curator of the Muncipal Gallery, organized at the United Arts Club, Dublin, a show of *Works by Post-Impressionist Painters*. This was the first time that such innovative paintings were seen in Ireland and they were of a style which superseded Hugh Lane's interests.

The previous November Roger Fry had opened his exhibition *Manet and the Post-Impressionists* at the Grafton Galleries, London, and Ellen Duncan, who must have seen the exhibition, arranged for a selection of the pictures to travel to Dublin. The exhibition comprised forty-seven paintings and drawings, namely one work each by Cézanne, Denis, Jules Flandrin, Pierre Girieud, Pierre Laprade, Henri Manguin, Signac (a *pointilliste* work) and Felix Vallotton; two works by Othon Friesz, Auguste Herbin, Maillol, Rouault and Paul Sérusier; three works by Derain, Marquet, Matisse, including *Landscape* (Belgrade), and Vlaminck; four by Van Gogh, including *Le Postier* (Boston) and *Jeune fille au bleuet* (later known as *Young Man* [sic] *with Cornflower*); five by Picasso, including his portrait of *Clovis Sagot*; and eight Gauguins, including *Tahitiens* (Tate Gallery) and *L'Arlésienne* (Chicago, now called

Picasso
Clovis Sagot, 1909
Courtesy Kunstalle, Hamburg

Portrait de Femme à la Nature Morte de Cézanne). At least thirty-nine of these works had been shown in Fry's exhibition, which closed on 15 January, but few of them can now be identified.[34]

Fry's exhibition caused a considerable and prolonged stir in London, many of the pictures being regarded by the press and public alike as outrageous and childish; and in Dublin, too, surprisingly after the accord given to previous exhibitions of modern paintings, this show evoked harsh criticism in the press. In the *Irish Times* George Russell (AE) who, it will be remembered, had promoted the 1899 Loan Exhibition and who was in favour of opening Irish art to external influences saw the pictures as lacking energy and vision. They were, he said, 'not decadent, but merely decrepit.' But he excepted Gauguin, Denis and Signac from this criticism and commented on the latter's 'unemotional and cold application of science to art'. Thus Russell demonstrated a familiarity with the theory of Divisionism, which was unusual in Ireland

15

at that time. However, as for the other paintings, they were, he felt, 'hardly to be spoken about' with their dull, pallid colours, incorrect drawing, even lack of pattern. 'There are no values in the universe to the Post-Impressionist eye', he judged.[35] Thus was revealed the innate conservatism even of one of the more liberal minds then in Dublin. In the *Freeman's Journal* Thomas Bodkin, too, had difficulty with the exhibition although he welcomed the opportunity to see such 'astonishingly novel' works. Gauguin gained most of his admiration for what he saw as sincerity and 'unity of purpose'. Van Gogh, Cézanne and Signac he also admired, although they, too, were discussed entirely in generalized terms. But Vlaminck, Derain and Flandrin he dismissed; Picasso's portrait of *Clovis Sagot* he thought was 'a depressing failure to rival Van Gogh', and Matisse he considered to be 'a mere artistic charlatan'.[36] Strangely, George Moore seems to have made no comments about this exhibition. Even though his taste for modern painting was firmly tied to Impressionism, one would expect him to have said something about such an eye-opening event, held at the very time he was deciding to return to live in London.

The reception of this exhibition by Bodkin and Russell was in many respects typical of that which the English critics had accorded to Fry's London exhibition two months earlier. Both men judged the works largely from a nineteenth century standpoint in which the cardinal rule was the Ruskinian maxim of 'truth to nature'. Having no alternative philosophy, they saw so many of the young painters as being insincere, incompetent and even childish. That was the judgement of the Irish and British press generally at the time and they did little to enlighten a public anxious to learn. In this respect the treatment by the Belfast press of Hugh Lane's 1906 exhibition was exceptional.

Later in 1911, in Belfast, Arthur Deane, curator of the Municipal Museum and Art Gallery, arranged an exhibition of *Modern Paintings & Early British Water Colours*, which was held from 4 August until 9 September. The pictures were borrowed in the main from commercial galleries in Paris and London and Deane undoubtedly built upon the foundation of Lane's 1906 exhibition. The modern section included works by the younger British and Irish artists—Mark Fisher, Gerald Kelly, Henry Lamb, John Lavery, Dermod O'Brien, William Rothenstein, Charles Shannon, Henry La Thangue, and others—as well as a group of French Impressionist paintings by Boudin, Jongkind, Manet, Monet, Pissarro, Renoir and Sisley. Unfortunately none of the French works can now be identified with certainty,[37] but the exhibition illustrates the diversity and range of interest in Modernism in Ireland at that time.

Maintaining the impetus of these events, in 1912 Ellen Duncan arranged another show of forty-eight *Modern French Pictures*, which opened at the United Arts Club, Dublin, on 29 March. Included were paintings by many of the artists seen previously, as well as Post-Impressionist works by Van Dongen and Van Rysselberg. But, more importantly, for the first time Cubist paintings were brought to Dublin.[38] Thus, in art-historical terms, the exhibition was an advance stylistically upon any previous show seen in Ireland. Regretfully we cannot identify these Cubist works either from the catalogue or from reviews of the exhibition; all we know is that they included works by Picasso, Gris, Marchand and Herbin. But the first two names especially, would suggest that they included some of the latest innovatory paintings and in reviewing the show the *Irish Times*, recalling the 1911 exhibition held at the Arts Club, said it contained 'yet more extraordinary works'.[39]

The next time we find such avant-garde paintings in Dublin is a decade later, in January 1922, when Paul Henry and Arthur Power arranged the exhibition, *Modern Pictures*, which was shown at Mills' Hall during Civic Week. Henry and Power hoped that their exhibition would stimulate Irish artists as the Literary Revival had stimulated the native writers[40] but, alas, this was not to be. In all, about thirty works were shown on this occasion, including some by Cézanne, Maillol, Marchand, Matisse, Modigliani (*Le Petit Paysan*), Picasso and Vlaminck. But the emphasis was on the work of the younger British painters, namely Robert Bevan, Vanessa Bell, Malcolm Drummond, Harold Gilman, Charles Ginner, Spencer Gore, Paul Nash and William Roberts. As is often the case with such exhibitions in Ireland, few of the works can be identified with certainty, although the Modigliani is now in the Tate Gallery and Gilman's *Mountain Bridge* was almost certainly the work by him now in Worthing Art Gallery. Looking back on the exhibition many years later, Henry thought it may have marked the beginning of a new era in Irish art,[41] and in this we must agree with him. Taken with the recently established Society of Dublin Painters and seen in the context of political independence, which came about at the same time, it gave a younger generation of artists their head.

* * *

In retrospect, it is clear that Ireland, in comparison with other countries, was not backward in aquainting herself with the Modern Movement. Indeed, in the light of the events which we have discussed, beginning with Dublin Sketching Club's extensive showing of Whistler in 1884, and remembering that London saw little avant-garde art until Fry's two Post-Impressionist exhibitions of 1910–11 and 1912, as did New York before the 'Armory' show of 1913, one may fairly claim that until the end of the first decade of this century the Irish were ahead of the times in recognizing the temper of the Modern Movement in its early years. Yet in Ireland, as elsewhere, many artists remained immune to or disdained the new movement. However, by the early 1920s, as the country achieved political independence, with all the hopes for a bright future which that implied, a new generation arrived on the scene. They had the advantage of growing up with the events which we have described and in several cases had studied art abroad, almost invariably in Paris. Thus they were both conversant with and sympathetic to modern painting. They were less concerned deliberately to create a distinct Irish school of art and preferred to align their work with more recent developments elsewhere, thus allowing a distinct school, if such should emerge at all, to emerge of its own accord. It is to their work and activities in the following decades which we must now turn our attention.

CHAPTER TWO

THE SOCIETY OF DUBLIN PAINTERS 1920-1932

'The French Impressionist movement which had left such a mark
upon the whole of European Painting, had passed without
leaving a ripple, apparently, upon the complacent
self satisfaction of this country'.

Paul Henry, *Further Reminiscences*
(Belfast: Blackstaff Press, 1973), p.68.

Background and contextual setting

PAUL HENRY (1876–1958) was one of a generation of Irish artists who came to prominence in the early 1920s. He had been in Paris as a student in the late 1890s and, there, was influenced by the work of the French painter of peasant life, Jean François Millet and, later, by James MacNeill Whistler at whose Académie Carmen he was a student. The influence of these two artists remained with him for the rest of his career and Whistler's teaching in particular firmly fixed his interest and attention on avant-garde painting.

In about 1900 Henry moved from Paris to London where he found employment as an illustrator on a number of journals; but he had little interest in such work and, as time went on, turned increasingly to painting and began to associate with other like-minded artists. From time to time he frequented Walter Sickert's 'at homes', held in the latter's studio at number nineteen Fitzroy Street.[1] Sickert, a friend of George Moore and of Hugh Lane, who also attended some of these meetings, was at the time the most sympathetic advocate in England of avant-garde painting. In his studio he gathered around him many of the young and progressive painters of his day and together they would discuss and evaluate one another's work. In 1907, from these friends emerged the Fitzroy Street Group which, focusing on Sickert, Spencer Gore, Harold Gilman, Robert Bevan and Charles Ginner—artists for whom Post-Impressionism had largely superseded the new orthodox interest in Impressionism—was for a short time the centre of English avant-garde art. Between them the members of the Group—Henry was just a casual visitor—shared equally the expenses of running the studio and a small store room in which they kept their work. In 1908, at the suggestion of the art critic Frank Rutter, a number of these artists formed the Allied Artists' Association in order to counteract the exclusiveness of the New English Art

Paul Henry R.H.A.
Ulster Museum

Club and as a sort of English version of the Salon des Indépendants. Henry was a founder member of the Allied Artists' Association and showed drawings and paintings at a number of its exhibitions.

At this same time, however, Henry was beginning to think again of Ireland, being influenced by the work of John Synge, whom he had earlier met in Paris. Synge's description in *Riders to the Sea* of life in the west of Ireland he found particularly poignant. 'There was something in Synge that appealed to me very deeply', he later commented. 'He touched some chord which resounded as no other music ever had done'.[2] Henry's friends in London included the essayist Robert Lynd and the journalist James Good, both friends from his school days in Belfast, and their close associations with Ireland at that time no doubt influenced him too. In 1909 Lynd married the writer Sylvia Dryhurst and they spent their honeymoon on Achill Island. It was the Lynds' enthusiasm for the west of Ireland, spoken of on their return, that convinced Henry and his wife Grace, whom he had married a few years earlier, that they too should go there. Thus in 1910 the Henrys visited Achill for the first time. They were captivated by it, and decided to stay there.[3] For the following decade the island, its people and the life which they led dominated Paul Henry's painting. It recalled in him the work of Millet in pictures like *The Gleaners* (Louvre), and, in his own compositions, such as *The Potato Diggers*, 1910–11 (cata. no.6), which shows a clear debt to Millet, he forged visual imagery close in feeling to that evoked by Synge's written word. But while Paul Henry was happy on Achill, Grace, who was also a painter, sought brighter lights and so in 1919 they moved to Dublin.

Henry found the art world in Dublin to be circumscribed and reactionary and he quickly became disenchanted with it. 'It is difficult to realise', he wrote many years later, 'how deep rooted was the ignorance and prejudice which existed at that time against any form of art which savoured, even remotely, of Modernism'. He continued: 'The French Impressionist movement which had left such a mark upon the whole of European painting, had passed without leaving a ripple, apparently, upon the complacent self satisfaction of this country'.[4] In Dublin it was almost impossible for a young artist with an interest in avant-garde painting to have his work accepted for the annual exhibitions of the Academy, the Water Colour Society of Ireland or the Dublin Sketching Club and, apart from these, there were few other venues in the city where pictures could be exhibited. Indeed, other Irish artists who had been interested in developments in contemporary painting had usually made their careers abroad.[5] Thus, confronted with these circumstances and with the examples of Sickert, the Fitzroy Street Group and the Allied Artists' Association in mind, in June 1920 Henry founded the Society of Dublin Painters in order to give young artists a venue at which to show their work.

In forming the new Society Henry was supported by a number of his contemporaries, including his wife Grace, E.M.O'R. Dickey, Countess Soumarokow Elston, Letitia Hamilton, Clare Marsh, Sir Frederick Moore, James Sleator, Mary Swanzy, Jack B. Yeats and James M. Willcox.[6] Of these people, Paul and Grace Henry, E.M.O'R.Dickey, Letitia Hamilton, Mary Swanzy and Jack B. Yeats were the most progressive in outlook; Sleator had only a passing acquaintance with the avant-garde[7] and little or nothing is known of the work of Countess Elston, Sir Frederick Moore[8] and James Willcox. However, Elston, Moore, Sleator and Willcox left the Society shortly after its first exhibition, which was held in August 1920, and their places were taken by Harry Clarke, Mainie Jellett and Charles Lamb. Thus the membership totalled ten persons, at which number it was fixed for more than a decade.

From the beginning the Society of Dublin Painters became synonymous with the best of avant-garde painting in Ireland and until the early 1940s, when the Irish Exhibition of Living Art was established, its members were at the forefront of developments in Irish art. The Society espoused no collective aesthetic, but rather sought to foster a spirit of broad-mindedness and sympathetic understanding in young artists of promise. Like the Fitzroy Street Group, on which it was modelled, its members elected a president, secretary and treasurer.[9] Group exhibitions of members' work were arranged in the spring and autumn of each year and each member was entitled to hold a one-man exhibition annually in the gallery at No.7 St. Stephen's Green, which the Society acquired in June 1920.[10]

The Dublin Painters' gallery was small. It measured only thirty-five feet by twenty feet and had a high, angled and glazed roof. Adjacent to it was a small store room in which the Society's records and other materials were kept. Before its occupation by the Dublin Painters, the gallery had an interesting history which might be recalled here. The building itself was erected in 1826. For a time in the 1890s an Italian artist called Antonio Barzaghi-Cattaneo worked there. The studio or gallery proper, however, situated on the first floor in the return of the building, was built in about 1869–70 by the painter Augustus Burke who occupied it until 1882 when he went to London. Briefly it was then used by the landscapist Colles Watkins before being taken over in late 1883 by John Butler Yeats. Yeats successor, in 1895, was the portrait painter Walter Osborne who remained there until his death in 1903, after which Yeats again occupied it until 1912–13.[11] Following Yeats, the Gaelic League used it for its meetings. Rooms adjacent to the studio also had from time to time an

James Sleator,
photographed in
about 1944
Photograph courtesy
Irish Times

artistic clientele, having been variously occupied by the Dublin Art Club, the portrait painter Sarah Cecilia Harrison, the Royal Society of Antiquaries (who let their room for the Hone-Yeats exhibition in 1901), Patrick Tuohy, the Royal Hibernian Academy's schools (c.1918–1939) and Sean O'Sullivan in the 1940s.

The new Society was established in unpropitious times. The revolutionary events which culminated in the Anglo-Irish Treaty of 1921 and the establishment of the Irish Free State in 1922 were of immediate threat; yet from its first exhibition the critics were enthusiastic about the Society. The *Irish Times*, referring partly to the exhibition and partly to what it called the 'arid field' of contemporary politics, found it at such a time 'full of hope and courage, full of promise and accomplishment'.[12] Both it and the *Freeman's Journal*, the more nationalist of the leading papers, admired the innovative qualities of many of the works on display and the artists' determination to face difficulties and not to evade them by resorting to stereotyped devices. Thus the aspirations of the Society were publicly acknowledged from the outset. But in the years after 1922 such aspirations were not easily maintained, for successive Irish governments were to pursue increasingly isolationist policies and deliberately promoted what was understood to be the ancient and pastoral culture of Gaelic Ireland to the exclusion of almost all other influences. That the Dublin Painters, in such a climate, had even limited success in stimulating public interest in modern painting is to their credit, for they alone among artists in the Free State at that time (in Northern Ireland the climate, as we shall see later, was less oppressive) kept an open mind to more liberal ideas than those fostered at home. Indeed in those years a template of social and cultural values was forged which, arguably, still directs the attitudes of a great many of the Irish people, even though in practice they have long since adopted the ways of the wider English-speaking world.

21

The quest for national identity, which was a motivating force behind much of life in Ireland during the 1920s, gained impetus, as we have seen, from the early days of the Literary Renaissance with Lady Gregory, W.B. Yeats and George Russell (AE). Yet in the Ireland of the twenties much of what they had achieved was eschewed as being Anglo-Irish in interpretation and therefore not *truly* Irish. The point was made by the novelist and short story writer Liam O'Flaherty in a letter to Russell criticizing his editorial policy in the *Irish Statesman*, a liberal paper, conscious of the different traditions within Irish society: 'I don't for a moment claim that your paper is not doing good work,' wrote O'Flaherty. 'But I do claim that it is not Irish, that it is not national, and that it is not representative in any respect of the cultural forces, in all spheres, that are trying to find room for birth in this country at present'.[13] In the visual arts the same spirits were at work. In 1929, for instance, George Noble, Count Plunkett, sometime director of the National Museum of Ireland and minister of Fine Art in the first Dail founded the Academy of Christian Art, membership of which was open exclusively to Roman Catholics, to promote what Plunkett termed 'the intellectual commonplaces of Catholic life'.[14] In painting in particular the clarion call at the time was for a 'national' art which would lay emphasis on life in the west, and much of

Sean Keating
The Race of the Gael, c.1939
Photograph Ulster Museum

22

the work of those artists who responded to this call was a kind of Social Realism, like Seán Keating's *Slán leat, a Athair/ Goodbye, Father*, 1935 (cata. no.7). Thus many painters echoed developments in contemporary literature, in the work of Daniel Corkery, Liam O'Flaherty, Frank O'Connor, and other young writers.

This was the opressive climate in which the Society of Dublin Painters was established. Few of its members, however, were concerned with matters of nationality and, indeed, as has been remarked of their generation, many of them felt a strain, a self-consciousness at what 'being Irish' meant,[15] a predicament aggravated in a number of cases by a background in the Protestant Ascendancy. They were the first innovators, however, to disregard the intransigence of the art establishment towards modern painting and for twenty years and more their gallery, small as it was, served as an important venue for exhibitions before other commercial galleries began to flourish. Moreover, the practice which they pioneered of holding frequent one-man exhibitions, which were almost unknown in Dublin before the Hone-Yeats show of 1901, and rare in the years immediately after it, later became commonplace.

The first decade

The Dublin Painters were more radical and influential during their first decade than at any other time. Being without a corporate manner they remained a loose association of individuals and it is thus that we must discuss their work. To begin with, Paul and Grace Henry, E.M.O'R. Dickey and Jack B. Yeats were the names most prominently associated with the Society's exhibitions. Few of the works which they exhibited were daringly avant-garde but they shared a keen awareness of recent developments in painting.

In his work Paul Henry reflected the Post-Impressionist stance of the Fitzroy Street Group. By 1920, of course, he was well-known in Dublin for both he and Grace had exhibited together regularly there and in Belfast during the previous decade. In the Dublin Painters' first exhibition, held in August 1920, Henry showed three paintings, including *The Potato Diggers* (possibly cata. no.6) and *A Western Village*, both of which had been painted on Achill Island a few years earlier, and two charcoal drawings. These paintings show him at the height of his powers; they are forceful, evoke pathos and symbolize the whole sentiment of the landscape with which he is perfectly in harmony. The bold simplicity of composition, with a few shapes juxtaposed one with another and a severely limited palette, except for one or two vibrant colours, he never surpassed. The harsh life evident in the *Potato Diggers* and the pose of the two figures toiling in unison, shows the influence of Millet, whom he had admired in Paris. Such paintings represent a dramatic contrast to the more sentimental pictures of the west of Ireland common before this time. Some of Henry's landscapes painted shortly after he settled on Achill are devoid of people and are characterized by a strong sense of tranquility. *Connemara Landscape*, 1913, is a good example of such works and here the influence of Millet has given way to that of Whistler. From about 1919, when he moved to Dublin, his compositions increasingly assume a sense of tranquility and are almost always empty of people. From now on he began to emphasize the abstract qualities of the composition, as can be seen in *Dawn, Killary Harbour*, 1922–3 (cata. no.8), one of his finest works. Henry often observed the landscape at dawn, savouring the stillness and purity of the air at that hour. Yet despite the abstract emphasis in many of his pictures of this time, Henry's response to the landscape was intuitive, guided—as was John Synge before him— by an omnipresent awareness of the fraility of human significance in the eternal conflict between man and the unpitying forces of nature. *Lakeside Cottages*, c.1923–7 (Lane Gallery), typifies the best of his work from the 1920s. Here is the quintessential Paul Henry, and in the sentiment for the landscape which it encapsulates it embodies those values which successive Irish governments and other bodies so eagerly promoted at the time.

In August 1922 Arthur Griffith, president of the new Free State government, died suddenly and at the Dublin Painters' autumn exhibition that year Henry exhibited a charcoal drawing (coll. Irish Government) of Griffith on his deathbed. Although never at his best as a portraitist, nevertheless here, as in some other charcoal studies made during his years in Achill, Henry captured the whole essence of his subject's persona and, with pathos, conveys the tragic sense of loss which the country felt at that time.

Paul Henry exhibited regularly with the Dublin Painters until 1926, usually giving a joint show with his wife in early summer and contributing to a group show in spring and autumn of each year. But thereafter he left the Society and went his own direction, although Grace continued to be an active member.

During her lifetime Grace Henry (1868–1953) was overshadowed by her husband. While she never equalled the best of his paintings, she was in many ways the more experimental and subtle painter of the two, always in search of something new. Her early Achill paintings have a distinctly personal style which at times is almost illustrative in manner, as in *The Top of the Hill* of about 1910–13 (cata. no.9), or again can be distinctly Whistlerian, as in her *Girl in White* (Lane Gallery). Figures, often of peasant girls, predominate in many of these early works and they frequently wear a coy expression which lends a sense of humour to the composition. Her landscapes of the same years, such as *Nightfall on a Mountain Village*—this may be the *Village by Night* which she exhibited at the Dublin Painters in autumn 1922—emphasize mood and atmosphere and are characterized, like those of her husband, by great economy of means both in conception and execution. In the early 1920s, however, Grace Henry became increasingly experimental and forged a distinctly Expressionist manner. Her practice at this time of juxtaposing bold shapes, using a severely limited palette and contrasting complementary colours illustrates her debt to Fauvism and recent French painting. Indeed, reviewing her work in the first Dublin Painters' exhibition, in August 1920, the *Freeman's Journal* commented that she had 'abandoned pure landscape', while her still lifes, it thought, showed a 'passionate delight in colour and form for their own sake'.[16] These characteristics can be seen in her *Country of Amethyst*, of about 1920, exhibited at the Dublin Painters early the following year,[17] as well as in *Spring in Winter, No.9* (cata. no.10), which probably dates from about 1920 or 1925. Her subject-matter here is still recognizably the west of Ireland, but with the brisk, assertive brushstrokes and piquant contrasts of colour it has been handled in a refreshingly novel way.

During 1924 and 1925, at a time when her marriage was under strain, Grace Henry stayed briefly in Paris and while there almost certainly worked with the Cubist painter André Lhote. She may have gone to Lhote at Mainie Jellett's suggestion, for by that time Lhote was well known to a number of Irish artists; but at any rate his teaching had little influence on her and her own free style prevailed. In 1930 Paul and Grace

Henry parted and, while Paul remained in Ireland, Grace spent most of the following decade painting in France, Spain and Italy.

Like Paul Henry, O'Rorke Dickey (1894–1977) was a Belfastman. On going down from Cambridge, where he read Moral Sciences, for a time under Bertrand Russell, he studied art under Harold Gilman at the Westminster School of Art and became a close friend of Gilman, Robert Bevan and Charles Ginner, all of whom influenced him. In 1920, the year in which he joined the Dublin Painters, he also joined the London Group and at the same time frequented the Bloomsbury Group and was a member of Vanessa Bell's Friday Club.[18] Thus he kept in touch with the latest developments in English painting.

Dickey was principally a landscapist, although he often painted architectural forms. He emphasized the structural and decorative aspects of his subjects and, notably in the early twenties, often imbued his compositions with a strong atmospheric quality. These were the characteristics which the critics noted in his painting *Slieve Donard*, which he exhibited at the Dublin Painters' first exhibition, and which may have been the picture now known as *Mourne Foothills*. Dickey was an active member of the new Society. He held a one-man show of paintings there in November 1920 followed by another in February 1922, when the *Irish Times* thought him to be possibly the most experimental painter working in Ireland.[19] The latter show coincided with the exhibition, *Modern Paintings*, held at Mills' Hall during Dublin Civic Week, which was arranged by Paul Henry and the critic Arthur Power. The emphasis in this show was on the work of the younger English painters, including Gilman, Bevan and Ginner, and the critics were quick to point out Dickey's affinity with them.

Dickey often painted in Italy in the early 1920s, having a predeliction for the mountains viewed in the early morning light, and many of his best compositions illustrate vast panoramas seen from a height. *San Vito Romano*, 1923 (cata. no.12), is one of his very best paintings. Here the emphasis on the formal structure of the landscape and the block-like shapes of the houses stepped up a hillside recalls Cézanne, but the detailed patterning of the foliage on the bushes in the foreground, the treatment of light and feeling of intense heat, coupled with the use of precise brush strokes closely woven together, betray the influence of Gilman and company. *Monte Scalambra from San Vito Romano* (Manchester City Art Gallery), also of 1923, and *Volscian Mountains* (Crawford Gallery, Cork), of about the same period, also show the mountains in the morning light. *From the Summit of Errigal*, which he painted in 1919 or 1920 (cata. no.11), treats the Irish landscape in a similar manner and lacks the sentimentality with which most of his contemporaries treated their native landscape.

In February 1923 Dickey held his last one-man show, this time of drawings and woodcuts, at the Dublin Painters' gallery. The exhibition included a number of prints of Irish scenes, including *Slieve Donard through the Cherry Trees*; *Newcastle Harbour, Co. Down*; *Errigal and Lough Nacung* and *Farmers in a Train*, 1922-3 (Lane Gallery), which demonstrate the concise but effective nature of his technique in the medium. As well as exhibiting with the Dublin Painters in these years he also showed regularly at the New Irish Salon, once, in 1921, at the Royal Hibernian Academy and annually at the Belfast Art Society. In 1924, however, Dickey moved to England where he remained for the rest of his life. His departure was a severe loss to the Dublin Painters' Society and to Irish painting in general.

E.M. O'R. Dickey
Farmers in a Train,
1922–3
Hugh Lane Municipal
Gallery of Modern Art

    Jack B. Yeats (1871–1957), the younger son of John B. Yeats and brother of W.B. Yeats, is the most important Irish painter to have emerged this century. Along with Paul Henry and Clare Marsh he was a signatory to the original lease of the St. Stephen's Green gallery. This is surprising, for although Yeats exhibited from time to time with a number of small groups and societies he never became closely involved with any of them. But his presence often lent authority to exhibitions which might otherwise have received little critical attention. As with Paul Henry, Yeats' pictures symbolize the character of Irish life but whereas Henry concerned himself mainly with the west, Yeats' is more universally Irish and has a strong sense of genre. His distinctiveness of concept and technique characterize his individuality and make him not easily classified with his contemporaries. Throughout his career Yeats' approach to picture making never changed. He was essentially an observer of events in the world around him, a recorder rather than a commentator and, despite what some critics have argued, there is nothing didactic in his work.

Yeats was an active member of the Dublin Painters' Society from 1920 to 1923. He exhibited at all their early mixed shows and held one-man exhibitions there in 1921, 1922 and 1923. In the group's first exhibition Yeats showed, along with two other paintings and a drawing, a composition called *The Dawn, Holyhead*, which he had probably only recently finished. Technically this picture is characteristic of his so-called 'middle period', in which the emphasis on line, which characterized his early work, slowly gave way to a more *malerisch* technique. The imagery shows three travellers huddled uncomfortably in the compartment of a train as they arrive to catch an early morning boat. Some months later, in his one-man show of February 1921, he exhibited *The Dark Man* in which he depicted a blind beggar being led across a busy street; while in another one-man show, held in April-May 1922, he included, amongst other works, *A Lift on the Long Car*, painted in 1914 (Temple Newsam, Leeds), *Bachelor's Walk, In Memory*, 1915, and *On the Racecourse*, 1922 (Mellon Collection, U.S.A.). *A Lift on the Long Car* was also shown in the Society's autumn exhibition in 1922. The imagery in these pictures, with their feeling for the isolation of the individual in society, veers towards Symbolism and pathos, and they illustrate the sense of romance and mystery with which Yeats could imbue commonplace scenes. They are the quintessence of Irish life at that time.

From the late teens until the mid-1920s Yeats recorded the political and social events which shaped the emerging Ireland. On the evidence of paintings like *Bachelor's Walk*, *On Drumcliffe Strand* (National Gallery of Canada), *The Funeral of Harry Boland* (Sligo County Library & Museum), or *Communicating with Prisoners* (Sligo), which crystalize much of the spirit of the times, he has been called the painter of nationalist Ireland, but that is to cast him in a role which he himself did not accept. Such pictures may have caught the mood of the times and evoke pathos, but that is not to say that they are statements of a political view, and while Yeats certainly sympathized with various factions, political and otherwise, none of their causes, *per se*, was the subject-matter of his art. Commenting, for example, at one time to his American friend and patron, John Quinn, about Sínn Féin and Nationalism, he said that he liked the 'idea' of what Sinn Fein stood for more than the organization itself.[21] Even in those works done after the mid-twenties, when his subject-matter was increasingly drawn from what one might call the 'human condition', he appears to stand aside as an observer.

By the mid-1920s, shortly after he stopped exhibiting with the Dublin Painters, Yeats' style reached its full maturity; idiosyncratic and Expressionistic in manner with forms more often hinted at than firmly established, the real meaning of his work hidden behind appearances and often culled from memory. This development is evident in *A Full Tram*, painted in 1923, and *The Breaker Out*, of 1925. These and other paintings of the time mark the onset of the more esoteric works of his later years.

It has been argued that Modernism was anathema to Yeats[22] but that is not so. In 1913, for example, he was happy to be included in the controversial Armory exhibition held in New York and at the time commented to his friend John Quinn: 'The great good these post-Impressionists and futurists will do will be that they will knock the handcuffs off all the painters';[23] and in 1929 he stated that painting had 'suffered terribly . . . from the admiration of the half-educated, from people who . . . cannot accept [it] on its own valuation, but always wish to see it as a vehicle for expressing something else'. 'Now the truth is,' he continued, 'a painting is not a vehicle for anything except itself. It is the memory of a moment . . . the eye is coming into its own. The innovator frees our eyes'.[24] From about 1914 Yeats was influenced by Walter Sickert and in the 1920s was directly in touch with him; moreover, influences are discernible, too, from Van Gogh and Rouault on his use of colour and from Ensor and Chagall on his composition.[25] In the early 1930s his friendship with Felix Hackett, professor of physics at University College, Dublin, influenced his experiments with primary and secondary colours and this largely accounts for the deliberate contrast of complementary colours, notably violet/yellow, in works such as *A Room*, of 1935, and other paintings of the period. Alongside this, in pictures like *Bachelor's Walk* there is evidence of an earlier, more intuitive approach to a similar juxtaposition of complementary colours. In addition, from the 1940s he was in touch with Oskar Kokoschka, whom he had met in Dublin through his dealer, Victor Waddington. It is thus clear that Yeats had developed an enduring interest in the ideas of Modernism and that his changing style resulted from contact with contemporary European artists and not from isolation.

Yet despite his stature and importance, Yeats had little influence on the development of Modernism in Ireland. Even at the beginning of the 1920s he was seen as standing apart from his contemporaries. As the *Irish Times* noted in reviewing the Dublin Painters' autumn exhibition in 1921, 'Yeats belongs to nobody but himself'.[26] Yeats' delight in the world around him is the key to understanding his art and career and it explains the ebb and flow of his support for diverse small societies and avant-garde groups such as the Dublin Painters and, as we shall see in later years, the White Stag Group and the Irish Exhibition of Living Art.

While it is true to say that in an Irish context Paul and Grace Henry, O'Rorke Dickey and Jack B. Yeats produced genuinely innovative work, nevertheless, when viewed in a European context it is clear that they were motivated by the artistic theories of the *fin de siècle* and the very early years of the twentieth century rather than by those of their own times. Conceptually they remained narrative painters, never becoming preoccupied with the aesthetics of medium, materials or theory as did the more progressive painters elsewhere. Indeed it was a refusal to become involved with such matters that distinguishes most of the Irish avant-garde painters from their British and Continental contemporaries, and, while they adopted techniques of composition, handling of paint and colour which were based on Post-Impressionism and, later, on the more Expressionist values of Fauvism, they retained a strictly nineteenth century sense of subject-matter. Until the 1940s Mainie Jellett, Evie Hone and Cecil Salkeld, as we shall see, were the only exceptions to this rule. But here we must also examine the work of a number of less innovative and influential members of the Dublin Painters' Society who were active in its early years for, in the long run, it was they who gave the Society it distinctive character.

* * *

The chief of these painters was Letitia Hamilton (1878–1964), and she worked loosely in an Impressionist manner. A pupil of Sir William Orpen at the Metropolitan School of Art, she later went to the Chelsea Polytechnic where she worked for a time under Frank Brangwyn, but neither Orpen nor Brangwyn seems to have had a strong

influence on her work. During the 1920s she travelled widely in France, Italy and Yugoslavia, painting mostly landscapes, and in the late 1930s she made regular visits to Venice and the northern Italian lakes: it was her travels which determined the development of her work. Throughout the twenties and thirties she exhibited almost annually at the Dublin Painters' gallery and also showed occasionally in England and abroad.

Letitia Hamilton was one of a number of prominent Irish women artists of her generation—others included her elder sister Eva, May Guinness, Mary Swanzy, Evie Hone and, in part, Mainie Jellett—who had sufficient private means to be able to travel and, to some extent, to paint for their own pleasure without having to worry unduly about more mundane matters. Usually Letitia Hamilton worked on the spot,[27] her paintings being characterized by bold brushwork, the frequent use of a palette knife to give a heavy impasto, and an emphasis on colour and light. Her manner was free from the rigidity of academic painting but unfortunately lacked direction or rigour so that the development of her style is difficult to plot. However, typical of her early work is a simplification of forms and shapes and the use of a limited palette, perhaps influences from Paul Henry, while later in her career her compositions became more cluttered, her colour richer and somewhat fussy. In the early 1920s country fairs and markets, usually in towns in the midlands of Ireland, were her principal subject-matter and led to works such as her *Irish Market Scene*, of about 1923 (Ulster Museum). In about the autumn of 1923 Letitia and her sister Eva visited Venice for the first time and in works such as *Venice*, 1923–4 (cata. no.14), which she exhibited at the Dublin Painters' gallery the following February, one can see the effect of the strong Italian sunshine on her painting, an influence which dominated the rest of her career. Although landscapes were her principal subject-matter she produced occasional interiors like that seen in *Cheyne Walk, Chelsea*, of about 1936–7. Many of these compositions have a strong sense of space and elaborate patterning of an almost Matisse-like character, the whole permeated by the sense of light which characterized all her work.

Eva Hamilton (1876–1960), who joined the Dublin Painters in 1922, exhibited less frequently than did her sister, Letitia, although she held a number of one-woman shows at the St. Stephen's Green gallery during the 1920s and 1940s and contributed regularly to the Society's group exhibitions in the 1930s. Until about 1925–6 she was best known for her portraits—indeed discussing her exhibition at the Dublin Painters' gallery in May 1925 the *Irish Times* noted that her study of the Rt. Rev. James Macmanaway, Bishop of Clogher, was by 'general consent' one of the best portraits exhibited in Dublin that year[28]—but thereafter she concentrated more on painting landscapes which she imbued with strong atmospheric effects.

Together with Letitia and Eva Hamilton, Harriet Kirkwood and Charles Lamb contributed to the conservative stance which the Dublin Painters' Society adopted in the late twenties and thirties but they also helped to sustain its popularity with the public.

Harriet Kirkwood (1880–1953) joined the Dublin Painters in 1922 and held her first one-woman exhibition there in November of that year. She soon became a prominent member, being elected secretary in 1930 and president in 1936, a position she held until 1948 when she was succeeded in office by Eva Hamilton. She painted a wide variety of subject-matter but is best remembered for her still lifes and flower studies, such as her splendidly vivacious *Still Life with Fruit and Flowers* of about 1940, and landscapes, like *House near Clondalkin*, c.1936 (cata. no.16). In both of these works the feeling for form and structure and the carefully considered relationship of object to object suggest the influence of Cézanne, whose work she greatly admired; although the latter painting, with its looser, more Impressionist manner, is reminiscent of Augustus John, whom she also admired. The feeling of light and atmosphere which is notable in the *Still Life* work pervaded all her painting, which was lyrical and strongly domestic in character. Contrary to what one might expect, the Cubist painter André Lhote, in whose studio she spent some time during the 1930s, seems to have had little sway with her and she was more influenced by her friends and contemporaries, especially Letitia Hamilton, Grace Henry and May Guinness in the twenties, and Norah McGuinness in the thirties. Like so many of her contemporaries, Harriet Kirkwood remained traditional in outlook. Her style, which lacked discipline, changed little over the years and she seems to have been motivated almost entirely by the pleasure which painting gave her. As the art critic of the *Freeman's Journal* commented on her works shown in the Dublin Painters' autumn exhibition in 1923, she 'too often stops short of achieving real significance',[29] although her work was by no means superficial. But unlike many Irish painters of her generation, Harriet Kirkwood was opposed to the narrow outlook of nationalism so prevalent in her time. Rather, she thought that if artists were truly to create a worthwhile and distinct

Irish art they should endeavour in their work to reflect the spirit of the times and to eschew mere symbols of nationality.[30]

Charles Lamb (1893-1964) also joined the Dublin Painters in 1922 and soon became one of the most regular exhibitors there. As well as showing in group exhibitions, he held one-man exhibitions almost annually throughout the 1920s and 1930s. Lamb was, perhaps, the most academic painter in the Society. Along with his contemporaries there—the later Paul Henry, William Conor, Maurice MacGonigal—and others outside the Society, including George Russell (AE), Seán Keating, Christopher Campbell and Seán O'Sullivan, whom we shall discuss elsewhere, he belonged to what Bruce Arnold has called the 'school of Irish academic realism'.[31]

A native of Co. Armagh, Lamb studied at the Belfast College of Art before going to the Metropolitan School in Dublin. In 1921, on the suggestion of the poet Pádraic Ó Conaire, he paid his first visit to the west, to Carraroe in Co. Galway, and although he did not finally settle there until 1935, the landscape of the area with its soft light henceforth dominated his subject-matter for the rest of his career. Lamb's best work dates from the 1920s and early 1930s. In those years people dominated his compositions and his style was economical and free from all superfluities as can be seen, for example, in *A Lough Neagh Fisherman*, painted in 1920 (cata. no.17), and *Hearing the News*, of about 1920–2 (cata. no.18). The latter picture he exhibited at the Dublin Painters' autumn show in 1922 and, in its depiction of a lone reader relating the news to a group of others, it represents a scene common in the west of Ireland at that time.

Along with Paul and Grace Henry and Seán Keating, Lamb was one of the first artists to discover the west of Ireland as a source of subject-matter. But he did not go there to escape the treadmill of urban life, as did Keating and so many others, rather he was captivated by the tranquility of the area and, in a way, that became the real subject-matter of his work. This concern for tranquility at times lent an abstract quality to his paintings—we have already observed the same trait in Paul Henry— expressed through a flattening of the picture-plane and an emphasis on the juxtaposition of shape and colour. In the mid-1920s Lamb spent some time painting in Brittany and, no doubt, the influence of French art contributed to these developments. Some of the works which he painted in Brittany, such as *Breton Market Place*, 1927, are similar in style to the paintings which other Irish artists—notably May Guinness and W.J.Leech—produced while working in the same area. Moreover, the composition of his *Breton Peasants at Prayer*, painted in 1926–7 (Garter Lane Art Centre, Waterford), is reminiscent of Paul Gauguin's *Vision after the Sermon (Jacob wrestling with the Angel)*, 1888 (Edinburgh), although the expression on the faces of the sitters has a more Irish piety. Later, in the 1930s, Lamb's work declined in quality and, notwithstanding his spirited brushwork and feeling for atmosphere, became repetitive and often little more than a cliché of his earlier themes.

Two other early members of the Society who should be mentioned here are Clare Marsh and William Conor. Neither of them, however, took much part in the Society's affairs and they had little or no influence on its development. Clare Marsh (1874– 1923), of course, was a founder-member of the Dublin Painters, and two months after the inaugural exhibition of August 1920 she held a joint show there with Mary Swanzy. On that occasion she exhibited mainly landscapes and urban scenes. After her early death, in 1923, she fell into obscurity and so her work is less well-known than it deserves to be. She is, perhaps, best remembered for her portraits such as that

Cecil Salkeld
Cinema, c.1922–5
Photograph Bryan Rutledge

of *Jack B. Yeats* (Drogheda), which was exhibited in her one-woman show at the Dublin Painters in February 1922. Her landscapes, which were much admired in her lifetime, are generally tranquil in mood and in them she often emphasized modulations of closely related tones, as can be seen, for example, in her nocturnal study, *Automobile Club*, of about 1922–3, which was shown in her Memorial Exhibition at the Dublin Painters' gallery in October 1923. Her untimely death was a loss to the Dublin Painters in particular and to Irish art in general. Much of her late work, like that of many of her contemporaries, betrays a French influence and the *Irish Times*, reviewing her Memorial Exhibition, noted that she had been 'an avid student of modernism', although only in so far as its methods matched her own ideals.[32]

32

William Conor
The Jaunting Car,
c.1933
Ulster Museum

William Conor (1881–1968) joined the Society in 1922, but apart from one-man shows held there in the spring of 1924 and 1925 he seems to have taken little further interest in it. Reviewing the former exhibition in the *Irish Statesman*, George Russell (AE) saw him as 'a Belfast counterpart to Jack Yeats',[33] and thought he recorded the rich character of the 'Northern Capital' with the same delight as Yeats depicted life in the west of Ireland. This was an apt observation, for the people of Belfast, going about their daily business, were the chief subject-matter of Conor's art throughout his career. Conor's early work is his most successful and he is best remembered for his figure compositions, such as the *Jaunting Car*, painted around 1933 (Ulster Museum), and occasional portraits. Early in life he developed an idiosyncratic technique which relied greatly on the use of wax crayons, which he had first used as a lithographer when working for a commercial art studio in Belfast. This technique dominated all of his work, but unfortunately in later years it became rather fossilized.

In looking to France for inspiration and example, the artists whom we have discussed continued a tradition amongst Irish painters which began in the nineteenth century. Nathaniel Hone, Sir John Lavery and Roderic O'Conor are, perhaps, the best known of their predecessors, but there were many others.[34] At home, the establishment of the independent Irish Free State in 1922 no doubt, in a wider setting, helped to reinforce links with France which have been a recurrent feature in Irish history in general.

* * *

As we have said, it was the more conservative members of the Dublin Painters Society who largely determined its character and development. But from the mid-1920s Mary Swanzy, Mainie Jellett, Evie Hone and Cecil Salkeld produced work which reflected more recent developments in Europe, although in the long run they were less influential than those whom we have already discussed in detail. Mary Swanzy was briefly influenced by Cubism, but Mainie Jellett and, to a lesser extent, Evie Hone became the only true Irish Cubist painters. In subsequent years, a number of others—notably May Guinness in the twenties, Doreen Vanston in the thirties, Ralph Cusack in the forties and Norah McGuinness, Louis le Brocquy and Colin Middleton in the fifties—were also influenced by Cubism but none of them embraced it as completely or with as much understanding as Jellett. Cecil Salkeld, however, was virtually the only Irish painter of his generation to look beyond France. With the possible exception of a few early works by Harry Kernoff, it is entirely due to Salkeld that any trace of the German *Neue Sachlichkeit* movement—or New Objectivity as it is usually termed in English—which originated in about 1920 and greatly influenced European art in the inter-war years, is to be found in Irish painting. Collectively, Swanzy, Jellett and Salkeld represent the pinnacle of achievement of the Dublin Painters' Society as far as avant-garde painting is concerned.

Cubism was the first great innovative movement in twentieth-century art. Essentially a representational art form, it became the parent of all abstract art. Its formative years lasted from about 1907 until 1914, although artists are still absorbing its consequences in terms of the freedom of concept which it permitted. The early development of Cubism has been described as falling into different periods, which have often been called by different names, but the most widely recognized divisions are, firstly, Analytical Cubism, spanning the years from 1907 to 1912 and principally concerning the work of Picasso, Braque and Gris; and, secondly, Synthetic Cubism, spanning the years 1912–14 and evolved in the main by Delaunay, Gleizes, Le Fauconnier, Léger and Metzinger. In the first of these two periods artists were concerned principally with the analysis and expression of forms and structures rendered without the aid of perspective, and colour was of little importance to them; while in the second period colour became all-important and often areas of different colours were juxtaposed one with another so as to create abstract compositions, often with an emphasis on qualities such as light or rhythm and movement.[35]

By the early 1920s, however, when Irish artists began to show Cubist works in Ireland, Cubism, in European terms, was no longer the dominant influence it had been before 1914, that role having passed to the Dadaists and the early Surrealists. Yet, with the exception of the Belfast painter Colin Middleton, in about 1936, Irish artists during the twenties and thirties ignored both Dadaism and Surrealism despite the fact that these movements, and Surrealism in particular, then dominated practically all forms of European intellectual expression. Indeed, as we shall see later, it was not until the White Stag Group began to exhibit in Dublin in 1940 that Surrealism showed a presence there.

Like many of her contemporaries, Mary Swanzy (1882–1978) studied art in Paris, during 1905 and 1906, and there she encountered the latest artistic trends at first hand. From the beginning her work showed a strong sense of structure derived both from her interest in drawing, an influence from John Hughes, whom she knew at the Metropolitan School of Art, and her admiration for Cézanne. But she soon developed a technique inspired by French Fauvism—she was in Paris when the Fauves caused a sensation at the Salon d'automne of 1905—and, despite other influences in later years, this prevailed throughout her life, even though for a time during the 1920s and early 1930s she adopted a Cubist manner influenced by the work of Robert Delaunay,

André Lhote and Albert Gleizes. By the late 1930s, however, Swanzy had ceased to be a Modernist in any real sense, although her use of Symbolism in the 1940s gave her work a certain topicality.

Mary Swanzy first showed avant-garde paintings in Ireland at her one-woman exhibition in the Mills' Hall, Dublin, in March 1919. She was then just back from a visit to eastern Europe. In the absence of the exhibition catalogue and judging only from press reviews of the show, it is impossible to be certain of what these works were like but they appear to have been mainly Fauvist in manner, although as she was at that time influenced by Cézanne the exhibition probably included pictures such as *Landscape*, of about 1918. The formal structure of the composition here represents the greatest state of advance of her work at the time, and was the closest she came to Cubism before the mid-1920s. Reviewing the exhibition, the *Freeman's Journal* commented: 'Some of the canvases inevitably recall the "flinging a pot of paint in the face of the public" criticism,' referring to the celebrated Whistler-Ruskin affair, 'for the artist works . . . with a breadth and baldness that challenge comment';[36] while the *Evening Mail* admired her use of colour by which it thought she achieved effects both original and bizarre. In particular it admired her *Interior I* and *Interior II*, considering them to be 'feasts of colour and of exquisitely handled effects of light'.[37] The works which she exhibited with Clare Marsh at the Dublin Painters' gallery in November 1920[38] appear, both from the catalogue and press reviews, to have been similar to those already mentioned and consequently not particularly avant-garde for that date. Similarly, the reviews of her one-woman show at the same gallery in May 1922[39] suggest essentially Fauvist works but with a clear emphasis on draughtsmanship.

This latter-mentioned exhibition was Swanzy's last show in Ireland for a decade,[40] during which time she travelled extensively in the South Seas, staying in Samoa and the Hawaiian Islands. There she made a number of paintings, such as *Samoan Scene*, c.1924, which are reminiscent of the work of Gauguin, whose pictures she had known in Paris. In these years she became interested in the effects of light on colour, influences which she incorporated in Cubist paintings which she first produced in about 1925. Although she was certainly one of the first Irish artists to be familiar with Cubism, it is unlikely, as is occasionally suggested, that she was the first Irish artist to adopt that manner, the latter distinction almost certainly belonging to Mainie Jellett who first showed works, which were developed out of Cubism, at the Dublin Painters' autumn exhibition in 1923. In any case Swanzy's was a decorative kind of Cubism and lacked the theoretical rigour of Cubism proper. Swanzy retained a strong element of representation, of recession borne through the use of perspective, and she emphasized firm draughtsmanship and a good colour sense combined with rhythm to suggest movement. In the later 1920s, however, she evolved a more formal Cubism where the emphasis on dynamic movement and energy as the principal subject-matter recalls Italian Futurism rather than the more passive tenets of Cubism proper. But such rigour and severity were not long maintained by her.

The names of Mainie Jellett (1897–1944) and Evie Hone (1894–1955) are inextricably linked. Hone studied at the Westminster School of Art—where she met Jellett—and, later, at the Central School, London, under Bernard Meninsky, on whose suggestion she went to Paris in the autumn of 1920 to study at the studio of the Cubist painter André Lhote. Early the following year she was joined there by Jellett and thus began their long association. In December 1921, seeking a more abstract and more spiritual art than that taught by Lhote, which was based on the study of natural forms, they went to work with Albert Gleizes and began an association with him which continued intermittently for almost two decades. During that time they worked in a manner similar to Gleizes,[41] and thus it was that Jellett, who was more prolific than Hone, first exhibited Cubist-inspired works, the fruits of her recent studies, at the Dublin Painters' autumn exhibition in October 1923.

Mainie Jellett[42] studied painting at the Metropolitan School, Dublin, before going in 1917 to the Westminster School where she worked under Walter Sickert. In 1921, as we have said, she joined Evie Hone at the Académie Lhote and, later, at the studio of Albert Gleizes. Sickert, Lhote and Gleizes were the three big influences on her career, her 'three revolutions' as she referred to them,[43] each of which caused her to re-think her ideas on art. Sickert brought drawing and composition alive to her and under his influence she decided finally to become a painter—hitherto she had also considered a career as a professional pianist. But her style at the time was strictly representational in manner as can be seen, for example, in her *Seated Female Nude Model*, painted in about 1919 or 1920. Lhote encouraged a type of Cubism based on the study of natural forms and encouraged his pupils, as Jellett later recorded, to use colour creatively and not merely descriptively; to emphasize organic colours and rhythmical forms and to think of a picture as an organic whole. *Seated Female Nude*, of 1921–2 (cata. no.21), shows the advance of her work by this time and in it the simplification of forms in both the figure and the background emphasizes the flatness of the picture plane, a characteristic of Cubism and a quality which was later stressed by Gleizes in his teaching. But Jellett remained dissatisfied with Lhote's approach and sought what she considered to be a purer, a more abstract form of painting, and so along with Evie Hone she persuaded Albert Gleizes to allow them to work under his guidance.

By 1923, when Jellett exhibited her first truly abstract paintings, which had evolved out of Cubism, in Ireland, she had already spent two years with Gleizes so that it is principally his influence and her subsequent work with which we need to concern ourselves here. Albert Gleizes was one of the major theorists on Cubism, his book *Du Cubisme*, written with Jean Metzinger and published in 1912,[44] at this time being regarded as the most important study of the theoretical principles of the Cubist movement. *Du Cubisme* was marked throughout by a strong rhetoric and emphasis on principles of colour and surface organization and, along with Metzinger, Delaunay, Duchamp, Léger and others, Gleizes was concerned to widen and develop the Analytical Cubism of Picasso, Braque and Gris. In 1917 he underwent a religious conversion and subsequently endeavoured to interpret the laws of art in terms of Catholic truth and religious experience of the Middle Ages. This stress on religion probably had much bearing on both Jellett and Hone, who became a convert to Catholicism late in her life, and may account for Jellett's quest of the universal, the 'inner principle and not the outer appearance', as she called it,[45] which so dominated her work. But Gleizes' art, especially by the time Jellett and Hone began to work with him, was in danger of becoming a sterile dogma and it is to the credit of the two Irish women that he himself probably avoided such extinction.[46]

Initially, and until about the time of the publication of Gleizes' later book, *La Peinture et ses Lois*, Jellett and Hone studied as Gleizes' pupils but they later worked alongside him in what became for them all a journey of self-discovery. Indeed, Gleizes later recorded[47] that the discipleship of Jellett and Hone compelled him to clarify his

Mainie Jellett
*Homage to Fra
Angelico*, 1927
Photograph courtesy
Pyms Gallery, London

working procedures and aims, notably with regard to his technique of 'translation' and 'rotation' (we shall discuss these terms in a moment) which, hitherto, he had practiced intuitively. The result of this activity was his book, *La Peinture et ses Lois. Ce qui devait sortir du Cubisme*, published in Paris in 1924, in which he outlined his recent thinking. But like much of Gleizes' art and writing done after the First World War, this book suffers from the dead weight of a too-rational doctrine.

Jellett's meeting with Gleizes began the third revolution of her life. With him, she later recounted:

> I went right back to the beginning . . . and was put to the severest type of exercise in pure form and colour, evolved on a certain system of composition . . . .I now felt I had come to essentials, and though the type of work I had embarked upon would mean years of misunderstanding and walls of prejudice to break through, yet I felt I was on the right track.

And she continued:

> . . . our aim was to delve deeply into inner rhythms and constructions of natural forms to create on their pattern, to make a work of art a natural creation complete in itself . . . based on the eternal laws of harmony, balance and ordered movement (rhythm). *We sought the inner principle and not the outer appearance.*[48]

This last sentence expressed what was to be her aim for the rest of her life. Jellett's words that she sought the 'inner principle' should not be taken to imply the existence of some eternal law which, if we can only find it, lies behind our knowledge of the world. In *Du Cubisme* Gleizes and Metzinger wrote that 'the visible world only becomes the real world by the operation of thought'; they did not believe in the existence of an objective reality towards which, by the use of reason, the painter might strive. And they continued:

> There is nothing real outside ourselves, there is nothing real except the coincidence of a sensation and an individual mental direction . . . .It therefore amazes us that well-meaning critics explain the remarkable difference between the forms attributed to nature and those of modern painting, by a desire to represent things not as they appear, but as they are . . . .An object has not one absolute form, it has several; it has as many as there are planes in the domain of meaning.[49]

The implication of this statement is clear: there exists no ultimate reality *per se*. But, Gleizes and Metzinger argued, only the artist, as a supremely sensitive individual, could bring meaning to the world and, therefore, by imposing his vision on us the artist compels us to see the world as he wishes us to see it.[50] That is the eternal law, the inner principle. It was the liberating message of Synthetic Cubism and its effects are evident in the subsequent Dadaist and Surrealist movements and, indeed, in the art even of our own times.

With Gleizes, Jellett evolved the principle of 'translation' and 'rotation', a method of dividing and sub-dividing the picture plane into juxtaposed shapes which echo the overall shape and proportions of the canvas.[51] Essentially, this process involved positioning a number of rectangles of different sizes concentrically on the canvas. These rectangles were then individually displaced both horizontally and vertically (that is, they were 'translated') and finally they were rotated to the left or right in order to emphasize diagonals. This technique, which emphasized rhythm and movement, became the basis of Jellett's subsequent abstraction and accounts for some of her finest paintings, including the two pieces which she exhibited at the Dublin Painters' autumn exhibition in 1923.

Perhaps predictably, these two works aroused considerable mis-understanding and antagonism in the press, a typical comment being that of George Russell (AE) who, it will be remembered, twenty years earlier had been a keen supporter of the avant-garde. Writing in the *Irish Statesman*, Russell found Jellett 'a late victim to cubism in some sub-section of this artistic malaria'; and after a few more discursive remarks on Cubism in general he concluded: ' . . . what Miss Jellett says in one of her decorations she says in the other, and that is nothing'.[52] To the *Irish Times* the pictures presented 'an insoluble puzzle' and it illustrated one of them in its issue of 23 October in the hope that some of its readers could 'provide a solution' to it. Only Thomas MacGreevy admired these paintings, recognizing their exhibition to be a major event; and in an article published in the *Klaxon*[53] he deplored the current quality of art criticism and lampooned his fellow-critics for their boorishness. *Abstract*, painted in 1922 (cata. no.22), is similar to the work which the *Irish Times* found to be 'an insoluble puzzle' and may possibly have been the other work exhibited in the Dublin Painters' exhibition.[54] It is one of Jellett's finest abstract paintings, the forms being concisely evolved and boldly placed and the colour and handling of paint are used in a manner complementary to the translation and rotation technique and do not detract from it. Its importance, too, lies in the fact that it is amongst the first one or two truly abstract paintings to have been produced by an Irish artist. It was, too, in terms of pure as opposed to figuratively derived abstraction, in advance of any similar work yet produced in the British Isles by that date.

In June of the following year, 1924, Jellett and Hone held a joint exhibition, almost entirely of Cubist works, at the Dublin Painters' gallery and thus began a number of exhibitions which they held there almost annually during the next twenty years. From the bold simplicity of her early abstracts Jellett's compositions became increasingly intricate. By about the mid to late 1920s paintings such as *Three Elements*, of about 1924, *Composition* and *Abstract* (cata. no.23), both of around 1925-30, were usual. Typical of such works is the combination of separate images, or 'voices' as Bruce Arnold has called them,[55] each evolved through the process of translation and rotation and related to one another within the overall composition but with a degree of autonomy in themselves. The use of muted colours and an emphasis on line are also dominant features of these paintings. Such works are reminiscent of some of Picasso's paintings of the same years, such as *Three Masked Musicians*, 1921, or *The Three Dancers*, 1925 (Tate Gallery), but we do not know if Jellett was familiar with these works.

It was not until 1928 that Jellett, again exhibiting at the Dublin Painters' gallery, began to receive praise for her work. On that occasion the *Irish Times* admired what it called the 'mystic fascination' of colour and subject in her *Homage to Fra Angelico*,[56] and George Russell (AE) also had a change of heart, finding the same painting 'most impressive', especially in the almost architectural construction of its composition.[57] The *Fra Angelico* composition is, too, a reminder of Jellett's occasional use of early Italian Renaissance paintings as inspiration—an influence from Lhote—for her own work. It also illustrates how she could combine representational images with Cubist forms and is a precursor of her later, more overtly religious, works.

In the early 1920s Evie Hone's work was very similar to that of Mainie Jellett, but she was never as fully committed to Cubism as was her friend and she seems to have concerned herself hardly at all with its theoretical principles. Moreover, from 1933 she devoted herself primarily to stained glass work to which, henceforth, her painting took second place.

With Gleizes and Jellett, Hone worked during the 1920s on the technique of translation and rotation, seeking 'inner principles' rather than the representation of visual appearances. But unlike Jellett, her work always retained a largely intuitive element which in the 1930s more or less ousted the Cubist influence. Hone first showed Cubist paintings in Ireland in her joint exhibition with Mainie Jellett at the Dublin Painters' gallery in June 1924. On that occasion she exhibited twenty–five paintings (Jellett showed thirty–four), but as both artists titled their works simply

'Tempera', 'Oil' or 'Gouache' the identification of individual works, even with the aid of the exhibition catalogue, is now impossible. However, the *Irish Times* captioned its review of the exhibition 'Cubist Paintings: Works of two Dublin artists' and the *Irish Statesman* headed its notice 'In the Modern Manner'[58] so we are in no doubt as to the nature of the works shown. At this time Hone's abstracts were almost indistinguishable from those of Jellett, although the *Irish Statesman* thought that while the latter possessed the 'surer brush, the firmer vision' Hone, nevertheless, was the 'purer artist'.

In these years Evie Hone maintained contact with certain avant-garde movements outside Ireland. From 1926 until 1931 she was a member of the 7 & 5 Society[59] in London and in 1932, along with Mainie Jellett, was a founder-member of the Paris-based group, Abstraction-Création,[60] whose aim was to promote a pure non-objective art. But despite these contacts Hone grew tired of the rather arid abstraction which she had developed and seems to have suffered some crisis of conscience at the time. By 1925 she had ceased painting and entered a community of Anglican nuns in Truro, Cornwall; but a year or so later she resumed her work, which now had an emphasis on representation and bright colours. *A Cherry Tree*, of about 1931, is an example of this new direction, although she did not abandon Cubism until the late thirties. In 1929, and again in 1931, she exhibited Cubist paintings at the Dublin Painters' gallery, but by then her work had become less austere and was more lively. The latter exhibition was probably her last show of Cubist paintings, properly speaking, for henceforth her work became increasingly figurative and, in 1933, in turning to stained glass, she found a medium which allowed her to develop her talents, especially for colour, more instinctively and completely.

Unlike her friend Mainie Jellett, Evie Hone was neither a major figure in the development of Irish painting—although for her stained glass she was a most important figure—nor was she particularly influential on others. Perhaps her authority emanates more from her role as a pioneer in introducing Cubism and pure abstraction to Ireland than from her works themselves which, with the passage of time, seem increasingly to have been largely preparatory for her stained glass activity. But it is in this last regard, as pioneers of a pure abstract art, that Hone and Jellett are of supreme importance to Irish painting. They, as we have seen, understood and wrestled with the implications of the theories of Cubism and Abstract Art in a way which none of their contemporaries did.

As well as Cubism, another major influence in European art in the inter-war years was the German *Neue Sachlichkeit* movement. In Ireland its influence can be found in the work of Cecil Salkeld (1904-69) and, to a lesser extent, in the early work of Harry Kernoff. The *Neue Sachlichkeit*—or New Objectivity—movement developed in about 1920 as a reaction against Expressionism. It represented a cold, descriptive linear style which, like its near counterpart in Italy, *Pittura Metafisica*, was a superficial and academic expression of a deeper trend towards the understanding of reality. But, like Expressionsim, it sought to render the full impact of spontaneous excitement and, with a penetrating exactitude, it pinched the shape of objects to illustrate the relevant experience with over-sharp forms. The resulting definition removed the object from its natural context and often imbued it with a somewhat Surrealist aspect.

Salkeld was a man of many parts. Primarily a painter and engraver, he later became an author, dramatist, poet and broadcaster. He was born in Assam, where his father

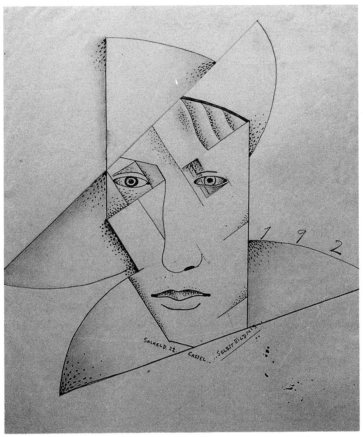

Cecil Salkeld
Self-portrait 1922
Photograph S.B.K.

was an administrator with the Indian Civil Service, but in 1909, after his father's premature death, he returned with his mother to Ireland. After studying under Keating and Sleator at the Metropolitan School of Art,[61] Salkeld went in 1921, at the age of seventeen, to Kassel in Germany to study at the Kunstakademie[62] and there encountered the *Neue Sachlichkeit* movement.

In Dublin Salkeld's training was strictly academic, as is evident in his life drawings done in late 1921 shortly after he arrived in Kassel. Here we can see the source of the emphasis on line and form which remained characteristic of his work. His *Romantische Szene* (Düsseldorf), an etching of 1921-2, also illustrates the traditional element in his training. But the influence of the *Neue Sachlichkeit* movement is clearly apparent in his work from 1922 and this shows his eagerness for the new art. In May of that year he attended the first congress of the Union of Progressive International Artists, an off-shoot of the Young Rheinland Circle of painters, who were based in Düsseldorf, and became its corresponding member for Ireland.[63] However nothing seems to have come from this and no other Irish member of the group is known. Also, in 1922, he exhibited at the first *Internationale Kunstausstellung* at Düsseldorf, where the exhibitors from other countries included, amongst others, Léger, Matisse and Vlaminck from France; Kees van Dongen, Theo van Doesburg and Gerrit Rietveld from Holland; and Umberto Boccioni from Italy.[64]

Composition, painted in 1922, clearly shows the influence of contemporary German art on Salkeld. Here the extreme stylization of forms, the flattening of the picture plane and diagonal thrust of the composition suggest an influence from the Bauhaus, then situated nearby at Weimar, and possibly of the work of Lyonel Feininger, who had taught there since 1919, and Oskar Schlemmer who joined the Bauhaus in 1920.[65] Salkeld may have been drawn to Schlemmer in particular, for in 1922 Schlemmer staged the *première* of his revolutionary 'Triadische Ballet' in Stuttgart and this event may also have influenced the young Salkeld who in later life became passionately interested in ballet.[66] Indeed ballet scenes often formed the subject-matter of his paintings in the 1940s and later. His *Self-portrait*, a pencil drawing, and *Figure Composition* (cata. no.26), a watercolour, both of 1922, further illustrate the speculative nature of his work at the time. The former reinforces the likely influence of Schlemmer, notably of his studies of figures in motion, while the more rounded forms of the latter, with a hint of Symbolism in the imagery, suggest an awareness of the Italian *Pittura Metafisica* painters, and de Chirico in particular. Even at this early stage in Salkeld's career one can see a number of features which remained characteristic of his whole *œuvre*, namely an emphasis on the importance of line over colour, a feeling for movement, the importance of figures to his compositions and, characteristic of his oils, the smoothly rendered surface of the canvas. Salkeld also produced a number of woodcuts in these years, of which *Cinema* (cata. no.27) is a good example. It shows his debt to contemporary German print-making and to his teacher in Kassel, Ewald Dulberg, a theatrical designer, who no doubt also influenced his later work for the theatre. But unlike many of his German contemporaries Salkeld did not concern himself with social criticism in these works, which are entirely decorative, although his *Death and the Maiden*, of 1923, has overtones of artists such as Grosz and Dix.

Salkeld probably settled permanently in Ireland in about 1925. The previous autumn he had held at the Dublin Painters' gallery what was probably his first one-man exhibition, although he did not become a member of the Society until about 1927. But his work had clearly been noticed even before this exhibition, for in his review of it in the *Irish Statesman* George Russell (AE) commented that he had 'emerged from the geometrical stage.' 'At present,' said Russell, 'the most powerful influence [on his work] is Indian painting and Irish tennis parties'.[67] From this remark we can assume that, by late 1924, the German influence on his work had weakened and that the exhibition included a number of lyrical pictures like *The Tennis Party*, of 1923. In the autumn term of 1926 Salkeld resumed his studies at the Metropolitan School[68] and the following year won the Royal Dublin Society's Taylor Art Scholarship for his composition entitled *The Builders*. The painting is now lost and is known only from an illustration in the journal *New Coterie* of spring 1927 and from a working drawing in the artist's papers, but in its emphasis on diagonals and the general upward thrust of the imagery we can detect the influence of his earlier work in Kassel. *The Builders* is similar in manner to his drawing of *Judith and Holofernes*, which he did two years earlier, probably while still in Germany, which was, perhaps, the first example of what became his mature style.

In these years Salkeld clearly felt confident about the progress of his career for in 1924 he published his philosophy of art in the journal *To-Morrow*. There he defined art as 'the crystallisation of idea into form, which [on the part of the observer] being comprehended by the senses, is transmuted into idea again'.[69] Actual forms around us, he said, are transmuted into ideas which can only be set-down on a flat surface by means of line and colour which subsequently 'live' only in so far as they symbolize real forms. And here he rejected photography and 'photographic' painting as not

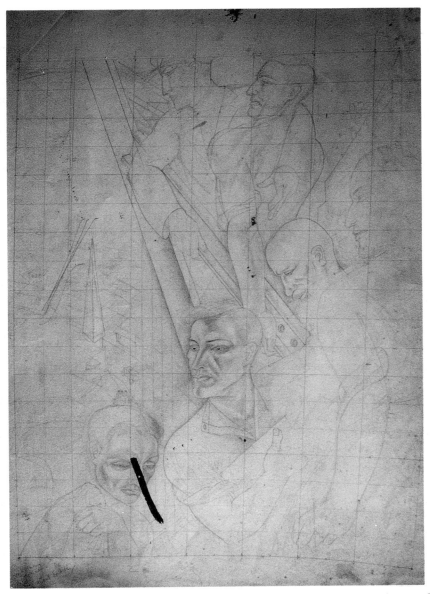

Cecil Salkeld
The Builders, 1920s
Photograph S.B.K.

being 'true art', but rather merely 'chromatic journalism'. In the next issue of the journal, published a month later, he continued his theory, saying that all forms must have universal rather than particular significance and that each picture should contain the solution to some formal problem, 'for it is this which gives a picture that intellectual unity which makes it always interesting'.[70] Technically, he said, colour should be applied smoothly in order to avoid distraction by a too subtle surface and he also recommended 'an incisive simplicity of drawing'. Salkeld maintained this philosophy of art throughout his career. Indeed, twenty years later he wrote in the *Bell*: 'I see no reason to alter my youthful definition of the principle of painting: [namely] *the minimum of form with the maximum associations*'.[71] Essentially Salkeld's theory of art was Expressionistic, as befitted his training in Germany, and it also reflected the spirit of the *Neue Sachlichkeit* movement with its emphasis on fidelity to tangible reality. In terms of Irish art he was one of the few artists of his time to hold a distinct theory of art and his views were different to those of any of his contemporaries.

Because of the multifarious nature of Salkeld's activities his career as a painter progressed erratically from the mid-1920s and after *The Builders* his most important works were the three compositions comprising the *Triumph of Bacchus* mural in Davy Byrne's public house, Duke Street, Dublin, completed sixteen years later. But during the twenties and thirties he exhibited periodically both in group and one-man shows. Noting his works in the New Irish Salon in spring 1924 the *Irish Times* thought, somewhat disparagingly, that along with Gleizes, Lhote, Evie Hone and Mainie Jellett he had 'advanced to second childishness'; although by the following October the same paper, commenting on his one-man show at the Dublin Painters' gallery, felt that he had the ability to 'tell the spectator more than is told by a picture constructed after the ordinary rules of perspective'.[72] Salkeld's association with the Dublin Painters was short-lived. He held a second one-man show there in November 1925, but the press passed little comment on it. The next occasion on which we see his work was a decade later in a mixed show with Grace Henry, Doreen Vanston and Edward Gribbon held at Daniel Egan's Gallery, Dublin, during February and March 1935. By that time his manner had become stylized and it remained so for the rest of his career.

Harry Kernoff (1900–74) joined the Dublin Painters' Society in 1927. After an initial flirtation with avant-garde ideas he lost his enthusiasm for the Modern Movement—and abstraction in particular—and turned to realism, striving to depict with verisimilitude life around him in all its aspects. Yet, despite his occasional rhetoric on the matter,[73] his early work, in its directness, was often similar to that of the painters of the *Neue Sachlichkeit* movement.

Only Kernoff's early work, done shortly after he left the Metropolitan School of Art, where his teachers included Seán Keating, whom he greatly admired, and Patrick Tuohy, shows any substantial influence of Modernism. Presumably he became aware of Modernism while a student in London and Paris,[74] where he went after winning the Taylor Art Scholarship in 1923 for his painting entitled *The Race*, although he would have seen avant-garde pictures reproduced and discussed in contemporary journals. At that time he was interested in Cubism, although he later, as we have seen, veered towards Expressionism.[75] Few of Kernoff's early pictures seem to have survived so that his most avant-garde works are known only from photographs extant in his papers. *Vortex*, of about 1923 (Kernoff papers, National Gallery of Ireland), and *Dance of Death*, 1923, are examples of two such works but others produced at about the same time were *Mascarade*, in which he symbolized different cultures of the world,[76] *War* and *Peace*. *Vortex*, which he exhibited in his one-man show at the Dublin Painters in May 1932, symbolizes Life, which is depicted by a woman holding a child in the centre of the composition, while grouped around her are figures representing some of the forces of life, namely piety and evil, law, learning, art, labour and wealth.[77] *Dance of Death* seems to represent some Mephistophelean domain inhabited by daemonic figures and wild animals. It may, in fact, be a composition which he exhibited in 1928 symbolizing Dogma seated chained while the world breaks at her feet, torn apart by figures representing her progeny—revolution, war, death, deceit, treachery—all arranged in angular rhythms. *War* and *Peace* are a pair of paintings, the former being a terrifying symbol of a mammon-ridden materialistic world caught in the grip of horror and desolation.[78] Other paintings

Harry Kernoff
Vortex, c.1923
National Gallery of Ireland

of these years which betray the influence of contemporary trends are *Extension in Time and Space*, of about 1926-8—Kernoff also made a woodcut of this composition—and three stage sets which he designed in 1928 for Georg Kaiser's play *Gas*,[79] (National Gallery of Ireland). The former composition depicts some sort of metaphysical world, possibly symbolizing Hope and Reality, through which man must pass but over which he has little control. The imagery—a massive viaduct leading only partly across an abyss, menacing skyscrapers and alien planets, all caught in an upward swirl—is, however, clearly Futurist in derivation. It recalls Fritz Lang's futuristic film, *Metropolis*, made in 1927, as well as the work of the Italian Futurist painters Russolo and de Chirico. On the other hand, his stage sets, especially the *Billionaire's Office* for act one of *Gas* and the *Workers' Hall* for act three, are pure Expressionism (he also did sets for Toller's Expressionist play, *Hoppla*,[80] for the Drama League), the latter in particular, with its crystal-like formations, perhaps

45

quoting designs of the German Expressionist architect Bruno Taut. After about 1930 or 1932, however, Kernoff turned aside from such influences and began to work in the realist manner for which he is most remembered.

* * *

As is by now evident, the Society of Dublin Painters, in providing a gallery where young and liberally minded artists could exhibit their work without having to submit themselves to a selection committee or other form of judgement, broke the stranglehold of academicism which the Royal Hibernian Academy and the other smaller bodies hitherto exerted on Irish painting. The Society quickly became a catalyst for all artists who had leanings towards the Modern Movement. Yet, strangely, in the light of the revolutionary nature of the times, there was never in its activities any move towards secessionism, which was a prominent feature of the development of the Modern Movement in other European countries. But when a secessionist movement, the Irish Exhibition of Living Art, did begin in 1943 many members of the Dublin Painters' Society exhibited at it. Those who belonged to the Society, however, remained individualists, each pursuing his or her own path. With the exception of Mainie Jellett, none of them was a crusader in any sense and the most we may say of them is that, as a group, their aim was passively to bring to Ireland an awareness of recent developments in European painting. The dominant influence amongst them of the School of Paris, their frequent adoption of a loose kind of Fauvism based on French examples and the widespread absence of a theoretical approach reflect their individuality. For many of them, especially the less influential whom we shall discuss in the next chapter, art was more of an avocation than a truly serious matter in their lives.

CHAPTER 3

THE SOCIETY OF DUBLIN PAINTERS 1932–1950

' . . . an institution of Ireland'

'The Dublin Painters', *Irish Times*, 3 February 1933.

THROUGHOUT the 1920s the membership of the Society of Dublin Painters had been limited to a maximum of ten persons, but in 1932 this number was increased to twelve and later, in about 1934, to eighteen.[1] However, with the departure of Paul Henry, O'Rorke Dickey, Jack B. Yeats and Mary Swanzy in the mid-1920s, all of whom were replaced by more conservative painters, much of the experimental work and excitement of the Society's early exhibitions fell away and, with the notable exception of Mainie Jellett, gradually it assumed the more cautious stance which marked its later years.

This growing conservatism reflects the widespread torpidity which took hold of Irish life during the 1930s. In the general election of February 1932 the Fianna Fáil party under Éamon de Valera became the largest party in the Dáil and thus formed the new government. De Valera and his followers had earlier opposed the terms of the Anglo-Irish Treaty of 1921, objecting principally to the partition of the country and to the requirement that deputies in the Dáil should take an oath of allegiance to the British monarch. In 1923 they had been on the losing side in the civil war, but in 1926 they formed the Fianna Fáil party and gradually began to enter the mainstream of Irish political life, first taking their seats in the Dáil in 1927. Fianna Fáil were committed to overthrowing the terms of the Treaty and after gaining office in 1932 they began to work towards a new Constitution, which was eventually adopted in 1937. In essence de Valera envisaged Ireland as a rural community whose values reflected those of the west, where the centuries of English domination had least affected the native population. The reality of these years, however, was a growing feeling of xenophobia and self-imposed isolation which ended only with the outbreak of the Second World War.

Throughout the 1930s and early 1940s the Society of Dublin Painters was held in good stead by the critics. The *Irish Times*, in an editorial in 1933, for example, wrote that it had become 'an institution of Ireland', and noted that its virtue was that it imposed no canons of school or genre upon its members.[2] A characteristic of the membership at this time is the preponderance of women, so much so that the same paper commented of the spring show in 1935 that it was the first time there had been in Ireland a women aritsts' exhibition, 'as this show virtually may be taken to be'.[3] From 1936 the Society was under the presidency of Harriet Kirkwood and, with the exception of Fr. Jack Hanlon, E.A.McGuire and Richard Finney, all of whom joined in the mid–1930s, all new members in subsequent years seem to have been women. The balance of the sexes was redressed, however, in the 1940s with the arrival of Ralph Cusack, Patrick Hennessy, Gerard Dillon, Thurloe Conolly and Robert Burke.

* * *

Mainie Jellett was perhaps the most progressive member of the Society during the 1930s and, in the light of her importance as a Cubist and an abstract painter, her work should be examined here in some detail. Jellett exhibited regularly at the St. Stephen's Green gallery throughout the thirties and in these years began to find recognition for her work. In 1930 three of her compositions—*Peinture No.1*, *Peinture No.2* and *Gouache*, probably all abstracts—were included in the important exhibition of Irish Art held at Brussels,[4] a show arranged with great diplomatic pomp and prestige and which may fairly be regarded as representing the officially accepted face of Irish art at that time. Later, the Irish government commissioned Jellett to design murals to illustrate the industrial development of the country for its pavilion at the Glasgow Exhibition in 1938,[5] and in 1941 Stephen Rynne felt able to write in the *Leader*: 'He who denies art to Miss Jellett denies his own times'.[6]

By the early to mid-1930s Jellett's compositions had become more formalized than hitherto and human figures, often with religious connotations, become apparent in them. Paintings such as *Composition*, of 1932–5, with its Madonna-like figure, are typical of her work at the time. This development culminated in the late 1930s and early 1940s, towards the end of her life, in a number of semi-abstract religious works, of which *The Assumption*, 1937; *The Ninth Hour*, 1939; *The Nativity*, 1941; *I Have Trodden the Winepress Alone*, 1943; and *Madonna of Eire*, 1943 (both National Gallery of Ireland), are the most important. Along with her *Homage to Fra Angelico*, these works, and especially *The Ninth Hour*, *Winepress* and *Madonna of Eire* have, in her use of colour and complexity of formal structures and rhythms, an amplitude and grandeur in excess of anything else she produced. These are devotional paintings and have a strong autobiographical quality to them; they evoke the spirit of the times in which they were painted and the latter work, in particular, recalls that imagined purity of Gaelic Ireland to which we have referred. Perhaps to an extent they were an act of catharsis, in part personal and in part for the times in which she was living. They seem, too, to stand at the end of a period of development and it is plausible to assume, both from the evidence of her work and her writing, that had she lived Jellett would have returned to a more representational kind of painting, probably of a form similar to her *Achill Horses* (National Gallery of Ireland).

But what, we must ask, was the substance of Mainie Jellett's contribution to the Modern Movement in Ireland? She herself wrote much about her approach to art and others, too, have written at considerable length about her work,[7] so that at times it is difficult to separate the word (which too often is rhetorical) from the work itself. Jellett, undoubtedly, is the most important Irish Cubist painter, yet there is still a lack of ease in her work. Perhaps she was consumed by a too rigid theory to the detriment of her own intuitive responses. Certainly the times in which she lived,

Mainie Jellett
Achill Horses,
c.1938–40
National Gallery of Ireland

especially the later 1930s and early 1940s, aggravated her sensibilities and thus made more difficult her work as an artist. She undoubtedly believed in Modernism and yet, referring to it in 1943, she wrote:

> This movement has been a means of purification a revitalisation [of art] . . . . I do not say it is a great art because I do not consider the present period is capable of producing great art . . . but it is a period when new foundations can be placed . . . . That, I feel, "The Modern Movement" in art is doing, and has done.[8]

Apart from her painting, Mainie Jellett's other major contribution to the development of the Modern Movement in Ireland was as a teacher, both of her own pupils and of the general public. Through her painting, writing and broadcasting—and the documents which she thus produced are the nearest we have to a manifesto from any Irish artist working in our period—she made plain to all that Modernism was not a passing fad, but was rather the serious attempt of a new century to create an identity for itself. Yet, for all her awareness, it is strange that she ignored completely Dadaism and Surrealism which, particularly as reflections of the times, were the real expression of the twenties and thirties.

Mainie Jellett's untimely death in February 1944 was followed in June of that year by a Memorial Exhibition held, appropriately, at the Dublin Painters' gallery and at the Waddington Galleries in South Anne Street, Dublin. The establishment that same year of the Mainie Jellett Scholarship for students[9] was another fitting memorial to her work as an artist and teacher.

Evie Hone appears to have exhibited little or nothing with the Dublin Painters after the mid-1930s. As we have said, from 1933 she worked principally in stained glass and the paintings which she did produce are largely Expressionistic in style

49

Grace Henry
The Red House at
Mougins, 1930s
Courtesy J.G. Cruickshanks

and show little trace of her earlier Cubist manner. Increasingly her subject-matter assumed a religious theme, which reflects the influence of Rouault on her at this time.

Of the original female members of the Society, Grace Henry also continued to exhibit there until at least the the mid-1930s. In these years she spent a considerable amount of time on the Continent painting in France, Spain and Italy where, stimulated by the exhilaration of gay colour under the southern sky,[10] she produced some of her best pictures, which are characterized by strong, vibrant colours, as can be seen, for example, in *The Red House at Mougins* of the early 1930s. Harbour scenes of boats with bright sails and light shimmering on the water typify her subject-matter and she also produced many still lifes and flower paintings. Stylistically these pictures are rooted in French Fauvism of the early twentieth century, a tradition which suited Grace Henry's personality, for nearly all of her work has a fluidity and restlessness determined, no doubt, by her temperament of which Máirín Allen noted in 1942 that she could be 'vivacious', at times with a 'youthful, irresponsible gaiety', but rarely philosophical or profound.[11]

Harry Kernoff, who had joined the Dublin Painters in 1927, exhibited there regularly until about 1933, after which time he turned to other venues. In 1935 he was elected an associate member of the Royal Hibernian Academy, became a full member the following year, and, henceforth, the Academy was his chief venue for exhibiting in mixed exhibitions. Although Kernoff began to reject avant-garde ideas in about 1930 or 1932, and adopted the representational manner for which he is best remembered, he never wholly embraced academicism, but retained a strong individuality which marks him from his contemporaries in the Academy. His approach to painting at this time is made clear in a number of aphorisms which he set down, of which the following are typical: 'Beauty is the artist's conception of nature in a rhythmic form, emphasizing his viewpoint with controlled emotion and with perfect

Harry Kernoff
W.B. Yeats, 1939
Photograph Bryan Rutledge

balance'; 'Just as a man is perhaps a symbol of a greater thing, so a picture should symbolize humanity'.[12] The sense of freedom, implicit in these statements, that the artist may approach his work as he will, was also typical of the approach to their art of many members of the Dublin Painters' Society.

From the early 1930s, portraits and landscapes became Kernoff's principal subject-matter and, as well as painting, he also produced numerous woodcuts for book illustrations. A characteristic of his work in general, as we noted earlier, is a fidelity to the world around him which he set down with a directness which at times makes his work close in feeling to that of the German Realists. This is especially true of his

Maurice MacGonigal
Inishmór, c.1930–5
Photograph S.B.K.

woodcuts, such as *We Want Work*, of about 1936, in which he captured concisely the prevailing mood of the times. In the early 1930s Kernoff began what was to become a long series of portraits of notable Dubliners of his day.[13] These were executed rapidly, usually with a maximum of about three sittings.[14] They are notable for their penetration of character, as can be seen, for example, in his drawing of the architect *Michael Scott*, 1930, with its expression of determination, and in his painting of the elderly *W.B.Yeats*, 1939, which conveys the strong personality of the sitter as well as the sense of foreboding which preoccupied the poet in his last years. Even in his woodcuts Kernoff could penetrate character as is evident in *Boon Companions*, 1934 (National Gallery of Ireland)—there is a watercolour of the same composition and title in the Ulster Museum—a self-portrait (seated right) with two friends. But despite his abilities at characterization, Kernoff does not rank highly as a draughtsman, as close scrutiny of his line and the modelling in, for example, his drawing of Michael Scott will indicate. Too often his portraits are of interest because of the identity of the sitter, rather than for technical or aesthetic reasons. Moreover, his style and technique changed little after the 1930s so that his later portraits often look repetitive.

Kernoff's landscapes, dating from the 1930s and later, are also well known. In these, unlike his Irish contemporaries who usually concerned themselves with the mood and atmosphere of the landscape, Kernoff emphasized the physical nature of the scene and often focused attention on aspects such as architectural features. His choice of subject, frequently drawn from the poorer areas of Dublin, was probably a reflection of his own humble origins. *Naylor's Cove*, probably done in the early 1930s, is one of his most successful landscapes and clearly illustrates his approach. Here the acute observation of figures engaged in diverse activities typifies his work as can be seen, too, in later pictures such as *Bend in the Road near Richmond, Surrey* of 1947 (cata. no.28). His landscapes are strongly linear, often with curves thrusting into the background, as does the roadway in the *Richmond* composition, and the almost naïve charm and gentle mannerism of the latter picture are also typical of many of his works. However, as with his portraits, Kernoff's technique in landscape changed little over the years and he was clearly at his best during the thirties. In terms of Irish art in general, Kernoff, as Brian Fallon has commented, was a 'Little Master',[15] but his strength and importance are as a chronicler of his times and of the world around him and that is what gives his work an enduring charm.

As a young man Maurice MacGonigal (1900–79) had sought a progressive style in his art. In about 1926 he helped to establish, and exhibited with, the short-lived Radical Painters' Group[16] and in the late 1920s joined the Dublin Painters Society. He held his first one-man show at the St. Stephen's Green gallery in 1929 and had similar exhibitions there in the ensuing years. From about 1933, however, he seems to have bothered little with the Society; this may have been due to the fact that, at heart, he was an academic painter and, as can be seen for example in his *Inishmór*, of about 1930–5, he was little influenced by Modernist trends. Also, in 1933 he became a member of the Academy of Christian Art, an ultra-conservative and chauvinistic body. With Seán Keating in these same years, and later, MacGonigal was a central figure in the movement which tried to establish a distinct 'national' art form, the sentiments of which were clear in works like his *By the Sea* of the late 1930s.

* * *

The most talented artists to join the Dublin Painters' Society in the 1930s were Nano Reid and Norah McGuinness, although neither of them took a leading part in its affairs. Also, their best work belongs to the 1940s and later. Nano Reid (1910–81) studied in Paris and London before settling in Dublin in about 1930. Her *Galway Peasant* (cata. no.29), painted in 1929, shows the bold simplicity and forceful character of her style at this time and recalls Paul Henry's paintings of Connemara peasants done almost twenty years earlier. Reid joined the Society in about 1934 and held her first one-woman exhibition there in May of that year, on which occasion she showed both landscapes and portraits, the latter (for economic reasons) being a prominent aspect of her work at the time. In the early thirties her style was fluid, but in 1934 she was influenced by the work of the Belgian artist Marie Howet, then on a visit to Ireland, which she saw at the Gresham Hotel, Dublin, and was encouraged to adopt a more forceful manner. This resulted in works like *The Lilter* (Ulster Museum), *The Bath* and her portrait of *Carl Hardebeck*, all painted in about 1936, and all of which are characterized by the use of a black line to separate the forms and a strongly gestural handling of paint. Throughout the late 1930s and early to mid-1940s she continued to hold regular one-woman exhibitions, as well as taking part in group shows, at the Dublin Painters' gallery, but she had little or no influence on her contemporaries there and overall her painting at the time had a melancholy feeling which remained characteristic of her for some time.

Norah McGuinness (1903–80) trained at the Metropolitan School of Art under Patrick Tuohy, Oswald Reeves and Harry Clarke, the latter having a strong influence on her early career as an illustrator.[17] However in about 1923 or 1924, while on a visit to London, she saw some French Impressionist and Post-Impressionist paintings and was so impressed by them that she decided henceforth to concentrate on painting,[18] although illustration work remained a source of income to her throughout her career. For a short time in the late 1920s she studied in London before going, on Mainie Jellett's advice, to Paris to work with André Lhote. Lhote, of course, emphasized Cubism, but McGuinness, who was by then already familiar with its theories, felt too set in her ways to embrace it as fervently as Jellett had done.[19] However, during these years her style changed considerably and one can see the influence on her of a number of artists, including Braque (whom she admired more than any other painter),[20] Lurçat, Dufy and Vlaminck. Vlaminck exerted a strong influence on a number of paintings which she did during the 1930s, notably on a group of gouaches inspired by the river Thames near to where she lived for a time at Hammersmith. These works are all handled with great bravura and combine brisk brushwork and a lively massing of tones in such a way as to contrast strongly with her more precise, linear work of the previous decade. Her colours, however, are less strident than one would expect from a French influence. In many respects she never surpassed these paintings, either in concept or execution, and some of them may have been seen at her one-woman show held at the Dublin Painters' gallery in March 1936, shortly after she joined the Society. *The Thames*, painted in about 1932–4 (cata. no.30); *Barges at Hammersmith*, 1932–6; *Still Life on the Thames*, 1932–6; and *Tower Bridge*, of about 1936, are amongst the best of these works. The medium, gouache, is perfectly suited to the spontaneity of approach, the dark hues and massing of juxtaposed forms such as barges and warehouses and the areas of contrasting tones ably convey the atmosphere of a great river at work and, although no figures appear, always one senses the bustle of the actual scene which is set down with great simplicity. There is, too, little attempt to suggest recession and, while the imagery is treated in a representational manner, she constantly reminds one of the flatness of the picture

N. McGuinness
A corner of the studio, 1980
Photograph S.B.K.

Moyra Barry
Rhododendrons,
c.1934
Ulster Museum

plane, an influence, no doubt, from her earlier Cubist studies. Norah McGuinness' treatment of landscape in general was as a breath of fresh air to Irish painting at this time, and those who were weary of the conventional scene of purple mountains and white cottages welcomed the freshness of her observation, her use of medium, mood and form. Yet paradoxically there is on occasions a tinge of melancholy about her paintings; but this may be seen as a metaphor for the times, for Norah McGuinness always reacted spontaneously to things around her.

Other women who joined the Society in the early-mid 1930s were Hilda Roberts, Moyra Barry, Lilian Davidson, Stella Frost, Joan Jameson, Brigid Ganly and Beatrice Glenavy. Along with Grace Henry, Letitia Hamilton, Harriet Kirkwood, Mainie Jellett and Evie Hone, all of whom remained from the previous decade, they henceforth set the tone and standard of the Society's exhibitions for the rest of the decade.

Hilda Roberts (1901–82) is best remembered as a portrait painter, although she also produced landscapes and some book illustrations. She first exhibited at the Dublin Painters' gallery in May 1928[21] after which she soon became noted for her portraits, of which those of the poet *John Lyle Donaghy*, 1928 (Ulster Museum), and *George*

Russell (AE), 1929 (cata. no.31), are good examples, if a little unadventurous. Moyra Barry (1886–1960) joined the Society in about 1934 but seems never to have held any solo exhibitions there, preferring to show in mixed exhibitions. Educated at the Royal Hibernian Academy schools and at the Slade School, London, she became best known and much praised for her flower paintings such as *Rhododendrons*, of about 1934 (Ulster Museum), in which her technique was to focus closely on the flowers and foliage, omitting all references to the surroundings, the composition being characterized by an emphasis on light and atmosphere. However, her work was often dull and repetitive and she contributed little to the avant-garde, although her early *Self-portrait in the Artist's Studio*, 1920 (National Gallery of Ireland), shows a vigorous use of brushwork and is Impressionist in concept. Lilian Davidson (1879–1954) joined the Dublin Painters at about the same time as Moyra Barry and exhibited there regularly. She is often remembered as a portrait painter, her best-known study possibly being that of *Jack B. Yeats* (National Gallery of Ireland), which captures the personality of the sitter but which is entirely traditional in concept. Some of her landscapes, such as *Low Tide, Wicklow*, of about 1934 (cata. no.32), show the influence on her of Jack Yeats, while others come close in feeling to the work of Paul Henry and J.H.Craig. Like so many of her contemporaries in these years, Lilian Davidson was a competent painter but had little originality.

Stella Frost was a close friend of Lilian Davidson. She became a member of the Dublin Painters in about 1935 but exhibited infrequently. However, she held what may have been her first one-woman exhibition, showing paintings of Yugoslavia and the Balearic Islands, there in October 1935. All in all, she had little originality and contributed little to the avant-garde in Ireland. In 1957 she edited the book *A Tribute to Evie Hone and Mainie Jellett* (Dublin: Browne & Nolan), which records her admiration of and friendship with these two artists. Like Stella Frost, Joan Jameson (1892–1953) lacked originality. A cousin of Harriet Kirkwood, who may have encouraged her to join the Society, she held her first one-woman exhibition there in November 1934 and, henceforth, for a decade or so, exhibited portraits, landscapes and flower paintings mainly in group exhibitions. However, she contributed little to the development of the group. Brigid Ganly (b.1909) and Beatrice Glenavy (1883–1968) came to the Dublin Painters in the mid-1930s, but they were more academic in outlook than their colleagues. With the former, perhaps, this is not surprising for she was the daughter of Dermod O'Brien, at that time president of the Royal Hibernian Academy. Her work is characterized by its variety of subject-matter and her range of media, which included tempera and pastel. Much of Beatrice Glenavy's work from the 1930s had an enigmatic, at times almost Surrealist quality, as can be seen, for example, in *The Intruder*, of 1932 (cata. no.115). She exhibited this picture in her exhibition at the Dublin Painters' gallery in February 1935, but she belongs really to the academic tradition[22] and we shall discuss her work in a later chapter.

With these painters, and others whom we have discussed, it will be seen that, by the early 1930s, the Dublin Painters had become unadventurous and lacked the rigour of their colleagues of the previous decade. Even those like Charles Lamb, a founder-member, who continued to exhibit in one-man and group exhibitions throughout the thirties, became mere shadows of their former selves, as can be seen, for example, in Lamb's *Taking in the Lobster Pots* of about 1947 (Armagh County Museum). In a way the apparent torpor which beset the Society in these years is a reflection of that condition which assailed Irish society at the same time. However, in the mid and late

1930s Fr. Jack Hanlon, Frances Kelly and May Guinness, all new members, brought a renewed vigour to the exhibitions and their presence was strengthened by the arrival of yet other talented young painters in the 1940s.

Fr. Jack Hanlon (1913–68) joined the Society of Dublin Painters in 1936. Contemporary with his studies for the priesthood he had studied art with Mainie Jellett and André Lhote, the latter influencing him towards Cubism. But Hanlon eschewed the more rigid theories of Cubism and developed a style which laid emphasis on colour and light, as can be seen, for example, in his *Still life with figure*, painted in 1945 (cata. no.34). Many of his best works are watercolours, such as *Maynooth College*, of about 1939 (cata. no.33), in which medium his style was both agile and delightfully economic, the subject-matter often treated, as here, with a sense of

Frances Kelly
Looking into the Garden, c.1938
Ulster Museum

Charles Lamb
*Taking in the
Lobster Pots*, c.1947
Armagh County Museum

humour. Both his oils and watercolours are characterized by brisk execution based on direct observation of his subject. While not an influential artist Hanlon's importance, as Cyril Barrett has noted,[23] lies chiefly in his support for those who spread the gospel of Modernism in Ireland.

Frances Kelly joined the Dublin Painters shortly after Fr. Hanlon. She had a brilliant career as a student at the Metropolitan School of Art and in 1932 became the first holder of the Henry Higgins travelling Scholarship.[24] With this award she went to Paris to study under the Cubist painter Léopold Survage,[25] although her style ultimately was little influenced by Cubism. Kelly became best known for her portraits and still lifes. Her work is characterized by lively brushwork and a strong feeling for light, air and space, often rendered in pale colours and with a predominance of greys, as can be seen in *Looking into the Garden*, of about 1938 (Ulster Museum), against which she would set bright reds, violets and other colours, which thrill with their radiance. Harmony is the prevailing quality in her compositions and, even in her portraits, the likeness of the sitter is subordinated to it. This can be seen clearly in her portraits of *George Furlong*, painted in the late 1930s, and *David Hone*, of the early 1940s. The latter two pictures also illustrate the probable influence on her of the French painter Marie Laurencin and this gives her work a distinctly international flavour.

May Guinness (1863–1955) joined the Dublin Painters' Society in the late 1930s but was never a prominent member. She had held a one-woman exhibition there in May 1922—showing, amongst other works, *Tugboat on the Seine* and *Procession at Josselin* (National Gallery of Ireland)[26]—and had another similar show in December 1935; but she exhibited in few of the Society's mixed exhibitions. Born in 1863,

May Guinness was a generation older than her colleagues. Besides her brief association with the Dublin Painters, she exhibited her work at various other venues in Dublin. However, despite her years, May Guinness was one of the most innovative Irish painters of her time and, though never at the forefront of the Dublin Painters' activities, we must nevertheless discuss her work in some detail.

May Guinness began painting in about the 1890s[27] but did not turn to art seriously until around 1905–7 when she went to Paris. There she was to work intermittently for more than twenty years under the Fauvist painters Ermenagildo Anglada-Camarosa and Kees van Dongen and, from 1922 until 1925, with André Lhote. She also greatly admired Matisse and her early work, done after her first visit to Paris, was much influenced by him. After the First World War she lived for a time near Dublin, at Marlay, beside Evie Hone, but in about 1932 she settled at Tibradden, Rathfarnham, Co. Dublin, although she continued to visit Paris regularly.[28] In these years there emerged a small group of admirers of her work who included Grace Henry, Evie Hone, Mainie Jellett and Mary Swanzy. Also, she assembled at her home a collection of avant-garde paintings by Bonnard, Dufy, Matisse, Picasso and Rouault, all artists whom she admired.

It is only with extreme tentativeness that we can hazard a guess as to the development of May Guinness's work. There are three main reasons for this difficulty: firstly, she rarely if ever dated her works; secondly, her career as a painter spanned only about thirty years of her adult life (she was already in her forties when she went to Paris and was seventy-two by the time of her last one-woman exhibition at the Dublin Painters' gallery in 1935) so that the normal lifetime's development is missing; and, thirdly, in all her one-woman exhibitions she showed a mixture of recent and past works executed in various styles so that neither the reviews of these exhibitions nor the catalogues are of much help in plotting her changing technique. However, with these difficulties in mind we may hazard describing her career as falling into three phases, namely early (pre-1922), Cubist (1922–5), and late (post-1925). Our main difficulty here is in distinguishing between the early and late phases, the Cubist works being more or less distinctive in manner.

As James White noted in the introduction to the catalogue of her Memorial Exhibition held in 1956,[29] May Guinness' early work was influenced by the broad decorative style of Matisse and Fauvism. Fauvism was at its peak at the *Salon d'Automne* of 1905 and the *Salon des Indépendants* of 1906, that is, at just about the time May Guinness arrived in Paris as a student. Her *Cathedral of Diest* (Lane Gallery) and *Procession at Josselin* (National Gallery of Ireland) both date from her early period,[30] and possibly illustrate her style before the onset of the Fauvist influence, which is reflected in her *Tugboat on the Seine*.[31] *Parisian Portrait Study*, *Girl with a Book*, *Woman Reading* and similar works, all executed with an emphasis on brisk brushwork, colour, mood and atmosphere, possibly also belong to her early period. But from 1922 until 1925 she worked from time to time with André Lhote[32] and was influenced by his approach to Cubism, which was to apply Cubist stylization as a formal discipline to scenes from everyday life. She produced several still lifes during these years, all very much in the manner of Lhote, in which stylized forms were arranged so as to make bold patterns but always with recognizable imagery. *Still Life* (cata. no.36) must date from this time and, in terms of the bold simplicity of the composition and the skilful use of an almost monochromatic palette, it is one of the most successful works she ever produced. Typical of such paintings is the use of a thin film of paint—which, with age, often becomes dry and paste-like in appearance—but which serves to emphasize the formal elements of the composition in contrast to the more *malerisch* approach of her earlier, and later, work. *Mother and Children*, a genre scene, probably dates from this period and embodies those characteristics which we have just mentioned. But this somewhat formulaic method of painting led to a certain aridity which was contrary to May Guinness' natural inclinations and, probably in about late 1924 or early 1925 (by which time she was already in her sixties), she returned to a more spontaneous method of painting which in manner was essentially Fauvist.[33] But occasionally in her later work, done after the mid-1920s, the influence of Cubism becomes apparent and *A Russian Cossack* may date from the beginning of the last phase of her development. Here, the bold simplification of forms and general flattening of the picture plane all betray Cubism, although the somewhat strident colouring probably came from Anglada-Camarosa. It was in this last period that she was undoubtedly happiest and at her most assured. Her best works of the time, such as *Outside a Paris Café* (Limerick Art Gallery) and *Mardi Gras* (cata. no.37), have a lyricism reminiscent of Marie Laurencin which gave her work a tenderness and which made it personal and unique. In these late works the act of painting and the medium itself became more important to her than any compositional or aesthetic theories and, especially in her pastel drawings such as *Athenian Evening* or *Les Amis* (Waterford Art Gallery), or in watercolours like *Roses in a Jug*, there is a *joie de vivre* never seen in her earlier work. Yet by the late 1920s and 1930s such works were hardly to be considered avant-garde, although in Irish terms they had a certain modernity.

As we have seen, May Guinness was one of the most innovative artists of her generation in Ireland, but nevertheless, her influence on the Modern Movement here was slight. Perhaps this was because she exhibited infrequently, although one senses too a latent privacy in her personality. Her work apart, she was undoubtedly a source of encouragement to those younger artists who gathered in her circle and because of this her place in the history of Irish art is greater than the works themselves might otherwise suggest.

In the late 1930s Dorothy Blackham, Margaret Clarke, Sylvia Cooke-Collis and Brenda Gogarty, who was a sculptor, all joined the Dublin Painters' Society. None of them brought anything new to the Society's exhibitions and Margaret Clarke, an academician of the Royal Hibernian Academy, worked in a straightforward academic manner. Dorothy Blackham (1896–1975) was a close friend of Mainie Jellett. Her early work is largely representational and is characterized by a tendency to flatten the picture plane and to emphasize shape, as can be seen, for example, in *The Nuns' Walk*, of about 1940. Her later work, however, was more decorative but had an emphasis on line, as in *House Painting in Paddington* (Lane Gallery). She was also well-known for her lino cuts of landscapes. Sylvia Cooke-Collis studied at the School of Art in Cork under John Power and, later, under Mainie Jellett in Dublin. She held her first one-woman exhibition at the Dublin Painters' gallery in June 1937,[34] showing works in which she emphasized rhythmical movements drawn from nature. Like Brenda Gogarty (b.1912), the daughter of Oliver St. John Gogarty, who seems to have been the only sculptor to have been a member of the Dublin Painters, she took little part in the running of the Society.

Thus was the membership of the Dublin Painters' Society in the late 1930s on the eve of the outbreak of war and of a period which was to be a watershed in the artistic,

Dorothy Blackham. *House Painting, Paddington*
Hugh Lane Municipal Gallery of Modern Art

61

as well as the social, development of modern Ireland. Despite its sluggish character, the Society was held in good stead by the critics in these years. In 1939 both the *Irish Times* and the *Irish Tatler & Sketch* thought that some of the members—in particular Mainie Jellett, Fr. Hanlon and E.A. McGuire—following the example of various European secessionist movements, might form an independent salon in opposition to the Royal Hibernian Academy.[35] This, in effect, they were to do by founding the Irish Exhibition of Living Art in 1943. The *Irish Times*, in 1939, also commented perceptively that while in other countries the lines had been drawn clearly between the Academicians and the Modernists, in Ireland the idea of creating a 'national school' had eclipsed all other developments.[36]

The pinnacle of critical acclaim for the Dublin Painters' Society came in 1942 at a time when the Academy, as we shall see later, was at its most intransigent and the younger, more radical artists were most vociferous in opposing its policies. That year Stephen Rynne wrote in the *Leader*:

> If a person wanted to make an annual check-up of Irish art and had few opportunities for seeing exhibitions then he would best achieve his end by attending the Dublin Painters. Here are the liveliest of the living painters, the explorers and experimentalists . . . . They paint what they will, for the most part their touch is light, airy, deft.[37]

In these years, too, a number of new members joined the Society and for a time they brought renewed vigour to it. But while the list of their names—Ralph Cusack, Patrick Hennessy, Gerard Dillon, Thurloe Conolly, Anne Yeats, Phyllis Hayward, Elizabeth Rivers—is impressive, in the main their influence on Irish art was brought to bear at other venues, notably, in the years after 1943, at the Living Art exhibitions.

* * *

Ralph Cusack (1912–65), a figure much overlooked in recent years, was a cousin of Mainie Jellett and possibly it was through her he joined the Dublin Painters in 1940. Self-taught as an artist, Cusack had begun to paint in the mid-1930s when, for health reasons, he was living in the south of France. With the approach of war, however, he returned to Ireland in May 1939. His style as a painter developed rapidly until about 1942 or 1943, but thereafter it remained static and from the late 1940s he painted hardly at all.

Until about 1943 boats and the sea were Cusack's principal subject-matter, but thereafter he turned to landscape, although occasionally he painted figure compositions and still lifes. *Fishing Boats, Loughshinney*, 1940 (cata. no. 131), with its clarity of expression, is typical of his early work and shows, too, the emphasis on line and pattern which was a characteristic of all his painting. It was exhibited in his first one-man show at the Dublin Painters' gallery in October 1940, along with a number of other paintings in which Stephen Rynne observed what he called 'queer juxtapositions' of imagery[38] which, he thought, gave the pictures a gentle Surrealist quality. In the late 1930s Cusack was influenced by Cubism, as, for example, *Nostalgia* of 1937 shows, and until the mid-1940s this was a recurring feature of his work. *Christmas in My Studio*, of 1943 (cata. no.38), which he exhibited at his third one-man show, held at the Dublin Painters that year, and *The Wreck*, 1943–4, both illustrate the point. In the former composition we can see the juxtaposition of diverse themes—an interior, a still life, landscape—which Rynne noted earlier, yet the whole has been treated formally in a manner which is clearly derived from Cubism. In the latter composition the image of the stricken boat with its structural ribs exposed—Cusack exhibited a similar work entitled *Scantlings* in the exhibition of Subjective Art, 1944—illustrates the Surrealist edge which his work so often embodied and which may have been in part provoked by the war which was then at its height.

From about 1943 Cusack turned increasingly to landscape for subject-matter and seems to have been influenced by the English painter Paul Nash, particularly in his choice of forms which often have a Surrealistic or metaphysical symbolism. Nash had greatly admired the work of the Italian metaphysical painter Giorgio de Chirico, which he had seen exhibited in London in 1928, and from that time in works such as *Northern Adventure*, 1929 (Aberdeen Art Gallery), *Landscape from a Dream*, 1936–8 (Tate Gallery), and *Sunflower and Sun*, 1942 (National Gallery of New South Wales, Sydney), his painting was metaphysical in character. These pictures were reproduced in a book on Nash, written by Herbert Read and published in the influential Penguin Modern Painters series in 1944, and Cusack would almost certainly have been familiar with that book.[39] Cusack's *Untitled*, of 1944, with its architectural structure which has been used to create ambivalent spatial relationships, suggests an influence from Nash's *Landscape from a Dream*; while *The Way to the World*, 1945 (cata. no. 132), with its symbolic architectural forms and metaphysical treatment of the landscape, is close in feeling to Nash's *Northern Adventure* and *Pillar and Moon*, 1932–42 (Tate Gallery). Moreover, many of Nash's pictures have a theatrical character and this is also true of Cusack's *The Way to the World*, which can be linked to his contemporary stage sets done with Anne Yeats for the Olympia and Gaiety theatres in Dublin.

Cusack last exhibited at the Dublin Painters' gallery in October 1945 when, in all probability, he exhibited works like those we have just discussed. In these years he occasionally made more directly representational pictures, although the metaphysical remained a dominant aspect of his work throughout the decade, as can be seen in *Summer Light*, exhibited at the Dublin Painters in November 1943, and *Queer Bird* of 1948. By comparison with these pictures his figure compositions, such as *Sleeping Nude* or *Seated Nude at Sea*, both of 1941, are less successful, the drawing of the figure in each case being clumsy and betraying his lack of training as a draughtsman, a deficiency which was, surprisingly, often less apparent in his pencil work than in other media. Overall, as a painter Cusack lacked a sense of purpose. It is said that he did not think highly of his work and in his semi-autobiographical book, *Cadenza: An Excursion* (1958), he did not even mention his painting.[40] With a little restraint and a sense of purpose Cusack could have been one of the most interesting and influential painters of his generation in Ireland.

Patrick Hennessy (1915–81), who came from Cork, studied art in Dundee before going to France and Italy in the late 1930s, but he returned to Ireland in 1939 and joined the Dublin Painters in about 1940. He held one-man exhibitions there every year until the late 1950s. Hennessy developed a superb technique as a naturalistic painter but, although he was little influenced by Modernism, his choice of imagery provokes a sense of mystery and intrigue which separates him from his academic contemporaries. *Kinsale Harbour*, of 1940 (cata. no.39), and *The House in the Wood*, of about 1941, which was almost certainly exhibited in his second one-man show at the Dublin Painters, in November 1941, illustrate the point. This sense of intrigue, at times almost Surrealist, was often effected through the bizarre placing of familiar objects in unlikely settings. This can be seen clearly in *Exiles*, of about 1943, in which two figures stand motionless like the columns of rock which mysteriously rise from the ground in the unreal landscape around them. The meaning of the picture is something which we, as spectators, must bring to it; it will therefore vary from person to person. This required act of participation by the spectator remained a characteristic of Hennessy's painting, but his best work dates from the 1950s and later and is therefore outside the scope of the present discussion.

Gerard Dillon and Thurloe Conolly came to the Dublin Painters in the early 1940s, but they rarely exhibited there. While they became important figures, their influence on the development of Irish painting came through the Living Art exhibitions and it is in that context that we shall look at their work in detail. Dillon seems not to have had any one-man exhibitions at the Dublin Painters' gallery and in the 1940s he preferred to exhibit elsewhere, notably at the Country Shop (where he held his first ever one-man show in February 1942), the Contemporary Picture Galleries and the Waddington Galleries. Conolly, however, held one-man exhibitions with the Dublin Painters in February 1945 and October 1946. In the first of these shows he included *Hall's Barn, Rathfarnham*, 1945 (cata. no.40), one of his finest paintings, which, acknowledging a debt to the English painter John Piper, whom he admired, typifies his work at the time.

Overall, during the 1940s, as in the previous decade, women dominated the affairs of the Dublin Painters' Society. With certain notable exceptions, as we have seen, they were strongly conservative in outlook although still beyond the pale of acceptability so far as the Royal Hibernian Academy was concerned.

The early 1940s briefly saw the return of Mary Swanzy to the Society. A founder-member, she had last exhibited there in 1922. In the intervening period she exhibited only once in Ireland, at an invitation exhibition in 1932 at Mespil House, the home of her friend Sarah Purser, but that exhibition was seen only by a few selected guests. In 1943, however, she exhibited at the Society's spring show, in February, and held a one-woman exhibition at the same venue a month later. During the 1930s Swanzy had turned from Cubism to a more allegorical kind of painting and, as the decade progressed, her work increasingly reflected the growing menace of war. Consequently, most of the pictures shown in 1943—*Praying Woman*, painted in 1939, *June 1940*, *The Sleepwalker*, for example—reflected this theme. But while these were powerfully evocative images of the times, aesthetically they represented a retreat from her more avant-garde work of the previous two decades.

Withal, Mary Swanzy's influence on the development of modern painting in Ireland was negligible. Even by 1919, when she first exhibited her new work in Dublin, the public were familiar with avant-garde painting and her later, Cubist, paintings were preceded by a number of years by Mainie Jellett's more rigorous and theoretically based Cubism. Also, her long absence from Ireland meant that she was less influential here than she might otherwise have been. Finally, Swanzy's eclecticism in the years before 1939 prompts speculation as to precisely what principles underpinned her art and, after that time, technically, she developed hardly at all.

Patricia Griffith (née Wallace) (1913–72), who began exhibiting with the Dublin Painters in 1941, was typical of many of the more conservative members. She was a close friend of Bea Orpen and Lilian Davidson, with whom she produced sets and costume designs for Dublin's Torch Theatre during the late 1930s. In about 1941

Patricia Griffith
Through the Window, Delphi Lodge, 1940s
Photograph S.B.K.

she married the architect William Griffith, owner of the Unicorn Restaurant, Merrion Row, Dublin, an early rendezvous for the artists of the White Stag Group with whom she occasionally exhibited. From the early 1940s Griffith worked mainly in gouache, painting landscapes in a semi-Impressionist technique which was influenced by Evie Hone, although occasionally she produced pictures like *Through the Window at Delphi Lodge* which are in the tradition of the English painters Paul Nash, John Piper and Edward Wadsworth. She also painted occasional portraits.

The 1940s also brought Anne Yeats, Phyllis Hayward and Elizabeth Rivers to the Society. Anne Yeats (b.1919) held her first one-woman exhibition at the St. Stephen's Green gallery in March 1946 and this was followed by a similar show at the same venue in April 1948. In the intervening period she had been in France studying contemporary French painting and the results of her studies can be seen in her *Woman Watching* (Ulster Museum) of 1948. Here she has used a combination of gouache and wax to form a style, similar to that of William Conor, which she retained, even in her later oil paintings, for much of the rest of her career. In 1943 Anne Yeats exhibited at the first Living Art exhibition and in 1947 she became a member of the organizing committee for the Living Art. Henceforth she directed her energies in that direction and her best work, perhaps, belongs to the 1950s and later.

Phyllis Hayward (1903–85) came to Ireland from England in 1940 in the wake of

65

Elizabeth Rivers
Photograph courtesy Gorry Gallery

the White Stag painters Basil Rakoczi and Kenneth Hall. She first exhibited her work in *Three New Dublin Painters*, a mixed show with Bobby Dawson and Cicely Peel,[41] at the Contemporary Picture Galleries in November 1941 after which time she was closely asociated with the White Stag Group. After the war she decided to stay in Ireland and joined the Dublin Painters in about 1948. She held a one-woman exhibition there in October 1949 but took little or no part in the running of the Society. Still life and flower paintings were her principal subject-matter and *Flowers in a Pot*, 1947, one of her very best works, may have been one of two flower pieces, in gouache, which she exhibited at the Dublin Painters in 1949.

Like Phyllis Hayward, Elizabeth Rivers (1903–64) was English.[42] She first came to Ireland in 1935 but settled here permanently after the Second World War. Her first one-woman exhibition in Ireland was held at the Contemporary Picture Galleries in April 1942 and this was followed by similar exhibitions at the Dublin Painters' gallery in April 1946, December 1947 and October 1949. Educated at Goldsmith's College and the Royal Academy Schools, London, Rivers studied for a time under André Lhote and Gino Severini in Paris in the early 1930s and it is their influence, and especially the Cubism of Lhote, which is most apparent in her work of the late 1940s. Paintings like *The Ark*, 1948 (cata. no.41), which she almost certainly exhibited at the Dublin Painters' autumn exhibition that year, and *Children at Hallowe'en*, 1948–51, show her at her best. Rivers was also one of the finest wood engravers and illustrators working in Ireland in her time. But although she exhibited regularly in Dublin from the late 1940s until her death in 1964, being reticent by nature, she was less influential than she might otherwise have been.

Despite the esteem in which the critics held the Society of Dublin Painters, throughout the 1930s and 1940s few of its members seriously concerned themselves

66

with recent developments in contemporary painting. They remained, by and large, rooted in the values of the *École de Paris* of the years before the First World War and, by later standards, were thus hopelessly outdated. By 1943, when the Irish Exhibition of Living Art was established, the Dublin Painters' role as leaders of the avant-garde in Ireland was effectively taken over and the Society went into permanent decline.[43] The loosening of discipline in its organization, the absence of any corporate aesthetic and the eclecticism of most of its members all contributed to its demise. Yet, to its credit, by the mid-1940s most of its aims had been achieved: there was greater public recognition of the merits of modern painting and several other venues, notably commercial galleries, where young artists could show their work had come into being as alternatives to the Academy.

Elizabeth Rivers
Winter Skies, 1960
Ulster Museum

CHAPTER FOUR

OTHER DEVELOPMENTS
1920–1940

'We can even be grateful for the extravagances of cubists, futurists,
and their kind, because they made us realise our complete boredom
with the careful, uninspired academic art.'

George Russell (AE), reviewing the New Irish Salon, *Irish Statesman*, 16
February 1924.

ALTHOUGH the Society of Dublin Painters represented the more avant-garde artists
working in Ireland during the inter-war years, other minor bodies were also formed
at the time and they too aimed to further the cause of Modernism by exhibiting more
radical works than could be seen elsewhere. Of these, the New Irish Salon, the Ulster
Unit and the Contemporary Picture Galleries were the most important. Also, during
these years patronage for art developed as never before with the foundation in both
Dublin and Belfast of public and private collections which emphasized developments
in contemporary art.

The New Irish Salon 1923–1928

James Crampton Walker (1890–1942) arranged the six exhibitions, each held annually
at Mills' Hall, Dublin, of the New Irish Salon in the years 1923–28.[1] As an artist,
Walker is best known for his still life and flower paintings executed in an academic
manner. In 1907 he had entered Trinity College, Dublin, to read medicine but
abandoned his course after three years to study art at the Metropolitan School and,
later, in Paris. He also studied for a time under Nathaniel Hone who greatly influenced
him. In 1925 he published *Irish Life and Landscape* (Dublin: Talbot Press), a book
of illustrations of paintings by his contemporaries. He was elected an Associate of
the Royal Hibernian Academy in 1931.

No documentation concerning the New Irish Salon appears to have survived so
that our knowledge of the six exhibitions is confined to press reviews of them. While
the exhibitions were not restricted to avant-garde painting, one can only speculate
that they may have been conceived as an Irish equivalent to the New English Art
Club,[2] that is, as an alternative to the Academy exhibitions, for most press reviews

over the years referred to them, one way or another, as exhibitions of 'modern' paintings.

Unlike the Academy, the New Irish Salon had no selection committee and artists could submit as many works as they wished so long as space was available to hang them. Each of the six exhibitions contained 250 to 300 paintings. Reviewing the first exhibition, 'the work of the modern school',[3] the *Irish Times* mentioned by name Paul Henry (*Spring in Wicklow*), Mary Swanzy (*In the South*), Harriet Kirkwood (*At the Mirror*), E.M.O'R.Dickey and Ossip Zadkine, 'a Russian'. From this list we can gauge the tenor of the exhibition and form a fairly clear idea of the nature of the works on show. The unidentified work by Zadkine was, presumably, lent by a private collector.

The 1924 Salon seems to have been the most avant-garde of the six exhibitions, with works by Gleizes and Lhote (presumably lent by Mainie Jellett and Evie Hone, who were also included), Cecil Salkeld, Paul and Grace Henry, E.M.O'R. Dickey (*View from Bellegra, Early Morning*), W.J. Leech and a group from England, including George Clausen, Augustus John and C.R.W. Nevinson. The traditionalists included Bingham McGuinness, H.W. Moss, Mary Barton, Sarah Cecilia Harrison, Howard Knee and Crampton Walker. Reviewing the exhibition in the *Studio*, Thomas Bodkin thought that while none of the works was of outstanding merit, overall the quality of the exhibits was high.[4] He also commented that the show was 'extensively patronized' by the public. It was this exhibition which prompted the *Irish Times* critic to suggest that in their work Gleizes, Lhote, Hone, Jellett and Salkeld had reached 'second childishness';[5] and in another example of the critical mood of the time, George Russell (AE), writing as 'Y.O.' in the *Irish Statesman*, expressed again his irritation at the Modern Movement. Likening Pointillism, Cubism, Fauvism and other trends to 'aesthetic bacteria', he commented:

We went into the New Irish Salon and saw the aesthetic bacteria at work, and the inflammations, ulcers and blotches they produced. The interest one felt was as much psychological as artistic. One speculated about the Gleizes, the Lhotes, the Salkelds and the Jelletts, wondering whether their decorations were reflections of thought forms or imitations of other cubists . . . . The only excuse for these patterns is a colour sense, and we regret to say that some of them had no more beauty of colour than is usual in a pattern on oilcloth.[6]

Later Salon exhibitions appear to have been less provocative. The 1925 exhibition, for example, caused no critical acrimony, the *Irish Times* merely noting that the Modernists were well represented, while in the *Studio* Thomas Bodkin reported that it had greater merit and interest than most recent Academy exhibitions, and he concluded by hoping that it would continue to be an annual event, 'if only for the stimulating effect it [has] . . . upon our lethargic Academy'.[7] In 1926 none of the really avant-garde Irish artists appears to have exhibited, O'Rorke Dickey, Paul Henry (*Potato Diggers*), Sean Keating (*'Twas a Lovely Funeral*), Sir John Lavery, W.J. Leech (*Olive Tree in Spring* and *Portrait of a Lady*), Dermod O'Brien and Leo Whelan (*Interior*) being the most prominent, while the following year, 1927, the Modernists were represented by O'Rorke Dickey (*Clayton Mills*), Grace Henry (*The Amethyst Country*), Mainie Jellett (*Oil Painting*) and Harry Kernoff. However, George Russell's review of the latter exhibition is notable for his change of opinion about modern

W.J. Leech. *The Cigarette.* Hugh Lane Municipal Gallery of Modern Art

painting. Writing in the *Irish Statesman*, he expressed reservations about the Jellett *Oil Painting*, and Henry's *The Amethyst Country*, which he considered to be 'as remote from realism' as was Jellett. But both works were 'justified', he said, because in looking at nature according to our mood, 'colours have a psychic appeal . . . quite apart from the place they have in . . . nature'. Thus, he continued, 'the artist is justified if the painting conveys . . . the psychological effect aimed at'.[8]

The last exhibition of the New Irish Salon was held in 1928. Apart from Harry Kernoff (*A Labour Meeting*) and W.J. Leech (*The Cigarette* [Lane Gallery], *L'Actrice*) the critics made no mention of the more innovative painters. Why the exhibitions were discontinued we do not know for they were successful both in terms of publicity and of sales, which amounted to over £500 annually for several years.[9] Perhaps Crampton Walker, who arranged them, wanted to devote more time to his own painting, or possibly, too, his health began to fail for he died in 1942 at the comparatively early age of fifty-two, having been ill for some time before his death.

* * *

No one artist or group of artists dominated the exhibitions of the New Irish Salon—strangely, Jack B. Yeats, who supported most of the smaller groups in his time, does not appear to have exhibited there—and, sadly, they little influenced the development of art in Ireland. This was due, perhaps more than anything else, to the absence of a selection procedure which might otherwise have given a sense of direction to the exhibitions. Yet we might pause here to look at the work of one or two of the more important artists who regularly exhibited at the Salon.

By the mid-1920s Paul Henry was at the height of his public esteem; but, paradoxically, from that time his work began to deteriorate to become ever more hackneyed. In about 1925 two of his paintings, *Connemara* and *A View of Lough Erne*, were reproduced as posters for the London Midland & Scottish Railway Company and were distributed to tourist bureaux throughout Europe and North America. The simplicity of Henry's style was well suited to the requirements of contemporary reproduction techniques—simplified shapes and the use of only three or four colours—as can be seen, for example, in the *Connemara* poster, but such widespread exposure created a stereotype of his work from which he never freed himself. This was also a time when his marriage to Grace was under strain and, significantly, he seems to have lost his interest in Modernism then too.

From the mid-1920s the often vibrant colours of Henry's early work give way to a more subdued landscape which at times becomes monotonous. Yet, despite this falling-off in quality, Henry never became an academic painter and his pictures are always somewhat abstract in spirit. Henry may be regarded as the father of the school of landscape painting which evolved in Ireland during the inter-war years which so greatly contributed to the development of a distinct Irish school of art.

W.J. Leech (1881–1968) was one of the finest Irish painters of his generation, but as he lived both in France and in England his work had little influence at home, although he showed regularly at the Royal Hibernian Academy and elsewhere.[10] A pupil of Walter Osborne, from about 1901 until 1916 Leech spent much of his time in France, where he encountered Impressionism and Post-Impressionism at first hand, the latter having a lasting influence on him. In about 1916 he settled permanently in England, although he continued to visit France for many years to come. Leech's

W.J. Leech
Self-portrait
Ulster Museum

mature works, such as *Un Matin: Waving Things, Concarneau* (Lane Gallery) or *Aloes* (Ulster Museum), both probably painted in the 1920s, are strongly Post-Impressionist in concept and execution. His style, always a trifle arid and somewhat eclectic, developed little from the twenties onwards and he seems to have been almost unaffected by advances in painting after the advent of Fauvism. Thus he had little by way of influence to offer other Irish painters who were interested in Modernism.

Sir John Lavery (1856–1941), who was born in Belfast, also lived in England. While he too exhibited frequently at the New Irish Salon and elsewhere in Ireland, he had little influence on artistic events here.[11] Lavery trained in Glasgow, London and Paris and was influenced by *plein-air* painting, eventually developing a style which, in Kenneth McConkey's words, was a 'decorative naturalism that synthesised the influence of Bastien-Lepage and Whistler'.[12] Although he was involved with Whistler in running the International Society of Sculptors, Painters and Gravers, by the turn of the century Lavery had little to offer artists interested in the more innovative trends of Modernism.

72

John Hunter
*Still Life &
Figures*, c.1945–50
Ulster Museum

The Ulster Unit 1933–1934

In 1921, shortly after the partition of Ireland, a number of Northern artists got together to form the Ulster Society of Painters in order to stimulate the development of painting in Northern Ireland. J.H. Craig was elected president of the Society, and the best known of its members, who were limited to twenty-five in number, were A.R. Baker, F.W. Egginton, David Gould, Theo Gracey, F.W. Hull, Hunter Jeffrey, Frank McKelvey, Stanley Prosser and Rendle Wood. These were mainly landscapists who worked in a traditional academic manner. The Society took rooms in Wellington Place, Belfast,[13] and held a number of annual exhibitions until the early 1930s, but it had little influence on the local art scene. However, in 1933 things began to change as a younger generation of painters, many of whom had studied and worked in London, came to the fore through the Northern Ireland Guild of Artists. The Guild, in turn, evolved into the Ulster Unit.

Unlike the members of the Dublin Painters' Society, whose interest in Modernism was entirely personal, the Ulster Unit was the first group of artists in Ireland to share, in effect if not by intent, a common aspiration of the role and purpose of art. For them Modernism symbolized the spirit of the age.

The Ulster Unit was founded in 1934 out of the short-lived Northern Ireland Guild of Artists, which had been formed in May of the previous year by John Hunter (1893–1951) as a forum in which young and progressive artists, who were usually excluded by the Ulster Academy, could meet and exhibit their work.[14] The Guild represented all that was unorthodox in Ulster art. Apart from Hunter, it included Lady Mabel Annesley, a talented printmaker; Kathleen Bridle, the future teacher of William Scott and T.P. Flanagan; Herbert Broderick (honorary secretary); Elizabeth Clements; William Conor; W.R. Gordon; the sculptor Morris Harding; Edward L.

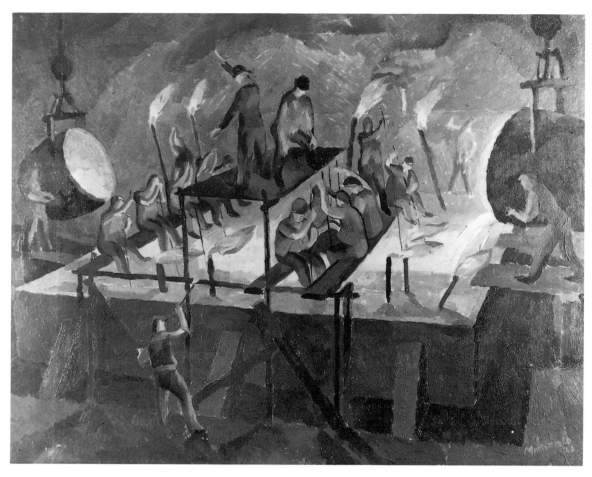

Edward Mansfield
Moulding Shop
1942
Ulster Museum

Mansfield, a Londoner who had come to teach at the Belfast College of Art; Edward Marr, a stained glass artist; Padraig Marrinan; Colin Middleton; Romeo Toogood; Anne and Margaret Yeames. They held one exhibition during the short existence of the Guild, in Arthur Street, Belfast, in November 1933 when the preface to the catalogue stated that their aim was 'to co-relate the various crafts of its members with one another, with the homes they are made to adorn and the age to which they belong.' And it continued to say that the Guild had 'no ism or schism to propagate or defend. It has no label for any or all of its members. It only demands that each of its members shall see with his or her individual vision and work with honesty and conviction.' The Guild did not long survive this exhibition but the emphasis which it placed on individual vision, albeit of an essentially corporate kind, was also a characteristic of the Ulster Unit which was formed late in the following year.

With the exceptions of Herbert Broderick, William Conor, Morris Harding, Padraig Marrinan and Anne Yeames, the members of the new group were as before and they were joined by the architect Denis O'D. Hanna, the painter John Luke, the sculptor and painter George MacCann, the potter Jean Macgregor and Crawford Mitchell, a print maker. In its aspirations the Ulster Unit was much influenced by the English group, Unit One, which had recently been founded by Paul Nash and some of his contemporaries.[15] The chronology of events leading up to the foundation of the Ulster Unit is interesting for it indicates the extent to which Hunter and his colleagues were

Sculpture studio,
Belfast College of
Art, c.1928.
Mercy MacCann, centre,
second row; George
MacCann and Seamus
Stoupe at back

familiar with the latest developments in English art, which they knew from first-hand experience gained both in London and from the pictures of the Lloyd Patterson Collection, lately assembled at the Belfast Museum and Art Gallery.[16]

As early as the spring of 1933 Paul Nash had approached several of his contemporaries with a view to establishing a group of like-minded artists who were interested not only in Modernism but also in applying Modernist ideas to industrial design. On the second of June that year he published a letter in *The Times* announcing the formation of the new group, named Unit One, and stating that its members supported no single aesthetic, no manifesto or declared programme of reform, but rather were a group of individuals united by what he called 'a quality of mind . . . a truly contemporary spirit'. Herbert Read in his book, *Unit 1: The Modern Movement in English Architecture, Painting and Sculpture*, published the following year, defined this spirit as an abandonment of the 'truth to nature' criterion in painting and of historical styles in architecture; of design considered as a structural pursuit; and of imagination explored apart from literature or metaphysics.[17] The emphasis which Nash placed on individual expression was indeed close to what emerged as an aim of the Northern Ireland Guild of Artists, which was formed a mere month before the publication of Nash's letter. Whether Hunter and his colleagues had any direct contact with Nash and company is both unknown and, perhaps, unlikely; but we may assume that the former, if he read Nash's letter, realized that it expressed concisely the views of his own group, and he presumably felt, too, that in effect he and his friends were part of a larger community of artists motivated by current trends. In April 1934 Nash staged what was to be the only London exhibition of Unit One—during the following twelve months it toured to Liverpool, Manchester, Hanley, Derby, Swansea and Belfast (March-April 1935)—and coinciding with it was the publication of Herbert Read's book on the Unit, which included a statement by each participant on his or her approach to art and reproductions of selected works.

The sense of community which we have suggested Hunter and his colleagues felt with Unit One is clear from the catalogue of the one and only exhibition held by the

Ulster Unit, which took place in the Locksley Hall, Belfast, during December 1934. This catalogue comprised a preface by John Hewitt, secretary to the Unit; notes on 'the Art of Picture Buying' which, amongst other things, urged the prospective purchaser to buy pictures 'to feed [the] soul'; and a symposium in which each exhibitor set down in aphoristic form what was for him the essence of his art. In his preface, Hewitt noted that for the first time Ulster had a body of artists alert to Continental influence, 'while that influence is still real and vital', that these artists did not accept 'the mere imitation of appearance' as being adequate to their purposes and that they emphasized in their work the 'supreme value' of individual experience. To some extent this rhetoric was not matched by the quality of the works shown which too often lacked originality.

The most influential contributors to the exhibition were Middleton, Luke, Toogood and MacCann. Of these, Middleton, as we shall see in a later chapter, was to become the most important in Irish terms, but Luke, Toogood and MacCann had a certain modernity in an Ulster context. One complete section of the exhibition, the *Northern Whig* tells us,[18] was reserved for abstract works by Middleton and MacCann, but none of these can now be identified. *Two Horses*, 1933, however, illustrates the nature of MacCann's painting at the time. Of Luke's works, the *Lustre Jug*, 1934 (Ulster Museum), and *Connswater Bridge*, 1934 (cata. no.42), are the best remembered. The latter is remarkable for its bold concept and precise draughtsmanship, but in it can be

George MacCann. *Reclining Nude*, 1930s

Photograph S.B.K.

R.C. Toogood
*Barge at
Edenderry*, 1936
Ulster Museum

seen the beginnings of the extreme stylization which characterized his later work and which ultimately stultified his development as an artist. Toogood also displayed a degree of stylization in the two works, *Theatre*, 1929, and *The Backyard*, 1934 (cata. no.43), which he exhibited. But although this development reached its peak in his *Barge at Edenderry*, 1936 (Ulster Museum), he returned to a more *malerisch* technique in later years. Other noted works in the exhibition were watercolours by Kathleen Bridle and Lady Mabel Annesley, linocuts by Hunter and Luke, etchings by Crawford Mitchell, sculptures by Elizabeth Clements, pottery by Jean Macgregor, and architectural designs by Denis O'D. Hanna.

The Ulster Unit dissolved shortly after this exhibition probably due to a lack of cohesion amongst the members. Nevertheless, they were the only artists in Ireland to espouse corporately a meaningful aesthetic based on contemporary trends. An important feature of Continental Modernism in the 1920s and 1930s, which is not reflected in Irish experience, was the urge to combine all the arts under a universal aesthetic, often in pursuit of a social ideal. In Germany, the Bauhaus sought to do this; in Holland, the De Stijl Group moved in roughly the same direction as did Le Corbusier and the Purists in France. The English experience of this momentum was milder than that of most Continental countries, but the Vorticists had earlier given a social edge to their art similar to that which Paul Nash and his contemporaries later attempted. In Ireland, however, despite the revolutionary nature of the period, only the Northern Ireland Guild of Artists and the Ulster Unit seem to have been aware of such a concept. Ironically, in looking only to London for their inspiration, these Ulster painters were intellectually more adventurous than many of their Southern contemporaries who looked directly to France.

Elizabeth Clements
Torso, c.1930s
Photograph Kinney Watters
Perry Photography Ltd.

The Contemporary Picture Galleries 1938–1948

As we have seen, by the late 1930s a considerable awareness of modern painting—
but not sculpture—had evolved in Ireland and this was due entirely to the effort of
individuals and not to any other pressures. Apart from the Belfast Museum & Art
Gallery, none of the public or commercial galleries had shown any interest in
promoting avant-garde painting. It was to rectify this situation that Deirdre
McDonagh[19] founded the Contemporary Picture Galleries in 1938. A year or so later
she was joined in the running of the business by Jack Longford.[20]

The Contemporary Picture Galleries were first established at number five South
Leinster Street, Dublin, but early in 1939 other rooms were acquired up the street at
number fifteen and the following October number 133 Lower Baggot Street was
added, although that became their sole address from about May of 1940. Like George

78

Russell (AE) in the late 1890s, McDonagh and Longford felt that the best way to stimulate the development of modern painting in Ireland was to expose Irish artists to the best of what was being done elsewhere. Thus they arranged a series of one-man, group and thematic exhibitions which, throughout the war-years, explored in a novel way various aspects of recent painting. Amongst the distinguished artists whom they introduced to the Irish public for the first time were Edward Ardizzone, Graham Bell, Vanessa Bell, William Coldstream, John Piper, Victor Pasmore and Claude Rogers.[21] They also promoted Jack B. Yeats before his rise to popular esteem during the 1940s.

Yeats' rise in popularity is usually associated with the Victor Waddington Galleries, where he first exhibited in 1943, but McDonagh and Longford were the first commercial dealers to recognize his worth.[22] Writing of the period many years later, the critic Stephen Rynne noted: 'Longford was a fine connoisseur and a picture vendor—head and shoulders above all his kind in Ireland at that time. No one did more for contemporary art or showed a better appreciation of good Irish artists than the gentle Longford'. He continued, referring to Yeats: 'The old man and young Longford were warm friends; there was something of a father and son affinity between them'.[23]

Throughout the 1930s Yeats had painted comparatively little but spent much of his time writing novels and plays. Towards the end of the decade, however, in the full flush of his maturity, he produced a number of memorable works such as *Once on a Day, A Race in Hy Brazil* (cata. no. 89), both 1937, and *High Water—Spring Tide*, 1939 (Boston Museum of Fine Arts). These compositions demonstrate his continuing emphasis on memory, set down in an inter-related web of experiences, narrative and stream of consciousness, as the central feature of his compositional technique. They, and others like them, often appear to be impenetrable, yet as Sir John Rothenstein noted after visiting the artist: 'The more broadly handled the later pictures, the more insistent he was that their subject should be clearly comprehended, and none of the accessory details, at first difficult to distinguish in a maelstrom of brush-strokes should be missed'.[24] Yeats always requires us to work to understand his subject-matter, but our reward, as the *Irish Times* recognized of his one-man show at the Contemporary Picture Galleries in October 1941, was that to possess a Yeats 'is to have something that will always be changing, something that may grow into what its creator never dreamt of'.[25] That is the universality of Yeats' art.

Thematic exhibitions were a feature of the Contemporary Picture Galleries. The best remembered of these shows are the *Loan and Cross-Section Exhibition of Contemporary Paintings*, held in October 1939; *Six Irish Artists from L'Académie Lhote*, November 1940; and *"In Theatre Street"*, November–December 1942.

The *Loan and Cross-Section* exhibition was a *tour de force*, with paintings by numerous Continental artists in the 'Loan Section', which drew on Irish private collections, and a 'Cross-Section' of works by Irish artists. Amongst the loans were works by Bonnard, Braque, De Chirico, Derain, Dufy, Gleizes (*Painting*, ? National Gallery of Ireland), Juan Gris (*Collage*, ? National Gallery of Ireland), Lhote, Moïse Kisling, Albert Marquet, Max Pechstein, Picasso (*Collage*, ? National Gallery of Ireland), Signac and Vlaminck. The English artists Mark Gertler, C.R.W. Nevinson, Sickert, Wilson Steer and Henry Tonks were also included as was Sir William Orpen. Of the Irish painters, who included many from the Dublin Painters' Society, the more avant-garde were Letitia Hamilton, Fr. Jack Hanlon, Paul Henry, Evie Hone,

C.E. Gribbon
Bowl of Carnations,
1930s
Photograph Dr. P. Gribbon

Mainie Jellett, Norah McGuinness and Jack B. Yeats; while Tom Carr, George Collie, Lilian Davidson, Lady Glenavy, Seán Keating, Harry Kernoff, Charles Lamb, Maurice MacGonigal, Dermod O'Brien and Seán O'Sullivan were the best of the more academic painters. This was the most important exhibition ever mounted by the Contemporary Picture Galleries. Not only did it bring together all the influential Irish painters of the time, but it served to illustrate once again the overwhelming dependence of Irish collectors on French painting.

Six Irish Artists from L'Académie Lhote comprised fifty-four works by Fr. Jack Hanlon, Evie Hone, Mainie Jellett, Eugene Judge, Harriet Kirkwood and Norah McGuinness, all of whom had studied with Lhote, although they did not all embrace the kind of Cubism which he encouraged.

"In Theatre Street" laid claim to be the first exhibition of theatre design ever held in Dublin. It aimed to stimulate an interest in such work by encouraging Irish artists to work in the theatre. Designs by Ralph Cusack, Mainie Jellett, Louis le Brocquy and Doreen Vanston demonstrated the wealth of talent already to be found in the Irish theatre and these were exhibited alongside sets by the theatrical designers Carl Bonn, Michael Clarke, Molly MacEwen and Micheál MacLiammóir. New names, of whom we shall hear more shortly, were the painters Stephen Gilbert, Basil Rakoczi and Anne Yeats. The exhibition also included paintings of theatrical subjects by le Brocquy, Norah McGuinness and Jack B. Yeats.

Referring to these exhibitions and the role which they played in promoting modern painting in Ireland, Stephen Rynne commented in September 1944, shortly after Longford's death: 'Art stepped out when Jack Longford launched his great educational shows at Contemporary Pictures. He is dead now . . . just when his efforts are producing results'.[26]

The Contemporary Picture Galleries remained in business until about 1948, but their influence waned after Longford's death. By then, of course, the artistic scene in

80

Dublin had changed: the White Stag Group were thriving and the Irish Exhibition of Living Art had come into being, thus providing other venues for young and avant-garde artists to show their work. Until the early 1940s, however, Contemporary Pictures were, in the words of Kenneth Hall, 'the only modern gallery that makes any attempt at advanced ideas in Dublin'.[27] Perhaps most significantly they paved a way which was taken up, to the advantage of Irish painting, by Victor Waddington in the later 1940s.

Other artists

Other artists not associated with these groups but whom we should mention at this point are Cecil Salkeld and three Ulster painters, Paul Nietsche, Edward Gribbon and Tom Carr.

Salkeld was less active as a painter during the 1930s than he had been a decade earlier. Nevertheless, by the late thirties he had developed the style—an emphasis on line, with forms precisely modelled and clearly delineated—by which he is best known. By this time he had lost the urge to experiment and his work developed little thereafter. Symbolism and allegory typify Salkeld's later work as can be seen, for example, in the three panels, completed in 1942, which comprise his well-known mural, the *Triumph of Bacchus*, in Davy Byrne's public house.[28]

Each of the Davy Byrne's panels is a separate composition, entitled respectively *Morning: Going to the Party with Bacchus*, *Noon: Joys of Enebriation in the Mid-day Sun* and *Night: Party at the End of Day*. Of these compositions, the second is perhaps the most satisfactory with its interesting group of well-known Dubliners of the day;[29] while the third is notable for its strong theatricality. Each composition shows a strong emphasis on line, mildly stylized forms and a smooth film of paint, all characteristics of Salkeld's mature style. While not amongst his very best works the compositions are, no doubt because of their location, the best known of his paintings.

Other allegorical subjects which Salkeld painted in these years include *Kali, Goddess of Destruction*, c.1945, a picture symbolizing the state of post-war Europe; *The Secret*, of about 1943–8, possibly a self-portrait with his wife; and *Leda and the Swan* (cata. no.44), painted at about the same time, which shows him at the height of his powers. As we shall see in a later chapter, he painted a number of excellent portraits at this time, but from the mid-1940s ballet subjects increasingly preoccupied him.

Paradoxically, Salkeld's greatest weakness as a painter lay in his easy technical fluency, for thereby he dissipated his energies in too many diverse activities and away from painting where his real talent lay. Thus the quality of his later work declined; he lost his clarity of vision, of form and precision of line and his use of paint often became laboured, devoid of its earlier subtlety.

* * *

Paul Nietsche (1885–1950), a Ukrainian who had studied art in Odessa, Munich and Paris, came to Belfast in 1926 on the invitation of a friend, Michael O'Brien, a Gaelic scholar whom he had met in Germany.[30] Nietsche was essentially an

Impressionist, but his strong extrovert personality, expressed in a bold handling of brush and palette knife, gave great character to all he did. True to the influences of his early training in Odessa,[31] his style was based on careful observation of the world around him. Nietsche was a fine colourist. He was at his best when painting still lifes, such as *Black Eve and Green Apples*, of 1949 (cata. no.45), flowers and portraits, of which his *Self-portrait*, 1947, now in the National Self-portrait collection in Limerick, is a good example. His landscapes by comparison are less successful, the compositions often lacking resolution while the colours are occasionally muddied and less boldly stated than in his other works. Perhaps the intimacy of a portrait or the exuberance of a group of flowers suited his temperament more than the panorama of landscape. Nietsche exhibited regularly during his years in Belfast and in the late 1940s he held a number of annual one-man exhibitions which were always well received. He exhibited at the Royal Hibernian Academy once, in 1930, and held a one-man show at the United Arts Club, Dublin, in June 1934.[32] A prominent member of Belfast's 'bohemia', he brought a touch of foreign colour to the city at a time when it was much needed. However, despite his somewhat eccentric personality, his work had little influence on his Irish contemporaries who, by and large, were more concerned with the native landscape and the traditional ways of representing it.

* * *

Edward Gribbon (1898–1939) was born in Belfast. He contracted tuberculosis, probably during the early 1920s, went to Switzerland to recuperate and while there began to paint. Although he paid periodic visits to Ireland, he spent most of his brief career working in Paris and, later, in the south of France.[33]

C.E. Gribbon
c.1930s
Photograph courtesy
Dr. P. Gribbon

Gribbon first exhibited in Dublin with a one-man show at Daniel Egan's gallery in January 1932, and in March 1935 he showed at the same venue along with Grace Henry, Doreen Vanston and Cecil Salkeld. Landscapes, often with buildings, and flowers were his principal subject-matter. He was, perhaps, at his best with the latter, as in *Bowl of Carnations*, painted in 1934, in which the exuberance of the flowers dominates the composition and gives it great vitality. The use of contrasting colours, such as we see here in the juxtaposition of reds and greens, is a notable characteristic of his work which, coupled with the feverish energy of his brushwork, is largely Expressionist in character and at times is reminiscent of Van Gogh whom he admired. His landscapes are typified by the use of strong colours and an emphasis on sunlight which gives to them a distinct Mediterranean character. This can be seen, for example, in *Ischia*, c.1934 (cata. no.46), one of his very best paintings.

That Gribbon did not exhibit more frequently in Ireland is a pity, for his work deserves to be better known. His Expressionist technique lent a sense of urgency to his work which was quite different to and refreshing from that of his Irish contemporaries.

* * *

Like Gribbon, Tom Carr (b.1909) was born in Belfast. He was educated at Oundle School, where his art master was E.M.O'R. Dickey, who had been a member of the Dublin Painters' Society. Later he went to the Slade School, London. Always a representational painter at heart, in the early 1930s, like many of his contemporaries, Carr experimented for a short time with a type of abstraction (none of his work survives from this period) and in 1934 he exhibited with Graham Bell, Ivon Hitchens, Rodrigo Moynihan, Victor Pasmore, Ceri Richards and Geoffrey Tibble in the *Objective Abstractions* exhibition at the Zwemmer Gallery, London. However, after the show Carr drew back from abstraction. During 1938 and 1939 he was associated with Victor Pasmore, Claude Rogers and others at the Euston Road School in London and that reinforced his adherance to representational painting. With Graham Bell, another member of the Euston Road School, he spent some time in Dublin in 1939 making paintings which were later exhibited in Jack Longford's *Loan and Cross-Section Exhibition* at the Contemporary Picture Galleries.

Patronage

The 1920s and 1930s in Ireland saw an upsurge in private patronage of the visual arts aimed at the acquisition of works for public collections. Until that time both state and local authority grants-in-aid of purchase to public art galleries had been either puny or non-existent[34] so that those galleries had to rely almost entirely on private funds. The first such fund to concern us is the Crawford Art Gallery's Gibson Bequest.

Joseph Stafford Gibson, a Cork man who had long resided in Spain, died in Madrid in February 1919 and in his will left to the Crawford Municipal School of Art—later Crawford Art Gallery—Cork, his collection of paintings, books, manuscripts and other objects along with a capital trust, the income from which was to be used to acquire works of art for the gallery. The will also made provision for a scholarship to allow a student from the province of Munster to study art on the Continent for up to a year. The capital sum bequeathed was £14,790, which was invested in the managing body of the School of Art who administered it, George Atkinson, headmaster of the Metropolitan School of Art, Dermod O'Brien, president of the Royal Hibernian Academy, and Lucius O'Callaghan, director of the National Gallery, being appointed to advise on acquisitions. Later, in 1929, Thomas Bodkin replaced O'Callaghan as an adviser.[35]

Purchases under the bequest were first made in 1920 and, in deference to the cultural introversion of the times, the advisers confined their selection largely to paintings by conservative Irish artists. Seán Keating's *Men of the South*, Frank McKelvey's *On the River Bann*, Dermod O'Brien's *Place de l'Eglise, Montreuil* and Leo Whelan's *The Kitchen Window* are representative examples of works acquired in the early years. During the late 1920s and early 1930s this selection was leavened by the acquisition of similar works by English painters, the most avant-garde of whom were Ambrose McEvoy, Wilson Steer and the Ulsterman O'Rorke Dickey who was then living in England. Thereafter acquisitions were confined almost exclusively to works by Irish artists. Consequently, the collection of paintings and sculptures bearing Gibson's name is narrow in scope and, from the beginning, did little either to encourage Irish artists in general or to stimulate interest in modern painting in particular.

* * *

In 1930 the Haverty Trust first became active. Established under the will of Thomas Haverty, a son of the painter Joseph Patrick Haverty, the endowment generated an income of around £550 per year which was to be used to encourage Irish art in the same way that the Chantrey and Turner bequests had been used to encourage English art.[36] Although Haverty's will appointed trustees of his endowment, a scheme for administering it was given legal force[37] and purchasing by the Trust began in 1930. With over £500 a year at hand, it was the largest endowment ever devoted to contemporary painting in Ireland.[38] The general tenor of works acquired over the years was conservative, although the selectors did at times try to be adventurous. Acquisitions were shown in a series of quinquennial exhibitions, beginning in 1935, after which they were dispersed to various public institutions. The first quinquennial exhibition, held in the Mansion House, Dublin, included Jack B. Yeats' *The Liffey Swim*, of 1923 (National Gallery of Ireland), one of the most avant-garde works ever acquired by the committee; William Conor's *The Jaunting Car*, 1933 (Ulster Museum); Seán O'Sullivan's excellent study of the poet *W.B. Yeats*, 1934 (cata. no.95); and three works illustrating the life of St. Patrick—*St. Patrick baptising the daughters of the Ard Rí Laoghaire*; *St. Patrick lights the Paschal Fire at Slane* (Irish College, Rome) and *St. Patrick Climbs Croagh Patrick* (Lane Gallery)—which were commissioned from Leo Whelan, Seán Keating and Margaret Clarke respectively. These are conservative in the extreme. From the second quinquennial exhibition, held at the National College of Art, we might mention Leo Whelan's *Interior of a Kitchen*, painted in about 1935 (cata. no.109); George Collie's *The First Three Trustees of the Haverty Trust*, of 1935–6; Keating's *Slán leat, a Athair/ Goodbye, Father*, 1935 (cata. no.7); and Mainie Jellett's abstract, *Painting*, 1938, now in the Ulster Museum, as being representative of recent acquisitions, of which only the last-mentioned was at all avant-garde.[39] Thereafter, acquisitions for the Trust reflect a cautious acknowledgement of the growing emphasis on modern painting in Ireland during the war years, which we shall discuss shortly. This change was apparent in the third quinquennial exhibition, held at the Municipal Gallery, which was distinguished not only by Sleator's portrait of *Sir William Orpen* and Seán O'Sullivan's *F.R. Higgins*, but also by the more avant-garde *Girl in White*, of 1941 (Ulster Museum), and *Variety Rehearsal at the Olympia*, of 1942 (cata. no.70), by Louis le Brocquy; as well as Norah McGuinness' *Four Courts*, and Laurence Campbell's *Pont de l'Alma, Paris* (cata. no.100). This trend was continued in the next exhibition, the last held during our period, which included paintings by Gerard Dillon, Dan O'Neill, George Campbell, Nano Reid and Thurloe Conolly.

As one looks back on the years from 1930 to 1950, it is clear that while the Haverty Trust did little to stimulate Irish painting as Haverty had wished, nevertheless, the acquisitions made under the Trust represent the changing trends of the period and in them we have a clear view of the developments that took place. Furthermore, apart from the Gibson Bequest, the Haverty Trust was at that time the only endowment which painters could look to for patronage.

* * *

In contrast to the Gibson and Haverty bequests which, as we have seen, were administered conservatively, the Friends of the National Collections of Ireland, founded in 1924, and Belfast Museum & Art Gallery's Lloyd Patterson paintings, assembled between 1929 and 1933, both greatly encouraged public interest in avant-garde painting.

The Lloyd Patterson Collection had a considerable influence on art in Ulster but, alas, was virtually unknown south of the border. The formation of the collection was due to Arthur Deane, the curator of the museum, who decided to use the proceeds of the Patterson bequest to form a collection of contemporary British paintings.[40] Unlike the authorities of the Municipal Gallery in Dublin, who in the late 1920s and 1930s still thought of 'modern' painting in terms of pre-First World War French art, Deane was interested in collecting the art of his own times. Consequently the Patterson collection had a direct influence on the Belfast painters, who would have been familiar with similar works to those represented in the collection from the pages of contemporary journals such as the *Studio*. This collection clearly influenced the members of the Ulster Unit.

That the Belfast museum should have acquired works by English, rather than Irish artists, was, happily, complementary to the activities of the Friends of the National Collections of Ireland. The Friends came into being largely due to the efforts of Sarah Purser, who almost certainly modelled the new Society on the National Art Collections Fund in Great Britain, of which she had been a member for several years.[41] The purpose of the Society, as set out in its constitution, was 'to secure works of art and objects of historic interest or importance, for the national or public collections of Ireland, by purchase, gift, or bequest, and to further their interests in other analogous or incidental ways'.[42] The Friends also dedicated themselves to the task of securing the return from London to Dublin of Hugh Lane's thirty-nine Continental paintings.

By the end of their first year, the Society had 112 members; by 1939 this number had risen to 325; and thereafter it settled at just under the 200 mark for the rest of our period.[43] For the first decade, membership subscriptions (one guinea per year) were the Society's only source of income, but from the early 1930s this income was enhanced by other monies derived from various sources. Thus, by way of purchase funds, almost £200 were to hand in 1926; £550 by 1939; almost £750 in 1943; and £1,100 by 1949–50.[44] As we shall see, that the Society should have accomplished so much over the years with such a limited budget is enormously to their credit.

Throughout their history the Friends have shown a catholic taste in their acquisitions.[45] Furthermore, unlike the trustees of the Gibson Bequest, they ignored the cultural pull of the 1920s and 1930s and decided that the best way to encourage Irish artists was to familiarize them with the work of their contemporaries elsewhere. Indeed, when the Haverty trustees, who were interested only in Irish art, began purchasing in 1930 the Friends decided to continue Hugh Lane's practice of acquiring mainly works by modern Continental and British painters[46] and in 1937 they reaffirmed their purchasing policy, stating:

> Familiarity with the art of our day in Europe is essential to the development and progress of our own. Without this constant familiarity taste is dulled and design stagnates. We are anxious that our chief Irish collection of modern art [HLMG] should provide this necessary contact. No state or municipal endowment is, at the moment, available in the Irish Free State to provide this vital stimulus . . . . To place good examples of the best foreign artists [and the desiderata cited included works by Cézanne, Derain, Gauguin, Matisse, Picasso, Rouault, Seurat, Signac, Utrillo, Van Gogh, Vlaminck] before our students and the public is a patriotic duty, and having regard to the splendid generosity of the late Thomas Haverty the duty may be discharged without any searching of heart.[47]

It is clear from the names on their desiderata list that the Friends were trying to proceed, as far as their resources would permit, in a methodical manner to remedy what they saw as shortcomings principally in the collections of the Municipal Gallery, Dublin. In their choice of artists there was a growing emphasis on innovative work, albeit of a somewhat dated kind for that period, and in succeeding years they purchased works by Picasso (*Les Orchidées*), Utrillo (*La Rue Marcadet*), Bonnard (*Boulevard de Clichy*), Rouault (*Christ and the Soldier*), Denoyer de Segonzac (*St. Tropez*, all Lane Gallery), and Vuillard (*Interior*, now called *A Man Seated on a Sofa,* National Gallery of Ireland). Of the younger British artists, many of whom were already represented in Belfast, they acquired John Nash (*Autumn Berries*), Duncan Grant (*Ships in Harbour*, both Lane Gallery) and Stanley Spencer (*Decoration*, now known as *Scene from the Marriage at Cana in Galilee* ,Ulster Museum), along with numerous works from the nineteenth century and earlier by Continental and Irish artists.

One event which is notable for the image which it conveys of the time was the rejection by Dublin Corporation's Art Advisory Committee of Rouault's *Christ and the Soldier* when first offered by the Friends to the Municipal Gallery in 1942. Officially no reason was given for the rejection of the work, but the ensuing lengthy discussion of the matter in the letters columns of the press makes it clear that it was considered by some to be irreligious, even blasphemous, while others delighted in it as a work of pathos. Ironically, however, the work was accepted 'with the greatest pleasure' by St. Patrick's College, Maynooth,[48] when offered there on loan. Later, in

1954, the Rouault, together with a *Reclining Figure* by Henry Moore, was again offered to the Municipal Gallery but the Advisory Committee once more rejected it along with the Moore. However, both works were finally accepted by a reconstituted committee in 1956.[49]

With regard to the advancement of Modernism in Ireland, the Friends introduced no works which—public outrage notwithstanding—were daringly avant-garde or innovative for the times; but they did continually warn against the effects of cultural isolation. To this end, in August 1944 they organized the exhibition, *Modern and Continental Paintings*, which drew on works in Irish public and private collections, and which demonstrated the wide range of modern paintings already in the country. The majority of works shown were French, namely Impressionist, Post-Impressionist, Fauvist (Vlaminck, *Fleurs*, ? National Gallery of Ireland) and Cubist paintings (Gleizes' *Painting*, Marchand, *Roofs of Paris*, Picasso, *Papiers Collés*, all National Gallery of Ireland), but also included were the Italian Giorgio de Chirico, whose *Dioscuri*, 1937 (Iveagh House, Dublin), was an example of his 'metaphysical' painting, and Expressionist works by the German artists Franz Marc, a member of the influential *Blaue Reiter* group, and Max Pechstein of the Dresden *Brücke* painters. This was the first exhibition of its kind to be held in Ireland since Ellen Duncan's shows of modern French painting in 1911 and 1912 and the Paul Henry/Arthur Power exhibition of modern paintings in 1922.

The exhibition attracted much comment and occasioned numerous letters to the press, including one from the poet Patrick Kavanagh[50] in which, like many commentators, he debunked almost the entire exhibition in the most flippant terms. But the *Irish Times* produced a leading article on the exhibition in which it praised the organizers and reminded everyone of the opportunity afforded them to make contact with an international standard, 'to see, at first hand, works by those artists whom critics of all nations rate most highly'. And it concluded: 'To a country which is pursuing cultural isolation, without seeing that it will mean cultural suicide, any breath from the outside is of value'.[51] The effects of the exhibition, however, were negligible, but following on the heels of the first *Irish Exhibition of Living Art*, held in September 1943, and the exhibition of *Subjective Art* of January 1944, it nevertheless did much to stimulate public interest in these years and later.

In their efforts to secure the return of Hugh Lane's thirty-nine Continental paintings to Dublin the Friends of the National Collections were also involved in the acquisition of Charlemont House as a permanent home for the Dublin Municipal Gallery. The history of their involvement here has been fully documented elsewhere[52] so that we need only discuss the matter in outline. As noted earlier, all attempts to have Lane's pictures returned to Dublin finally failed in 1926 with the publication of the British government enquiry into the affair. Following this President Cosgrave told the Dáil that his government considered the issue to be an international matter, and he reaffirmed his support both for those who argued for the return of the pictures and that Dublin Corporation should build a gallery to house them. At a meeting on 31 March 1927 the Friends passed a resolution welcoming Cosgrave's statement, but they also suggested that any gallery should in part be financed by the government.[53] At their annual general meeting held a year later, neither the corporation nor the government having done anything to bring about such a gallery, the Friends decided to act unilaterally on the matter, arguing that not only would the erection of a gallery be the best way to secure the return of the Lane pictures, but that such a gallery would represent the greatest service which could be rendered to the Irish national collections. At this, Sarah Purser suggested Charlemont House, then recently vacated by the Register General's department, as a suitable place for the gallery and, after much lobbying, it was eventually handed over in September 1929 and opened to the public in 1933.[54]

The (Hugh Lane) Municipal Gallery of Modern Art has often been surrounded by controversy. In many instances this has been self-provoked for, certainly in our period, the authorities responsible for it appear to have had no clear view of its function, of the role which it should play in the artistic life of the community or, indeed, of the kind of work which—if funds had been available—it should collect, apart from what others were willing to give to it. Thus, it has always been at the mercy of one faction or another. As far as modern art is concerned, until the 1950s its enthusiasm halted, as did Lane's, too, with the Impressionists, later developments being treated with the utmost suspicion or even hostility. To those who ran the Gallery modern art had no continuing chronology; it was—in so far as they thought about it at all—merely an art freed from the formalism of previous ages and left, presumably, in limbo. Consequently they invited criticism from all shades of opinion, from those who were opposed to Modernism in principle and from the more forward looking to whom the Gallery appeared moribund. Reviewing the new premises in 1936 John Dowling thought that in Lane's time the collection, although smaller, had been more coherent. The loss of the Lane pictures, he said, greatly reduced the value of the collection, but he argued that the protestations against these pictures being in England would have carried more weight if the corporation had shown the 'slightest indication' in the previous twenty-five years of adding to the splendid nucleus gathered by Lane or of replacing the lost examples by others. And in conclusion he rebuked the corporation for being represented in the art market 'only as a mendicant'.[55] Terence de Vere White, too, who did much for the Gallery through his work with the Friends of the National Collections, was able to write as late as 1957 that it was 'to a great extent hung with pictures more than half a century old'; which situation, he said, 'meets with the approval of those who manage the Gallery who have shown a marked aversion to paintings of the modern school'. As examples of this boorishness, he cited the rejection of Rouault's *Christ and the Soldier* in 1942 and Henry Moore's *Reclining Figure* in 1954 and noted works by Picasso and Bonnard which had been accepted with 'little enthusiasm'.[56]

The Municipal Gallery has never been in the forefront of developments in Modernism in Ireland; that role belongs to the smaller groups such as the Contemporary Picture Galleries, which we have already discussed, and others who came to prominence during the war years. It is to them that we must now turn our attention.

CHAPTER 5

THE WHITE STAG GROUP

' . . . as we were getting away from the war we would get away from it
and be in the country away from it then in those days we did not
know where the war was or what it would be it might be in
Ireland any time . . . '

(Kenneth Hall, autobiography, p.54).

As the war clouds gathered over Europe in the course of 1939, the reaffirmation by the Irish government of a policy of neutrality presaged for many an even greater sense of isolation than that experienced in the previous two decades. As early as April of that year the Taoiseach, Mr. de Valera, had told the Dail that his policy was to keep Ireland out of the impending conflict. He had successfully pursued a similar policy with regard to the Spanish Civil War, although upwards of one thousand Irishmen fought in Spain.[1] But whereas the Spanish Civil War was a struggle for power in one country, it would be more difficult to remain neutral in a wider conflict. However, Ireland did remain neutral, although during those years of the 'Emergency', as the war was called in neutral parlance, there was always a possibility that either the British, and later the Allies, or the Germans would invade her for tactical reasons. In F.S.L. Lyons' words, 'Irish neutrality depended not alone upon the Allies observing it, but upon their forces being strong enough to prevent the Germans from infringing it'.[2] Avoiding the war, therefore, was not entirely within Irish control. Moreover, throughout the war both the Allies and the Axis Powers maintained diplomatic representation in Ireland, with the result that Dublin became a centre for espionage and conspiracy.[3] It is against this background of uncertainty and intrigue that we must view the activities of the White Stag Group.

Despite these circumstances, the war-years in Ireland were a watershed between the early self-conscious years of independence and a more certain identity. As far as the visual arts and Modernism in particular are concerned, the time saw a tacit acceptance of many ideas which had evolved during the previous two decades. It was this willingness to consider new ideas, in the main alien to Ireland, that distinguishes the 1940s from previous decades.

The outbreak of war in 1939 compelled several Irish painters to return home from abroad—we have already mentioned Ralph Cusack and Patrick Hennessy in this respect and others included Norah McGuinness and Louis le Brocquy—but with them arrived a number of English artists, who from 1940 exhibited together under the name of 'The White Stag Group'. They, being outsiders, were free of the social and other prejudices which pressed upon their Irish contemporaries and consequently they brought a much needed freshness of approach both in their work and other activities.

Background in Bloomsbury

Basil Rakoczi (1908-79) and Kenneth Hall (1913-46) formed the core of the White Stag Group. Rakoczi's interests, however, originally lay in psychology as much as in painting. In fact, with a friend, Herbrand Ingouville-Williams, he had founded the Society for Creative Psychology in the Bloomsbury district of London in the early 1930s. Ingouville-Williams was then reading psychology at Cambridge, but Rakoczi was self-taught, basing his ideas of the subject and the practice of psychotherapy on personal experience with his own analyst, the Freudian, Karin Stephen.[4] Meetings of the Society, which usually took the form of lectures and group work, were held at Rakoczi's rooms in number 8 Fitzroy Street.[5] In July 1935, at one of these meetings, Rakoczi met Kenneth Hall, then a struggling artist, and they immediately became close friends. Rakoczi shared Hall's interest in art, having been a student for a time at both the Brighton School of Art and the Académie de la Grande Chaumière in Paris—later, after the Second World War, he worked under Ossip Zadkine, who no doubt stimulated his interest in psychology.[6] Later that same year, 1935, Rakoczi and Hall founded the White Stag Group for the advancement of subjectivity in psychological analysis[7] and art. Rakoczi and Hall were, strictly speaking, the only 'members' of the Group[8] but they were joined by associates—Friends of the Group— including Ingouville-Williams, who lent much financial support. The emblem adopted by them, a white stag set on a dark ground, was Hungarian in origin and signified creativity. For much of his life Rakoczi used it as a personal symbol, for it appears on a range of his publications dating from the 1930s until the 1970s.

To begin with the activities of the White Stag Group were orientated towards psychology, and Rakoczi earned a meagre living as an analyst. Only later did he and Hall concentrate on painting. Rakoczi had been married and had one son, Anthony, but the marriage had failed in 1932, although Rakoczi retained custody of the child. In the mid and late 1930s he travelled a great deal in Europe and Egypt, and in 1934 visited India, where he spent a time of retreat at Ghandi's ashram and met the writer Tagore. In the late 1930s he was often accompanied on his travels by Kenneth Hall and Ingouville-Williams. Rakoczi, Hall and Ingouville-Williams were pacifists and in August 1939, sensing the inevitability of war, they decided to come to Ireland where they hoped to find conditions in which they could continue their work undisturbed.

The White Stag Group in Ireland

Having arrived in Ireland Rakoczi and Hall took a cottage near Delphi in Co. Mayo, about six miles from Leenane on the northern side of Killary Bay. In his autobiography Hall details their movements at this time and describes their feelings, in a style delightfully reminiscent of Gertrude Stein:

We met in Galway and as we were getting away from the war we would get away from it and be in the country away from it then in those days we did not know where the war was or what it would be it might be in Ireland any time and any place might be bombed so Benny [Rakoczi] looked at a map for Connemara . . . and we would get away from the war . . . on Killary Bay.[9]

They travelled the area by bicycle, sight-seeing and sketching, and remained there until early in 1940 by which time it seems they missed the contact with others offered by city life to which they were accustomed. Also, Anthony Rakoczi's education had to be considered and Dublin offered better schools than could be found in the west.

Thus Rakoczi and Hall moved to Dublin, where they took rooms at number 34 Lower Baggot Street. The city provided an environment conducive to their activities and they soon gathered around them a small circle of friends who shared their interests. As in Bloomsbury, they arranged lectures and discussion groups, which were open to all-comers, under the auspices of the Society for Creative Psychology, the first meeting of which was held on 26 April 1940 at number 25 Lower Baggot Street in a flat belonging to a friend, René Buhler. On that occasion Rakozi spoke on 'The Structure of the Mind', while a month later he gave three talks entitled: 'The Practice of Psychological Analysis', 'The Psychology of the Numen in Relation to Medicine, Religion, Art and Politics' and 'The Acquisition of Happiness'.[10]

René Buhler, whose flat was used on these occasions, was a linguist and salesman. German by birth, he had for several years lived in England with his French wife, Georgette (Zette) Rondel. Together with Nick Nicholls, a mutual friend, they came to Dublin in about August 1939 and for a time lived in Lower Baggot Street.

Throughout the winter of 1940 and during 1941 the Society for Creative Psychology held meetings, at which Rakoczi was a regular speaker. The last we hear of the Society, however, is in September-October 1941, when Rakoczi gave two lectures, on yoga and the development of personality, entitled 'Yang and Yin' and 'Ri and Ki'. These topics illustrate his interest in subjectivity which came to dominate his painting.

The English expatriates who gathered around Rakoczi and Hall in Dublin were Nick Nicholls, a poet and painter of abstract works; Georgette Rondel, a painter; Stephen Gilbert, a painter, and his Canadian wife Jocelyn Chewett, a sculptor; and Phyllis Hayward, a painter and former member of the Society for Creative Psychology in Bloomsbury, who came to Ireland in 1940. Herbrand Ingouville-Williams was also in Dublin by early 1940. Their Irish associates were Dorothy Blackham; Ralph Cusack; Bobby Dawson, a painter and photographer; Paul Egestorff, a painter (his father was German, his mother Irish);[11] Evie Hone; Mainie Jellett; Nano Reid; Patrick Scott; Doreen Vanston, who first showed with the group at the invitation of Rakoczi in 1942; and Patricia Wallace. Others, who occasionally exhibited at White Stag exhibitions, were Barbara Bayley; Leslie Birks; Brian Boydell, a painter and musician; Thurloe Conolly; Phyllis Eason; Humphrey Gilbert; May Guinness; Eugene Judge; E.A. McGuire; Ann Miller; Elizabeth Ormsby; Conor Padilla; Cicely Peel; Nelson Pollard; Anthony Reford; Endre Roszda; Henri Silvy and Donald Teale (husband of Phyllis Hayward).[12] Still others, not all artists and largely on the fringe of this company, were René Buhler; Noel Moffett, a Dublin architect, and his wife Margot; Patricia Griffith; Nigel Heseltine, son of the composer Peter Warlock, he took the pseudonym 'Michael Walsh' and produced plays at the Olympia Theatre with Shelah Richards as 'Shelah Richards, Michael Walsh Productions';[13] Ronald Macdonald Douglas, a playwright and short-story writer; Victor Meally, a Dublin mathematician, much interested in Eastern philosophy;[14] and the writer Olivia Manning Robertson. Due to the uneasiness of the times, one or two of those mentioned were occasionally under surveillance by the gardai Special Branch. One correspondent, Vaughan Biscoe, said that this was ' . . . if only because of the famous parties in no. 25 Lr. Baggot St. It was not unknown for Cauvet Duhamel, of the French Embassy, and Dr. Karl Peterson (German "Press Attache") to be present at the same time tho' at different ends of the room, and things got pretty hairy at times. There were, to my certain knowledge, at least two "spies" always around—really not much more than paid agents posing as students and reporting to various Embassies'.[15]

* * *

The first exhibition in Ireland of paintings by the White Stag Group was held at number 34 Lower Baggot Street, Dublin, during April 1940. Ten artists took part on that occasion, namely Basil Rakoczi, Kenneth Hall, Nick Nicholls, Mainie Jellett, Georgette Rondel, Patricia Wallace, Barbara Bayley, Anthony Reford, Elizabeth Ormsby and Endre Roszda. Also included were sketches by Rakoczi's son, Anthony. In the absence of the exhibition catalogue it is impossible to know what pictures were shown, but Rakoczi's *Cottages, Carna*, and other similar works done shortly after his arrival in Ireland, may well have been included. Hall's *Doorway, Lower Baggot Street*, of early 1940, which is similar in style to Rakoczi's *Dublin Alley* (cata. no.48), may also have been included. The *Irish Times* praised the exhibition, commenting that the artists all shared 'a fundamental freshness and originality of treatment'. And it singled out Kenneth Hall as a welcome change from the more hackneyed interpretations of Irish scenery.[16] The inclusion of such a prominent artist as Mainie Jellett, who showed an abstract composition and a *Virgin and Child*, in this early exhibition of the Group suggests that Rakoczi and Hall lost little time after their arrival in Dublin in seeking-out kindred spirits in the local art scene.

The next White Stag exhibition, also a mixed show, was held at number 30 Upper Mount Street, Dublin, during October 1940. By then the original circle had been joined by several others, including Dorothy Blackham from the Dublin Painters' Society, Jocelyn Chewett and her husband Stephen Gilbert, Bobby Dawson, Paul Egestorff and Eugene Judge. In all, sixty-nine works were shown on this occasion, and opening the exhibition Mainie Jellett said that those participating aimed 'to interpret the times in which they live,' without being 'hidebound to any particular school or cramped by academic conventionality'.[17]

Of the exhibits, Rakoczi's *The Curragh* and *Farm, Slievemore* testify to his recent spell in the west, but in *Dublin Alley*, which was painted soon after his move to the city, we have a good example of his technique at the time, which was to draw with a pencil into the still wet paint, a technique which Kenneth Hall tells us he acquired from his friend Helmut Kolle and which he first employed early in 1939.[18] This technique gave great spontaneity of execution, which is clearly evident here. Kenneth Hall's *Dublin Barge* demonstrates his use of the same technique, although line is important in all his work. In the absence of formal training it is not surprising that Hall should have adopted such an Expressionist approach to painting. 'For me [life] was to be an artist,' he wrote, 'and what I knew as an artist would be in my work . . . that and life and living and loving and sunshine'.[19] Few of the other pictures shown in this exhibition can now be identified, but Mainie Jellett's *Horses from the Sea*

Basil Rakoczi
Cottages Carna,
c.1940
Photograph Bryan Rutledge

was almost certainly similar in style to her *Achill Horses*, now in the National Gallery of Ireland. Stephen Gilbert was represented by a group of figure compositions which were almost certainly Expressionist in execution, while his wife, Jocelyn Chewett, showed one work, *Fish*, in alabaster. Dorothy Blackham showed *The Nuns' Walk* and Patricia Wallace and Paul Egestorff each showed a number of landscapes. *Still Life with Fish*, 1940-2, is characteristic of Georgette Rondel's work at this time and may have been included in this exhibition. It shows the French influence of Braque and others in her training. Georgette Rondel (c.1915-42) was born in France and educated at art school in Paris. She worked as a commercial artist in Paris, London and Dublin where she also produced some theatrical designs. Rondel was a fine draughtsman with a bold, authoritative line, and a good sense of design. She had a difficult personality, however, and from time to time tended towards schizophrenia. In 1942 she returned to England to be with her husband, René Buhler, who had gone there the previous year, but died that autumn. Nick Nicholls' poem 'My Love is Dead', published in the *Bell* in November 1942, was written in memory of Zette Rondel.[20]

As the chronology (Appendix 2) of the activities of the White Stag Group makes clear other exhibitions, including a number of one-man shows, now followed at frequent intervals. These exhibitions are often notable for the inclusion of works on loan by well-known painters, such as those by Dufy, Gleizes, Juan Gris, Frances Hodgkins, Helmut Kolle, Picasso, Rouault, Sickert and Christopher Wood which were included in the exhibition of December 1940.[21] Such pictures gave authority and an international dimension to the early White Stag shows. Lectures by guest speakers were from time to time also held in association with these exhibitions. Mainie Jellett,

Georgette Rondel
In the Green,
c.1940–3
Photograph S.B.K.

for example, gave a talk (almost certainly about Cubism and abstract painting) at Rakoczi's exhibition in November 1940 and on 20 December that year, Henri Silvy of the French Legation gave a lecture entitled 'The Legacy of Cubism' at number 30 Upper Mount Street.

The first one-man show by a member of the White Stag Group was Rakoczi's exhibition of paintings, held in November 1940. On that occasion he exhibited almost forty works which, according to a press review,[22] ranged in style from Expressionist to Surrealist. Clearly some of the pictures, such as *James's Street* and *Fitzwilliam Lane*, must have been similar to his *Dublin Alley*, but also included were Continental scenes such as *Drying the Nets, Tréboul* and a number of figure studies. The range and choice of subject-matter in these works demonstrates that at the time Rakoczi continued to make largely representational paintings as well as more abstract or Subjective[23] ones, the latter being a mode which he had first begun to explore while living in Paris in the autumn of 1938.

* * *

Numerically the White Stag Group was at its largest during 1941. Two group exhibitions were held that year, in February and November. The first of these comprised fifty-one works by eighteen artists, of whom E.A. McGuire, Cicely Peel, Nano Reid and Patrick Scott were showing with the Group for the first time. Three paintings on loan by Albert Gleizes (*Abstract*), Jean Marchand (*Houses*) and Max Pechstein (*Landscape*) were also included. Even with the aid of the catalogue few of the exhibits can now be identified, but the general tone of the exhibition was in line with the already familiar White Stag style. Rakoczi showed mainly Subjective works, including a picture entitled *Three Heads*, the subject-matter of which, as we shall see shortly, was to preoccupy him later. Hall was represented by a flowerpiece and two Dublin street scenes, which were no doubt executed in a similar manner to his *Dublin Barge* of the previous year. Mainie Jellett showed two works, *Composition* and *Painting 1923*, the latter almost certainly being similar to the severly abstract pictures which she first showed at the Dublin Painters' Society in autumn 1923. The other exhibits included still lifes, landscapes, figure compositions, two nude studies by Georgette Rondel, Expressionist pieces by Stephen Gilbert (*Fantasia*) and Nick Nicholls (*Still Life*), an abstract by Patrick Scott, and two works by Bobby Dawson (*Still Life*, *Head of a Girl*), who veered towards Surrealism. Other events that spring were a talk on sculpture given on 9 May by Jocelyn Chewett and Mainie Jellett's lecture, 'The Spiritual Force in Art', also given in May.

The spring exhibition was followed in October 1941 by a one-man show of paintings by Kenneth Hall. Although he had been painting since the early 1930s, Hall turned seriously to art only after a visit to Spain with Basil Rakoczi in 1935. From then until 1939 he travelled and painted intermittently with Rakoczi in several European countries. In April 1939 he underwent an operation for mastoiditis but it was not entirely successful and the ailment was to plague him for the rest of his life.

As we have said, on arriving in Ireland, Hall and Rakoczi settled in the west. 'Life is very primitive but also nice and homely, oil lamps, peat fire, and water from a stream', he wrote to Lucy Wertheim on the second of October; and a few weeks later, on 27 November, he told her: 'We have the Studio, the Times Literary Supplement and the New Statesman so I hope not to turn into a complete turnip while here'. Hall was happier and more content in Connemara that he had been for a long time and was rather pleased with several of the twenty or so paintings he did during his stay there. However by March of 1940, by which time he had moved to Dublin, he was in low spirits as he told Lucy Wertheim on 12 March.[24] Also, he found Dublin provincial, which he did not care for. But despite his difficulties, on 30 March he told Mrs. Wertheim that he was busy arranging the exhibition subsequently held at number 34 Lower Baggot Street that April. In January 1941 Hall took a flat at number 18 Upper Fitzwilliam Street and remained there for the rest of his time in Ireland. During those years he often travelled to the west, staying with friends[25] and painting the landscape.

Kenneth Hall was to begin with principally a landscapist but animals, particularly birds and fish, dominate his later work. His painting evolved through two distinct phases. The earlier phase, of the years 1935-41, comprises mainly landscapes which are characterized by the use of a black line to describe and delineate forms; while the latter phase, 1941-6, contains mainly Subjective paintings in which the black line is often retained but in which he has emphasized abstract qualities such as shape and colour. The development of his painting before he came to Ireland can be briefly summarised. Until about 1937 his compositions were conceived almost as flat patterns, with little suggestion of recession in space, the forms and shapes being outlined with a thin black line of constant weight and thickness and the colours laid flat with no attempt at modelling, the whole often having a child-like simplicity of concept. There is a light-hearted humour in these early works which later gave way to a more sombre note which, with few exceptions, remained for the rest of his career. Three pictures which stand out from the body of his work at this time are *Boats at Glyfada*, 1937, *Old Phaleron, Greece*, 1938 (cata. no.50) and *Itea*, 1939 (cata. no.51). They are amongst the best of his paintings from any period and illustrate how his style had developed by the time he arrived in Ireland. All three were painted briskly and with great

97

assurance. The two first mentioned are probably the closest Hall ever came to naturalistic work and, with the splendidly Dufyesque *Itea*,[26] are more light-hearted in mood than was the case in almost any of his later work.

Hall's one-man show of October 1941 comprised fifty-one pictures, many of which had been painted before he came to Ireland. He prefaced the exhibition catalogue, which was in French throughout, with a poem describing the Baudelaireian nature of his artistic ethos and which rather poignantly betrays his mood at the time:

> Je ne suis pas la lune
> Je ne suis pas de bois
> Sans mon âme
> Je veux échapper
> Et je veux monter aux arbres
> Pour y chercher la Beauté.[27]

Opening the exhibition, Jocelyn Chewett praised his use of colour and the sensitivity of his drawing. Figure compositions and landscapes dominated his subject-matter and the former included a number of early Subjective pieces—on the day before the exhibition closed Basil Rakoczi gave a lecture entitled 'Subjective Painting'. A number of the pictures were lent by other artists, including Stephen Gilbert, Evie Hone, Basil Rakoczi and Patrick Scott, thus testifying to the esteem in which they held his work. As with so many White Stag exhibitions, few of the works shown can now be traced, but *La tête grecque* and *Après la guerre* (cata. no.52) were included. By 1941 the war was beginning to take its toll on Hall and, along with the last mentioned painting, *Little Bird* (cata. no.53), also painted that year, shows his anxiety at the time.[28] The handling of paint in the latter is strongly gestural and the use of colour, conspicuous brushwork and emphasis on the existential act of painting anticipate post-war Abstract Expressionism, while the symbolic image of a bird (a dove?) suggests a moral commitment to peace by the artist. This painting also marks the beginning of Hall's interest in birds, fishes and animals, an influence from Patrick Scott,[29] which are central to his later compositions. There is a bird-like image prominent in *Après la guerre* and its rather amorphous shape recalls the biomorphic images of some of his later abstracts. In the feeling of desolation conveyed *Après la guerre*, perhaps, evokes greater despondency than any of Hall's other paintings.

The group show of November 1941 comprised sixty-eight works by twenty-four artists and was the largest of all the White Stag exhibitions. Newcomers to the Group on this occasion included, amongst others, Phyllis Hayward and Doreen Vanston. Rakoczi and Hall were both well represented with by now familiar works, and of the Irish painters Patrick Scott and Bobby Dawson were prominent. An architect by training, Scott (b.1921) was self-taught as an artist, the sea, close to his childhood home in Co. Cork, having first stirred him to paint.[30] Other early influences on him were Cézanne, whose work he saw in London in 1939, and Matisse, whom he he knew from reproductions and whom he admired for the freshness and freedom of his colour.[31] None of the works which he exhibited on this occasion can now be traced, but from this time dates his preoccupation with birds and animals as subject-matter in his paintings. His earliest extant pictures date from about 1940 or 1941. In them birds, fishes and other creatures are reduced to symbols; the flatness of the picture plane is acknowledged, there being no attempt to suggest recession; there is a concern for the texture of the canvas, the pigment is thinly applied and translucent[32] and in places the canvas has been left unpainted to make lines which give an architectural element to the work. Neither can the two pictures by Bobby Dawson (b.1920s) now be identified, but we can assume that in style they would have been similar to *We Are Ready* and *Untitled*, both of about 1941. In terms of subject-matter and the Surrealist approach adopted, these are characteristic of Dawson's work at the time and were influenced by Picasso, whom he knew from illustrations. Both compositions are linear in structure and although the imagery is bizarre they have a strong element of humour.

Amongst the newcomers to the Group, Phyllis Hayward and Doreen Vanston were the most important. Phyllis Hayward, as we have noted earlier, had come to Dublin in 1940. She soon became a prominent member of the art scene, exhibiting from time to time with the White Stag Group, at the Contemporary Picture Galleries[33] and, from 1944, at the Irish Exhibition of Living Art. French Impressionism, Fauvism and Cubism were the early influences on her,[34] and flowers and still life were her favourite subject-matter. She also painted some portraits, but these are often dull and depend for their interest on her handling of the medium rather than a likeness of the sitter. Of the four pictures which she showed on this occasion, one, *Growing Seeds*, was almost certainly a flower piece. Such works by her are predominantly linear in technique and have a freedom and spontaneity derived from her experimental use of mixed media whereby she often combined gouache, ink, crayon, pastel and occasionally monotype in the one work. *Still life with Guitar* (cata. no.54), which dates from the early 1940s, illustrates this method and shows too her debt to Cubism. *Flowers in a Pot*, painted in 1947, is exuberant and shows her at her best. Doreen Vanston (1903-88), a Dubliner, studied art in London and under Roger Bissière at the Académie Ranson in Paris, where her mother sent her on the advice of Paul Henry.[35] It was no doubt Bissière who encouraged the independence of spirit that characterizes all her work. She spent most of the 1930s living and working in France and for a short time studied with André Lhote. Back in Dublin, in 1941, she met Basil Rakoczi and thus became associated with the White Stag Group. *Keel Dance Hall*, which she exhibited in November 1941, indicates that she had recently spent some time in the west.

Late in 1941 Basil Rakoczi held another one-man exhibition. It was officially opened by the playwright Lennox Robinson on 21 November and Mainie Jellett also spoke on the occasion. In the absence of both the catalogue and press reviews of the exhibition we cannot know which works were included, but almost certainly they would have been Subjective in manner, as in *Untitled*. Here the subject-matter is derived from the imagination but seems to relate to some dream or allegory of life. Colour is less important than form and shape and there is an emphasis on line, as with the representational works previously discussed. Pattern and decoration are also important to these early Subjective works, the general structure of which owes much to Cubism. Other works of the period, such as *Kether*,[36] painted late in 1941, introduce us to Rakoczi's interest in philosophy and mysticism and in them we can see the beginnings of the fantasy figures which are so prominent in his later compositions.

Other events organized by the Group in 1941 were lectures by Mainie Jellett in October and December and, from November, life classes were held at number 30 Upper Mount Street every Monday evening. These activities demonstrate a growing interest amongst many Irish artists in the avant-garde and clearly there was at the time a need for a forum, unfettered by any conditions or limitations of number, in which to show such work. Moreover, we may fairly claim that the activities of the White Stag Group must, to some extent, have encouraged the foundation of the Irish Exhibition of Living Art in 1943.

* * *

After 1941 the activities of the White Stag Group settled around a smaller number of artists, principally Rakoczi, Hall, Nicholls, Gilbert, Chewett, Hayward and the Irish painters Patrick Scott and Doreen Vanston, although from time to time others exhibited with them. From early 1942 until the end of the war most of the exhibitions and other events arranged by the Group were held at number 6 Lower Baggot Street, which became known as the White Stag Gallery.

The exhibition in February 1942 of works by Jocelyn Chewett, Stephen Gilbert, Hall, Rakoczi and Patrick Scott was the only mixed show held by the Group that year. Alas, we have neither the catalogue nor press reviews of it and so must speculate as to the nature of the works shown. Jocelyn Chewett (1906-79) was the only sculptor to exhibit with the White Stags. A Canadian by birth, she had lived in England from 1913. In 1927 she enrolled at the Slade School to study painting under Henry Tonks, but after a time turned to sculpture, becoming a pupil of A.H. Gerrard. In 1931 she left the Slade[37] and went to Paris to work with Brancusi and Zadkine. Four years later, in 1935, she returned to England and married Stephen Gilbert, whom she had first met while at the Slade. The Gilberts then moved to Paris and remained there until 1940 when they came to Dublin. It was through Mainie Jellett that they met Basil Rakoczi and other members of the White Stag circle.[38]

Her stay in Ireland was a happy period for Jocelyn Chewett. She found many friends, including Evie Hone, with whom she felt much in common. Her approach to sculpture was through material and form, which she held to be more important than conceptual ideas,[39] and she worked always to reveal as concisely as possible the inherent characteristics of the material she was using, employing 'pure' or simplified geometrical forms purged of all inessentials such as decoration.[40] 'Je m'intéresse aux proportions essentielles trois dimensions,' she wrote, continuing: 'Les époques dans l'histoire de la sculpture qui m'attirent le plus sont celles où on a recherché la qualité fondamentale de la forme'.[41] *Le Pendu*, 1942, which she may well have shown in Dublin, is typical of most of her work and shows the influence of Zadkine.

Shortly after he arrived in Ireland Stephen Gilbert (b.1910) began to make Expressionist paintings, which he later referred to as 'Cobra-type' paintings. Of these works he wrote:

> I do not know how this esoteric painting produced in Ireland without influence or followers was in fact essentially what the artists of Cobra were producing . . . contact with Celtic art similar to the original art of Denmark might well have been an unconscious influence.[42]

Expressionism dominated Gilbert's work throughout the 1940s and into the 1950s and during that time his subject-matter and technique changed little. *Painting 1940* (Court Gallery, Copenhagen) is our earliest example of his Expressionist work. The

100

Jocelyn Chewett
Le Pendu, 1942
Photograph courtesy Stephen
Gilbert

image is in part Surrealist and, notwithstanding the animal-like features, one cannot be sure of its derivation. The range of colours is limited, a black outline gives definition, and the handling of the paint suggests that it was done briskly. However, *Painting 1942*, with its image of an insect-like creature, is more typical of the bulk of his work done in Ireland and indeed until after 1950, in which butterflies, dragonflies, spiders and other such insects seem often to have been the source of the imagery. The emphasis given to the head in this last mentioned painting is also characteristic of Gilbert's work throughout the period.

From about this time, 1942, Patrick Scott's compositions, while retaining the characteristics already mentioned, became increasingly geometrical. *Untitled*, is a good example of such work which was influenced by Ben Nicholson, whom he knew from reproductions seen in books.[43] But whereas Nicholson was concerned mainly with shapes, Scott was more interested in line, which always assumes an importance over colour or other elements in his compositions. The use of a circle or sphere as a dominant element, as in *Untitled*, was to preoccupy him for the next thirty years.[44] In *Three Painters* Scott described how he worked at the time:

I have no aim in my painting, other than my own happiness. I am not seeking to express any truths . . . .
    Material is collected at odd moments and in different places. Pieces of wrought-iron seen here and there. Pictures sketched out roughly; canvas chosen for its texture; design worked out more fully on canvas; composition charted on paper to retain its details while the background is being painted . . . .

101

I am interested chiefly in simple forms, such as fish and birds, rather than in the complex forms of human beings or flowers.[45]

The only other exhibitions which appear to have been held by the White Stag Group in 1942 were one-man shows by Basil Rakoczi in May and December and a similar show by Kenneth Hall in September. There was, however, a steady stream of other events, including lectures on art, life classes, poetry readings and musical recitals.

* * *

In early April 1943 Phyllis Hayward, Kenneth Hall, Basil Rakoczi and Patrick Scott held a joint exhibition of watercolours. The show is notable in that it marked the beginning of the most Subjective phase in Hall and Rakoczi, while Scott exhibited pictures of fish and animals, themes which were to preoccupy him increasingly for the next few years. This exhibition was followed later that same month by another with works by Hall, Rakoczi, Scott, Stephen Gilbert and Doreen Vanston. Few of the works shown on this occasion have been traced, but Rakoczi's *Child Flying* was included. In its dream-like wistfulness[46] and Surrealistic use of imagery *Child Flying* is a good example of Rakoczi's early Subjective paintings and recalls the lyrical fantasy evoked by the work of his teacher Ossip Zadkine.

In May 1943 Nick Nicholls (1914–91) held his first one-man show, of sixteen works, at the White Stag Gallery, the exhibition being opened by Ralph Cusack. Nicholls was born in Salisbury, Wiltshire, his father being English, his mother Irish,[47] from a family in Co. Cavan. A quantity surveyor by training, he was self-taught as an artist. Nicholls came to Ireland in June 1939 and remained here until 1946, when he returned to England. As well as being a painter, he also wrote poetry.

Landscapes, still lifes, figure and animal compositions are Nicholls' principal subject-matter. His early work was precise in manner and much influenced by Cézanne, but by the time he arrived in Ireland it had become freerer, more spontaneous, as in *Stephen's Green*, where the paint has been applied briskly with a scumbled technique, there being no attempt to model forms, even in the figure, and the range of colours is kept to a minimum. The whole painting has a loosely Subjective feeling, an aspect which dominated his work from about 1942 onwards, notably under the influence of Miró.

As we have seen, there was in these years a steady stream of events at the White Stag Gallery. We know the date of few of these events, most of which were informal, but the references which we do have testify to their range and tempo. Basil Rakoczi was a good impromptu speaker on occasions, although he also gave more formal lectures, but other speakers, from time to time, were Mainie Jellett, H.F. Norman and Dr. Ingouville-Williams.

Exhibition of Subjective Art

The most important event to be arranged by the White Stag Group was the *Exhibition of Subjective Art*, held at number 6 Lower Baggot Street in January 1944. With the first Living Art exhibition, which took place the previous autumn, it was one of the most notable art exhibitions to be held during the war years in Ireland. The exhibition attracted widespread press coverage, provoked considerable public comment, occasioned several lectures and publications and spawned a similar exhibition in London, in 1945.

The exhibition was arranged by Margot Moffett and its origin is set-out clearly in a letter of 22 June 1943, which she wrote to Patrick Scott inviting him to take part in it. Because of the points raised in the letter and the impression which it gives of public apathy towards contemporary art it is worth quoting at length:-

Dear Pat,

A few weeks ago Kenneth [Hall], Stephen [Gilbert] and I were talking about the old problem, namely, the utter lack of awareness in Dublin's cultural life of the significance of the contemporary trends in the arts (and in non-representational painting in particular), and the resultant lack of a high standard of informed, reliable art criticism. Between us we came to the conclusion that the time had come when modern painting in Ireland had reached a stage of development which justified bringing pressure to bear on public opinion, through an organized programme of activity, thereby creating a stimulus for a deeper appreciation of the place of modern painting in the community. If the artists do not look after their own interests no one else will.

The result of this discussion was that a General Committee was formed consisting of: Jocelyn [Chewett] and Stephen

                Kenneth and Benny [Rakoczi]

                Brian [Boydell] and Thurloe [Conolly]

                Nick [Nicholls], and myself as secretary.

We have drawn up a programme of activities whose main points are:

1 Renting a large, centrally-situated hall.
2 Holding an exhibition representative of the best non-representational painting and sculpture in the country.
3 Organizing public lectures to be held during the exhibition.
4 Arranging for Herbert Read, to come over from England to open the show and to lecture.
5 Issue an illustrated catalogue of the programme of activities, which, it is suggested, might form the basis for a book on modern painting in Ireland to be published later.

I am writing to ask you whether you would be willing to join in with this scheme. The other painters who are to be approached are: Doreen Vanston, Bobby Dawson, Paul Egestorff, Frank Callanan, Phyllis Teale [Hayward], Ralph Cusack, Mainie Jellett and Evie Hone. If you are in sympathy with the idea, the General Committee would be very glad if you would set aside not more than 6 paintings which you would like photographed for reproduction in the folio which will be sent to Herbert Read when we write inviting him over . . . .

In order to finance this scheme we are getting in touch with a number of people who might feel sympathetic enough to subscribe. We are aiming at £100 .'

Yours,

Margot.

From this letter it is clear that the purpose of the exhibition was didactic, that the organizers aimed to stimulate public interest in and acceptance of contemporary art. In asking Herbert Read, who was a friend of Margot Moffett and her husband, Noel,[48] to associate himself with the exhibition they hoped to make it as prestigeous as possible. Eventually the exhibition opened with fifty-six works by thirteen artists.[49] They were, in the order of their names appearing in the catalogue: Jocelyn Chewett, Paul Egestorff, Bobby Dawson, Nick Nicholls, Doreen Vanston, Stephen Gilbert, Ralph Cusack, Brian Boydell, Thurloe Conolly, Phyllis Hayward, Basil Rakoczi, Kenneth Hall and Patrick Scott. With the exception of Thurloe Conolly they had all shown before with the White Stag Group.

Herbert Read planned to be in Dublin from 1-8 January and an elaborate programme of events was arranged for that period. His most important engagements were to have been the opening of the exhibition on the afternoon of the 4th, followed that evening by a public lecture entitled 'The Social Foundations of Architecture', given in conjunction with the Architectural Association; while on the 7th he hoped to give another lecture, 'The Nature of Subjective Art', in the Country Shop at 7.30pm.[50] However, at the last minute Read was unable to come to Ireland[51] and this programme of events had to be altered. At the opening of the exhibition on the 4th Margot Moffett read a message from Read, partly based on his introduction to the catalogue. Read also sent the text of a lecture, 'Art and Crisis', which was read in place of his advertised lecture on the evening of the 7th at the Country Shop. Also at the Country Shop, on 17 January John Hewitt, then curator of art at Belfast Museum & Art Gallery, gave a lecture entitled 'The Adventure of Subjectivity'.

As with previous White Stag exhibitions no single style encompassed all the works on show and the word 'subjective' in the title signified the freedom of each artist to express himself as an individual. The works exhibited may, however, be divided loosely into three categories: those tending towards Surrealism; those either abstract or formalized; those semi-representational or Symbolist.

In the first category were paintings by Rakoczi, Hall, Nicholls, Dawson, Gilbert and Boydell. We have already commented on the nature of Rakoczi's early Subjective paintings, and *Child Flying* and *Three* (cata. no.55), both exhibited here, typically show his interest in psychological fantasies and dreamlike qualities, although in the latter work the composition is more formally arranged than before. There is also in it a greater emphasis than before on texture, surface and the play of one colour with another. *Bird and Fish* and *Bird Turning in Flight*, both painted in 1943, are typical examples of Kenneth Hall's contemporary work and are similar to *Sleeping Duck* (cata. no.57), of 1944. Hall simplified the appearance of the creatures he painted to a near symbol of their species, but emphasized their natural attributes and habitat. Nick Nicholls' use of line and symbolic gestures sugests a likely influence from Paul Klee, and *Lovers*, of about 1943, the present whereabouts of which is unknown, is similar to his *Contemplation* (cata. no.58), painted the following year. In a statement about *Lovers*, Nicholls said:

 Two animal-like figures, male and female, whose giant heads are locked in a kiss. The crosses and circles on their bodies are emblematic of their sexual ideas. The tails join to complete their happiness. The world is represented by three stars.[52]

Bobby Dawson, the youngest of the White Stag painters, was perhaps the most abstract

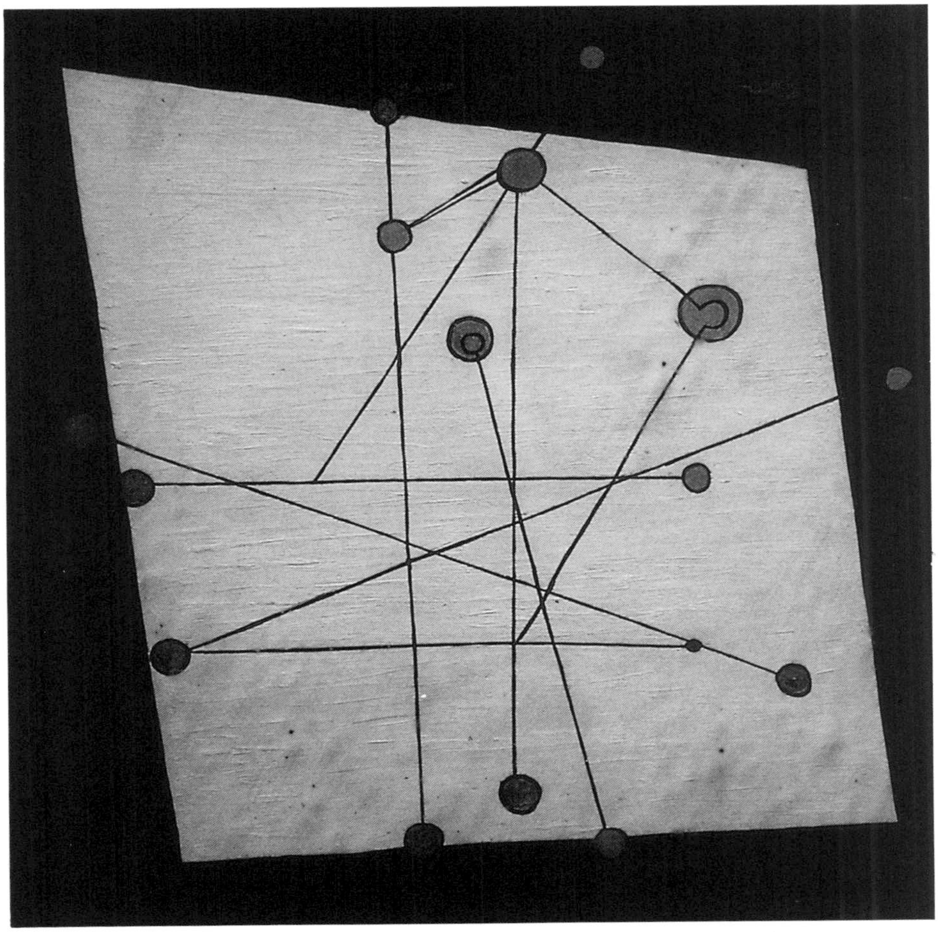

Bobby Dawson
*Head in
Equilibrium*,
c.1941
Photograph S.B.K.

of this group who veered towards Surrealism. *Head in Equilibrium*, of about 1941, is typical of his work at this time and, as was usual with him, would have been developed from a number of preliminary studies in pencil or ink. Dawson admired the work of Paul Klee, which he had seen in exhibitions,[53] and his own paintings often recall Klee's famous remark about 'taking a line for a walk'. Moreover, in Dawson's pictures colour is almost always secondary in importance to the linear structure. Stephen Gilbert's *Flux of Form*, alas has not been traced, but judging by the illustration in the catalogue, it was similar to his Cobra-type paintings which we have already discussed. Brian Boydell's *The Return of the Wood* and *Atlas Approached* (cata. no.59), both 1943, illustrate the way in which he used—in an idealized manner—the branches of trees, worm-like creatures and other organic matter which often appears to writhe, to suggest an imaginary hostile landscape of impassable terrain. Colour, which is usually pale in tone, is less important than the linear design in these works.

In the second category, that is of abstract or formalized works, were paintings by Scott, Egestorff and Vanston, and sculptures by Jocelyn Chewett. On first sight Patrick Scott's studies of birds and other animals appear largely humorous but careful study reveals the precise geometry behind the division of the canvas, as, for example, in the use of the Golden Section in *The Zoo* and *Renvyle*, both dating from 1943. Despite the recognizable imagery these paintings have a formal structure close to abstraction. Paul Egestorff studied under Mainie Jellett and her influence is evident in works like

105

Composition, c.1942, or *Vortex*, 1949 (cata. no.60), although the latter was not included in this exhibition. Like Jellett, Egestorff emphasized the structural element in composition, concerning himself with tone and prismatic colour progression to produce what he calls 'adequate provision of *passage*' to enable the eye to move freely around the picture.[54] Egestorff was more interested in formal structures and theories of composition than any of the other White Stag artists for whom such things approached anathema. *Head*, c.1943 (cata. no.61), by Jocelyn Chewett is largely Cubist, but also shows an element of subjectivity in the simplification of the features. It may also owe something to the African and Oriental wooden masks which Chewett would have seen in the Trocadéro Museum in Paris, which also influenced Picasso and other Cubists in the early 1900s. In a statement printed in the *Bell*, 1944, to which we have already referred, Chewett described what she considered to be the achievement of the sculptor:

> The medium a sculptor works in gives him an emotional incentive equal to that given by the idea. Hard stones need few incisions, soft ones large and deeper hollows and furrows. The sculptor's achievement is the synthesis in his work of his feeling for his medium, his understanding of natural form, and his romantic or symbolic idea. Of these three points of departure the idea must be subservient in the plastic arts, if it is to have a full expression.
>
> Ideas are universal; but understanding of material and three-dimensional feeling must be achieved, and united with the idea.[55]

Like Jocelyn Chewett, Doreen Vanston was influenced by Cubism, especially by the work of Picasso, which she encountered before the war in Paris. Figure compositions and landscapes with figures and animals were her principal subject matter. *A Dying Animal* (cata. no.62), painted in about 1943 and shown on this occasion, is one of her best works of this period.[56] The picture is composed of semi-representational forms set down in a Cubist manner. The colours are bold but the handling of the paint is unobtrusive and does not interfere with the design, so that our attention is directed principally to the feeling of agony evoked by the death-throes of the animal.

In the third category of works, those semi-representational or Symbolist, were paintings by Cusack, Conolly and Hayward. Cusack's *Scantlings*, which is now lost, is known only from the illustration in the catalogue, but it was typical of his work at the time. The symbolism in Thurloe Conolly's *Painting*, c.1943 (also lost), which depicts a bride and her bridegroom standing mysteriously in an almost empty landscape seems to relate to the war then raging. Conolly wrote in the *Bell* about this painting:

> In this picture I have not set out merely to show a bride and bridegroom. I have tried to make everything in the picture work towards the expression of possibilities surrounding the marriage of an insensitive, possibly brutal man to a girl diametrically opposed in spirit.
>
> Ideally I should like my painting to react, not away from humanity but away from universal oppression, towards humanity. At the same time using painting as an extension of personality, based on sensations reacted and interpreted through the imagination and through the harnessing of dream images.[57]

Phyllis Hayward was more representational in manner than any of her White Stag colleagues. Her flower and still life pieces are her most successful works of the 1940s.

The catalogue of the exhibition of Subjective Art was more elaborate than any previous White Stag publication. Patrick Scott designed the cover, Herbert Read wrote the introduction and there was an illustration of one work by each artist, except Phyllis Hayward. The list of subscribers at the end included the architect Michael Scott, a staunch supporter of Modernism in Ireland. In his introduction Read praised the 'fresh vigour' of the works on show which seemed to him 'to belong to the main stream of European culture', and he saw the exhibition as being 'representative of the latest phases of the contemporary movement'. Modern art, he said, was a challenge to lazy habits of thought, to tired senses and uneasy minds, and to complacency of vision. An artist is one who looks at the world with unclouded vision and his work should express that vision. We, when we look at the work, should wait for it to appeal to our senses, for good art is sensuous; 'We do not go far astray,' he said, 'if we keep to that simple level of appreciation'. Finally, he suggested that painting was a language which could be understood in all places and at all times. The artist does not merely record what the camera can record; rather, with imagination, he can pierce 'the superficial veil of appearances and reveal the inner structure of what the eye sees'.[58]

Herbert Read's remarks and the exhibition were a challenge to the more conservative elements in the Dublin art scene and caused considerable stir in the press. Those who admired the show voiced reasoned enthusiasm, while those who opposed it did so usually in terms of unqualified generalities cloaked as indignation. The *Evening Mail* of 4 January was enthusiastic, saying that while Subjective art might puzzle the traditionalists, the general effects of the exhibition would be to stimulate other artists to work in that manner. The *Irish Times* critic was also keen on the show, describing it as a 'lively exhibition', although he took exception to Herbert Read's suggestion in the catalogue that this was probably the first time that works from 'the mainstream of European culture' had come from Ireland in modern times, citing the exhibition of works by Mainie Jellett and Evie Hone at the Dublin Painters' gallery in 1924 as a harbinger 'of what Irish painters could do with the . . . avant-garde'.[59] However, the *Independent* was scathing in its criticism, categorizing Subjective art with Dadaism, Cubism, Vorticism, Futurism and Surrealism as 'the periodic outcropping under a new name of the fantastic and the grotesque. The movement,' it declared, 'has wound its way from Zurich to Paris, and from the Butte of Montmartre to New York's Greenwich Village. It has been laughed away in every capital of the world'.[60] The *Irish Press*, too, was unhappy with the show which it thought lacked direction.[61] But perhaps the most hostile opposition came in a letter to the *Evening Mail*, in which the writer referred to Subjective art as 'Art in aesthetic rags and tatters; the antithesis of art. A veil of imbecillic mystery, to cover up paucity of inspiration . . . . A puerile attempt to gain publicity or notoriety without true artistic effort'.[62] These comments stirred the *Mail* to produce a leading article in defence of the exhibition in which it declared: 'Properly speaking, all art is subjective art . . . . If the new "subjective" artists find that their emotions draw them away from naturalistic representations they are as much entitled as . . . any other painter of the orthodox style to paint as the spirit moves them'.[63] More reasoned criticism, however, came from Theodore Goodman, writing in *Commentary*. 'Whatever one may think of their aesthetic value,' he said, 'Dublin should be grateful to the group for the spade-work they have done in preparing a reactionary public to receive some of the really important experimental work of the last forty years when at last it reaches these shores after the war'.[64] And he reproved those who scorned the exhibition by saying that it was typical of outdated movements such as the *École de Paris*, Vorticism, Futurism and Dadaism, by reminding them that abstract art in general, and Surrealism in particular, had been dominant trends before the war and that, in any case, Dublin had seen few works from any of these schools. Edward Sheehy, writing in the *Dublin Magazine*, also gave a more considered opinion of the exhibition, although he was less enthusiastic about it than was Goodman. While accepting the efficacy of abstract art in general, he was uncertain about the worth of Subjective art in particular, which he felt to be merely 'subjective idealism translated into art', with the solipsism which that implied.[65]

* * *

Other publications followed on the heels of the exhibition of Subjective Art. In its issue of February 1944 the *Bell* published Herbert Read's introduction to the catalogue, unchanged, as 'On Subjective Art',[66] and accompanied it—as we have already noted—by illustrations of works by Thurloe Conolly, Jocelyn Chewett and Nick Nicholls. In Cyril Connolly's influential review, *Horizon*, in May 1944, Read published an article entitled 'Art in Crisis'[67] which, he said, contained the substance of the lecture he had been prevented from giving in Dublin the previous January, but the text of which had been read in his absence. In this article, which had a political slant, Read argued in favour of Subjective art, for a spontaneous, unpremeditated art based on the artist's 'gift' for perception, which, he said, could be either a conscious or an unconscious act. Art should stem from the artist's personality rather than the application of strict rules, as was the case with arid academicism, in which art lost its sensitivity and became a 'thumb-ruled' copy of nature. He saw vitality in art as steming from two possible alternatives, either as part of a general cultural pattern, or from a quality of the individual, the expression of the artist's personality. But he saw the former possibility leading to some sort of state worship, to totalitarianism; consequently the second possibility was the only viable alternative. Besides, he argued, 'Art . . . is not the by-product of a culture; rather, a culture is the end-product of the outstanding personalities of a number of artists'. And he concluded by saying, almost certainly with Ireland in mind: 'There still exist in the world a few small nations which have stood out against the mass neurosis of our time—that mad obsession for power and wealth which is bringing destruction to our civilization. If such nations can preserve their independent identity, then it is a situation which has great possibilities for art'.[68]

For the April 1945 issue of *Horizon*, Margot Moffett contributed a short essay, 'Young Irish Painters',[69] in which she discussed the work of the White Stag Group and the exhibition of Subjective Art. She saw the Group as building upon the pioneering work of Mainie Jellett and Evie Hone and bridging the 'cultural time-lag' in Irish art from 'early Gleizes' until the mid-1940s. The 1944 exhibition and the attendant activities had been arranged, she said, in order to make a 'complete statement' about the development of the Modern Movement in Ireland at that time and to stimulate critical and informed opinion. Her article was illustrated with pictures by Patrick Scott, Kenneth Hall, Doreen Vanston and Stephen Gilbert.

One of the aims behind the exhibition was the hope that it might lead to the publication of a book on avant-garde painting in Ireland. *Three Painters*, a study of the work of Basil Rakoczi, Kenneth Hall and Patrick Scott, published in Dublin in 1945, was the fulfillment of that aim. The book had a preface by Herbert Read and an introduction by Herbrand Ingouville-Williams.[70] It may be regarded as the definitive statement of the philosophy of Subjective art as interpreted by the White Stag Group.

In his preface Herbert Read saw developments in modern art—in particular the rejection of naturalistic representation based on the laws of perspective—as giving greater freedom of means for the expression of content and form. It was 'the imagination itself that [had] lost its shackles', he said, and Freud was the source of that release.[71] In Ingouville-Williams's words such developments allowed the three artists under discussion to realize 'a fresh vision of life', and as a group he thought they represented the beginning of a new trend in twentieth century painting in which themes—whatever their source, either in nature or in the subconscious—would be of secondary importance to the aesthetic language of architectural structure and formal relations. It was, he said, a regard for the latter qualities that distinguished the Subjective artist from the strict Surrealist, who dispensed with them, and who in their place brought together objects in incongruous proximity to shock the spectator. But, he continued,

> In Subjective Art . . . order and emotion are synthesized . . . but the theme, instead of being drawn from objects in the external world, is elaborated by the workings of the imagination turned inwards upon the memories, dreams and phantasies of the Unconscious. Objects which appear in Subjective paintings, such as a bird, a fish, a figure, or a garden, are not represented in a realistic manner, but as dream-images, as conceptual memories, as the eidetic phantasies of the child-mind.[72]

To Ingouville-Williams the unconscious, and in particular the creative power of the numen, 'the fountain-head of all artistic and cultural achievement', was the source of such activity, and it was the insensible character of this creative power which gave art 'its elusive, magical quality'. He also felt that when we look back at every period of history the greatest artists, without any conscious knowledge of direction, seem to have been in accord with the *Zeitgeist*, the spirit of their age. And so, he concluded:

> To-day the field of the Unconscious, the conflicts and phantasies engendered within it, the troubling contrast between this almost-unrecognised world and that of surface-appearances, the attempt to resolve the dissonances between these two aspects of the psyche—these would seem to be the trends of the *Zeitgeist* in 1944, which are giving birth to the Subjective Art of our time.[73]

As to giving a title to one of his paintings, the Subjective artist could do so only in retrospect after studying the finished work. Thus he could say, with Picasso: *Je ne cherche pas, je trouve.*[74]

Having defined Subjective Art, Ingouville-Williams went on to discuss briefly the work of Rakoczi, Hall and Scott. He considered the subject-matter of each of

Patrick Scott
Renvyle, 1943
Photograph Bryan Rutledge

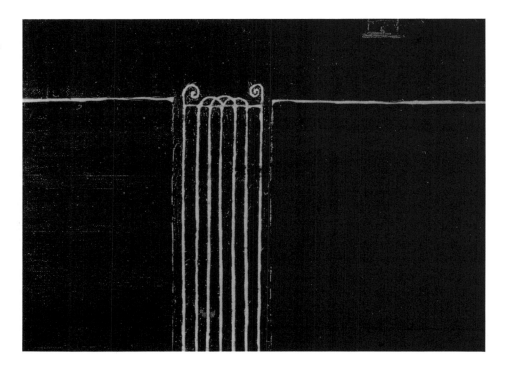

them, discussed their handling of materials, and included a brief statement by each on his approach to painting. The book was illustrated with a frontispiece by Basil Rakoczi and six works by each artist, many of which had been seen in the exhibition of Subjective Art. Generally speaking, the book was poorly received in Ireland, with disparaging reviews in the *Irish Press* (22 November 1945), the *Irish Times* (29 December 1945) and the *Standard* (4 January 1946). However, Maurice Collis in the *Observer* (16 December 1945) admired it and thought the artists concerned constituted 'a cosmopolitan corner in Dublin life, not without influence, probably, for its future'; and the reviewer in the *Listener* (16 May 1946) found the book both 'useful and convincing'.

Another result of the exhibition of Subjective art was the White Stag show, *Young Irish Painters*, held at the Arcade Gallery, Old Bond Street, London, during April-May 1945. Of the artists who had shown in the earlier exhibition only Brian Boydell, Thurloe Conolly and Paul Egestorff did not participate on this occasion and no others took their places. Forty works were exhibited but only ten had been shown before, thus suggesting that all had been painting steadily during the previous fifteen months. That the subject-matter with each was by now familiar also suggests a period of steady development. Once again the catalogue contained an introduction by Herbert Read, in which he repeated his previously expressed sentiments for Subjective art. John Russell, reviewing the exhibition in the *Listener*, was enthusiastic about the 'abundant vitality and curiosity', and the 'engaging diversity of influence' in the works.[75]

* * *

There seems to have been a lull in the activities of the White Stag Group after the Exhibition of Subjective Art, for the only other recorded event in 1944 was a one-man show of paintings by Patrick Scott held during November and December of that

110

year. This was Scott's first ever one-man show, and the pictures, some of which we have already noted, reflect his continued concern for landscape, fish, birds, and animals—'a nursery world', Edward Sheehy later called it.[76] The catalogue of the exhibition notes that the works were arranged in chronological order, so we know the precise development of his work at this time. In compositions like *The Zoo* and *Birds on the Shore 2* (cata. no.63), both painted in 1943, we have a combination of all those features of his painting which we have already discussed. *Birds in the Trees*, 1944, is an almost identical composition to *Birds on the Shore 2* and was painted shortly after it. Here, as in most of these pictures, the birds were derived from models, although Scott occasionally drew live birds and other animals at Dublin zoo.[77] As usual, the pigment was applied thinly and the forms of the birds determined by scraping through the pigment to reveal the canvas. These forms were then emphasized by a peripheral line scored with a sharp instrument, and highlights—small dots of brighter colours—were added to emphasize the heads and tails. Colour is still second in importance to aesthetic considerations to do with the linear divisions of the picture plane. *The Sun, Evening Landscape*, (cata. no.64) and *Cow looking out of a Cornfield*, all of 1944, post-date *Birds in the Trees* and are among the last of Scott's work done in such a formal geometric manner. The use of a horizon line in *Evening Landscape* and other works of the period may have been induced by his childhood by the sea, but he did not use it consciously for that reason.

* * *

During January and February 1945 Kenneth Hall held a one-man show of *Paintings of Birds and Fishes* at the White Stag Gallery. Several of the paintings had been shown before and, as with Patrick Scott, the titles confirm his continued interest in this subject-matter. As we have said, after 1941 Hall's work became increasingly Subjective, and in *Three Painters* he defined concisely what he meant by this:

> In a painting, or indeed in any work of art, there is an objective and a subjective element, which are collected into the mind and personality of the artist and fused into the one form that they bear in the finished picture.
>
> The objective element is that which is observed in or drawn from the external world by the artist. The subjective element is that which is contributed by the artist from the depths of his own nature with little or no reference to outside reality. When the subjective element predominates over the objective element in this sense, the painting may be said to be a Subjective painting.
>
> In paintings such as those that I have done of birds and fishes the means of expression are reduced to a minimum; and, in so reducing them, one has to aim at complete expressiveness in each of the means employed. The contribution to be made by colour has to be completely stated in most cases by two colours only, and the relation of each to the other must be accurately gauged if a poverty or thinness is not to result; and the line must be completely felt and the form completely expressed by it throughout. If the line becomes mechanical at any point, the expressiveness of the whole painting will almost certainly be lost.[78]

Bird and Fish and *Bird Turning in Flight*, 1943, both exhibited again on this occasion, demonstrate clearly this phase of his work and exemplify his conditions governing the use of colour, line and form. In the latter picture the symbols used for the bird's legs, feet and tail are derived from the *Little Bird* composition and the sensitivity of line is increased by juxtaposing, in several areas, a painted line with lines scored through the thick impasto. He probably used a stuffed bird as a model for these pictures because the shapes, especially of the heads and beaks, are often similar. Concurrent with these paintings of birds and fishes Hall produced some abstract works in which the painted forms have a biomorphic character.

Kenneth Hall was not an intellectual painter motivated by theory, as was Basil Rakoczi. He was at his best when working directly before his subject and none of the pictures which he painted in Ireland suggests the feeling of gaiety and discovery which we feel if front of his *Old Phaleron, Greece* or *Itea*: the war, exile and alienation from his family bore heavily on him.

Early in 1945 Stephen Gilbert held an exhibition at the White Stag gallery. The catalogue has not survived, but we can be sure that the exhibition included a number of his Cobra-type paintings. As well as insect-like creatures, semi-human forms dominate in many of these compositions, and *Mandala* (cata. no.65), 1944, illustrates the development of his work on the eve of his departure from Ireland. Here, the figure is more representational than those in his earlier paintings, though the construction of forms is still quite Surrealist. Here too, as before, few colours are used and the conspicuous brushstrokes betray the briskness of execution.

These paintings, which were all done in Ireland, provoke a sense of anguish which is probably due to their having been painted in war-time. Indeed the anguish and turmoil of war provided a stimulus for all the artists of the Cobra Group, whatever country they were working in. Besides some pictures by Jack B. Yeats and Kenneth Hall, Stephen Gilbert's were the only boldly Expressionist paintings to be made in Ireland before those done by Colin Middleton in the late 1940s.

Amongst the last White Stag exhibitions to be held in Dublin were a show of paintings by Nick Nicholls and Ann Miller, held in May 1945, and one-man shows by Basil Rakoczi held in February and October 1945.

Only one of Nicholls' pictures, *Contemplation*, 1944 (cata. no.58), included here has been traced, but the others would certainly have been executed in a similar style. Along with this work, which was exhibited under the title *Foetus, Lovers*, of around 1943, and *Untitled*, of 1944 (cata. no.67) belong to the last phase of his development before he left Ireland after the war. In *Lovers* the imagery is emblematic of sexual desire, while in *Contemplation* it symbolizes the unity of the soul and the individual. In *Untitled* the image of a bird represents peace, a symbol which often occurred in Nicholls' work until the late 1950s. Nicholls' co-exhibitor on this occasion, Ann Miller, was his fiancée, whom he married in 1947. Born in about 1927 of Irish-Jewish extraction, Ann Miller lived with her parents in Dublin. Her father was an industrialist, with business interests in Ireland and England. She met Nicholls in about 1943 or 1944 and began painting under his guidance.[79] Apart from this exhibition, nothing seems to have been recorded about her career as an artist.

Rakoczi, no doubt, showed recent paintings in both one-man exhibitions held in 1945. They would, therefore, almost certainly have been in his Subjective manner. As we noted earlier, *Two Heads* and *Three* mark the maturing of the Subjective phase of Rakoczi's work in Ireland. They have a boldness of concept and simplification of imagery and form which distinguishes them from his earlier works and which links them with later ones such as *Feeding a Bird*, 1944. The use of colour in these works is still subordinated to form and the composition is dominated by bold shapes which

Basil Rakoczi
c.1960s
Photograph courtesy
Jacqueline Robinson

divide the picture plane and which occasionally, as in *Three*, are used to produce a feeling of movement. Rakoczi also employed a mixture of painted and incised lines to give a graffiti-like texture and to imbue these 'figures' with an animate feeling. *Chess Players* probably just post-dates *Three* and illustrates the speed with which his work was developing at the time. The Cubist forms in this picture are devoid of the graffiti-like texturing hitherto employed and, in their simplicity of shape, presage works such as *Child Flying*, which was probably painted in late 1943. The dreamlike wistfulness, to which we have referred already, in the latter picture may indicate a feeling of alienation in Rakoczi resulting from four years' exile in Ireland. This contention is reinforced by *Prisoner* (cata. no.56), which was probably painted early in 1944, in which the head on the left of the composition is clearly derived from that in *Child Flying*. *Prisoner* marks the final stage of development of Rakoczi's work before he left Ireland. In it there is a greater awareness of the flatness of the picture plane and less emphasis on receding space than hitherto; and there is more reliance on strong colours, thinly applied, to emphasize the forms, which are segregated from one another by hard edges and straight lines. In places, Rakoczi has used a sharp instrument to score a line close to the boundary of each form in order to emphasize it. In *Three Painters* he spoke about his method of painting in terms which might well be a description of the creation of this picture:

Having established the eyes as whitish ovals with dark pupils added, I feel along the profile upon the left side. I place a centralising line, and I then draw in

113

the profile on the right. One side of the face has light preponderating, the other dark.

Colour-bands, passing horizontally, tie this dual face to the background or to other faces, or birds, or planet-shapes. An interchange of light and dark, of transparency and opaqueness, is worked out in pigment; and the incised lines are drawn in waves and patterns much as children draw in the sand or primitive people practise tattooing.

The sky, the middle-distance and the foreground are established with bands of colour and lines. Sometimes paths of a violent or distorted perspective lead the eye inwards to some distant door or gate, and out beyond it to the sea. The conception thus grows out of the mind meditating upon the shape, texture and colour at my disposal, nourished as I have been by a study of children's drawings and the carving, painting and textiles of primitive or peasant races. By such a method of meditation art becomes purged of all inessentials and robbed of the meritorious and superficially attractive.[80]

* * *

At the end of the war, in 1945, the English and other expatriate friends of the White Stag Group left Ireland and returned, in most cases, to where they had been before hostilities began. In late 1945 Stephen Gilbert and Jocelyn Chewett moved to Paris. Basil Rakoczi left Ireland in March 1946[81] and returned to England, as did Kenneth Hall who settled in London where he died in July that year. Nick Nicholls remained in Ireland for a short time before returning to London and Phyllis Hayward, who stayed in Dublin until about 1950 or 1951, also settled in London.[82]

With the exodus of these figures the White Stag Group in effect ceased to exist. However, Rakoczi kept in touch with friends in Ireland and paid periodic visits here. In January 1949 he gave a lecture entitled 'The Artist and Contemporary Art' to the so-called Friends of the White Stag Group in Dublin, but those in attendance were a very different audience from the original group of admirers. Rakoczi also continued to exhibit at the Irish Exhibition of Living Art until the early 1950s and held a one-man show at the Dublin Painters' gallery in spring 1954.

As we have said, the White Stag artists brought a welcome freshness to the art scene in Dublin. They were not great innovators; indeed they were largely eclectic, but they were willing to experiment and by asserting their independence they were an example to others in their quarrels with the establishment. Nonetheless, their influence did not last, and we must finally agree with Edward Sheehy, as he wrote in 1945, that although the war years had a considerable effect on the development of painting in Ireland, 'the refugees [doing] a good deal of evangelising in the cause of variety of modernism', they had, as far as he could detect, little influence on the native painters who preferred 'to work out their own salvation or damnation'.[83] This they did through the annual shows of the Irish Exhibition of Living Art and the Royal Hibernian Academy. With the departure of the White Stag artists these exhibitions, and the former in particular, dominated the future course of Irish painting. It is, therefore, with them and the two streams of development—the Modernist and the Academic—which they represent that our discussion must henceforth concern itself.

CHAPTER 6

THE IRISH EXHIBITION OF LIVING ART

'Let us open our eyes and our minds and
form our own honest opinions .'

(Mainie Jellett, *Commentary*, May 1942, p.7).

Background

THE first Irish Exhibition of Living Art was held in Dublin in 1943. It was in effect, though not by intent, a belated assertion of secessionism similar to those movements which had earlier manifested themselves in other European countries; movements which involved a tussle for surpemacy between the avant-garde and the more academic establishment.

In Ireland this tussle was particularly acute in the early 1940s at a time when criticism of the Royal Hibernian Academy had become more rigorous, especially among young painters of whom several were again living at home, having fled the war in Europe. Moreover, as we have seen, the exhibitions of the White Stag Group had stimulated an awareness of Modernism as, too, had the activities of the other independents such as the Contemporary Picture Galleries. The time also saw a general improvement in the standard of published art criticism over the merely descriptive reportage which typified the 1930s. Among the newer critics, Stephen Rynne began a regular column in the *Leader* in 1940; Theodore Goodman contributed to *Commentary* from 1941; and A.J. Leventhal and Edward Sheehy wrote regularly in the *Dublin Magazine* from 1943, Sheehy being especially influential even until the 1950s. Art criticism also appeared from time to time in other periodicals, notably the *Bell*, and, from 1949, *Envoy*.

Criticism of the Academy reached a climax during the years 1942 and 1943, a time when its fortunes were at their lowest ebb since the late nineteenth century. In a sense, the institution was helpless in the face of its enemies. It was, after all, an academy, and the business of academies is not to be innovative; yet it had failed, as Paul Henry earlier commented,[1] to take *any* notice of the artistic revolution which began with Impressionism in the late nineteenth century. Matters came to a head in 1942. That year two paintings by Louis le Brocquy, namely *The Spanish Shawl*, which had been painted in 1941 (cata. no.69), and *Image of Chaos*, were rejected by the selection committee,[2] despite the fact that le Brocquy had exhibited at the Academy every year since 1937. His work, therefore, was not unknown to the selectors. Indeed in 1941 he had exhibited *A Picnic* (cata. no.68) at the Academy, a painting much more radical in its disposition of mass and form and a more penetrating study of human relationships than was *The Spanish Shawl*. Le Brocquy's rejection coincided with a critical article about the Academy which Mainie Jellett published in *Commentary*, the magazine of the Picture Hire Club.[3] This article was the first piece of reasoned criticism of the institution to be published other than the usual journalistic judgements and because of its rigour and the points raised it is worth quoting at length:

Every year I go to the R.H.A. exhibition in a spirit of hopefulness, expecting there may be some change for the better, some new young head pushing . . . up through the miasma of vulgarity and self-satisfaction which is the general impression I unfortunately register each year. I have come away mortified at what I have seen, not minding for myself and older artists . . . but worried for the younger generation and what sort of an example they were being shown. When they looked at the work hung on the line, were they to consider that that was the best their country could produce, and, if it was, were they to form their taste upon it?

Then I looked at the work hung on the line from year to year. With the exception of Jack B. Yeats and an odd work here and there, bad craftsmanship, vulgarity, and faulty weak draughtsmanship were its main characteristics, and, in the cases where there had been any standard maintained in technique, it merely resulted in a coloured photograph void of any creative element either of colour or form. I ask an institution like the R.H.A., which is capable of being a force for good in our country, at least, if it can do nothing else, to give us good academic work . . . .

Then one looks for some sign of nationality, something that would tell the onlooker that these pictures were by Irish men and women. The only artist who could stand this test is Jack B. Yeats . . . . This quality of nationality is something lacking in Irish art as a whole. It is a quality that cannot be studied and self-consciously looked for; it will show only if we artists are working creatively with our whole capacity of body and soul, and not if we continue to paint complacent coloured photographs of cottages and Irish scenery, without delving deeper into the inner consciousness of our country and its natural rhythm of life. I appeal to the young painters and students; I ask them to open their eyes, to wake up, to produce work that at least has the characteristics of youth, energy and life, and to become creators, not bad colour photographers.

This year's Academy seems to suffer even more from the faults I have mentioned than last year's [but she excluded specifically from this judgement the portraits exhibited by Margaret Clarke and James Sleator, and she concluded] . . . the R.H.A. must not shut its doors to life, otherwise it will of necessity die of senile decay. This present exhibition is, with very few exceptions, an all Irish exhibition, therefore we are in a position to take stock of what academic art is and what it stands for in this country. Let us open our eyes and our minds and form our own honest opinions and ask ourselves: is this what we want as Irish art?[4]

In this statement Mainie Jellett not only took issue with the standards of the Royal

Hibernian Academy, but in effect exposed the poverty of the prevailing social attitude of the day. She was, in fact, cautioning against isolationism, as George Russell (AE) had done twenty years earlier in his editorials in the *Irish Statesman* and as Seán O'Faoláin currently was doing in the *Bell*. Russell always argued that Ireland was not a society unified by one culture, but was rather a synthesis of different cultures. O'Faoláin took up this point when he asserted in the *Bell* in 1943 that Irishmen should cease deluding themselves and recognise the fact that 'long before 1900' they had become 'part and parcel of the general world-process'.[5]

This attack on the Academy produced a reply by Brigid Ganly, published in the next issue of *Commentary*. She wrote ostensibly in defence of the Academy but was, in fact, apologetic in tone. She argued that the Academy could only exhibit what was submitted to it; that its commitment to teaching and its 'official' status gave it a social dimension, and that the range of works which it might thus exhibit was necessarily curtailed in comparison to the freedom enjoyed by the independent groups. Its social role, she said, meant that the largest pictures were usually given pride of place while the brightest coloured ones drew most attention. To attract attention, therefore, artists were forced to make larger and louder pictures, especially, she added, as the selectors for the Haverty Trust sought out certain types of composition. Consequently, with one eye on the Haverty Trust and the other on a possible portrait commission many artists, she argued, had developed 'a moral squint' which had a deplorable effect on their work. In conclusion, she was even more apologetic:

> I think Miss Jellett is over anxious for the artistic youth of Ireland. If they are to become fine artists, they will study the classics in the National Gallery. They will study contemporary form in the one-man shows, where it will not clash with the work of the elder generation. *They need not take the Academy too seriously* . . . they will be inspired, not by other pictures, but by life itself. That is the only way to achieve a National and Individual Art . . . . But the Hibernian Academy is no worse than other academies, is more catholic than most.[6]

In its July issue *Commentary*, doubtless acting in the interests of impartiality, published an independent view of the Academy in which the writer, however, largely endorsed Mainie Jellett's views.[7] He was, too, more specific in his criticism than either of the previous writers had been. He saw too many artists trying to outshine one another in their use of vivid colours and in too many cases thought oil paint had been treated as if it were something to be 'thrown about in lumps'. Most of the portraits he thought were 'inevitably' uninteresting aesthetically, the exceptions being Seán O'Sullivan's *J.J. O'Connor* (Crawford Gallery, Cork), 'a sparkling bit of work', and James Sleator's *Mr. Justice Thompson* (Law Society of Northern Ireland) 'painted with obvious enjoyment and a sense of character'. Seán Keating's seascapes showed 'neither sense of composition, nor power to make water liquid and transparent'. Even Jack B. Yeats failed to thrill and Frank McKelvey was in a rut, although he liked his *Evening* and *West Coast* for their marvellous effects of light on water. Among the watercolours he found Helen Pennefather's *Rainy Morning* and *Sunlit Road* outstanding for their treatment of atmosphere and also remarked on works by Theo Gracey, Tom Nesbitt, Dorothy Blackham and Bea Orpen. In the sculpture section everything to him seemed to be comparatively insignificant beside the group of works by the late Oliver Sheppard, although he quite admired Jerome Connor's *Pikeman*

(cata. no.128). But more importantly, he said, the 'up-to-the-minute' school was hardly represented at all, while several academic painters—notably Maurice MacGonigal and Herry Kernoff—seemed to have made conscientious efforts to 'go modern' but with disasterous results. Reviewing the exhibition in the *Leader*, Stephen Rynne broadly concurred with these views, saying that the show was bad, with hardly anything worth a second look. Even Yeats, Dermod O'Brien, Kernoff and McKelvey were rather boring. While many of the works were technically satisfactory, too often, Rynne thought, they suggested a desire to please at any cost.[8] As these comments show, although the Academy was by definition conservative, many academicians undoubtedly felt that they should take *some* notice of recent trends in art, but often the results of their labours only belied in them confusion, if not bewilderment.

For its 1943 exhibition the Academy, perhaps feeling that it should make a determined stand for the values which it espoused, dismissed the Modernists almost to a man.[9] However, their absence was apparent, for the *Irish Times*, noting the rejection of Nano Reid and Louis le Brocquy, asked:

118

Is the Royal Hibernian Academy going to close down on modernistic painting? The fact that at least two of Ireland's best-known modern painters figure among the 'rejects' this year would seem to suggest that such is the case.

And in a later review the same 'paper commented that the exhibition was

... hardly Hibernian in its comprehensiveness, for such distinguished and successful exponents of contemporary tendencies in art as Mary Swanzy, Grace Henry, Evie Hone, Mainie H. Jellett, Nano Reid, Norah McGuinness, Yvonne Jammet, Frances Kelly, Jack P. Hanlon, Louis le Brocquy and Ralph Cusack are entirely unrepresented.[10]

In the *Leader* Stephen Rynne also mentioned the young painters and was astonished in particular at the rejection of le Brocquy. 'His is [an] aristocratic sort of painting,' he wrote, 'fitted for the fine room and the cultured taste; his work is well plotted and well wrought'.[11] Generally speaking, however, he thought the Academy was beginning to feel the strain of war with a 'pinched' look about many of the exhibits. Once again Brigid Ganly came to its defence in *Commentary* arguing, somewhat gratuitously, that a conscientious academy of arts was perfectly right to exclude work it thought to be incompetent until the artist had proved the seriousness of his intention.[12] A.J. Leventhal also sided with the Academy on this issue. Reviewing the exhibition in the *Dublin Magazine*, he reminded us that it should promise no shocks against established order 'since its hierarchy is based on the ruling art dogma'. Thus, he said, the RHA offers 'the best the country can produce in the traditional mode';[13] and he concluded with the opinion that the 1943 show was one of the most interesting in the history of the Academy.

Thus was rested the Academy's case on the issue. However, the struggle between it and the Modernists petered out later that year when a number of the younger artists, led by Louis le Brocquy, Mainie Jellett and Norah McGuinness, founded the Irish Exhibition of Living Art, which was to become an annual event sympathetic to the avant-garde. Significantly, the 'Living Art', as we shall henceforth refer to these exhibitions, and the Academy were never mutually exclusive and many artists, including academicians and others, patronised both venues. Moreover, le Brocquy was elected an associate member of the Academy in 1946 and a constituent member in 1948, and Norah McGuinness became an honorary member in 1957. While the Living Art exhibitions were born out of a justified frustration at the reactionary course pursued by the Academy, they represented also a climax of awareness for the Modern Movement which had been growing in Ireland since the 1920s and earlier.

The first Irish Exhibition of Living Art

The first Irish Exhibition of Living Art was held at the National College of Art in Dublin from 16 September until 9 October 1943. The declared aim of the organizers was that it should be 'a comprehensive survey of significant work, irrespective of School or manner, by living Irish artists'.[14] The immediate events which led to the exhibition can be easily stated. They were, firstly, the rejection by the Academy of le Brocquy's *The Spanish Shawl* and other paintings in 1942; secondly, Mainie Jellett's

article 'The R.H.A. and Youth', published in *Commentary* in May 1942; and thirdly,
the Academy's rejection early in April 1943 of works by le Brocquy and most of the
other avant-garde painters. As a result of these events le Brocquy's mother, Sybil,
suggested holding another exhibition, with official backing as opposed to a *salon des
refusés*, and, acting on her suggestion, Louis broached the idea to Mainie Jellett who
was enthusiastic about it.[15] Indeed Mainie had herself for some time been thinking
along broadly similar lines. Later le Brocquy approached Fr. Jack Hanlon about the
matter and he agreed to join what was in effect a steering committee and became its
chairman. The first meeting of the new committee took place on 21 April 1943 in le
Brocquy's studio at number 13 Merrion Row, those present being le Brocquy himself,
his mother Sybil, Mainie Jellett, Evie Hone and Jack Hanlon. Laurence Campbell
was later asked to join them but he refused, as did Jack B. Yeats, although the latter
agreed to exhibit and he did so.

   One of the first things the committee had to do was to find a venue for the proposed
exhibition. Le Brocquy and Mainie Jellett approached the Department of Education
about the matter and, having assured them that they had the support of certain

120

individuals and guarantees against financial loss,[16] it was agreed that it might be held at the National College of Art, that is, the same venue as was then used for the annual exhibitions of the Royal Hibernian Academy. Another meeting of the steering committee was held on 12 May, when it was resolved that, 'owing to a growing demand from a large public for an exhibition giving a comprehensive survey of the work of living Irish artists', they would constitute themselves formally into a committee 'to organize a public Exhibition to be called "The Irish Exhibition of Living Art"'.[17] Those present at this meeting were Jack Hanlon (initially in the chair), Mainie Jellett, Norah McGuinness and Louis le Brocquy. They were all, said le Brocquy later, 'aware of the urgency of establishing an exhibition further to the R.H.A. The little societies—and premises—(Dublin Painters) were of no use'.[18]

Having so constituted itself, the new Committee elected Mainie Jellett to be chairman and co-opted Laurence Campbell, Margaret Clarke, Ralph Cusack and Evie Hone to serve on it. James Sleator, was invited to attend meetings to give advice when necessary. Louis le Brocquy became honorary secretary and Jack Hanlon honorary treasurer of the committee.[19] Finally, Elizabeth Curran was engaged to help with the exhibition and a list was compiled of artists who were to be asked to submit work for selection.[20] Entry forms to accompany submissions were drawn up inviting each entrant to submit a maximum of five works 'which in view of the special character of this Exhibition,' it was stated, 'the Committee hope will be recent and important examples of your work'.[21] While invitations were issued to certain artists to submit work, nevertheless, any resident Irish artist was eligible to put his work forward for the selection which took place at the National College of Art on 30 August.[22] The Press View was arranged for 15 September and the exhibition opened the next day.

* * *

Thus opened what was probably the most consequential art exhibition to have been held in Ireland during the first half of this century and certainly the most 'eye-opening' show since the Hone/Yeats exhibition of 1901. Commenting on the latter, George Russell (AE) had hoped it would attract 'in a mood of true understanding, those who would like to believe in the existence in Ireland of a genuine art'.[23] Arguably the first Living Art exhibition was the most positive indication that Ireland did, indeed, foster a 'genuine art', albeit of a kind which few had anticipated or worked to achieve.

The first Living Art exhibition comprised 168 works plus a memorial section of 22 sculptures by Jerome Connor. Those taking part in it represented the best of Irish painting and sculpture at the time. The public evidently thought well of the exhibition for, by its close, a total of £289 worth of pictures had been sold and the exhibition had been seen by 3,000 adults and more than 2,000 school-children.[24]

In general the press received the exhibition well. The *Irish Times* critic going so far as to suggest that it was 'the most vital and distinguished exhibition of work by Irish artists that has ever been held'.[25] The *Irish Independent*, too, was full of praise, commenting: ' . . . it is an unusually stimulating show. One went expecting to find Academy rejects that would imbue respect for Academy decisions, and one found instead a large proportion of unexpectedly interesting new work'.[26] Arthur Power, writing in the *Bell*, also spoke highly of the show saying that it gave much food for thought and was long overdue, but he wished that it had been more retrospective in concept.[27] The critic who voiced the strongest misgivings of the exhibition was Máirín

Allen who thought it lacked a national character, an often remarked criticism of Irish art at the time, as we shall see later when we come to discuss the academic tradition. Writing in the *Father Mathew Record* Allen commented:

> If any exile visited the *Irish Exhibition of Living Art* recently held in Dublin . . . he must have emerged bewildered . . . by the utter foreign-ness of so much presented to him as Irish art . . . the mass of the painting shown is affected, imitative, and empty . . . .rightly or wrongly one gets the notion that the strange foreign-ness . . . is the result of an absence of contact between these artists and the normal, native cultural background.[28]

By 'normal' native cultural background, Allen of course referred to that sentiment for Gaelic Ireland which so pervaded the times. However, A.J. Leventhal, in a more considered review of the exhibition written the following spring, commended its lack of chauvinism saying that there was on view 'nothing that smacked either of insularity or of narrow regionalism. On the contrary,' he said, 'European influence was the dominant note'.[29]

The work of the younger artists dominated the exhibition. In the *Leader* Stephen Rynne praised le Brocquy's *Spanish Shawl*, considering it to have been 'most skillfully treated . . . for all its fragility, its almost papery quality . . . it has peculiar strength deriving from the masterly pre-planning';[30] attributes which, evidently, had little impressed the Academy judges a year earlier. The *Irish Times*, too, thought well of le Brocquy, commenting that he, Gerard Dillon and Jack Hanlon had broken 'new ground . . . to fine effect'.[31] As well as being the prime mover behind the Living Art exhibition, le Brocquy was also the most important painter to emerge from its ranks. Much has already been written about him,[32] so that here we need only plot the chief points in his development, our main concern being to assess his contribution to the Modern Movement in Ireland.

Louis le Brocquy (b.1916) is self-taught as an artist. As a young man he was influenced by Rembrandt and Manet,[33] both of whom he knew from reproductions and whom he admired for their subtlety of tone; but in 1938, in Geneva, he saw Spanish paintings from the Prado and was enthralled by Velázquez and Goya. Later, he came under the spell of Degas and Whistler as well as the Japanese painters Kiyonaga and Utamaro. From these influences stems his fascination with tone, which led in the 1940s to a number of almost monochromatic paintings. From this time, too, can be traced what was to be the real subject-matter of his work for the rest of his career, namely the isolation of the individual and the impossibility of our ever really knowing others. This sense of isolation can be seen, for example, in *Southern Window* (Lane Gallery), which was painted in Menton in 1939 and which is, perhaps, his earliest surviving painting. Here, the soft light which pervades the composition, the richness of the shadows and the figure standing with her back to us betray the influences which we have mentioned. These themes were developed after his return to Ireland, notably in *A Picnic*, of 1940. Here the isolation of the individual is personified, the three people in the picture bear no relationship to one another save as elements in the composition and as such they have been distributed on the picture plane almost as flat pattern. Line is the dominant element in the composition, which clearly shows the influence of Whistler and Degas, and the painting was, in fact, based on Degas' *Sur la Plage*, which le Brocquy knew from the Lane collection.[34]

An unusual composition for le Brocquy, in that it is perhaps the closest he has ever come to portrait painting in the traditional manner, is *Girl in White*, 1941 (Ulster Museum). The sitter for this study was the actress Kathleen Ryan, and the composition—which was based on Whistler—and almost monochromatic range of colours clearly reveal the early influences on him. The clumsily resolved lower part of the composition and the hesitancy widely evident in the handling of the paint show it to be an early work; but, nevertheless, the assurance of line in the profile of the face and hands is remarkable for a painter so early in his career, the more so as it is perhaps only the seventh picture le Brocquy had painted.[35] Le Brocquy's later portraits, such as that of *Niall Scott*, 1945, or his *Self-portrait*, 1947, a drawing in the National Gallery of Ireland, are interesting as revelations of character and personality, but are distinctly non-academic in approach. His later 'heads' or 'images' of various personalities—Yeats, Joyce, Beckett and others—all of which greatly post-date our period, are also not portraits properly speaking.

The Spanish Shawl, 1941, may just post-date *Girl in White*. In it the painting of the shawl closely resembles the treatment of the bodice and sleeves in the latter painting, but a thicker impasto is employed than hitherto. In many respects the composition of *The Spanish Shawl* is close to that of *The Picnic*, but whereas in the latter le Brocquy emphasized the flatness of the picture plane, in the former he has treated space in a much more three-dimensional manner. The work is clearly experimental, the artist is still seeking a meaningful subject-matter, but his interest in the individual is overt and from now on that increasingly preoccupied him.

Ralph Cusack showed five works in the first Living Art exhibition. Amongst them were *Christmas in My Studio*, which we have discussed elsewhere, as well as the more Surrealist composition, *The Road*, which illustrates the change of style which occurred in his work at about this time. Mainie Jellett was greatly admired by the critics, her *Ninth Hour* (Lane Gallery) and *Madonna of Eire* (National Gallery of Ireland) attracting most attention, although A.J. Leventhal thought her approach to Cubism was 'a little out-moded'.[36] Leventhal also admired the Surrealism of Nick Nicholls and the Cubist-inspired works of Doreen Vanston, which included *A Dying Animal*, a picture we have already encountered. Of the other progressive artists Norah McGuinness was held in high regard.

While living in London during the 1930s Norah McGuinness had exhibited at the Wertheim gallery. There she was a member of Lucy Wertheim's Twenties Group which included, amongst others, Christopher Wood, Victor Pasmore, Barbara Hepworth, Roger Hilton, Elizabeth Rivers and Kenneth Hall.[37] Later she also showed with the 7 & 5 Society and with the London Group. Thus her inclinations were clearly for the avant-garde. In 1939 she returned to Ireland and settled here permanently. Norah McGuinness was primarily a painter of landscapes and still lifes, although from time to time she painted some portraits such as her splendidly vivacious study of *Ida McGuinis*, done in 1930, and her later study of the actress *Shelah Richards*, 1942 (Abbey Theatre). As with her landscapes, in both of these works she has clearly concentrated instinctively on the existential act of painting rather than on trying to arrest a likeness of the sitter. Throughout the 1940s she continued to paint in a rather Fauvist manner, increasingly handling oil paint much as she had earlier used gouache. In these years she lightened her palette and her work generally assumed a strong lyricism, a characteristic which remained even when she returned to Cubism in the late 1950s and early 1960s.

123

Mainie Jellett
I Have Trodden the Winepress Alone
National Gallery of Ireland

Norah McGuinness was not a boldly avant-garde painter; but, as Anne Crookshank has remarked,[38] her expressive use of colour and frequently arbitrary handling of space separate her from the academic tradition. It is surprising that she was never tempted by abstraction—'pure abstraction would be an empty field for me', she said[39]—but rather remained faithful to the tradition of her early friends and contemporaries such as Frances Hodgkins and John Piper. Her main contribution, perhaps, to the Modern Movement in Ireland lay less with the influence of her own work, which is mildly conservative, although it reflects the overall tenor of the early Living Art exhibitions, than in her openness towards others and her rejection of cant from whatever quarter it might come.

Thurloe Conolly (b.1918) was one of a generation of young artists who came to prominence through the Living Art exhibitions. Self-taught, he had more or less drifted into painting,[40] and in 1941 decided to devote himself full-time to it. He was a regular exhibitor at the Living Art exhibitions and became a member of the organizing committee in 1947. His career as a painter may be divided into four distinct periods,[41] namely: the years 1942–5, typified by figure compositions and romantic landscapes, reminiscent of the English painter Christopher Wood; 1945–8, when he was much influenced by the work of John Piper, notably in his use of materials and choice of subject-matter which usually referred to derelict buildings and ruins; 1948–52, when he often assumed a sort of mathematical abstraction, at times with a hint of Paul Klee; and finally, 1952–6, when he became completely abstract. The two paintings which he showed in 1943, *Sailor at Night* and *The Yellow Tower*, in both subject-matter and narrative treatment are close to Christopher Wood, although Conolly lacked Wood's sensitivity. Other painters of the same generation as Conolly, who were well represented in the 1943 exhibition and who made their mark on it, were Nano Reid, Gerard Dillon and Patrick Scott.

In reviewing the exhibition A.J. Leventhal praised Mary Swanzy, who showed a number of recent works, and May Guinness, whose *Golden Wedding in Belgium*— a picture similar to her *Religious Procession in Brittany* (National Gallery of Ireland)—he thought referred 'straight back to the Douanier Rousseau'.[42] Margaret Clarke and Jack B. Yeats were the most admired of the academicians, Leventhal describing the former's *Young Girl with a Cat*, almost certainly the painting now known as *Ann with a Cat*, as a *tour de force*. Yeats' *Homage to Bret Harte*, a composition devoted to the idea of freedom, was to the *Irish Times* one of his greatest achievements in expressing romantic tragedy, a view which Máirín Allen endorsed in the *Father Mathew Record*.[43] These were the years of Yeats' elevation to popular esteem, the onset of a finale in which images, set down in a riot of colour and form, became gay amusement for his imagination. From the late 1930s, when Jack Longford had shown him at the Contemporary Picture Galleries, through the early forties under Victor Waddington's sponsorship, and culminating in his joint show with Sir William Nicholson in London in 1942 and the Yeats National Loan Exhibition in Dublin in 1945, Yeats achieved a strong measure of universality in his work and was increasingly regarded as an artist of international standing. Characteristics of his technique at the time are animated brushwork, a reliance on the palette knife and, frequently, paint applied directly from the tube and modelled with thumb or finger.

Other academicians who attracted comment included Dermod O'Brien, the president of the Academy, and Seán Keating. O'Brien, although himself an academic painter, was nevertheless sympathetic to the younger artists and encouraged them as best he could, often by buying their work for his own collection. Keating on the other hand was more hostile and it is surprising that he even exhibited at a venue such as this, although his *Tip Wagons at Poulaphouca* (Electricity Supply Board) was widely admired.

Of the sculpture included in the first Living Art exhibition, the memorial section to Jerome Connor drew most attention, his work expressing, in Máirín Allen's view, deep pathos and a noble vision of his people.[44] Laurence Campbell was also praised, although Leventhal thought he could have sent more important works, while Melanie le Brocquy he felt was 'yet to come'. To Stephen Rynne, on the other hand, the sculpture was 'quite the best exhibition we have had for many a year'.[45]

An annual exhibition

From the beginning it was the intention of the organizers that the Irish Exhibition of Living Art should be an annual event.[46] Thus, encouraged by the success of the 1943 exhibition, they decided to press ahead with a similar show the following year. The general arrangements for the submission and selection of works remained as before, but it was decided that non-Irish artists should be allowed to exhibit.[47] Changes to the committee that year included Laurence Campbell, who resigned, and Mrs. A. le Brocquy who was appointed honorary exhibition secretary. Further, at a meeting on 5 September 1944 the committee unanimously elected Norah McGuinness their permanent chairman, a position which she was to hold until 1972. Thus both the organizing committee and the exhibitions were constituted in a manner which, in all but matters of detail, were retained for the rest of the decade.

* * *

The 1944 Living Art exhibition opened on 14 September and ran until 6 October. It comprised 157 paintings and sculptures and nine pieces of stained glass. There was a similar representation of academic and non-academic artists as in the previous year and nine works were included by some of the more avant-garde English artists, namely Frances Hodgkins, Henry Moore, Ben Nicholson, John Piper, Matthew Smith, Graham Sutherland and Julian Trevelyan.[48] The presence of most of the White Stag artists was also noticeable in 1944.

As before, the exhibition was well received and £420 worth of paintings were sold, including four purchased by the trustees of the Haverty Trust.[49] The press, by and large, thought the exhibition even better than the previous one. The *Irish Independent* felt that in its short life it had given 'a decided stimulus' to the art scene and Stephen Rynne, commenting on the growing appreciation of Modernism generally in Ireland, said in the *Leader*:

> Six or seven years ago shows like this were few, haphazard, take-it-or-leave themes. To-day they are frequent, fashionable and . . . popular. There is anxiety to show, to be seen, to advertise in catalogues, for people have become picture conscious and picture buyers. Never before has art made such strides in Ireland as it did in the last six years; from being a footling thing, or a thing to tickle the vanity of the very rich, art has become something with a meaning for every man.[50]

For many visitors, the centre of attraction that year was Mainie Jellett's *Homage to Fra Angelico*, a composition based on Angelico's *Coronation of the Virgin* in the Louvre. It was included as a memorial to Mainie who had died the previous February. Other widely acclaimed works were Jack B. Yeats' *A Palace*, 1943, which to the *Irish Press* showed 'magic borrowed from no master',[51] a comment which illustrates Yeats' increasing stature at the time; and le Brocquy's *Alone* and *Tennis Courts in April*, which Rynne thought had 'harmony and . . . suavity [as with] no other painter of his generation', although to Edward Sheehy they betrayed a 'residue of dilettantism'.[52] The theme in *Alone* emanates from Siegfried Sassoon, as the accompanying couplet in the catalogue makes clear: ' . . . the word is life endured and known. It is the stillness where our spirits walk .'[53] Here le Brocquy's concern for the solitude of the individual is clear and it is evident too even in his contemporary landscapes, such as *Famine Cottages, Connemara*, 1944, where the figures in the background are depicted as onlookers, strangely detached from the landscape, rather than participants in the historiography of the scene.

Thurloe Conolly's *Watch-tower: Aran*, Jack Hanlon's *Annunciation*, Ralph Cusack's *Thirst in the Forest*, Norah McGuinness's *The Ferry Harbour, Youghal* and Phyllis Hayward's *Flowerpiece*, ' . . . so lacy, graceful, and vivacious', thought Rynne, were all widely commended. Of the White Stag artists, Rakoczi, Hall, Nicholls, Gilbert, Scott and Paul Egestorff were well represented with characteristic works, of which we have already encountered Rakoczi's *Prisoner* and Scott's *Birds in the Trees*. The Dublin Painters' Society were also well to the fore, with a number of works each from Grace Henry, Letitia Hamilton, Harriet Kirkwood, May Guinness, Evie Hone, Joan Jameson, Frances Kelly, Hilda Roberts, Pat Griffith, E.A. McGuire and Cecil Salkeld, whose *Ballerina* typifies his subject-matter from that time. The academicians were poorly represented, but Dermod O'Brien, Beatrice Glenavy and, of course, Jack B. Yeats were all there.

Few of the pictures shown by the English artists can now be identified, but Graham Sutherland's *Pembrokeshire Landscape* was lent by Sir Kenneth Clark. Surprisingly, perhaps, little emphasis was placed on these pictures by the press. Theodore Goodman, in *Commentary*, was alone in thinking that their inclusion improved the show, while to the *Irish Times* they were 'not more searching or of more lively interest than those by our own artists',[54] a view representative of most comments.

* * *

For the 1945 exhibition it was hoped to bring pictures from Belgium and France but war-time restrictions prevented this. However, the French Provisional Government in London lent a number of works and others were borrowed from English artists and from private collections in England and Ireland.[55] As with the previous exhibitions sales were good in 1945, £456 worth of paintings being sold.[56] Generally the press again thought well of the exhibition and now regarded it as part of the social 'Season'. Edward Sheehy remarked that if it remained an annual feature it would 'certainly outdo the Academy in significance if not in popularity';[57] while Stephen Rynne, with the French and English artists in mind, felt:

> We have not been so dumb here at home after all and Neutrality has suited our art as much as it has suited our consciences . . . . It is . . . solace and encouragement to know that we here in Ireland have now safely and soundly established our own Living Art . . . [as] proof of the liveliness of our artists.[58]

The artists who dominated the exhibition were by now familiar names. Le Brocquy was developing both in depth of expression and range at the time, as his *Condemned Man* and portrait of *Master Nial Scott*, both painted in 1945, show. In the former composition the sense of isolation is overwhelming and the sitter's gaol seems to be more mental than real. In the latter, his ability to simplify forms in the extreme is a foretaste of his more Cubist-inspired works of the end of the decade. Norah McGuinness showed a number of landscapes, and Grace Henry, Joan Jameson, Cecil

Galbally, Evie Hone, W.J. Leech (who was showing with the Living Art for the first time), Phyllis Hayward, Raymond McGrath, Ralph Cusack (whose *The Way to the World* was to Rynne 'a reverie of great charm') and Frances Kelly were all well represented. The latter's portrait of *Mrs. Seán T. Ó Ceallaig* Sheehy thought to be the *chef-d'œuvre* of the exhibition, being well composed and boldly painted. *Hall's Barn, Rathfarnham*, 1945, although not included in this exhibition, is one of Thurloe Conolly's most successful paintings of that year. The prominent surface texture of thick gesso covered with thin glazes of colour wrought with a precise linear definition, represents an enormous improvement in his powers as a draughtsman over earlier works, and the strikingly theatrical contrasts of light and dark tones typifies much of his work from the time. Of the then lesser known artists Sheehy thought, prophetically, that Daniel O'Neill promised well for the future, and he also praised Colin Middleton's 'consumate technique' in *The Dark Tower* and *The Mirror*.

Colin Middleton (1910–83) was the most important of the group of Northern artists who came to prominence at the Living Art exhibitions. Although he had shown in the *Ulster Unit* exhibition in 1934, Middleton first drew attention as an artist of consequence in 1943 with his one-man exhibition held in the Belfast Museum & Art Gallery. This exhibition was followed in quick succession by a joint show with Nick Nicholls, at the Grafton Gallery, Dublin, in May 1945 and another one-man show in Belfast the following autumn. We are here, of course, only concerned with Middleton's career until 1950, but even in these early years the central problem for the historian in assessing his *œuvre* is apparent, that is, to judge the real nature of his notorious eclecticism. As early as 1943, reviewing his exhibition in Belfast, the *Northern Whig* commented on the variety of styles to be found in the works, which he had produced during the previous four years. 'Mr. Middleton,' said the 'paper, 'is undoubtedly our boldest and most individual painter and it may be doubted whether any other local artist could stage a show of 100 pictures with so many characters but of no one type'.[59] Although the writer went on to admire the works on show, he was clearly uneasy about the meaning of such variety. Similarly, the *Irish Times*, reviewing Middleton's 1945 exhibition in Dublin, was disturbed before such a variety of styles, 'which at different times, remind one of Piper, German Expressionism, Pointillism, and of Cubism', although it concluded that fundamentally he was a Surrealist. By 1949, when he again showed in Dublin, the same profusion of styles was noted but the *Irish Times* now saw him as having progressed to another stage of development in which, with pictures such as *Teresa* and *Jacob Wrestling with the Angel*, painted in 1948 (cata. no.73), he seemed to concern himself with what it called the 'lost hopefulness' of so many refugees from the recent war.[60]

A closer look at Middleton's work of the time clearly illustrates the source of such opinions as these and highlights our difficulty in accounting for the development of his style. In about 1937, in compositions such as *Spanish War*, Middleton began to experiment with Surrealist imagery and the following year, motivated by the untimely death of his first wife and the approach of war in Europe, he developed his ideas in a number of studies in pen, ink and collage, of which *Vogue*, 1939, is representative. But concurrent with these he made paintings of Belfast street scenes in a semi-Expressionist style, as in *Street Corner Shop*, 1939. By 1941 he had produced *Lagan: Annadale, October* (Ulster Museum) and a number of other works, all executed in a loose Impressionist manner. Yet in these same years he also painted *The Fortune Teller*, *The Yellow Door* and *The Dark Lady*. The first two of these pictures, with their emphasis on carefully delineated forms, were clearly influenced by Salvador Dali, while the latter, with its emphasis on line, is indebted to Miró and Picasso. To further complicate this diversity of manner we have other pictures such as *White Geese*, which is strongly Yeatsian with its broken patches of colour applied with a palette knife, and *March Landscape*, 1942, which recalls Ivon Hitchens, as well as other more Surrealist studies of the time. In 1946, however, Middleton painted *Our Lady of Bikini* (cata. no.72), a composition inspired by the atomic tests held at about that time at Bikini attol in the Pacific ocean, which is one of his most important works and, being essentially Surrealist in concept, would lead one to assume that he had at last settled on a particular manner of expression. Other similar works include *Columbus*, painted a year later, in 1947, and *The Toy Box* and *Visitation*, both of 1948. Yet just when we begin to feel thus assured he reverted to a more Expressionist technique of bold brushwork and emotionally evocative colours, as in *Jacob Wrestling with the Angel* or *Nelson Street*, 1948, a manner in which he continued to work until the mid-1950s when he became much more concerned with landscape and geological structures. However, in the early 1970s he returned to Surrealism and produced a number of works in which many of his earlier concerns returned and coalesced.

Throughout his career Middleton was questioned from time to time about his eclecticism and the reasons for it. In reply he always said that he saw it as being a perfectly natural reaction to external influences. Indeed in 1967 he said that a period as psychologically complex as the late twentieth century demanded that an artist be diverse and versatile in his manner;[61] and at the end of his life he said that other painters had 'opened the gates' which he walked through. He didn't try to impose his style on the things he painted, rather, he said, he preferred to allow the subject to impose itself on him.[62] His friend, the poet and writer, John Hewitt always upheld his views on this matter, referring to the 'fecundity' of his 'invention' as early as 1942 and his 'alertness', his 'readiness of response' in 1976.[63] Earlier Edward Sheehy, who also greatly admired his work, commented that Middleton's notebooks represented an 'unsatisfied pilgrimage through the devious ways of modernism'[64] and he described what we might term 'the human condition' as being the enduring subject-matter of his work. Middleton, he said, seemed to be seeking an incorruptible sense of order, to synthesize various experiences into a private world so as to challenge the world of reality. Yet at the outset one is thwarted by the impossibility of escaping from oneself, within the bounds of reason; and this, he argued, led him to a form of Symbolism in which the symbol, usually an archetypal female figure, is the precursor of meaning and derives validity from its roots in a universal subconscious. Futhermore, he said, Middleton embraced the human condition with love, understanding and charity and thus in paintings such as *Jacob Wrestling* or *William and Mary*, which he exhibited at the Living Art in 1949, he achieved 'a profound and universal greatness'. Far from being imaginative and remote, said Sheehy, these works were 'passionately human . . . [with] a sustained emotional grandeur'.

While agreeing with Sheehy's assessment of these works and others of the same period such as *Our Lady of Bikini*, one feels there is something less than convincing about Middleton. Despite all the reasons proffered for his versatility one finds oneself continually questioning its rigour, wondering how *purposeful* was his adoption of external influences, for at each stage of his development he refused to consolidate his achievement. He was undoubtedly sensitive to events in the world around him as, for example, in his Surrealism of the late 1930s and early 1940s with its references to war or, later, in his condemnation of atomic weapons with the concomitant clash of technical achievement versus moral values, which stated the human predicament concisely, and he confronted these difficulties as none of his Irish contemporaries did; yet withal one feels that he failed to develop the full rigour of his stance. Perhaps this impasse is explained by his technical virtuosity. Trained as a linen damask designer, he always emphasized the technical aspect of painting and from his earliest exhibitions the critics praised his technical skill. So maybe, when all is said and done, Middleton was in love with his materials, with oil paint in particular and with the techniques of handling it, for all his work exhibits a sensuousness of execution. But as historians assessing his work we must not be blinded as to content by an adroit technique. Middleton had little influence on others and in many respects was a loner. He was certainly, as John Hewitt suggested, Ireland's greatest Surrealist painter,[65] but for all his outgoingness he remained provincial and timid.

Nano Reid was of the same generation as her friend Norah McGuinness and, like her, was a member of the Dublin Painters' Society. Her real claim to prominence, however, came with the Living Art exhibitions where she was a regular exhibitor. Nano Reid was a fine draughtsman, as the boldness of line and general economy of means in her drawing of *Edward Sheehy*, done in about 1944 (cata. no.75), for example illustrate. From about this time the melancholy of her earlier work gave way to a more lyrical approach, which can be seen in *Friday Fare* and *The Hanging Gate*, both painted in 1945, the latter being exhibited at the Living Art that year. In these years she also adopted a bird's eye view of things, which often gives her compositions a pictographic effect and characterizes her work thereafter. As the 1940s progressed her style became increasingly Expressionist and her work varied in manner from the Germanic *West Cork Mountains*, of about 1945, or *Forest Pool*, 1946 (cata. no.76), both of which with their harsh, angular forms recall the Brücke painters, to the Matisse-like *Girl with a Scarf* of 1947.

Of Colin Middleton's Northern confrères who exhibited at the Living Art exhibitions Gerard Dillon, Dan O'Neill, George Campbell and Nevill Johnson were the most important, although Campbell and Johnson did not exhibit there until 1947 and 1948 respectively. This group of Northerners not only dominated the later Living Art exhibitions, but largely determined the development of Irish painting throughout the 1950s.

Gerard Dillon (1916–71) was born in Belfast. After leaving school in 1930 he spent seven years, principally in London, as a painter and decorator and only towards the late thirties decided to devote himself to painting, in which he was almost entirely self-taught. Dillon was caught in Ireland by the outbreak of war in 1939 and, as he could not return to England because of travel restrictions, he decided to live in Dublin. He held his first one-man exhibition at the Country Shop on St. Stephen's Green in February 1942, the exhibition being opened by Mainie Jellett. Reviewing the works on display the *Irish Times* commented that, despite his manifest lack of art-school training, he could 'put the breath of life' into his painting and it admired his vivacity, his good colour sense and his ability to catch the essential movement or gesture to invoke drama.[66] In the absence of the exhibition catalogue—if one was produced, which is doubtful—and judging only by the titles of those works mentioned in the *Irish Times* review, it seems that the paintings exhibited represented what became Dillon's usual subject-matter, that is, folk-scenes often heavily laden with sentiment and nostalgia. This review singled out for attention *Forgive Us Our Tresspasses* and

Gerard Dillon
*Angels with Split
Voices*, early 1940s
Photograph S.B.K.

Result of a Raid, the latter conveying with a sense of pathos his feeling for those 'little shuffling people', as John Hewitt once called them,[67] whose homes had been destroyed.

From the early 1940s Dillon's subject-matter increasingly reflected the west, particularly the Aran Islands and Connemara. But whereas Paul Henry, for example, and so many others had been enchanted by the landscape itself Dillon was taken by its people and their customs. Writing in 1951 about what had first motivated him to paint, he said that Seán Keating's illustrations for Synge's *The Playboy of the Western World*[68] and the work of Marc Chagall, which presumably he knew from reproductions, had first stimulated him.[69] The influence of Chagall is clear in several aspects of his work, notably in his use of strong, often vibrant colours, his technique of rendering a bird's eye view of his subject, as in *The Black Lake*, of about 1940 (An Chomhairle Ealaíon), and in his practice of combining various sequences of a narrative in one composition, as in the *Goat Herd*, which he exhibited at the Living Art in 1950. This last-mentioned trait, however, was influenced too in the late 1940s by the similar narrative technique found in the carved decoration on Irish High Crosses.[70] Also, *Yellow Bungalow*, 1954 (cata. no.77), which is arguably his masterpiece, clearly resembles Chagall's *La Chambre jaune* of 1911, not only in its title, but in the overall composition, the strange tilting of the floor, the window to the right hand side and the predominant use of yellow, although where Dillon might have seen this painting we do not know. Despite his deficiencies as a draughtsman some of his early drawings, such as *Angels with Split Voices*, of about 1940–4, have a remarkable assurance of line, and in this case, the break-up and overlapping of forms show him to be experimenting with certain aspects of Cubism. But the main thrust of Dillon's work was with peasant life, although as he returned to London in late 1945 or early 1946 the west of Ireland did not quite monopolize his work as it might otherwise have done.

Like Dillon, Dan O'Neill (1920–74) was a Belfast man. Apart from a few life classes which he attended at the Belfast College of Art and a short time spent at the studio of his friend Sidney Smith,[71] he was self-taught as an artist. While working as an electrician he began, in 1939, to paint in the evenings, at first working intuitively but Smith and Dillon, whom he met at about this time, introuced him to the work of Cézanne, Rouault and other modern French painters and consequently his style, which matured with prodigious speed—Cecil Salkeld described him as a 'late prodigy' who 'sprang into the arena fully armed'[72]—became Expressionistic and strongly Romantic in character, his subject-matter generally drawn from the universal themes of life, birth, love and death. His first important exhibition was a joint show with Gerard Dillon at the Contemporary Picture Galleries in December 1943, when he showed his *Head of a Clown*, c.1940–3, a composition which is clearly indebted to Rouault but which, for so early a work by a self-taught painter, shows great simplicity of form, dexterity of technique and a strong tactile awareness of surface. The feeling of pathos, which characterizes nearly all of O'Neill's work, is also evident. Another early work, *Madonna*, of about 1940–4, demonstrates O'Neill's familiarity with early Italian painting, which he knew from reproductions. Such pictures are often characterized by simplified, though carefully modelled forms rendered with smooth brushwork over which he would paint, frequently with a palette knife to give a heavily textured effect, clothes in strongly contrasting tones. The mood of these paintings is usually one of calm serenity tinged with gloom.

* * *

No Living Art exhibition was held in 1946 as the Thomas Davis Young Ireland Movement centenary exhibition, *Pictures of Irish Historical Interest*, occupied the National College of Art that summer. The organizing committee hoped that the Living Art might instead be shown in the gallery at Brown Thomas & Co., but a prolonged docks strike that year put paid to these plans. However, the situation was to some extent saved by the exhibition of *Living Irish Art* shown at the Leicester Galleries, London, in October 1946. Cecil Phillips of the Leicester Galleries had visited the

132

Living Art the previous year when it was hoped that he would take a selection from that exhibition to London, but war-time conditions prevented this. The following year, however, seventy-six works by those artists who showed regularly at the Living Art were exhibited in London.

* * *

The Living Art exhibitions were by now well established and had become an important part of the annual calendar. From 1947 the exhibitions were again held at the National College of Art. Changes to the organizing committee in these years included Anne Yeats, Thurloe Conolly and Michael Scott, who joined it in late 1946; Ralph Cusack, who became treasurer in August 1947 in place of Jack Hanlon; and in March 1948 Norah McGuinness, the chairman, asked to have the title of her office changed to president, and this was agreed unanimously.[73] Once again, the press had a high opinion of the exhibition in both 1947 and 1948. 'It is hardly necessary to state that the standard here is higher than in any other group show', wrote James White in 1947;[74] while the following year Edward Sheehy opined: 'The Living Art Exhibition has become an institution and is to-day a far more important artistic event than the Academy'.[75] And that same year, in an unpublished note on the exhibition, the writer and philosopher Arland Ussher commented that it 'may turn out to be one of the beginnings of Irish Cultural History'.[76]

In these years we find, by and large, the same names dominating the exhibitions as before. From about 1945 le Brocquy had been preoccupied with the theme of travelling people, or tinkers, and this preoccupation is reflected in a number of works which he showed at the Living Art and elsewhere at the time. *Travelling People* and *Tinkers Resting* (Tate Gallery), both painted in 1946, and *Tinker Woman with Newspaper*, 1947, all illustrate this line of development, which still centred on the isolation of the individual. In these pictures, however, the tinkers symbolize the individual mis-placed in an organized, settled society, and they may also be regarded as metaphors for the then displaced persons of war-torn Europe. Le Brocquy's tinker paintings preoccupied him until the early 1950s and led to a number of works in which he explored human relationships within the family. His large composition, *A Family*, painted in 1951 (La Praelpina, S.P.A., Milan), is one of the most important works from any period of his career, but also marks the development of his art at the end of our period of study. A characteristic of these last-mentioned paintings is his adoption of a semi-Cubist structural discipline expressed in angular shapes and forms which were derived from Cézanne and Picasso and which were later influenced by the Polish painter Jankel Adler, with whom he became friendly after his move to London in 1946. A sense of underlying structure, in one form or another, remains an essential part of le Brocquy's work.

Le Brocquy in the 1940s was not an avant-garde painter in any revolutionary manner. Being self-taught his approach to art was at first intuitive rather than theoretical. Later, however, he became more analytical; observing, uncovering, people repeatedly his centre of interest. Le Brocquy has always followed his own path, but the originality of his thinking distinguishes him from his Irish contemporaries. As we have seen, his subject-matter is traditional but is treated in such a way as to reflect the times. From our present viewpoint, looking back over forty years, we can see a consistency in le Brocquy's development which is firmly rooted in his early

133

Norah McGuinness
The Four Courts,
1940
Ulster Museum

work. It is this consistency which makes him one of the few Irish painters of international rank to have emerged this century. Aside from his own work, le Brocquy's great contribution to the development of the Modern Movement in Ireland was in liberating other artists from established convention for, in founding the Living Art exhibitions, he created a forum in which others could express themselves freely.

Norah McGuinness, too, was moving forward in the mid-1940s. In works like *Swans Nesting* and *Mill on the Nore*, both painted in 1947, or *Bachelors Walk*, of 1949, she employed a delightful lyricism in which her use of the medium was—like her work of a decade earlier—perfectly in keeping with her mood. Nano Reid was preoccupied with watercolours in these years, and, with pastels and drawings, they often predominated over oils in her exhibitions. Increasingly at this time she painted landscapes of her native Boyne valley, which evoke a feeling of nostalgia and have an element of mysticism about them, as can be seen, for example, in *Mellifont Abbey* of 1947. However, her portraits retained a more direct approach and simplicity of style. She was, too, as we have seen, an active member of the Dublin Painters' Society at the time and there held a number of one-woman exhibitions before transferring her allegiance to the Dawson and Waddington galleries in 1947 and 1950 respectively. Also in 1950, with Norah McGuinness, she represented Ireland at the twenty-fifth Venice Biennale, where her works included, amongst others, *Forest Pool* and *Friday Fare*.

Like Norah McGuinness, Nano Reid was a conservative painter and while she is rightly termed a Modernist, she was not a pioneer in any sense. Nevertheless, she was one of the best Irish painters of her generation. As Jeanne Sheehy has pointed out,[77] she was a realist, and in her manner, which was largely intuitive, she had something of the energy of the post-war Abstract Expressionists.[78]

Jack Hanlon, a member of the original exhibition committee, was also was widely admired in the mid-1940s, particularly for his simplicity of composition and use of colour. Jack B. Yeats, however, was greatly under-represented at the time, showing only one work each year from 1945. May Guinness, by then in her eighties, showed in 1947 and Cecil Salkeld regularly contributed, although by this time his work had become somewhat stylized and repetitive in manner. Of the White Stag artists, Basil Rakoczi, Nick Nicholls, Paul Egestorff, Phyllis Hayward, Doreen Vanston and Patrick Scott all continued to exhibit regularly.

Doreen Vanston is best remembered from these years for her landscapes of South America. In 1926, while in Paris, she had married a Costa Rican student and, after a brief stay in Italy, they settled in Costa Rica. However, the marriage broke-up during 1932 or 1933 and Vanston returned to France and later to Dublin. But in 1947 she returned briefly to Costa Rica and there made a number of watercolours, including *Untitled*, 1947, and *El Carruno de San Antonio*, 1948 (cata. no.78), which, in their sensitive handling of washes and juxtaposition of colours and tones are typical of her work until the late 1960s. Her oils, however, were often more Expressionist in treatment than her watercolours.

Patrick Scott seems to have painted little during the mid-1940s and of the four works which he exhibited with the White Stag artists at the Arcade Gallery, London, in 1945, at least three had been done during the previous two years. By 1947, however, his style had changed, although his subject-matter remained as before. He retained a formal manner of composition but became more concerned with textures and patterns which disguise the underlying geometry. There is a suggestion of mood and atmosphere in works of this period, such as *The Sea Wall*, which he exhibited at the Living Art in 1947. Here, as before, the paint has been applied thinly and scored through to reveal the canvas and define the imagery. A similar technique is evident in *Wet Day*, 1949, and *Bird Nesting*, 1950, although in these he outlined certain forms with a black line. The treatment of foliage in these two last-mentioned pictures may owe something to the influence of Nick Nicholls' later work.

The most notable thing about the Living Art exhibitions in the mid-1940s is the number of new names which came to prominence. We have already mentioned Thurloe Conolly, Colin Middleton, Dan O'Neill and Gerard Dillon and have noted the fact that, with the exception of Conolly, they all came from Belfast. But in 1947 and 1948 respectively George Campbell and Nevill Johnson, who were also from Belfast, began to exhibit and, with their Northern contemporaries, exerted a strong influence on an otherwise almost exclusively Dublin scene.

George Campbell (1917–79) although born in Co. Wicklow, spent his formative years in Belfast. He was a close associate of Dillon and O'Neill and, like them, was self-taught as an artist. His mother, Gretta Bowen (1880–1981), also became a painter as did his elder brother, Arthur. George Campbell first began to paint in 1941, having been spurred by the Blitz to record the damage wreaked on Belfast by the Luftwaffe.[79] In about 1943 he decided to devote himself full-time to painting. He held his first exhibition, a joint show with his brother, in Mol's gallery, Belfast, during February–March 1944 and another, with Gerard Dillon, at John Lamb's gallery in Portadown the following July. From July until December 1945 he was in London preparing for an exhibition at Waddington's Gallery in Dublin the following spring. Thus began a

George Campbell
Spanish Gypsies
Photograph S.B.K.

number of exhibitions which he held there in subsequent years, during which time he also exhibited at the CEMA gallery, Belfast and at Heal's Mansard Gallery, London, where in 1948 he joined with Dan O'Neill, Nevill Johnson and Gerard Dillon in the exhibition *Four Ulster Artists*. In these years he was also active with his brother in Belfast art circles and was a founder-member of both the Progressive Painters Group and the Northern Ireland branch of the Artists International Association,[80] which was formed in November 1944 in an attempt to raise public awareness of art. In about 1946 Campbell met a group of Spaniards, who had come to Dublin as refugees during the Spanish Civil War, and through them he developed an interest in Spain which was further stimulated a year or so later when, during a visit to London—possibly at the time of the *Four Ulster Artists* exhibition—he painted several pictures of Spanish gipsy dancers from the Carmen Amaya dance troupe

136

George Campbell
*Slack Day,
Smithfield*,
c.1941–2
Ulster Museum

who were then performing at the Princess Theatre.[81] Of these works, *Gitana* and *Matador* were exhibited in *6 Painters* at the CEMA gallery, Belfast, in October 1948 and *Gitana*, *Consuelito*, *Carmen*, *Malaguena* and *Jota* were exhibited in his one-man show at Waddington's, in Dublin, in May 1949. In 1951 he paid his first visit to Spain,[82] and thereafter the mood and atmosphere of that country, its people, their music and traditions and the landscape itself, especially of the area around Malaga, were to be important stimuli for his art.

Campbell exhibited regularly at the Living Art exhibitions from 1947. The subject-matter of his early painting was, as we have said, principally concerned with the Blitz, with shabby city streets and the hardship of civilian life in war-time. These were the themes of his exhibition at Mol's gallery in spring 1944 when several of the pictures were titled 'Belfast Commentary', and number twenty-five, *Belfast Commentary (6)—Easter, 1941*, confirms that he was painting from at least that year and not 1943 as has been suggested by some sources. Reviewing this exhibition most of the critics admired his 'social conscience' and the suggestion of emotion and sense of pathos which characterized many of the works.[83] His *Slack Day, Smithfield*, of about 1941–2 (Ulster Museum), while not included in this exhibition, typifies his early work[84] and its dark tones and muted colours remained a feature of his painting until the late 1940s. Reviewing his exhibition at Waddington's in 1946 for the journal *Commentary*, Theodore Goodman suggested that this characteristic was an influence both from the English painter John Piper, whom Campbell then admired, and from the prevailing mood of the times, for, said Goodman, unlike so many Irish painters who had lived in relative isolation during the war, Campbell 'had worked, and felt in a country at war, his work reflects the contemporary spirit'.[85] The paintings shown at Waddington's included street scenes, circus and theatrical subjects and landscapes. In the *Irish Times*, Arthur Power noted Campbell's sense of

137

intimacy in pictures such as *Madge in the Mirror*; he praised his vitality and observation and commented that, in contrast to many of his contemporaries, he 'has always something to say'.[86] His handling of paint at this time is characterized by short, often uncertain brushstrokes which produce an effect of fussiness, and his technique changed little until about 1948, when he adopted a mildly Cubist approach. We can see the beginnings of this change in some of his Spanish gipsy paintings, such as *Gitana*, and it is more pronounced in *Tinkers, Kilkeel* and *Kilkeel Harbour*, both painted in about 1949 or 1950, where there is a distinct tendency to emphasize planes which are often elongated. But Campbell never became obsessed with technique and in paintings like *Claddagh Duff, Connemara*, c.1950–1 (cata. no.79), which is one of his best pictures of this period, a strong sense of spontaneity remains as does a feeling for the existential act of painting which also characterizes so much of his work in general. This last-mentioned painting is, too, a welcome change from the more hackneyed interpretation of the west of Ireland common to so many of his contemporaries.

Campbell's best work belongs to the 1950s and 1960s and is thus outside the scope of this study; but his themes, drawn particularly from music and set down in vibrant colours, often with a semi-Cubist awareness of structure, increasingly reflected his time spent in Spain and his later landscapes had a strong sense of patterning which had its source in works such as *Claddagh Duff* and others of around 1950.

Nevill Johnson (b.1911) came from Buxton, in Derbyshire. On leaving school he went into business and, in 1934, his business activities brought him to Belfast where he was to live for the next fourteen years.[87] During his early years in Belfast he began to paint in his spare time, taking lessons from John Luke, with whom he had become friendly. In about 1936 he and Luke visited Paris where they saw Cubist paintings in the Musée d'Art Moderne and, during the trip, they also chanced upon an exhibition of Surrealist pictures,[88] both styles later influencing Johnson's own work. In 1946 he took part in what was probably his first exhibition, a group show with Olive Henry, Gladys and Max MacCabe and Aaron McAfee at the MacGaffin Gallery, Belfast,[89] and later that same year met Victor Waddington, who offered him a gallery contract, thus allowing him to paint full-time. In September 1947 he joined, as we have seen, with George Campbell, Gerard Dillon and Dan O'Neill in the exhibition *Four Ulster Painters* at Waddington's, the show being transferred to Heal's Mansard Gallery the following May. Also in the following year, 1948, he settled in Dublin.

Nevill Johnson has always been something of an outsider, an observer of events preferring, in his own words, 'to walk against the wind'.[90] His earliest extant paintings, such as *Linenscape*, 1945, are strongly Surrealist in concept. Here there are clear influences from Salvador Dali in the sense of timelessness and silence which is evoked by the setting, of Yves Tanguy in the disposition of imagery and of Giorgio de Chirico—all artists whom Johnston acknowledges as having influenced him—in the overall metaphysical nature of the composition. The choice of images was suggested by Edwin Bryson, who commissioned the painting, and the handling of the paint, with a thin film of colour glazed over a tempera base, shows Johnson's debt to his teacher, John Luke, and was a technique which he retained until the early 1950s when his impasto became a little heavier. Johnson's work at this time combined a mixture of poignancy and wit. *And the Sixth Day*, painted in about 1947, for example, depicts two semi-organic 'figures' as if coming to life upon a flat and desolate plain, the whole pregnant with the horrors of the recent past. Johnson exhibited this work at Waddington's in 1947 along with other contemporary pieces, including *The Year of Grace 1945* and *A Voice Crying*. Writing of them, the *Irish Tatler & Sketch* thought they were macabre symbols of the post-war atomic age and of the follies of materialism and it admired the seriousness of his thought.[91] These works catalogue Johnson's acute sensitivity to contemporary events, a sensitivity which provoked a crisis which led him to destroy so much of his work in the later 1950s. 'These silent surreal wastelands,' he later wrote, 'these mute bones and raven skies—whom was I addressing? Of what relevance [were] these Arcadian shores to a world of blackmail and bombs?'[92] Or in H.R.F. Keating's phrase, such pictures exposed 'the prickly conscience' of the times[93] which so many tried to ignore. Along with Jack B. Yeats' *Tinker's Encampment: The Blood of Abel*, 1940, Kenneth Hall's *Après la guerre* and Middleton's *Our Lady of Bikini* they are amongst the most poignant images of war and its effects painted by any artist in Ireland in the modern period. In about 1947, however, Johnson adopted a more Cubist manner, influenced by Braque and Gris, which we first see in *The Family*, which he exhibited at Heal's Gallery in 1948. Here, in contrast to his earlier works, he has used opaque paint but has retained his sensitivity for the tactile nature of the canvas. The forms of the figures and what appear to be circus tents in the background have been rigorously simplified and he has continued to use the sombre colours of his earlier works. In concept and treatment the picture recalls le Brocquy's composition of the same title, painted in 1951, and one is tempted to wonder if le Brocquy might have seen it at some time, perhaps in the Waddington Gallery. Johnson's Cubist style is seen at its most advanced stage in *The Clown* (cata. no.80), which dates from about 1950. The relative flattening of the picture plane, as here, remained a feature of his work until the mid-1950s as did his dominant use of yellow and tones of grey. Johnson's best works, of which *Landscape, Rock Pool* (cata. no.81) is a good example, date from the years after 1949–50 and thus are outside our period. Yet in them, despite—or perhaps because of—his relentless questioning of the nature of things around him, one can often sense the paucity of content which eventually troubled him so that perhaps it is not entirely surprising that he suffered a period of intense self-doubt in the late 1950s.

In the 1948 Living Art exhibition Thurloe Conolly showed his recently painted *Man with a Draughts Board*. This picture represents a change of subject-matter for him and, with a greater degree of abstraction than hitherto, a growing interest in pattern and an emphasis on the flatness of the picture plane, we have in it a number of characteristics which he developed later. This tendency towards abstraction typifies the third period of his development as a painter, namely the years 1948–52, in which he produced some pictures akin to the mathematical abstractions of Ben Nicholson. But at the same time he also painted a number of fantasy compositions—which he rather dismissively referred to as 'aesthetic nonsense'[94]—including *In the Forest, The Royal Hunt* and *A Very Powerful Queen*, which he exhibited in his one-man show at Waddington's in November 1949. These paintings, with their graffiti-like drawings of figures and animals, were the outcome of a growing interest at the time in native Oceanic, American and African art.[95] To his purely abstract compositions done now and later he gave titles such as *Painting XLII*, 1953, or *Composition 2*, 1956, for they were explicitly non-figurative, being composed in the main of interlocking geometrical shapes, although they sometimes convey a suggestion of Indian or tribal symbolism. *The Juggler*, 1953 (cata. no.82), is one of the few semi-figurative works

from this last period and shows the characteristics which we have mentioned as well as recording his continued concern for texture and pattern.

That Conolly should have been light-hearted about his painting is a pity for he was a fine technician and his later work is characterized by a continually developing sensitivity. Yet his aptitude to become a serious painter must remain in doubt, and his eclecticism, which was often more sub-conscious than intentional, betrays the lack of rigour of his viewpoint.

By the late 1940s Gerard Dillon was maturing as a painter, as can be seen, for example, in his *Fish Eaters* of 1946 (Arts Council of Northern Ireland). Here we have the already familiar characteristics of his work, a bird's eye view and a narrative format, but there is also a curious distortion of perspective which serves in part to flatten the picture-plane and to give a hint of symbolism to the composition. Another feature which is common to his work and which we see here is an unexpected degree of sophistication, for on the table, amid what appears to be a quasi-monastic group of peasants eating a basic meal, is a bottle recognizably of Chianti wine and hanging on the wall in the background is a painting of a Madonna and Child in the manner of Evie Hone or Mainie Jellett. *Fish Eaters* reveals Dillon as a *faux naïf*, as Brian Fallon once called him, and points to a major weakness if we are to consider his art as being in any way important other than for its inherent charm for, despite his professed 'Irishness', in Fallon's words, 'One does not find a nation's "soul" by painting her peasantry'.[96] Pictures such as *Fish Eaters*, despite their appeal, convey more about the painter than his subjects.

Many of Dillon's best remembered paintings—*Self-contained Flat* (Arts Council of Northern Ireland), *Yellow Bungalow*, *Connelly's Bar, Inishlacken* (Arts Council of Northern Ireland), *The Brothers* and others from his series of paintings of clowns—

Gerard Dillon
Fish Eaters, 1946
Arts Council of
Northern Ireland

date from the years after 1950 and are therefore outside our period; but arguably his early works, with their directness, sense of discovery and the freshness of his handling of paint and colour, are his best. Like his later works, too, they are strongly autobiographical which is, perhaps, what makes them so attractive to us.

Apart from these attributes the substance of Dillon's contribution to Modernism in Ireland was slight. As a self-taught painter it was perhaps inevitable that he should work loosely in an Expressionist manner, progressing intuitively under the guidance, in his case, of a gentle, pathos. Like his contemporary and friend, Dan O'Neill, and to a lesser extent George Campbell, he represents a period which went quickly out of fashion, being overtaken during the late 1950s by the new art from America so willingly embraced by a younger generation. Thus at our present remove in time, in all but his best paintings Dillon appears to lack rigour and while his work has individuality and charm it is, perhaps, too self-indulgent for a more cynical age.

Like Dillon, Dan O'Neill also quickly matured as a painter in these years. In about 1945 or early 1946 he met Victor Waddington who greatly admired his work and encouraged him to paint full-time, giving him his first one-man exhibition in Dublin in October 1946. In 1948 he exhibited in a mixed show at the CEMA gallery in Belfast and at Heal's Mansard Gallery along with George Campbell, Nevill Johnson and Gerard Dillon. In late 1948 or early 1949, almost certainly aided by Victor Waddington, O'Neill spent a brief period in Paris as a result of which his style, both in concept and execution, for a time resembled that of Vlaminck and Utrillo, whose work he must have seen there. We can see this influence in, for example, his *Place du Tertre*, 1949 (cata. no.83), which is one of his very best pictures. Here he perfectly captures the mood and atmosphere of night life in bohemian Paris, which is perfectly suited to his familiar nostalgia. He was well represented at the Living Art exhibitions in these years. In 1947 the Haverty Trust purchased his *Cityscape* from that year's exhibition and in 1948 they acquired *The Mirror* and, a year later, bought *The Blue Skirt* (cata. no.84)—which the critic Kenneth Jamison once called 'a kind of northern odalisque . . . [which] seemed to belong to the great European tradition and yet to be something excitingly new'[97]—thus giving a seal of official approval to his work. He held another one-man exhibition at Waddington's in October 1949 when the works on display included *The First Born*, 1949 (Ulster Museum), and *The Matador*. In the latter picture the lace-like patterning on the bull-fighter's jacket, which was produced by squeezing paint directly from the tube to the canvas, became a familiar feature of his style. In 1950 two of O'Neill's paintings, *Near Culdaff, Co. Donegal* and *Artist and Models*, the latter work still very Parisian and with a Picassoesque quality to the figure in the foreground, were shown in the exhibition of Irish art which toured in the U.S.A. and Canada.

In the early 1950s O'Neill reverted, to some extent, to his earlier technique and among his best remembered works from the period are *Knockalla Hills, Donegal*, 1951 (Ulster Museum), and *Birth*, 1952 (Arts Council of Northern Ireland), which is full of drama and emotion rendered with all the spontaneity of quick brushwork and occasional use of the palette knife which one associates with him. Landscapes always featured prominently in O'Neill's subject-matter, but whereas those of the 1940s were treated in a fairly representational manner, with much emphasis given to the mood and structural aspects of the scene and with rather subdued brushwork, in the 1950s he produced much more Expressionist works, such as his *Knockalla Hills* or *Figure in Snow*, of about 1952–4. He also painted some portraits, such as that of *Katherine, Lady Nelson*, c.1950, but these are less satisfactory than either his landscapes or semi-mythological figure studies, such as *Flora*, 1954, in which he was free to interpret the subject-matter as he wished.

Like Dillon, O'Neill made a useful contribution to modern painting in Ireland by helping to break the academic grip of the times, but he contributed little to the wider cause of Modernism. In retrospect he appears excessively romantic with insufficient intellectual discipline to forge a progressive method. It is not surprising, therefore, that he was unable to sustain the quality of his output after the mid-1950s, by which time his best work was long behind him. In a sense he was trapped by his own prodigiality and suavity.

Notable aspects of the Living Art exhibitions at this time were a lecture by Herbert Read, given in 1947, and the inclusion of thirty-one French Impressionist and other paintings from the Bomford collection[98] which were hung alongside the Irish works in 1948. Read's lecture, entitled 'The Present Situation of Art in Europe', was almost certainly a draft of his later paper, 'The Situation of Art in Europe at the end of the Second World War', which he gave in the United States and, later, in Germany and which was eventually published in the *Hudson Review* (New York) in spring 1948.[99] The Bomford pictures comprised one work each by Bonnard, Braque, Daubigny, Degas, Matisse, Modigliani, Picasso and Vuillard; two each by Daumier, Derain, Klee, Rouault and Soutine; three Manets; five Cézannes and five Renoirs. While such works no doubt added to the stature of the exhibition, paradoxically, for a group of progressive artists, they had a distinct period appeal.

* * *

In 1949 a number of changes were made to the composition of the organizing committee, the most important being the resignation of Louis le Brocquy that March. As le Brocquy was the prime mover in establishing the Living Art exhibitions his resignation was an important event and his reasons for leaving the committee, as well as his impressions of the exhibitions at that time, are set out in a letter of 21 January 1949 to Norah McGuinness and should here be recalled.

Le Brocquy had been thinking about his role on the committee for some time and had discussed the matter with Norah McGuinness the previous Christmas. He felt that an assessment of the exhibitions, both of their past and future, was then due. Looking to the past, he felt that the committee had been almost completely successful in their objective in creating conditions wherein the 'most vital painting and sculpture in the country' was regularly exhibited to a wide public. Moreover, he said, the Exhibition of Living Art and all it stood for was recognized and respected as an annual event. He continued:

> I dare say no one could have known the utter necessity for such an Exhibition other than we painters nor would anyone else have had the incentive to create such a controversial show as that in '43 in face of such difficulties. We did what had to be done and now today our aims or raison d'être and even our artists are widely accepted. My only regret is that Mainie is not here to witness it.

Looking to the future, he went on, they had no aim other than to keep the exhibitions alive. But he himself did not want to continue indefinitely sitting in judgement on the work of other artists and so felt he should resign from the organizing committee. The alternative, as he saw it, was that the Living Art exhibitions would become repetitive and eventually just another sort of academy.

> This is not what we have aimed at [he wrote], and I feel accordingly that in future we painters should be *sending* our work in like anybody else not *putting* it in. We've done our job in establishing I.E.L.A. and I would propose that in the future it should be organized by a committee excluding painters and sculptors. Whom we might nominate is a matter for discussion. I have thought of the advisability of appointing the Friends NCI[100] with a view to their taking over the Exhibition as an annual or two yearly event. Should they wish to include some painters on their judging committee—well and good—such a committee would not be self-appointed and would probably differ in composition each year. I don't think we should worry unduly about abandoning our role as custodians of a very high standard of work. I.E.L.A. always aimed to be a comprehensive forum—not necessarily an exquisite affair.[101]

The committee considered the recommendations expressed in le Brocquy's letter, but decided that the Living Art exhibitions were not sufficiently well established to be handed over to another group, as he had suggested. However, recognizing the need for a wider representation of interests, they invited Lt.-Col. R.K. Knox and R.R. Figgis to join them. They also felt that closer links with the Northern artists were desirable and asked J.A.S. Stendall, curator of the Belfast Museum & Art Gallery, to become a patron, but he declined the offer.[102] Other changes in the committee that year were Jack Hanlon, who again became treasurer, and Patricia Rushton, who was appointed exhibition secretary in place of Sybil le Brocquy, who resigned the post. As it was again their intention to bring pictures from France for the next exhibition, Major W. Kirkwood, the Earl of Rosse, Sir Basil Goulding and Lord Moyne were invited to become additional guarantors because of the expense involved. Later, Evie Hone and Anne Yeats went to Paris where they selected fourteen pictures by contemporary artists and five Aubusson tapestries by Jean Lurçat, all of which were hung in that year's exhibition.[103]

As in previous years, the press were unanimous in their praise of the 1949 exhibition. To the *Irish Times* it abounded in vitality in comparison with the recent Royal Hibernian Academy show, and Edward Sheehy thought it simply 'the best . . . yet'. The critics all admired Jack B. Yeats, his *Left-Left*, 1948, being one of the finest pictures in his late manner, thought Sheehy. Louis le Brocquy was again well to the fore, the *Tatler & Sketch* considering his *Madonna and Child with St. Anne* to be the most striking picture in the exhibition, superbly composed and with splendidly harmonized colours. Norah McGuinness' *Bachelors Walk*, 1949, was praised for the way in which it perfectly captured the spirit of the Dublin quays; and Nano Reid's *To Drogheda*, Doreen Vanston's South American landscapes and Anne Yeats's *Woman Watching*, 1948 (Ulster Museum), were all much admired.

Of those young artists whom the Living Art exhibitions brought to prominence in the late 1940s, mention should be made of Anne Yeats, although her work really belongs to the 1950s and later. Anne Yeats, the daughter of W.B. Yeats, studied drawing and painting under Dermod O'Brien and Maurice MacGonigal at the Royal Hibernian Academy schools from 1933 until 1936[104] but spent the first years of her career as a stage designer, working mainly at the Abbey Theatre. However, she turned seriously to painting in 1942. Her first exhibited works were shown at the Living Art in 1943 and she held her first one-woman exhibition, at the Dublin Painters' gallery, in March 1946. She had a similar show at the same venue in April 1948 and this was to be her last such exhibition until 1963, when she showed at the Dawson Gallery in Dublin. The Haverty Trust's acquisition of her *Woman Watching* from the 1949 Living Art exhibition was her first taste of official recognition. Here, her technique is rather crude, the colours are garish and the whole composition has an Expressionist feeling, which was no doubt derived from her theatre work. Until the late 1940s Anne Yeats painted mainly in watercolours and gouache, which she often combined with wax, as in *Woman Watching*, and which she used in an experimental manner—similar to that adopted by the Belfast painter William Conor—to give a general effect of texture rather than to model forms. But in about 1948 or 1949 she turned to oils, although her subsequent technique often resembles her use of wax, as is evident in *One Room*, of about 1954 (cata. no.85). Although she painted still lifes and landscapes, the subject-matter of her early work was mainly concerned with the human condition and in particular with the isolation of the individual and this, too, is evident in *One Room* and other works of that period.

Other artists singled out for mention by the critics in 1949 included Colin Middleton, beside whom, wrote the *Irish Times*, all of the French paintings 'pale into insignificance',[105] and it particularly liked his *Woman with Roses* and *William and Mary*; while in the *Dublin Magazine* Edward Sheehy called Middleton an 'emotional

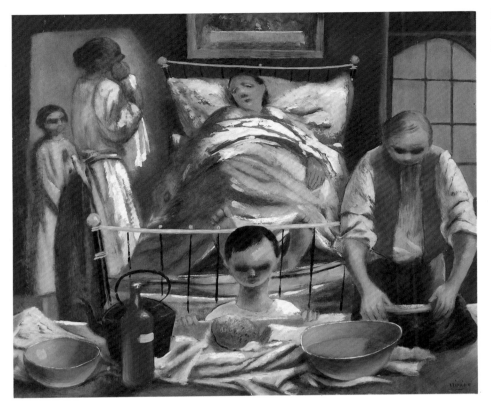

Dan O'Neill
Birth, 1952
Arts Council of Northern
Ireland

and exuberantly colourful humanist'. Thurloe Conolly was also admired for his use of colour, his *Composition* to the *Tatler & Sketch* being one of the best works in the exhibition.[106] Dan O'Neill was generally well liked, the press admiring in particular *The Blue Skirt*, 1949. Other outstanding works were Nevill Johnson's *Crucifixion*, 'his most impressive picture yet', thought Sheehy; George Campbell's *Shawled Women, Night*; Gerard Dillon's *Memory Pool* and works by Patrick Scott, Frances Kelly, Joan Jameson and Cecil Salkeld were all noted. Of the sculpture, Hilary Heron's *Danaan Woman* was to Sheehy[107] the outstanding work and Oisin Kelly's *Masters in Chapel* and *St. Genesius the Comedian* (Abbey Theatre) also drew comment.

In passing we should mention the more academic painters who exhibited at the Living Art for, as we have said, these exhibitions and those of the Royal Hibernian Academy were not mutually exclusive. Dermod O'Brien, the president of the Academy until his death in 1945, was a patron of the Living Art and also exhibited there; Margaret Clarke was a member of the original organizing committee; Jack B. Yeats, as we have seen, also exhibited regularly as did Seán Keating, Laurence Campbell and Beatrice Glenavy, all full members of the Academy. These people we shall discuss in detail in a later chapter. The sculptors, too, who exhibited at the Living Art—including Peter Brennan, Hilary Heron, Oisin Kelly, Melanie le Brocquy—we shall discuss later, although it is fair to say that sculpture never featured very prominently at these exhibitions.

* * *

The Irish Exhibition of Living Art was a much needed forum in the 1940s and annually it did a great deal to proselytize the public to the cause of Modernism. Yet many of those who exhibited there were not so much Modernists as merely non-academic painters with little chance to exhibit elsewhere. Too often there was little development in their work which, while it may have been avant-garde in the early or mid-1940s, had by the end of the decade become merely repetitive. But the early success of the Living Art exhibitions and the esteem in which they were held by the press and public was due, as Brian Fallon has said, to the fact that it was recognized that 'here at last was an "Irish school", not in the chauvinistic or Made in Ireland sense, but a new and vital generation with something of its own to say'.[108] It is a pity that the organizing committee did not follow le Brocquy's advice in 1949 and hand over, in some purposeful way, the running of the exhibitions to another body. For by continuing during the 1950s more or less without change, the later exhibitions lost much of the vitality and sparkle of those of the previous decade. But perhaps the greatest achievement of the Living Art exhibitions was in demonstrating irrefutably that, despite the tenor of the times, Irish art was not immune to the mainstream of European intellectual endeavour. By the early 1940s the era of nationalistic isolation, in the fine arts at least, had ended.

CHAPTER 7

OTHER DEVELOPMENTS
1940–1950

'We emerge a little dulled, bewildered, deflated.
There is a great leeway to make up . . . .'

(Seán O'Faoláin, *The Bell*, July 1945, p.288).

THE years of the 'Emergency' were a watershed in the political and social life of
Ireland. 'We emerge,' wrote Seán O'Faoláin in 1945, 'a little dulled, bewildered,
deflated. There is a great leeway to make up, many lessons to be learned, problems
to be solved which, in those six years of silence, we did not even allow ourselves to
state'.[1] Politically the country had survived the crisis, but socially and culturally the
xenophobic policies pursued by successive governments since independence had
produced a sense of fatigue which bordered on despair. To relieve this situation
economic growth was henceforth to be the new imperative. At the same time large
numbers of people began to move from the countryside to the towns and cities and
there was a rise in emigration. Thus for a time post-war Ireland was in a volatile state
although, surprisingly, the changes which emerged little altered the basic ideological
conceptions of the mass of the population. The declaration of a Republic, outside the
British Commonwealth, in 1949 bonded social attitudes which changed little until
the 1960s.

* * *

The early 1940s saw a considerable increase in the number of works of art sold at
exhibitions in Dublin. We have already noted this in connection with the Living Art
exhibitions and shall shortly observe the same phenomenon at the annual exhibitions
of the Royal Hibernian Academy. To some—perhaps even a considerable—extent
this increase in picture buying was a consequence of the absence of other consumer
goods brought about by the war. This increase in demand for works of art of all
kinds both stimulated and coincided with the development of a number of exhibition
venues.

In Dublin, the most important of these venues were the Victor Waddington
Galleries; the Contemporary Picture Galleries, which we have already discussed;
the Gorry Gallery, which in 1939 transferred from Upper Ormond Quay to
Molesworth Street, to a studio recently vacated by Seán O'Sullivan, and which

147

concentrated on picture restoration rather than exhibitions;[2] the Picture Hire Club; the Grafton Gallery, which opened in 1944[3] and which regularly exhibited the work of young artists; the Dawson Gallery; and the Country Shop in St. Stephen's Green, which showed paintings throughout the 1930s and 1940s. However the period also saw the demise of the Angus Gallery, in about 1936; of Daniel Egan's Gallery in about 1940, and of the Mills' Hall from about 1944.

The Picture Hire Club was an interesting, and possibly unique, experiment in Ireland. Run by Sean and Margaret Dorman, the Club first opened in March 1941 in rooms above Trueman's art shop at number 24 Molesworth Street, Dublin. Dermod O'Brien was its president, Hilton Edwards, Lady Glenavy, Maud Gonne MacBride and Lennox Robinson were vice-presidents, and Margaret Dorman was secretary. The idea behind the venture came from the artist Richard Kennedy and it was modelled on a similar club run by Harrods in London. As well as holding exhibitions and selling paintings the Club offered its members pictures which could be hired over an agreed period of time after which the hirer was free either to return them or to purchase them at their original price, less the hire fees already paid. However, despite being well patronized, the Club had a small financial turn over and so, after a short life, it closed in about April or May 1942.

But of greater duration than the Picture Hire Club itself was the monthly journal *Commentary*, edited by Sean Dorman, which was the voice of the Club. First published in November 1941, *Commentary* ran until 1946. As well as carrying articles on the fine arts—to several of which we have already alluded—it contained literary and theatrical criticism.[4] The artists associated with Picture Hire—Dorothy Blackham, Sylvia Cooke-Collis, Lilian Davidson, Brigid Ganly, Stephen Gilbert, Jack P. Hanlon, Grace Henry, Evie Hone, Mainie Jellett, Seán Keating, Richard Kennedy, Harry Kernoff, Maurice MacGonigal, Norah McGuinness, Kitty Wilmer O'Brien, Dermod O'Brien, Seán O'Sullivan, Basil Rakoczi, Dolly Robinson and Georgette Rondel— reflect its style and demonstrate its affinity with other progressive groups such as the Dublin Painters' Society, the White Stag Group and the early Living Art exhibitions.

In Belfast, too, despite war-time conditions, the period saw increased interest in art exhibitions and in picture-buying, with frequent shows at the CEMA gallery from the mid-1940s and occasional shows at Messrs F.G. Davis, John Magee, Mol, Pollock, Robinson & Cleaver and Rodman. From about 1936, however, few exhibitions were held in the Carlton, which had earlier been a popular venue. Elsewhere in Ireland exhibitions were held at local art societies and occasionally in department stores and hotels, while in Limerick the Goodwin Gallery opened in about 1944.

Of all of these venues, the most consequential for the future development of modern painting in Ireland were the Waddington and Dawson galleries in Dublin and the CEMA gallery in Belfast. Significantly, too, many people who at this time began to buy pictures continued to do so after the war, and the practice of holding regular one-man exhibitions usually of recent work, which later became the normal practice of commercial galleries, had its beginnings, in Ireland, at this time.

Paul Henry
*Old People
Watching a Dance*,
1910–11
Photograph Bryan Rutledge

The Victor Waddington Galleries

Victor Waddington was born in about 1906. His family were Scottish but came to Ireland in 1916.[5] Waddington began to deal in pictures in about 1921 and opened his first gallery, in Dublin, in 1925,[6] financing it from money which he had earned as a prize-fighter.[7] The gallery occupied two rooms on the first floor of number 28 South Anne Street and in later years expanded to other premises at number 19 Nassau Street (in about 1938) and at 8 South Ann Street (in about 1942).[8]

In opening his gallery Waddington's policy was to stimulate interest in the visual arts through exhibitions and to encourage patronage. In the late 1920s, with a show of works by Seán Keating, he initiated a regular pattern of one-man exhibitions, which usually lasted about ten days. Exhibitions of this kind, as we have noted, were then unusual in Dublin. In the late 1930s and 1940s he toured exhibitions of paintings by gallery artists to the provinces, to Galway, Limerick, Thurles and Cork and he also took pictures to New York[9] and London. In the 1940s works by foreign artists were brought to Dublin thus familiarizing the public with contemporary trends from abroad. The most important and influential of these latter exhibitions were the *School of London* and the *French Exhibition*, both held in the spring of 1947.

The *School of London* exhibition was of works by the most avant-garde British artists of the day and included, amongst others, John Armstrong, Edward Burra, Robert Colquhoun, Jacob Epstein, Barbara Hepworth, Ivon Hitchens, Robert MacBryde, Henry Moore, Ben Nicholson, John Piper, Ceri Richards, Matthew Smith, Stanley Spencer, Graham Sutherland and Oscar Kokoschka, who had become a British subject that year. The exhibition was well received by the press, the *Irish Times* feeling that the artists had more vitality than their Irish contemporaries, although it thought they lacked the 'beauty and profundity of a Maillol or a Modigliani, or the delicacy of a Chagall'. But, it concluded, 'the drive and force of this [group] . . . should shake the easy-going complacency of our artists, and they will ponder on such pictures as "Caernarvon Castle," by Piper, "Woman and Tric-Trac Game," by Robert MacBryde, the works of Ivon Hitchens, Kokoschka, John Armstrong and others, who lift art to a higher grade than we are accustomed to here'.[10]

The *French Exhibition* followed a month after the *School of London* show and included over seventy works by French artists, the best known being Bonnard, Braque, Lhote, Masson, Matisse, Picasso, Rouault and De Staël, although the majority of the works were by relatively obscure painters. It is now impossible to trace most of the works shown, but Lhote's *Fille de Cuisine* may have been his *Femme dans sa Cuisine*, which is now in the Ulster Museum. Reviewing the exhibition in the *Irish Times* Arthur Power was clearly disappointed with it overall, his main concern being that too many artists, in rejecting nature as their guide, had produced merely decorative pictures, often with a crude sense of colour. However, in concluding his review he considered the works to be 'gayer and more advanced' than those recently shown in the *School of London* exhibition and he congratulated Waddington on his enterprize in bringing such works to Dublin at a time when foreign travel was still difficult.[11]

Waddington also produced a number of influential publications under the imprint of his gallery. Of these, the most notable are *Twelve Irish Artists*, 1940, which had an introduction by Thomas Bodkin, and Thomas MacGreevy's *Jack B. Yeats: An Appreciation and an Interpretation*, 1945, which did much to popularize Yeats' work. The twelve artists included in the former title, and the name of the one work by each which was reproduced, were: Paul Henry, *Old People Watching a Dance*; J. Humbert Craig, *Coming from Mass* (Crawford Gallery, Cork); William Conor, *The Low-backed Car*; Seán Keating, *Half Flood*; Frank McKelvey, *On the Lagan*; Harry Kernoff, *Naylor's Cove, Bray*; Charles Lamb, *Hearing the News*; Grace Henry, *The Top of the Hill*; Maurice MacGonigal, *By the Sea*; Dermod O'Brien, *Scuffling the Mangolds*; Seán O'Sullivan, *William Butler Yeats* and Leo Whelan, *A Kerry Cobbler*. In his introduction Bodkin thought the book fairly represented the present state of development of what he called the 'modern school' of Irish painting. The cosmopolitan character of modern art as it had developed in other European countries was, he thought, 'superficial rather than essential'; whereas these works, by comparison, illustrated the character of Irish life and were clear evidence of the existence of a distinct Irish school of painting, although, somewhat reluctantly, he admitted his difficulty in describing 'with satisfactory words the subtle workings of the Irish national spirit in pictorial art'. However, he did reflect with insight that Irish painters are seldom or never rhetorical in concept, but prefer to be lyrical and nostalgic rather than didactic.[12]

The illustrations in *Twelve Irish Artists* do, as Bodkin said, give a good idea of the state of development of painting in Ireland at the time of publication—Mainie Jellett is a glaring omission—that is, on the eve of the arrival of the White Stag Group and the early Living Art exhibitions. Moreover, they are also typical of the type of art sponsored by Waddington until that time. In the light of the book, therefore, when we reflect on those artists who came to the fore during the 1940s we can see clearly the nature of the changes which occurred during the war-years.

In many respects the heyday of the Waddington Galleries coincided with the early Living Art exhibitions. From those years stems Victor Waddington's close association with Jack B. Yeats, who first exhibited with him in 1943.[13] Also in those years, Waddington initiated the practice of placing gallery artists under contract. By this means, in return for a regular income which left the artist free to paint full-time, Waddington had title to his complete output and guaranteed him regular one-man exhibitions while, at the same time, he established a clientele who were interested in the work of the artists whom he promoted. Thus, when Waddington closed his Dublin gallery in 1957 and moved to London[14] not only was it the end of an era in the development of Irish art, but a number of artists suddenly found themselves without a steady income or a venue to exhibit in and were compelled to reassess their activities. However, by that time Leo Smith had opened the Dawson Gallery and recruited many artists who had previously shown with Waddington.

Leo Smith, a Dubliner, was born in about 1910. In about 1926 he went to work for Victor Waddington and eventually became his gallery manager.[15] Later, in 1944, he opened his own gallery in Dawson Street, Dublin, handling the work of, amongst others, Gerard Dillon, Evie Hone, Louis le Brocquy, Norah McGuinness, Nano Reid and Mary Swanzy. From the time of Waddington's departure to England until the early 1960s the Dawson Gallery was, perhaps, the foremost commercial gallery in Dublin dealing in contemporary art. Leo Smith died in 1977.

* * *

While a number of Northern artists, as we have seen, largely dictated the development of painting in Ireland in the mid and late 1940s, most of these artists, like their colleagues of the Ulster Unit a decade earlier, also looked to England for inspiration. Thus, in many respects, they were more outward looking than their Southern contemporaries. The brief flourish of the Progressive Painters Group and the Northern Ireland branch of the Artists International Association are two examples of such outwardness.

The Progressive Painters Group was established in Belfast in the summer of 1944. Its members were George Campbell, Gerard Dillon, Dan O'Neill and John Turner and their aim was to stimulate public awareness of the Modern Movement in painting. However, they appear to have had little success and held only one exhibition, at number 46 Upper Queen's Street, Belfast, in August 1944.[16] In November of that year Campbell and Turner were drawn into the Northern Ireland branch of the Artists International Association and that may account for the demise of the Group.

The Artists International Association (AIA) was first formed in England in 1935 from the Artists International, which had been founded by the illustrator Clifford Rowe in 1933 to promote a Marxist view of art. The new Association was a response to Soviet policy that the Communist Party should form as many fronts as possible to resist Fascism and it aimed to recruit members from those who opposed the rise of

Kathleen Bridle
*Lough Erne from
Rossfad*, 1945
Ulster Museum

Fascism in Europe. Within the Association the emphasis was on the 'raising of consciousness'. Amongst others, Herbert Read was loosely associated with the AIA.[17]

The Northern Ireland branch of the Artists International Association was formed at a public meeting in Clarence Place Hall, Belfast, on 9 November 1944. Joan Loewenthal, who may have made contact with the AIA while a student at the Royal College of Art in London, was instrumental in forming the branch, of which Mrs. T.D. Day became honorary secretary. They took rooms at number fifty-four Royal Avenue, Belfast, where from time to time they held exhibitions. The only 'official' exhibition to be held, however, was *Belfast Commentary*, which—surprisingly for such a radical group—took place in association with CEMA at the Belfast Museum & Art Gallery during March and April 1945. On that occasion the following artists exhibited: Kathleen Bell, Doris V. Blair, Arthur Campbell, George Campbell, Tom Carr, R. Taylor Carson, K.E.A. Crozier, Louis N. Davis, Joan Day, Patricia Hacking, Denis O'D. Hanna, Marjorie Henry, Olive Henry, Gladys Maccabe, Max Maccabe, Aaron McAfee, James McIntyre, Marjorie McMullan, Colin Middleton, Trude Neu, Sidney Smith, John Turner and Maurice C. Wilks.[18] The press were little enamoured with the exhibition, the *Irish News*, for example, describing the group's purported internationalism as mere 'ballyhoo'.[19]

At heart, the majority in the Northern Ireland branch of the AIA were neither politically motivated nor interested in proselytizing on behalf of the Communist

C.E. Gribbon
Ischia
Photograph Bryan Rutledge

Party. Indeed, the branch broke up after a short time when Miss Loewenthal moved to England and, with her possible exeption, they seem to have had no purposeful contact with the AIA in London.[20]

The CEMA gallery, Belfast

The Council for the Encouragement of Music and the Arts (CEMA), Northern Ireland, was first established in February 1943 for an initial period of two years.[21] To begin with it was funded jointly by the Pilgrim Trust and the Northern Ireland government, but after the initial period it was funded entirely by the latter. Its job was to provide art exhibitions and dramatic and musical performances of the highest standard which could be enjoyed throughout the Province. From the outset, the Council began to assemble a collection of paintings and sculptures by living Irish artists from both north and south of the Border and, along with exhibitions from other countries which it arranged, it toured these to centres in Northern Ireland. The first of these exhibitions, held in late 1943 or early 1944, was entitled *Work of Living Irish Artists (Series I)*, and contained paintings by the following artists whose names serve to illustrate the kind of art which the newly established Council was keen to promote: Kathleen Bridle,

153

F.E. McWilliam. *Collage*, 1946. Ulster Museum

J.H. Craig, William Conor, Lady Glenavy, Paul Henry, Seán Keating, Frances Kelly, Harry Kernoff, Charles Lamb, Louis le Brocquy, John Luke, J. Langtry Lynas, Violet McAdoo, Maurice MacGonigal, Norah McGuinness, Colin Middleton, Seán O'Sullivan, Hilda Roberts and Jack B. Yeats. Such exhibitions served well in promoting contemporary art, but it soon became apparent that the Council required a permanent exhibition venue in Belfast. Thus the gallery at number 55A Donegall Place was acquired and opened in about February 1947. For the following decade it was to be a major influence in the development of painting in Ulster.

The decade beginning in the mid-1940s was dominated by George and Arthur Campbell, Gerard Dillon, Thomas McCreanor, James McIntyre and Leslie Zukor. The CEMA gallery was host to a variety of exhibitions. Apart from the work of local artists other displays included *Photographs of Irish Georgian Architecture*, put on in May 1947; Maurice MacGonigal, *Paintings*, November 1947; and *Modern Turkish Art*, *Soviet Architecture*, *Soviet Theatre*, *Modern Hungarian Paintings* and *Modern Dutch Art*, all seen in 1948 and 1949. Also, in May 1947, in association with the British Council, CEMA arranged an exhibition of Czechoslovakian art which was held in the Belfast Museum & Art Gallery and which subsequently travelled to the Municipal Gallery, Dublin, where it was shown under the auspices of the Friends of the National Collections of Ireland.[22]

In 1958 the Donegall Place gallery was closed and, after a break of two years, during which time exhibitions were sponsored by CEMA at the Piccolo Gallery in Wellington Street, the Council opened a new gallery nearby in Chichester Street. In 1962 CEMA was re-named the Arts Council of Northern Ireland. In terms of the development of art in Ulster, CEMA saw the beginning of regular sponsorship of the arts by the state and thus marked the commencement of a new era in patronage, a similar era being initiated, as we shall see later, south of the Border with the acceptance of Thomas Bodkin's *Report on the Arts in Ireland* in 1949.

* * *

Two Ulster artists who came to prominence in Britain in the 1940s and who should be mentioned here in passing are the Sculptor F.E. McWilliam and the painter William Scott.

F.E. McWilliam was born in Banbridge, Co. Down, in 1909. He studied art at the Slade School from 1928 until 1931, before settling permanently in London. He was associated with the British Surrealist Group in the late 1930s and served with the Royal Air Force during the Second World War. His post-war work retained a strong Surrealist edge, as can be seen in his *Collage*, 1946 (Ulster Museum), *Man and Wife*, 1948 (cata. no.86), and other works of the period.

William Scott was born in 1913 at Greenock in Scotland, but grew up in Enniskillen, Co. Fermanagh. There he studied art under Kathleen Bridle before going to the Belfast College of Art in 1928 and to the Royal Academy Schools, London, in 1931. He lived and worked in Italy and France during the late 1930s before serving with the Royal Engineers from 1942 until 1946. After the war he settled in England. His early work is figurative, with greatly simplified forms which in time became virtual symbols of the objects from which they were derived. Later, with an added emphasis on the flatness of the picture-plane, his work became abstract. William Scott died in 1989.

While McWilliam and Scott both retained close personal links with Ulster, their exile in London meant that neither of them influenced the development of the Modern Movement in Ireland as they might otherwise have done.

CHAPTER 8

THE ACADEMIC TRADITION

'The Academy is the perfect answer to the opponent of modern art . . . .
But for the general influence of the Impressionistic palette . . .
we might still be in the nineteenth century.'

(Edward Sheehy, *Dublin Magazine*, July–September 1946, p.42).

THROUGHOUT the period which we have been discussing the more academic painters
in Ireland continued to work apparently oblivious of the at times momentous changes
which were taking place around them. Yet, as we have seen, their conservatism was
also a yardstick with which we have been able to measure the progress of the Modern
Movement. The main body of academic painters in Ireland was, of course, the Royal
Hibernian Academy, but the Ulster Academy of Arts, the Watercolour Society of
Ireland and the Dublin Sketching Club also helped to sustain the academic tradition.

The Royal Hibernian Academy of Arts:
the institution and its fortunes

The Royal Hibernian Academy was first incorporated by Royal Charter in 1823.[1]
Although it has had a stormy history, it has served the arts in Ireland well, and,
despite its relative decline in the late nineteenth century, it occupies an important
place in the country's art affairs. As is well-known, Academy House in Abbey Street,
Dublin, its home since 1826, was destroyed by fire at Easter 1916 and from then
until 1939, when the house at number fifteen Ely Place—formerly the residence of
Oliver St. John Gogarty—was acquired the Academy had no permanent abode.[2]
During those years its business was carried on by the secretary, Richard Caulfield
Orpen, from his office in South Frederick Street.[3] But the acquisition of Ely Place,
while providing a home for the Academy, did not satisfy its exhibition needs and
plans were laid to erect a gallery in the garden to the rear. However the outbreak of
war in September 1939 brought restrictions which put paid to these plans and by the
late 1940s when the idea was revived the Academy had insufficient funds to erect a
gallery. In December 1947 it petitioned the Oireachtas for a grant of £50,000 towards
the cost of the proposed building, but the request was refused.[4] Throughout the period
the Academy's income was meagre. In 1941 the government withdrew its annual
subvention of £300, an amount first voted by parliament in 1831,[5] and thereafter
income was limited to fees and commissions from the annual exhibitions.[6]

Like its sister academies elsewhere, the Royal Hibernian Academy was driven by a sense of tradition. Its approach to all issues, especially the debate over Modernism, was determined by a perceived need to safeguard standards of artistic skill and craftsmanship. Its model in such matters was its illustrious son, Sir William Orpen (1878–1931). Orpen, a Dubliner, had studied art at the Metropolitan School before going to the Slade. Thereafter he settled in London and remained there for the rest of his life, becoming celebrated as a portraitist and painter of genre scenes. From 1902 until 1914 he taught part-time at the Metropolitan School and, besides these commitments, was frequently in Ireland working on portrait commissions. He was, too, one of the first painters at the time to address the issues of Irish identity and tradition in his work. Thus, as we shall see, he exerted a strong influence on a generation of students at the Metropolitan School and at the Academy, where he exhibited regularly, and of which he had become an academician in 1907. However, Orpen never returned to Ireland after the First World War.[7] Writing about the Academy as late as the 1950s, Terence de Vere White was able to comment that even then it had not recovered from the impact of Orpen, whom its members followed so slavishly that they became sterile and impoverished. The 'Oliver Twist' in the institution, he said, was Jack B. Yeats.[8] The Academy had no truck for the more cerebral or Expressionist art of Modernism which it regarded as synonymous with lower standards. But the main indictment against it is that it proffered no idea as to its future development if sterility was to be avoided.

* * *

The fortunes of the Academy during our period fall into three distinct phases, namely, the years before 1941, 1942–3 and 1944 till 1950. We shall examine each phase in turn.

As early as 1913, reviewing the Academy exhibition, Thomas Bodkin noted a 'dearth of all fresh talent' and a large amount of 'rubbish' which, he said, disgraced the exhibition.[9] This excess was due to the size of the exhibition, which comprised 558 works, and such large shows were characteristic of the Academy throughout our period, despite the fact that the critics often called for smaller, more judiciously selected displays. A decade later, in 1924, Bodkin thought the Academy was still in decline, although he exempted from his criticism portraits by Estella Solomons, Patrick Tuohy's *Stephen Joyce, Esq* and Leo Whelan's *Gipsy*.[10] By 1926 George Russell (AE), too, was clearly depressed by the state of the Academy, as he commented in the *Irish Statesman*:

> Nothing which has happened in Ireland or the world has perturbed this amazing body of men, not the burning of their own premises, not the world war, nor the example of the aesthetic revolutionaries of other countries, pointellists [sic], post-impressionists, cubists, futurists, and other rebels against tradition.

And he continued, lamenting the lack of imagination among the academicians, whom, he said, 'catch no fire from the literature or the movements of their time'. 'All I desire,' he concluded, 'is that . . . painting should be intellectually alive'.[11] In 1932 Bodkin returned to the fray. Writing in the Official Handbook of the Irish Free State, he thought that the Academy had 'fallen upon evil days', although with a little more

J.H. Craig
*The Crolly,
Co. Donegal*, 1930s
Photograph Bryan Rutledge

encouragement or a little more opposition, it would probably be stimulated into a period of vigorous achievement.[12] However, judging by press reviews of its subsequent exhibitions, the Academy merely continued as before.

The period, however, saw little constructive art criticism either in the press or elsewhere and such reviews as did appear usually took the form of descriptive reportage rather than critical analysis.[13] The general clamour from the mid-1920s was for a 'national' art. Reviewing the 1924 Academy exhibition, George Russell (AE) observed that there was still no national tradition in the visual arts in Ireland. The general impression of the exhibition, he said, was of 'art without national roots'.[14] But while Russell saw a national art as the distillation and expression of the national essence, most critics took it to refer solely to those themes and subjects which laid emphasis on life in the west. Reviewing the 1932 Academy the *Irish Times* correspondent, for example, wrote: 'Unfortunately, the show is less than ever representative of national art. If it were not for Mr. Seán Keating's pictures there would be hardly any specimens of the "national" group—the only group that really matters in Ireland at present'.[15] Keating's *Slán leat, a Athair/Goodbye, Father*, painted in 1935 and exhibited at the Academy the following year, is a good example of such so-called national art. The composition depicts a parish priest leaving Aran for the mainland, and writing of the picture years later, Keating expressed what for him had been the significance of the west and his views are typical of the romanticism of the period. In Aran, he wrote:

The contrast between the . . . decayed grandeur and second rate provincialism of Dublin; the riches, wastefulness, and utter conventionality of upperclass

London life repelled me. By contrast Aran, wrenching an existence from the sea, against a background of endless labour, danger, poverty, ignorance, patience and religious belief; charming gentle manners, the sonorous musical cadences of spoken Irish . . . all these things decided me that here was where I wished to live and work.[16]

In 1934, in an editorial entitled 'Art in Ireland', the *Irish Times* again appealed to the notion of a national art, but saw the Academy as being central to it. 'For all the short-lived mutinies and "rebel" *salons* which have excited Dublin's artistic circles at various times in the past few years,' it commented, 'the mutineers are generally anxious and eager to have their work hung on the Academy's walls'.[17]

Chief among the so-called mutineers was Ben O'Hickey, who in 1931 founded the Associated Irish Artists' Society—publicly dubbed the 'Rebel Artists'—a *salon des refusés* for those whose work had in recent years been rejected by the RHA. In 1934 the Society became the Academy of Irish Art, of which the founder-members were O'Hickey (honorary secretary and treasurer), Michael O'Beirne (president), William Brett (vice-president), Marion King, Mary Power and J. Fitzpatrick. Their declared aim was to promote the development of a 'national' school of art, with an emphasis on historical and sentimental works.[18] Of the other members of the new Academy, Seán Keating, a close friend of Ben O'Hickey, was the best known. The Academy of Irish Art ceased to exist in about 1939, having contributed little to the development of art in Ireland. Its very title was pretentious and it remained, in a pejorative sense, a *salon des refusés*.

Through its inertia, the RHA in these years invited criticism from all shades of opinion. The 1938 exhibition, for example, brought protests on the one hand because many of the Modernists had been 'thrown out',[19] while, on the other hand, the sculptor Albert Power declined to exhibit in protest against the Academy's lack of emphasis on a national art. Sympathising with Power's feelings, Dr. Ethna Byrne, reviewing the exhibition in the *Leader*, roundly declared:

Not long ago Mr. L.S. Gogan addressing the Academy of Christian Art . . . gave good advice to Irish artists in general; he recommended them to steep themselves in Gaelicism, to go back to traditions to the great Gaelic past for their inspiration . . . .

It is a pity that such excellent advice is not followed. Mediaeval Ireland produced works of art so beautiful that they are among the most precious treasures of subsequent civilization and models of the highest artistic ability. Modern Ireland can do the same—if she will consent to *be* Irish, if her artists will work for an *Irish* art.[20]

The Academy of Christian Art, to which Dr. Byrne referred, is another example of the chauvinism of the period. Founded in 1929 on the initiative of George Noble, Count Plunkett, sometime director of the National Museum of Ireland and Minister of Fine Arts in the first Dail, its stated purpose was 'to give a free voice to a Catholic community . . . to deal with the intellectual commonplaces of Catholic life, while recognizing Theology in its relations with the ordinary incidents of civilization'. The Academy embraced art as 'an aid to spiritual knowledge and spiritual thought' and, it argued, 'Christian Art is a faint reflection of God's Beauty'.[21] For reasons of doctrine and ritual only Roman Catholics were eligible for membership. Of the better known artists, George Collie, Seán Keating, Maurice MacGonigal and Albert Power were full members and Margaret Clarke was an associate member. The Academy of Christian Art ceased to exist in about 1950 or 1951.

Besides these developments, in the early 1940s criticism of the RHA grew in severity especially, as we have seen, with the younger painters recently returned to Ireland from abroad. Also, other activities at the time, such as the exhibitions of the White Stag Group, undermined its authority to arbitrate on artistic matters. The events of 1942–3, the second of our three phases in the Academy's fortunes, which led to the inauguration of the Living Art exhibitions, mark the lowest ebb in its affairs since the late nineteenth century. Yet, sadly, by refusing to take *any* cognizance of changing attitudes towards art, the Academy brought many of its difficulties upon itself.

With the advent of the Living Art exhibitions, which mark the beginning of the third phase of its development in our period, the Academy settled again for a cosy complacency. Reviewing the 1945 exhibition, Stephen Rynne lamented the dominance of pictures relating to the west of Ireland. Led by Charles Lamb, he said, the Academy was 'threatened by peasant habitations' which seemed to oust all others, and he pleaded with the authors of such works to 'eschew Connemara, cancel reservations in Aran and have a think about the whole matter'.[22] Rynne was also depressed by the following exhibition, which he thought was almost devoid of pictures of distinction. The Academy, in his opinion, had become 'quite unimportant from every point of view'.[23] Discussing that same exhibition Edward Sheehy noted:

The Academy is the perfect answer to the opponent of modern art. There, in most of the exhibits, you have respect for technique, for natural appearances, appreciation of rural beauty, an unobtrusive morality and a careful avoidance of the more unpleasant aspects of life. But what is said that has not been better said before. What a concentration of sweet, cloying and soporific dullness in most of this garniture and household stuff. But for the general influence of the Impressionistic palette, and a freerer application of paint, we might still be in the nineteenth century.[24]

Despite more favourable reviews in 1947 Sheehy, alas, felt able to write at the end of the decade that the Academy exhibition suggested 'a catastrophic decline in the art of painting in Ireland'.[25]

For the Academy these years were the end of an era and it never regained its pre-eminence of earlier days. The growing fashion in the period for one-man shows in the private and commercial galleries was a trend, too, which may have adversely affected it, as Stephen Rynne suggested in 1945:

This year's Academy is not only shabby but bad .... Why all these secondary paintings from men who we know are doing better work? I fancy that the reason lies in this craze for private and one-man shows. The artists feel that they do better—sell better, get more publicity—in the small and fashionable galleries .... The result is that the Academy gets a specimen of the artist's work, not the chief d'œuvre which is its due tribute.[26]

In effect, during the late 1940s the Academy was by-passed by events. For too long it had held firmly to anachronistic principles which led at length to sterility.[27]

The academicians and their work

Despite the inertia of the Royal Hibernian Academy as an institution, individually its members produced much excellent work. The dominant categories of works exhibited each year in our period were portraits and landscapes but a small number of genre or 'subject' pictures were also produced. Surprisingly, still life works were comparatively few in number as were overtly religious subjects.

Jack B. Yeats was the outstanding, if the least typical, academician of the time. But, in the light of his later celebrity, it is easy to forget that even in the late 1930s and early 1940s he was treated by the critics and others with a degree of caution. To the *Irish Times* in 1938 he was a mystery, but always exciting; and Stephen Rynne that same year had reservations about him, referring to several of his paintings as 'messy smears'. Rynne, however, thought his *In Memory of Boucicault and Bianconi*, 1937, 'a gorgeous . . . omnibus, full of stories and romances, exploits, and eerie happenings . . . [with] ten years unravelling in it for the lucky purchaser'.[28] By the mid-1940s, however, Yeats was indisputably the doyen of Irish artists. He had recorded the dramatic intensity of his time and, in compositions such as *By Streedagh Strand* and *Tinkers' Encampment: The Blood of Abel* (cata. no.90), both painted in 1940—

162

Dermod O'Brien
Lennox Robinson,
1918
Ulster Museum

not to mention others like *On Through the Silent Lands*, 1951 (Ulster Museum), still to come—set down images redolent of the universality of human experience. Yet although Yeats exhibited regularly at the Academy and elsewhere, his idiosyncratic style ensured that his work was less influential on his contemporaries than might otherwise have been the case with an artist of his stature.

Dermod O'Brien (1865–1945) became president of the Academy in 1910 in succession to the architect Sir Thomas Drew. He remained in office until his death, the longest presidency in the history of the institution. Noting his election, the *Studio* commented that he was 'full of zeal on behalf of all progressive movements' and it ventured that under him the Academy ought to gain in prestige and efficiency. The keynote of his work, it continued, was 'sincerity' and it admired his feeling for form and balance and his manner of painting the Irish landscape, free from the sentimentality and rhetoric so dear to some painters.[29]

The son of a landowner in Co. Limerick, O'Brien was brought up in a strict Anglo-

Irish atmosphere. His father intended him for the Foreign Office or the civil service, but O'Brien was intent on becoming an artist. Educated at Cambridge, he then studied painting in Antwerp under Charles Verlat[30] from 1887 until 1891. There he acquired a solid academic style which was little tinged by the French tradition which he later went to the Académie Julian in Paris. In 1894 he was briefly at the Slade School, London, a spell which no doubt reinforced his academic bent. O'Brien settled in Dublin in 1901, at a time when the Irish Literary Renaissance was at its height.[31]

Dermod O'Brien's early compositions are formal in manner as, for example, in *The Jewel*, of 1903 (National Gallery of Ireland), and have about them a feeling of reserve which remained a characteristic of his whole *œuvre*. Even his early landscapes such as *Sheep-shearing* (Lane Gallery) and *The Sand Pit*, of about 1908, evoke this feeling. For almost three decades after he settled in Dublin—and particularly after he became president of the Academy—O'Brien, along with Sarah Purser, was one of the leading portrait painters in the city. His early portraits, such as that of *Alderman W.F. Cotton, MP*, c.1905–15 (Lane Gallery), reveal a high degree of craftsmanship, notably in the modelling of the features and in his rendering of the different textures of the sitter's clothing. Yet the picture as a whole is stiff and lacks vitality which, sadly, was too often the case with O'Brien's work. Even in later studies, such as that of *E. Magawley Banon*, painted in 1934 (National Gallery of Ireland), and his group portrait of the *Executive of the Royal Dublin Society*, 1940 (cata. no.92), we see these deficiencies, the latter work lacking cohesion amongst the members of the committee who are treated merely as individuals. But in less formal works O'Brien could be more at ease, as his study of Barry Fitzgerald as the King in Lady Gregory's play *The Golden Apple* (Abbey Theatre) and his portrait of his friend and biographer Lennox Robinson, 1918 (Ulster Museum) show.

From the mid-1920s, however, O'Brien concentrated more on landscape painting, the genre for which he is best remembered. These late landscapes, which are usually small in size, are much less academic in execution than his portraits and often have an ease and fluidity which reflect his innate love of pastoral countryside. *The Deer Park, Powerscourt*, of 1925 (National Gallery of Ireland), *The Estuary of the Shannon*, 1935 (cata. no.91), and *Golden Falls, Ballymore Eustace, Co. Wicklow*, 1936, are typical of such works in which he draws attention to both the physical structure of the landscape and the fertility of the land, the whole being rendered in loose, semi-Impressionist brushwork and with less concern for detail than in his early landscapes. In the 1920s and 1930s he paid a number of visits to the south of France and painted in the area around Cassis where the warm Mediterranean light and the atmosphere precisely suited his mood. In these works, perhaps more than in any others, as his biographer noted, he reached an easy confidence in himself.[32]

O'Brien was one of the best still life painters of his generation, and in compositions such as the floral *Arrangement* (Crawford Gallery, Cork), his precise technique was perfectly suited to rendering the delicacy of flowers and distinguishing between textures of plant, pot and surface.

Viewing O'Brien's work as a whole, however, one feels he never realized his full potential as a painter. His awareness of background and tradition seems at times to have held him captive for he was self-conscious in his own work and felt a civic duty for the arts in the community. Regarding the Royal Hibernian Academy, one is tempted to suggest that he remained president longer than was his due; yet had he resigned at any time after the mid-1920s the institution would almost certainly have fallen into the hands of those who called for a narrow-minded national art and would thus have atrophied even more quickly than it did. Yet it is surprising that O'Brien, who was liberally minded and not opposed to innovation, despite his own work, did not steer the institution towards a more sympathetic accomodation with Modernism.

* * *

Portraits were a constant feature of the Academy's exhibitions and this differentiates them from all other shows of the period. Apart from Dermod O'Brien, the other

Sir Gerald Kelly. *Goyesca III*, c.1930s.

Hugh Lane Municipal Gallery of Modern Art

outstanding portraitists year after year were Sir William Orpen (until 1917 when he last exhibited), Sir John Lavery and Sir Gerald Kelly, but as they lived in England their influence in Ireland was less than it might otherwise have been. Of the resident artists, Leo Whelan and Seán O'Sullivan increasingly dominated the scene from the mid-1920s and James Sleator, O'Brien's successor as president of the Academy in 1945, came to the fore in the 1940s after his return from London.

Born in 1856, Lavery was one of the older generation of painters exhibiting in our period. His portrait of *Cardinal Logue* (cata. no.93), painted in 1920 and exhibited at the Academy in 1921, is a fine example of his work at the time. A penetrating study in character, it has a breadth of concept, a spontaneity of execution and freedom from unnecessary detail which distinguish Lavery from his home-bound Irish contemporaries. In the early 1920s he painted many of the most eminent Irish men of the time, including community and church leaders, such as Cardinal Logue and Charles Frederick D'Arcy, and politicians from both parts of the country, including Michael Collins—*Love of Ireland*—William T. Cosgrave, Éamon de Valera, Arthur Griffith and Kevin O'Higgins (all Lane Gallery), and Lord Carson, Viscount Craigavon and Joseph Devlin (all Ulster Museum). In these years he also painted a number of subject pictures which have a distinct Irish interest, notably the *Ratification of the Irish Treaty in the English House of Lords*, 1921 (National Gallery of Ireland), *Blessing the Colours*, 1923 (Lane Gallery), and the *Dublin Horse Show*, 1928.

Gerald Festus Kelly (1879–1972), a Londoner, studied art for a time in Paris before settling back in London, where he had a distinguished career. Early in the century he had been friendly with Sir Hugh Lane who invited him to exhibit in his exhibition of Irish paintings at the Guildhall, London, in 1904 so he may have had Irish connections. He exhibited regularly at the RHA from 1905, was elected an associate member in 1908 and an academician in 1914. In 1920 he married an Irish woman, Jane Ryan, and thus cemented his association with Ireland. Kelly excelled as a portraitist and is best remembered for his numerous pictures of his wife, which he titled simply, 'Jane I', 'Jane II', 'Jane III' and so on. In all he painted over fifty portraits of her, many of which were exhibited at the RHA. His work is characterized by a precise academic technique with a clear emphasis on draughtsmanship and line, the whole invariably having an air of accomplishment and dignity.

Of portraitists working in Dublin, Leo Whelan (1892–1956) was arguably the most important of his generation. 'The brilliance of Leo Whelan we have come to take as a matter of course', the *Irish Times* felt able to comment in 1942,[33] a remark which speaks for his stature. Whelan trained under Orpen at the Metropolitan School. In 1916 he won the Royal Dublin Society's Taylor Art Scholarship for his painting *The Doctor's Visit* (National Gallery of Ireland) and eight years later, in 1924, was elected an academician of the RHA, filling the vacancy created by the death of John Butler Yeats. In 1926 he was awarded a medal at the Tailteann Games for his distinguished portrait of Dr. Claude Louis Purser, Vice-Provost of Trinity College.

The overbearing force of Orpen's influence on Whelan can be seen in his early portrait of an unknown sitter entitled *The Gipsy*, 1923. Exhibited at the RHA the following year, it firmly established his reputation. Here, the pose and the dress of the figure clearly resemble several of Orpen's portraits of Beatrice Elvery (later Glenavy), such as *Brigit—A Picture of Miss Elvery*, 1909, which was almost certainly painted at the Metropolitan School during the time Whelan was a student there. The even distribution of light and relatively smooth film of paint in *The Gipsy*—Whelan

always employed a direct technique with little underpainting—remained characteristics of his portraiture throughout his career, although the landscape setting in which the figure here is placed was rarely repeated in his major portraits.

Whelan's portraits were conventional and unimaginative in concept, but at his best were executed with great dexterity and technical accomplishment and he could penetrate outward appearances to capture character and personality. Apart form Orpen, he greatly admired the seventeenth century Spanish painter, Velázquez, and his own slightly earlier contemporary, John Singer Sargent.[34] Usually adopting a three-quarters view of his subject, Whelan placed emphasis on the sitter's face and hands and played down other aspects such as the clothing and the surroundings. One can see these traits in works from different stages of his career, such as his studies of *Louis Claude Purser*, 1926—which the sitter described as 'absurdly like me'[35]—and *E.H. Alton*, c.1943, both of which belong to Trinity College. They are also evident in what is undoubtedly one of Whelan's best works, and arguably the finest portrait painted in Ireland during our period, namely his *Lord Dunraven*, 1933 (cata. no.94),

167

which he exhibited at the RHA in 1934 and at the Royal Academy, London, in 1936. Here the modelling of the head and hands is masterly, the figure is firmly seated in his chair and Whelan has concisely, but with great authority, portrayed his personality and character. During the 1940s Whelan retained this approach to composition but increasingly placed his sitters in context so as to indicate occupation and lifestyle— he had occasionally done so earlier, as in his portrait of the *Countess of Dunraven*, 1934. His 1946 portrait of the *Hon. William Evelyn Wylie, K.C.*, a prominent member of the Royal Dublin Society, for example, depicts the sitter seated at his desk surrounded by the trappings of office, and his study of *Gladys MacCabe*, also painted in 1946, has the sitter in her own home, the somewhat spartan arrangement of the furnishings echoing her taste.

Seán O'Sullivan (1906–64) was a contemporary of Leo Whelan and, like him, studied at the Metropolitan School, although he later spent some time in London and, from 1927, in Paris at La Grande Chaumière and Colarossi's.[36] In about 1928 he returned to Dublin, taking a studio at number 20 Molesworth Street. In September 1939 he moved to number 6 St. Stephen's Green and there remained for the rest of his career.

O'Sullivan's early career was precocious. In his twenties he became well-known for his portrait drawings, such as those of *F.R. Higgins* of the Abbey Theatre, 1926, *Jack B. Yeats*, 1929, and *Éamon de Valera*, 1931,[37] all of which demonstrate his ability to establish a good likeness and his dexterity as a draughtsman. He continued to execute similar studies with great bravura throughout his career, but his technique changed little over the years and, sadly, his later drawings became repetitive; as Anne Crookshank noted, they were often excellent individually, but *en masse* tend to form a monotonous row of images.[38] Some of O'Sullivan's best portraits in oils, too, were done when he was in his twenties and early thirties. His study of *W.B. Yeats*, 1934 (cata. no.95), painted when he was twenty-eight, is a good example. Here, the great poet is depicted deep in thought, in a pose which appears natural and not contrived. The painting is executed with bold brushwork and a judicious use of colour which complements the mood of the sitter. The composition is roughly triangular—a common device with O'Sullivan—and the emptiness of the background also serves to heighten the feeling of meditation. *President Douglas Hyde*, 1936 (Áras An Uachtaráin), is another excellent portrait, and by showing the sitter in profile (a bold but unusual concept for an official portrait) O'Sullivan has ably captured Hyde's personality. As before, the brushwork has vitality and the range of colours is discreet.

In the 1940s O'Sullivan's best portraits were those of *F.R. Higgins*, c.1940 (Abbey Theatre), *Eoin MacNeill*, 1941 (University College, Dublin), *An Taoiseach, Eamon de Valera*, of about 1943 (cata. no.96), and the actor *F.J. McCormick*, 1949 (Abbey Theatre)—he also did a superbly penetrating character study of McCormick in pencil in 1942 (National Gallery of Ireland). The earliest of these works is a profile view of a seated figure and, unusual for a portrait, the canvas is of greater width than height. The second picture is a three-quarters view; painted with flair, good use has been made of the bright colours of the sitter's academic robes and the play of shapes created by the books on shelves behind him. That of An Taoiseach, a front view, depicts the sitter as a man of action and purpose. By contrast, F.J. McCormick is shown surrounded by personalities in the theatrical world in such a way that the composition almost suggests a feeling of animation. By constantly adopting a variety of poses, as in these works, O'Sullivan brought vitality to his work, in contrast to Leo Whelan who, as we have seen, was more conservative.

Seán O'Sullivan once said that a portrait was a statement of what the artist thought of his sitter. In a successful portrait, he continued, the sitter should be regarded 'as dispassionately as a piece of still life'.[39] His *Mother Mary Martin*, painted in 1954 (Drogheda Hospital, Convent), to some extent illustrates this thesis and shows, too, that at his best O'Sullivan maintained a high standard of execution and of characterization. Unfortunately, however, the strain of constant commissions, especially the never ending number of pencil studies which he undertook, began to tell on him and from the early 1950s or so his work became increasingly stereotyped.

On the death of Dermod O'Brien, in October 1945, James Sleator (1885–1950) became president of the Academy,[40] and remained in office until his own death some four years later. It was Sleator's job in those bleak days to bring stability and a renewed sense of purpose to the Academy, although in truth the institution was impotent in a changing world. A quiet, retiring man, Sleator was well suited, both through his work and temperament, for this task.[41] Trained at the Metropolitan School under Orpen, for whom he later worked on a number of occasions as a studio assistant,

169

Sleator never deviated from the academic manner. Between 1915 and the early 1920s he taught for a time at the Metropolitan School, where his pupils included Cecil Salkeld; during the mid-1920s he was for a time in Florence and for most of the thirties he pursued his career in London. In 1941, however, with the London Blitz at its height, he settled in Dublin and soon became well-known as a portraitist.

Alas, as with Whelan and others, Sleator was overwhelmed by the force of Orpen's example and personality and never developed his full potential as an artist. Orpen's influence is evident in the concept and execution of his early *Self-portrait*, painted in about 1914–15 and now in the National Gallery of Ireland, a work which brought him his first success when exhibited at the Academy in 1915.[42] His portrait of *Mrs. MacNamara* (Armagh County Museum), which he exhibited at the RHA in 1918, is also Orpenesque, bearing a close resemblance to the latter's *Mrs. St. George*, of about 1906. Here Sleator's restrained use of colour and differentiation between the textures of the sitter's clothes is a virtuoso performance and, as with the Orpen picture, the painting evokes the social climate of the times. A relatively youthful work, it shows the precocious maturity of his technical ability and represents a peak beyond which he never progressed. His study of the author *Forrest Reid*, 1924 (Ulster Museum), is an important work but its execution in a loose, almost Impressionist, manner is unusual for him. Although he was abroad for most of the 1920s and 1930s, Sleator continued to exhibit regularly at the Academy, yet the most fruitful period of his career came after 1941 when he settled in Dublin. In these years the list of his sitters reads like a 'Who's Who' of Irish society and is indicative of his social and artistic standing. *The Hon. Mr. Justice Thompson, KC*, 1942, exhibited at the Academy in 1942, illustrates his technical competence and ability to portray personality, although it otherwise lacks originality. On the other hand, his study of *Lennox Robinson* (Abbey Theatre), painted at about the same time, displays great character and a bold use of colour and his *Jack B. Yeats*, 1943 (Crawford Gallery, Cork), also demonstrates his skill at characterization. Of his later portraits, those of *Rutherford Mayne*, done in about 1944 (Abbey Theatre), *Ninian McIntyre Falkiner*, 1948 (Rotunda Hospital, Dublin), and *Dr. Alex Spain*, 1948 (National Maternity Hospital, Dublin), are amongst the best. They combine vigorous brushwork and a good colour sense to produce lively images. The even spread of light common in all these works was characteristic of Sleator and that, perhaps, he might have used to more striking effect.

Seán Keating (1889–1977) was another prominent portraitist. A native of Limerick, he too was a pupil of Orpen—whom he idolized—and, like Sleator, worked for a time in Orpen's studio. He was, moreover, Sleator's successor as president of the Academy. As we have seen, Keating was eager to establish a 'national' art in Ireland, his feelings for this being stimulated by a visit to the Aran Islands in about 1913 or 1914. There he was so taken by the way of life of the islanders that he returned frequently for many years to come and, indeed, the rugged character of the people and the landscape there he later portrayed as an idealized and heroic Gaelic Ireland. Keating held his first one-man exhibition in Dublin in 1921. The following year he was represented in the Irish exhibition at the Galeries Barbazanges, Paris, and in 1927 showed in the exhibition of British Art at Brussels, from which his painting *The Mountainy Men* was purchased by the Belgian government. During the 1920s he was a frequent exhibitor at the Royal Academy in London and in 1929 held his first one-man exhibition in the United States, at the Helen Hackett Gallery, New York. Back in Dublin, during these years he exhibited regularly at the Waddington Galleries.

Between 1926 and 1929 Keating was often in Co. Limerick painting scenes for the Electricity Supply Board of the Shannon hydro-electric scheme then under way, his theme being 'The Dawn of a New Ireland'.[43] In 1939 he won first prize in an international competition organized by the IBM Corporation in New York for his painting, *The Race of the Gael* (IBM, New York), in which he eulogized the rugged character of the gael. His work always had a strong element of patriotism, as expressed in his *Men of the West*, of 1916 (cata. no.97), and *Men of the South*, 1922 (Crawford Gallery, Cork), and he celebrated the traditional virtues of Irish life in compositions such as *An Aran Fisherman and his Wife*, painted in the 1920s (Crawford Gallery, Cork), *Half Flood*, probably of the 1930s, and other similar works.

Keating was never at his best as a portrait painter; rather he needed a narrative to sustain him. Many of his most successful subject pictures such as *Men of the West*, *Men of the South* or *The Race of the Gael* contain portraits of individuals whom he knew,[44] but their strength, nevertheless, derives from the narrative. His portraits proper are often stiff and have a formality which betrays his lack of ease with them. For example, in his *Homage to Sir Hugh Lane*, c.1920 (Lane Gallery), the various figures remain as individuals and do not cohere as a group within the composition. Amongst his most successful portraits, however, are those of his friend Ben O'Hickey, painted in about 1932 and known as *The Tipperary Hurler*[45] (Lane Gallery), *The Most Rev. Dr. O'Dwyer, Bishop of Limerick*, painted in about 1943 (Limerick Art Gallery), *The Most Rev. Dr. O'Neill, Bishop of Limerick*, of about 1947 (Limerick), and *The Limerick Girl*, probably painted in the late 1930s or early 1940s. In the robust figure of *The Tipperary Hurler* we have another example of Keating's adulation of 'the gaelic race', whereas in his portrait of Dr. O'Dwyer he is much less at ease and appears too deferential

Sean Keating painting at Poulaphouca, Co. Limerick, 1920s.   Photograph courtesy E.S.B.   171

Seán Keating
*Most Rev.
Dr. O'Neill, Bishop
of Limerick*, c.1947
Photograph Bryan Rutledge

before his sitter, the work having the air of a business-like commission. However, his painting of Dr. O'Neill, no doubt also a commission, is more successful and in it he has captured the strong character and intellect of the sitter.[46] In these works Keating's technique was direct, with very little underpainting, but while his colour and brushwork have about them a suggestion of economy they do not express form as concisely as one would expect from an artist of his stature and they lack the ease, say, of Leo Whelan. Perhaps this discomfort was due to the constraints of a formal commission, for in *The Limerick Girl*, maybe the nearest Keating ever came to a casual—almost wistful—portrait, we have a delightfully poetic figure perfectly relaxed in mood as is the artist in execution. Perhaps, too, Keating was at times over conscious of his considerable technical ability, especially as a draughtsman, for as the *Irish Statesman* perceptively commented with regard to his *Homage to Sir Hugh Lane*, which he exhibited at the Academy in 1920, he was 'in love with brilliance and cleverness, not with nature'. And it continued: 'He puts people in studios, and hangs up sheets beside them, and paints academic landscapes behind them. It is all false and dead and means nothing'.[47] In short, too often what is missing is the narrative element.

Of the many other portrait painters who exhibited at the Academy George Collie, Margaret Clarke and Christopher Campbell regularly produced notable work. Collie, especially, earned a high reputation for his commissioned portraits.

George Collie (1904–75), was born in Carrickmacross, Co. Monaghan. He studied at the Royal Hibernian Academy school and under Tuohy, Sleator and Keating at the Metropolitan School. He won the Taylor Art Scholarship in 1927 and again in 1929 and this enabled him to continue his studies at the Royal College of Art in

London and, later, in Paris at the Académie de la Grande Chaumière and Colarossi's. After his return to Dublin he taught for a time at the Metropolitan School before opening his own school in the early 1940s and he ran it for over thirty years.

George Collie
First Three Trustees, 1935–6
Hugh Lane Municipal Gallery of Modern Art

Despite his time in Paris, Collie worked in a strict academic manner. Over the years he painted many civic dignitaries, including *George Noble, Count Plunkett*, 1933–4, and *The First Three Trustees of the Haverty Bequest* (Lane Gallery), as well as a number of churchmen, of whom his studies of *The Most Rev. Dr. Farren, Bishop of Derry*, 1941–2, and *The Most Rev. Dr. Lyons, Bishop of Kilmore, Cavan*, 1946, are the most outstanding from our period. Later, in the 1950s and 1960s, he succeeded Leo Whelan as the leading portrait painter in Dublin. None of his portraits, however, has the firmness of style or assurance of Leo Whelan or Seán O'Sullivan.

Collie's teacher, Patrick Tuohy (1894–1930), should be mentioned here. He also was a pupil of Orpen at the Metropolitan School, and later taught there for a short time, during which he had a strong influence on a number of his contemporaries. In the 1920s, however, he spent long periods in Paris, where he knew and painted James Joyce, and in 1927 went to the United States and, with the exception of one brief visit to Ireland, remained there for the rest of his life. Thus he had less influence in Ireland than would otherwise have been the case. Tuohy is chiefly remembered for his portraits, such as that of Joyce's father, *John Stanislaus Joyce*, 1923–4 (cata. no.98), and figure studies, of which his *Mayo Peasant Boy*, painted in 1914 and *The Little Seamstress*, of 1914–15 (both Lane Gallery), are good examples.[48]

173

Margaret Clarke (1888–1961) acquired a reputation as a portraitist early in her career. Her study of her infant son, the future artist, *David Clarke*, painted in about 1920, shows her at her best and puts her work clearly in the tradition of Walter Osborne and William Orpen. Here she has rendered beautifully the expression of wonderment on the child's face as he sits in the strong sunshine in a garden. Her brushwork is unobtrusive and conveys the richness of texture, notably in the child's dress. In contrast to the serenity of this work, her portrait of *Lennox Robinson*, c.1920–7 (Crawford Gallery, Cork), is mildly Expressionist in appearance, a result of the contrast between the academic treatment of the face, the starkness of the setting and the abrasive effect of the colours—a strikingly red shirt, black tie and jacket with ascetic blue walls behind. Other portraits of these years, such as that of her daughter, *Ann Clarke*, c.1922 (National Gallery of Ireland), are more in the Orpen tradition, although *Ann with a Cat*, of about 1930, is again more Expressionist. Her *Archbishop McQuaid*, 1941–2 (Archbishop's House, Dublin), on the other hand, is strictly academic in both concept and execution. This mild variance between the academic and the avant-garde in Margaret Clarke—one should recall that she was a member both of the Dublin Painters' Society and the organizing committee of the Living Art exhibitions—was a consequence of a tug between her training under Orpen and her own intuitive responses and, as her son remarked,[49] she was often uneasy about it.

Although Christopher Campbell (1908–72) was not a member of the Academy, he exhibited there regularly and deserves to be better known than he is. Born in December 1908, he lived all his life in Dublin. Together with his brother, the sculptor Laurence Campbell, he attended the Metropolitan School of Art, studying under Patrick Tuohy and George Atkinson. Campbell was at his best as a portrait painter, although he also painted figure compositions, still lifes and a number of religious subjects. He was a shy, retiring man and apart from the annual Academy exhibitions he exhibited rarely if at all. Thus his work is relatively unknown.

Campbell's portraits exude energy and vitality and in concept and execution are quite distinct from those of any of his Irish contemporaries. That of his brother, Laurence, for example, the work possibly exhibited at the Royal Hibernian Academy in 1937 as *Laurence of Sculpture*, depicts the sculptor standing before one of his own relief panels, his black smock and beret contrasting boldly with the cream of the panel, the flesh tints of the face and hands the only warm tones in the picture. The brushwork is bold and the impasto of the paint has been used to good effect to simulate patterning on the sculptor's smock. By the 1940s, however, Campbell's style had become more precise and his brushwork less obtrusive, although his use of colour and sense of pose were still distinctive. His study of *Desmond Finlay Green, Esq.*, painted in about 1947, illustrates these developments which are even more apparent in his *Self-portrait* of 1950 (cata. no.99), a strikingly candid work. His use of colour in the latter picture—a rust hued jacket contrasted strongly with an ultramarine blue shirt and greens and umbers in the background—is most daring and accomplished and the painting of the face consists of soft modulations of flesh tints interspersed with juxtaposed greens and reds in a manner unequalled by any of his contemporaries.

Two Northern painters, William Conor and Frank McKelvey, who are better remembered for their genre scenes and landscapes also exhibited portraits from time to time. William Conor (1881–1968) studied art in Belfast before becoming an apprentice lithographer. From his lithographic work he developed a technique of handling materials which dominated his whole *œuvre*. In about 1912 he paid a brief

visit to Paris, where he met André Lhote and in whose studio he worked for a time, but he was little influenced by what he saw there. In the early 1920s he moved to London and was in touch with his fellow-Ulstermen E.M.O'R. Dickey and Sir John Lavery, and they introduced him to Augustus John and others of his circle. In 1926–7 he visited New York but, as with Paris and London, the experience had little influence on him. From the late 1920s, when he settled permanently in Belfast, his style and subject-matter changed little.[50]

Conor was not at his best as a portraitist. Too often his handling of paint, which is characrerised at times by an almost animated frenzy, distracts our attention from the subject and compels us to read the work in purely *malerisch* terms. This is evident, for example, in his portrait of *R.V. Williams (Richard Rowley)*, painted in 1920 (Ulster Museum). His study of his mother (Ulster Museum), which dates from about 1919, and that of *Dr. Douglas Hyde* (cata. no.101), commissioned in 1938, however, are more successful, and in these he has captured the personality and expression of the sitters with much feeling. In the *Douglas Hyde* picture the strong colours of the

175

academic robe in which the sitter is attired bring vitality to the composition, and the paint surface is less agitated than before.

Frank McKelvey (1895–1974) was highly regarded in the North of Ireland for his portraits and he painted many eminent people there. Born in Belfast, McKelvey studied art at Belfast College of Art, where he won several awards, including the Taylor Art Scholarship in 1918. His portraits are strictly academic but at their best are very accomplished and, as in that of *William Blair Morton, MA, D.Sc*, 1945 (cata. no.102), he could achieve a penetrating characterization of his sitter. At other times, however, although he invariably achieved a good likeness, his work was more stereotyped.

In the 1940s Cecil Salkeld produced some excellent portraits. Of these, *The Birthday Gift*, of about 1947, a study of his daughter Celia, and *Mrs. Maureen Doran*, painted in 1948 and exhibited at the Academy that year, are good examples. The latter is, perhaps, Salkeld's finest ever portrait. Another work of the same period, *'The Vacant Throne', in memory of F.J. McCormick*, 1948–9 (Abbey Theatre), a multiple study of the well-known actor in different roles, which was exhibited in 1949, shows the still imaginative quality of Salkeld's later work.

Unfortunately Harry Kernoff's portraits, as we noted earlier, were often repetitive in both concept and execution and, while he painted many notable Dubliners of his day, too often the finished works are memorable only for the sitter and not for aesthetic reasons.

* * *

Landscapes comprised the other major area of works exhibited each year at the Academy. Here Dermod O'Brien, W.J. Leech, Paul Henry, Charles Lamb, J.H. Craig, Frank McKelvey and Maurice MacGonigal set the standard for others to follow.

Dermod O'Brien's landscapes we have already discussed, but his craftsmanship should be emphasized for it was always held in high regard. As one of his many admirers commented: 'In an age of slovenly painting . . . O'Brien is outstanding . . . diligent application, delightful elegance, unvarying good taste . . . goes into all his work',[51] qualities which can be seen to good effect in his *Estuary of the Shannon*, 1935. W.J. Leech was an individualist and, of course, lived in England. His palette was brighter than that of most of his contemporaries and his outlook less introspective. By the 1930s the Post-Impressionist influence which was prominent in his earlier works, such as *Aloes*, of 1922–3, had given way to a more pastoral treatment. Stephen Rynne, in 1945, thought him 'one of the great painters of our time' and remarked the following year that he 'almost carries the . . . Academy on his shoulders'.[52] *The Bridge, Regents Park*, painted in about 1935 (cata. no.103), is typical of his work in these years and, as here, the strong sunlight percolating through the trees is characteristic of his compositions in general. Yet his exile from Ireland meant that Leech had less influence here than his work warranted.

In landscape, Henry, Lamb, Craig and McKelvey were the leading exponents in the depiction of the west and Co. Donegal. Henry, as we have noted, discovered the west of Ireland in 1910 and almost single-handedly forged a school of painting based on the landscape there which, in the hands of Lamb, Craig and McKelvey, dominated the period between the wars and, perhaps more than any other, approximates to a genuine Irish school of painting.

The best of Henry's work was already behind him by the early 1930s and as the decade progressed he only rarely visited the west. Many of his compositions of the time were almost certainly made from sketches done earlier. But occasionally he produced a work, such as *Connemara Landscape*, of 1943, which was published as a poster by Bord Fáilte, and which demonstrates the vitality of his residual feelings for the area. To a large extent Lamb, like Henry, became repetitive in these years and while he had a considerable following, he never regained the vigour of his early work done for the Dublin Painters' exhibitions in the 1920s.

If J.H. Craig and Frank McKelvey were less innovative than either Henry or Lamb at their best, they, nevertheless, produced work which was consistent in quality and which, with realistic fidelity, conveyed the character and mood of the western landscape. Through frequent exhibitions, perhaps more than anyone else, they popularized the landscape tradition begun by Henry.

James Humbert Craig (1878–1944) was born in Belfast. Apart from an uncompleted term spent at the Belfast College of Art, he was self-taught as an artist. Craig was a regular exhibitor at the Academy, from 1915, and his work was included in the prestigious exhibition of Irish Art in Brussels in 1930. He was almost exclusively a landscape painter, working predominantly in the Glens of Antrim—where he had a house—Co. Donegal and Connemara, although from time to time he travelled and painted on the Continent.

Craig reacted directly to the landscape, working quickly in a loosely Impressionist manner which was characterized, as John Hewitt observed, by 'the swift notation of the insistent effect, the momentary flicker, the flash of light, the passing shadow'.[53] These qualities are clearly apparent in *Glendun, near Cushendun* (cata. no.104), probably painted in the early 1930s, and they demonstrate the subtlety of his brushwork and feeling for the ever changing mood of the landscape. He also made wide use of a palette knife which at times gave his work an almost monumental effect, as can be seen, for example, in *The Crolly, Co. Donegal*, which too was probably painted in the early 1930s. This work is typical of his output of the 1920s and 1930s and the emphasis on the sky, the prominent mountain with hills beyond and the isolated habitation caught in sunlight show the influence of Paul Henry. The meandering stream in the foreground, which has eroded its way through the soft bogland, illustrates his skill at representing water and the dankness of such terrain. His later pictures, done in the last decade of his life, by which time he painted only for pleasure and not to satisfy demand, are mainly pastoral scenes—at times reminiscent of Corot—characterized by luxuriantly rich vegetation, often with a deep, shaded pool with cattle grazing nearby. Such compositions were always based on directly observed scenes and, while they are occasionally sentimental in feeling, at their best they show Craig's understanding of the countryside and, being invariably modulated in shades of green, demonstrate his skill in manipulating tones.

Craig was not a successful figure painter and in those works where figures are prominent, such as *Going to Mass* (Crawford Gallery, Cork), which dates from the 1930s, they merely become subsumed into the overall landscape.

In comparison with Craig, Frank McKelvey placed less emphasis on the structure, mood and atmosphere of the landscape and concentrated more on capturing the essential visual effect of the scene. In appearance, his work is in the tradition of Dermod O'Brien and has less of the romantic feeling associated with Craig and other of his contemporaries. An indication of his stature is the fact that he had three landscapes in the exhibition of Irish art at Brussels in 1930 and another in the similar exhibition which toured north America in 1950. Early works such as *Evening, Ballycastle*, of about 1924 (cata. no.105), or *Cross Channel Steamers at Donegall Quay, Belfast*, 1929 (Belfast Harbour Commissioners), which are characterized by a sense of tranquility and close observation of the scene, show him at his best. Often his landscapes have a genre feel to them, as can be seen in *Leinster*, one of a quartet of paintings commissioned in 1945 to symbolize the four provinces of Ireland, and in his numerous farmyard studies of chickens and hens pecking for food. In concept these last mentioned works recall similar subjects by Augustus Burke and Joseph Malachy Kavanagh and suggest that McKelvey may have been influenced by the tradition of late nineteenth century Irish painting of which they are a part. However, as John Hewitt remarked,[54] McKelvey never made the most imaginative use of his great technical ability so that too often his work was repetitive.

J.H. Craig and Frank McKelvey were often grouped together by the critics when reviewing the Academy exhibitions, where their works would have been easily comparable one with another. In 1925 the *Irish Times* referred to them and some of their fellow-Northerners, including Rendle Wood, Theo Gracey and Stanley Prosser,[55] as virtually forming a 'Belfast school' of painting which, it thought, 'surpasses the Southern painters.'[56] Indeed, it is interesting to note that that school of landscape painting which we have described as descending from Paul Henry through Charles Lamb, J.H. Craig, Frank McKelvey, and which was continued in later years by Maurice Wilks (1910–84) and numerous others, was an almost entirely Northern-inspired affair.

Of the remaining, southern based landscapists, Maurice MacGonigal and Seán Keating were the most influential, although in this context one should also recall Harry Kernoff's urban scenes of the 1930s and 1940s, works like *Naylor's Cove* and *Bend in the Road near Richmond Surrey*, which we have discussed elsewhere.

Maurice MacGonigal was born in Dublin. After a brief apprenticeship in the stained glass studio of his uncle, Joshua Clarke, he joined the Na Fianna Éireann and then the IRA, for which activities he was later arrested and interned. In the 1920s he turned his back on politics and henceforth devoted himself entirely to his art. From 1923 until 1926 he studied at the Metropolitan School under Tuohy and Keating. Tuohy greatly influenced him and imbued him with a liking for clean, pristine colours and a cool palette.[57] In 1924 he won the Taylor Art Scholarship and had his first works accepted by the Academy. Three years later, in 1927, he visited Holland, where he admired Rembrandt and Vermeer, and the experience decided him to concentrate on landscapes and genre works, although he painted portraits from time to time.[58]

During the 1930s MacGonigal often visited the west of Ireland, painting in Achill, Aran and the area around Renvyle. Until late in his career, he was an academic painter although he greatly admired Cézanne, Braque and Picasso for the emphasis which they placed on formal structures, an approach which, applied to landscape, freed him from the nostalgia and romance endemic in Irish painting. MacGonigal never lost his love of landscape. 'I'm never very happy painting portraits', he once said, 'but I'm perfectly content painting in the open air, particularly when painting the sea'.[59] His unease in portraiture is apparent in *By the Sea* and *Mother and Child* (Crawford Gallery, Cork) which in subject-matter and treatment show his sympathy for a national art. Painted in about the late 1930s, each of these compositions is almost certainly a portrait of his wife. In each case the landscape, which ostensibly is merely a background, is rendered in considerable detail and thus becomes as prominent in the composition as the figures themselves and, furthermore, because of this, the picture plane appears shallow, with limited recession. Often, too, MacGonigal's brushwork, which as here consists of small strokes coupled with strong juxtapositions of tone, is restless and, while this technique worked satisfactorily in landscape, where it contributed a feeling of freshness, it was not so appropriate to portraiture. By comparison, his landscapes appear full of fresh air and vigour, as in *Inishmór*, c.1930–5, in which he is clearly in control and at his ease. In this work we have all the characteristics of MacGonigal at his best, a cool palette dominated by blues and greys, a pristine, almost luminous quality to the paint effected by working on a white ground, and an emphasis on the physical structure of the landscape and not the romance associated with it. These same attributes are present in a later landscape, *Garden, A Summer's Day*, painted in about 1948, which is one of his very best works and which has an almost animated liveliness brought about by his use of small dabs of colour and strong juxtapositions of tone. MacGonigal's feeling for landscape is seen to advantage, too, in *Errigal, Co. Donegal*, painted in about 1950 for the Electricity Supply Board. Here the workings have become subsumed into the overall landscape, the treatment of the subject being quite distinct from Keating's Ardnacrusha paintings of the 1920s.

Seán Keating, on the other hand, was not prolific as a landscape painter. He was happier when utilizing the landscape as part of a wider narrative. Indeed, reviewing the Academy exhibition in 1927, when he showed a number landscapes recently commissioned by the Electricity Supply Board, the *Irish Times* commented that his style was 'hardly suitable' for such work, lacking the decisive touch characteristic of his figure painting.[60] This judgement is clear to be seen if we compare the dryness of landscapes, such as *Teas Mór* (Waterford Art Gallery) or *The Meeting of the Waters, Leixlip* (Electricity Supply Board), with the vitality of narrative pictures like *Half Flood* and *Mere Irish*, both dating from 1935–6, in which he extols the simple virtues of life in the west.

From time to time Seán O'Sullivan painted landscapes, but generally these are somewhat sentimental and occasionally illustrative. In the early 1950s, however, encouraged by a private collector, he turned forcefully to landscape and painted a number of scenes of the west of Ireland and Co. Donegal which show him in a relaxed mood. These pictures were executed briskly, with bold colouring which at times gives them an almost theatrical quality. Occasionally, too, he painted genre scenes, such as his *Studio Interior*, of the late 1930s, and *A Kerry Pub*, 1939 (Limerick Art Gallery), but these are less important as are his religious compositions, many of which were done for the *Capuchin Annual* during the 1930s.

* * *

Genre, and what one might call 'subject' pictures, along with still lifes and occasional paintings of religious subjects, were a regular feature of the annual Academy exhibitions. Moreover, commissions for such works were a welcome source of income for many painters.

Seán Keating, as we have seen, was at his best as a painter of subject pictures; yet overall there is something less than satisfying about his work which frequently is overburdened by sentiment. One of his best ever compositions, however, is *Men of the West*, 1916 (cata. no.97). It is a concise statement of character and resolution; but, unusual for Keating, our attention is held by the boldness of the composition and not the narrative. In this and later works on a similar theme, as Anne Crookshank and the Knight of Glin have noted,[61] Keating forged from the west of Ireland propagandist imagery which was adopted by the independence movement in an attempt to force Irish art into line with nationalist thinking. *Men of the West* was followed in 1922 by a companion work, *Men of the South* (Crawford Gallery, Cork), but the latter does not have the concise rigour either in concept or execution of the earlier picture.

One of Keating's most allegorical compositions is *Night's Candles are Burnt Out* (cata. no.106), which was painted in 1928–9. Two or three years earlier, in 1926, he had been commissioned by the Electricity Supply Board to execute a series of pictures recording the development of the hydro-electric scheme on the river Shannon at Ardnacrusha in Co. Limerick. This composition, one of twenty-odd subsequently completed, is an allegory of Keating's hopes for the new Ireland then just emerging after 1922. In it we see the advancing power of electricity about to oust the candle, which is placed beside a priest at the bottom right-hand corner, and the oil lamp, held by a workman to the left of centre. This change is epitomized in the figures of a mother and father with their children in the top right, the latter representing the new generation. The hanging skeleton at the left-hand side of the composition represents the death of the old era, while the workmen to the left of centre and the contractor in the foreground, represent latent entrepreneurial skills. The contractor's contemptuous stare at the gunman to his left is an historical reference to the recently ended civil war of 1922–3 and also symbolizes the birth of the new era and confidence in the future. The immensity of the whole Shannon project and the determination with which it was carried through are vividly illustrated in *The Key Men*, of about 1928–9 (Institution of Engineers of Ireland), another work in the series, and one which is strongly rhetorical.

Throughout his life Keating maintained a strong dislike of avant-garde art. For him, true art meant solid craftsmanship based on a thorough understanding of the academic tradition which he saw as having been handed down like a torch from generation to generation. Writing of this tradition towards the end of his life he said: 'I may fairly claim to have inherited a share in Latin culture & civilization via the Beaux Arts & the Prix de Rome, from the man who taught the man who taught Tonks who taught Orpen who taught me'.[62] To break this tradition, as he considered the Modern Movement had done, was, to Keating, sacrilege and, indeed, his resignation as president of the Academy in 1962 came about because he saw his colleagues there, in reaching an accomodation with the avant-garde, as compromising step by step with what he called 'anarchy'. To him the function of an academy above all was to preserve standards of technical ability; 'Art is skill,' he said in 1965, 'modern art will go down the drain'.[63]

Maurice MacGonigal, too, did a number of subject-pictures. The best of these are *The Irish Captain*, painted in 1933 (McKee Barracks, Dublin), which depicts a soldier fully accoutred in combat outfit—'the picture of the year', said the *Irish Times*[64] when it was exhibited at the Academy—and *Dockers* (cata. no.107), painted the following year, 1934. The first of these works, no doubt painted to symbolize the new National Army, is in fact a rather stiff, lifeless composition and the infantryman portrayed (there is no suggestion of a setting or context which is unusual for MacGonigal) looks decidedly apprehensive. The latter picture, depicting three dock workers seemingly drawn from the context of a mass meeting, is also stiff and a bit lifeless so that one is unsure as to what prompted the picture unless, perhaps, it is defiance in the face of adversity. *The Olympia*, painted in about 1935 or 1936 (cata. no.108), on the other hand, is a much more successful composition, the strong theatrical lighting creating atmosphere and the colour and bold contrasts of tone are put to good effect. As a subject, it is in a long tradition stretching back to Sickert, Toulouse-Lautrec, Degas and many others.

Withal, MacGonigal appears to have never quite reached his full potential. There is too often a hint of gloom in his work which may be due to the fact that he saw himself as an isolated figure.[65] Also, notwithstanding the fact that he himself was an academic painter, he did not agree with Keating's views of immutable standards, and that of course raised the problem of finding acceptable alternatives.

As a genre painter Leo Whelan made his name in 1916 with *The Doctor's Visit*, which won him the Taylor Art Scholarship that year. Whelan was greatly influenced by the seventeenth-century Dutch painters, notably Vermeer. However, as with his portraits, his style and compositional approach to genre work changed little with the passage of time and eventually became repetitive. He painted a number of interiors, often kitchen scenes, in which he usually depicted a figure[66] at work preparing food, surrounded by cullinary utensils and vegetables, all of which he painted with great realism. Perhaps the most accomplished and the most Vermeer-like of these genre works is *The Kitchen Window*, 1927 (Crawford Gallery, Cork), which is executed with great assurance and, for Whelan, is unusual in the skillful use of light to create a somewhat theatrical effect. *The Fiddler*, of about 1932 (Crawford Gallery, Cork), and *A Kerry Cobbler* are other examples of his genre work at its best.

In his early years, Whelan painted some landscapes in a manner similar to that of Corot, but they are quite unimportant. Along with Keating and Margaret Clarke, he was one of three artists commissioned by the Haverty Trust in 1931 to paint an incident from the life of St. Patrick in order to mark the Eucharistic Congress planned for Dublin the following year. Whelan's picture was cumbersomely entitled *The Baptism by St. Patrick of Ethna the Fair and Fedelmia the Ruddy, daughters of the Ard Rí Laoghaire* (whereabouts unknown), Keating's was, more simply, *St. Patrick Lights the Paschal Fire at Slane* (Irish College, Rome) and Margaret Clarke's was *St. Patrick Climbs Croagh Patrick* (Lane Gallery). Sadly, however, these paintings are all dull and are of little interest aesthetically. Whelan's *Blessed Virgin Mary, Queen of Ireland* was also painted to celebrate the Eucharistic Congress and was widely reproduced and distributed in Ireland. But it, too, is of little significance.

A Dublin Interior, painted in about 1915 or 1920, *Ceramic Figure and Self-portrait in a Convex Mirror*, done in the early 1920s, and *Interior*, 1931 (cata. no.110), demonstrate James Sleator's skill as a genre painter, although he worked little with such themes. The former work is firmly in the tradition of Walter Osborne and late nineteenth-century Irish painting. It is also one of the few works in which Sleator made good use of an almost theatrical play of light. The composition of his *Ceramic Figure* recalls Velázquez and the latter work, which not only depicts Orpen at his easel but is extremely Orpenesque in style, owes much to the seventeenth-century Dutch painters Vermeer and De Hooch. Sleator was most at ease with the intimacy of a still life or flower piece, and *Still Life with Flowers*, 1949 (cata. no.111), shows

George Collie
Blighted Hopes,
c.1933
Ulster Museum

him at his best. Here he excells at distinguishing surface textures and his masterly brushwork, subtle use of colour and sensitivity to medium were unsurpassed by any other painter in Ireland at the time.

Sleator possessed a superb—perhaps a too easy—technical fluency which meant that he did not often have to strain himself. This was unfortunate for he was not particularly imaginative in his range of composition or interpretation of subject-matter and, like so many of Orpen's pupils, one feels he never reached the heights which he might otherwise have done.

George Collie also painted genre and subject pictures, which often have a social dimension to them. These include *The Midday Meal*, 1927 (cata. no.112), with which he won the Taylor Scholarship that year, and which verges on social realism in its representation of the spartan surroundings and the frugal meal which is being served. *Blighted Hopes*, of about 1933 (Ulster Museum), a study in character, and *This Generation*, c.1946, are other examples of his genre work. The latter, depicting two rather bored children before an industrial landscape, may be a symbol of a generation in Ireland which, sadly, looked to emigration for its future. Occasionally Collie produced still life and flower pieces and religious works, including several sets of Stations of the Cross for churches and colleges, but these are not memorable.

The technique of using a heavy impasto developed by William Conor was well suited to subject painting. In his early days Conor excelled in depicting and capturing

the mood of those around him, although as time progressed his style atrophied. The dress and mien of the bandsmen in *The Twelfth*, painted in 1918 (Ulster Folk & Transport Museum), capture precisely the character of the subject and the era; but less convincing are *The Jaunting Car*, of about 1933, or *Men of the Home Front*, 1940 (both Ulster Museum). Conor worked from drawings of individuals and groups of people observed in the street, and he later turned these drawings into compositions merely by adding a convenient background. Thus, frequently his subjects and the background scene bear only a superficial relationship to one another. This is noticeable in, for example, *The Jaunting Car* where the figures in the foreground and the street behind appear to be on different planes. Of Conor's landscapes, another early work, *City Hall under Snow*, done in the 1920s (Ulster Museum), is one of the most successful. The scene has been concisely observed and executed and the limited palette of cool colours ably conveys the mood of a winter day.

Two of Margaret Clarke's figure compositions should be mentioned here, namely, *Strindbergian*, 1927 (cata. no.114), and *Mary Magdalen*, 1927–8. Along with

183

St. Patrick Climbs Croagh Patrick, commissioned by the Haverty Trust in 1931, these are examples of the least satisfactory aspect of her work, for her style was unsuited to the demands of a narrative composition. *Strindbergian* is in effect a group portrait, the most recognizable figure being that of Lennox Robinson at the right-hand side. The composition is enigmatic and Expressionistic in concept and if, beyond its theatricality, it relates directly to the work of the writer August Strindberg this is not clear. Neither the *Mary Magdalen* nor the *St. Patrick* composition is memorable, although Clarke was awarded a gold medal for the former at the Tailteann Games in 1928.

Still lifes and occasional figure compositions, however, show Beatrice, Lady Glenavy (née Elvery),[67] at her best. Born in Dublin in 1883, she attended the Metropolitan School of Art where she studied sculpture under John Hughes, although she later turned to painting and became a close friend of Orpen, who painted her several times. She was elected an associate member of the Academy in 1932 and a full member in 1934[68] and was from about the same time a member of the Dublin Painters' Society, where she held her first one-woman exhibition in February 1935.

Beatrice Glenavy's compositions often have a sense of drama and an enigmatic or near-Surrealist appearance, although she never thought of herself as being a Surrealist painter.[69] Perhaps her most interesting and ambitious picture in this regard is *The Intruder*, of 1932 (cata. no.115), which she exhibited at the Academy that year. Here is a sort of Thessalian allegory of desire in which a female centaur, having galloped through the scene, stops to beckon a young man from a group of figures who are picnicking, while other pairs of figures (lovers?), clearly disturbed by the event, attend with mild surprise. Writing of the picture in her autobiography, Beatrice Glenavy said that its meaning, 'if any', was that 'the unknown was more interesting than the known'.[70] The range of colours in this picture—which is unique in Irish painting in our period—with bold reds and greens in the foreground and red, yellow, violet, blue and orange on the distant hills is also unusual in Glenavy's work. More typical of her output is *Enigma* (Ulster Museum), which was probably painted in the 1930s, in which by placing an autumnal garland of corn sheaves, foliage and a rose, all tied with a ribbon from which hangs a watch, before an empty landscape, she has created a strangely mysterious picture. Indeed no other Irish painter made such near-Surrealist images as these until the late 1930s and early 1940s.

Other academic societies

Other groups and societies which helped to sustain the academic tradition in our period were the Ulster Academy of Arts, the Water Colour Society of Ireland, the Dublin Sketching Club and, in the 1940s, the art exhibitions held in association with the annual Oireachtas festival. Individually none of these bodies was of great importance or influence, but collectively they perpetuated a conservatism which was remarkably resilient.

The Ulster Academy of Arts was created in 1920 from the Belfast Art Society, which had formerly been known as the Ramblers' Sketching Club.[71] Although membership of the Academy was not restricted to Ulster artists—the president of each of the other art academies in the British Isles was elected an honorary academician as were Sir John Lavery, Sir Gerald Kelly, Leo Whelan and Seán

Keating—as the majority of its members and other exhibitors came from Northern Ireland it was, in effect, provincial in scope. By and large the works exhibited each year at the Ulster Academy were similar in subject-matter and kind to those shown at the Royal Hibernian Academy, although the better known Dublin painters rarely exhibited in Belfast. Sir John Lavery, however, was a regular exhibitor until the late 1930s. Of portraits, James Sleator's *Forrest Reid*, 1924 (Ulster Museum), John Luke's self-portrait, better known as *The Tipster*, 1928 (Ulster Museum), and Lavery's self-portrait entitled *The Silver Casket*, 1935, are typical of the better works shown. Landscapes, particularly in watercolours, however, accounted for the majority of pictures exhibited each year and here J.H. Craig and Frank McKelvey were, as one would expect, pre-eminent; but Kathleen Bridle's *Lough Erne from Rossfad*, 1945 (Ulster Museum), Theo Gracey's *Scene on the Antrim Coast*, probably of the late 1920s, and A.R. Baker's *Cornish Cliffs*, 1922, are more typical of the majority of exhibits. Some genre pictures such as William Conor's *The Jaunting Car*, A.P. Jury's *At work on the Bog*, possibly done in the late 1930s, Romeo Toogood's *Barge at Edenderry*, 1936 (Ulster Museum), and Maurice Wilks' *Turf Gatherers*, 1945, were included from time to time. As these examples show, little work of an experimental kind was exhibited at the Ulster Academy. Romeo Toogood's *Barge at Edenderry* illustrates the extreme formalism of his work at the time and Colin Middleton exhibited Surrealist studies from 1938 and in the mid-1940s showed *Our Lady of Bikini* and similar works. But generally the Ulster Academy, to an even greater extent than the Royal Hibernian Academy, lacked rigour and purpose. The academicians appear to have been not at all concerned with any vision or theory of art, but rather used their academy merely as an exhibition venue.

Over the years many influential Irish artists exhibited with the Water Colour Society of Ireland. In the 1920s and 1930s the best known of these included Rose Barton, Mildred Anne Butler, Lilian Davidson, May Guinness, Letitia and Eva Hamilton, Evie Hone and Mainie Jellett; and from the 1940s Moyra Barry, Dorothy Blackham, Sylvia Cooke-Collis, Paul Egestorff, Stella Frost, Fr. Jack Hanlon, Bea Orpen, Helen and George Pennefather and Patricia Wallace are best remembered. Apart from these people, the other exhibitors were mainly amateurs who painted only for pleasure. Each year the Society's exhibitions were dominated by landscapes, still lifes, flower pieces, occasional genre works and portraits, but the standard overall was low, and those whom we have mentioned usually saved the exhibitions from being entirely mediocre. In 1941 the *Leader* critic clearly conveyed the prevailing character of the Society's recent exhibitions when he said that they were 'a sort of artistic conversazione'.[72]

The Dublin Sketching Club, whose annual exhibition of 1884 began our survey, unfortunately did not sustain the enthusiasm of its early promise. At one time the Club counted amongst its members such eminent artists as Augustus Burke, Nathaniel Hone, Bingham McGuinness, Walter Osborne, Sarah Purser, Colles Watkins and John Butler Yeats, but after its early efforts on behalf of the avant-garde it settled into semi-obscurity and from about 1900 went into decline. By the late 1930s it had almost ceased to exist[73] and it continued thus until the late 1940s when it rallied again, although it never regained its early vigour.

The Oireachtas art exhibitions were inaugurated in an effort to integrate art with the Irish language movement and were combined with the annual Oireachtas festival. Although this festival was first held in 1897, the art exhibitions were launched, in

Dublin, in 1905 and thereafter others were held in 1906, 1907, 1911 and 1920 after which time, although the festival was occasionally celebrated, no exhibition was held until 1941 when it was established as an annual event.[74] From 1941 until 1943 only invited artists were permitted to send works for selection for the exhibition, but thereafter all Irish artists, or those resident in Ireland for at least ten years, could submit works.[75]

By and large the standard of work exhibited at the Oireachtas exhibitions in the 1940s differed little from that seen at the Royal Hibernian Academy. By the mid-forties the movement had lost its sense of purpose and the exhibitions did little to stimulate the emergence of a distinct Irish school either in painting or sculpture.

CHAPTER 9

SCULPTURE 1920–1950

'[Before 1950] there was little impact of the new materials and
aesthetic of Continental "modernist" sculpture'.

John Turpin, 'Sculpture', in Brian de Breffny (ed.), *Ireland:
A Cultural Encyclopaedia* (London), 1983, p.215.

THROUGHOUT the period under discussion sculpture in Ireland was little influenced
by the growth of the Modern Movement and remained largely academic in character.
The exceptions to this rule, all of whom we have mentioned already, are George
MacCann and Elizabeth Clements, who were active in Belfast during the 1930s, and
Jocelyn Chewett, who exhibited in Dublin with the White Stag Group during the
war-years. The doyen of Irish sculptors in the first decades of the century was John
Hughes (1865–1941), but as he had lived in France and Italy from about 1903 his
influence at home thereafter was negligible. However, in the absence of Hughes
Oliver Sheppard (1865–1941), his exact contemporary, and Albert Power, who had
studied with both Hughes and Sheppard, were pre-eminent amongst sculptors until
the late 1930s.

Oliver Sheppard's status by the 1920s was based largely on work done close to
the turn of the century, and it is for his memorials to the 1798 Rebellion at Enniscorthy
and Wexford[1]—*The Insurgent* or *Pikeman*, 1903, in Wexford, is the best known of
these—and his *Death of Cuchulain*, 1911–12, works which are strongly evocative
of the national consciousness, that he is best remembered. Indeed, in a supplement
to the *Irish Times* published in January 1932 the unidentified critic, reviewing the
state of sculpture in Ireland in the previous decade, noted that Sheppard had done
'little or nothing', but commented that, as a teacher at the Metropolitan School, he
had been responsible 'in one way or another' for nearly all the recent sculpture
produced in Dublin.[2]

While the 1920s brought Sheppard recognition of his earlier work, the selection
in 1936 of his *Cuchulain* as a memorial to the 1916 Rising, and its subsequent placing
in the General Post Office in Dublin, put a seal of approval on his whole career.
Originally modelled in plaster and later cast in bronze, *Cuchulain* is perhaps, both
literally and metaphorically, the most heroic of all Sheppard's work. The mood of
the dying hero is rendered with great pathos and the composition has a sense of
universality which fits it admirably for its present role. Of new work done in the
1920s and 1930s, however, Sheppard's two Tailteann Medals of about 1922 (Lane
Gallery), his plaque to the Earl of Iveagh, 1929 (Trinity College, Dublin), and busts

of John Joly, 1930 (Royal Dublin Society), and Pádraig Pearse, 1936 (cata. no.116), are the most important. Of these works, the plaque is uninspiring and lacks flair, although it is technically competent, but the busts of Joly and Pearse show Sheppard at his best, the latter being rendered heroically. Also, in the 1930s, other early works in plaster, including *Inis Fáil*, 1906 (Lane Gallery), and *'In Mystery the Soul Abides'*, of about 1920–8 (National Gallery of Ireland), were cast in bronze.

Of his contemporaries elsewhere, Sheppard greatly admired Jacob Epstein, although he seems not to have been influenced by him. Rather, he was affected by 'Belle Époque' sculpture in general—as his *Cuchulain* and bust of Pearse show— and Rodin in particular and these were the models he passed on to Albert Power, his most illustrious pupil.

Albert Power (1883–1945) was born in Dublin. He was first apprenticed to a monumental sculptor before studying under John Hughes and Oliver Sheppard at the Metropolitan School, where he won several prizes, including the National Gold Medal for Sculpture in 1911.[3] Elected an associate member of the Royal Hibernian Academy

188

Albert Power,
*1916 Memorial,
Limerick*, 1919–39
Photograph Bryan Rutledge

in 1911, he became a full academician in 1919. He was represented in the exhibition of Irish art in Paris in 1922 and at the similar exhibition in Brussels in 1930.

Power continued the sculptural tradition of Sheppard although his work was more naturalistic and lacked completely the romantic and heroic qualities of his teacher. The difference between them can be seen, for example, by comparing Power's 1916 Memorial in Limerick—original study 1919, finished monument c.1938—or his bust of the Nationalist, *Austin Stack*, 1939 (National Gallery of Ireland), with Sheppard's *Cuchulain* or *Pearse* of the same period.

Power's work falls into three categories, namely portrait busts, which he produced throughout his career and which seem to have been his main source of income; ecclesiastical works; and what one might loosely call genre pieces. His style changed little during our period and the main characteristics of his portrait work are an emphasis on naturalism and good characterization of his subject. These qualities are evident in his head of *Archbishop Mannix*, 1921, which shows him at ease with the sitter and confident in his manipulation of the medium, marble, which has been worked in

189

considerable detail. His *Blessed Oliver Plunkett*, 1921 (Lane Gallery), also demonstrates his skill in marble and here, no doubt because of the subject-matter, the feeling of pathos evoked by the piece is greater than one usually finds in his work. In his head of *Bethel Solomons*, 1933 (Rotunda Hospital, Dublin), which is cast in bronze, Power has polished the surface of the metal to a high degree and the piece has been modelled with flair and a feeling for spontaneity which is also unusual for him. But perhaps his most successful bust, in which the fluid modelling and use of the medium, bronze, are perfectly matched with the personality of the sitter, is that of *W. B. Yeats*, executed in 1939 (cata. no.117). This is one of the very best portrait studies, in any medium, done in Ireland during the years which we have been studying. Other portraits by Power, such as those of *Sir Hugh Lane*, 1933 (Lane Gallery), a posthumous work, or *Austin Stack*, however, are more pedestrian in execution and lack vitality.

Of Power's ecclesiastical pieces, his *Madonna and Divine Child*, 1921–2, and *Christ the King*, 1934–6, done for the tympanum of Mullingar Cathedral, are the most important. The former, carved in limestone, evokes more pathos than, as we have said, is usual for Power, and the whole—as befits the medium—has been rendered in boldly conceived forms with no undue detailing, although the complication of limbs and drapery at the front of the piece might have been more succinctly resolved. The Mullingar tympanum was the foremost ecclesiastical commission of the 1930s and, surprisingly, was the only major commission which Power ever received. But sadly he was not at his best on such a scale or with the subject-matter. Power was commissioned to do this piece in 1934 on the recommendation of the architects of the cathedral which was then under construction.[4] The subject-matter represents the Blessed Virgin handing over a model of the old Cathedral of St. Mary's, which formerly occupied the site of the new building, to Christ the King, the central figure in the composition. The other figures beside the Virgin are SS. Patrick and

Rosamond Praeger
in her Holywood
studio
Ulster Museum

Peter, while the group on the right represents Pope Pius XI, at whose request the cathedral was dedicated to Christ the King, the Most Rev. Thomas Mulvany, Bishop of Meath, and Cardinal MacRory, Primate of All Ireland.[5] The figures, which were carved on site in Portland stone, are in high relief but, although executed with great realism, they lack vitality and animation. Sadly, as we have said, Power was not at his best on such a scale or within the limitations of a commission of this kind. Power worked better when free to choose his own subject-matter, and other of his commissions, such as the 1916 Memorial in Limerick or the *Croppy Boy*, c. 1938–9, in Tralee, are equally stiff and formal. On the other hand, when free to please himself, as in *The Fall of Icarus*, done in about 1940 (cata. no.118), or his *Connemara Trout*, 1944 (cata. no.119), which are domestic in scale, he exploits with ease the inherent qualities of material and subject and his sense of realism comes into its own.

Overall, Power's achievement is difficult to assess. He stands at the end of a tradition, although at a point where its successor, the Modern Movement, had not yet begun to encroach upon it. He had a good technical facility, yet was unadventurous except, perhaps, for the degree of naturalism which he brought to a scene hitherto preoccupied by nationalist-inspired sentiment.

Other, more minor, sculptors working in Ireland in the 1920s, 1930s and later who continued the academic tradition included Rosamond Praeger, Frank Wiles and Morris Harding, all Northerners, and Joseph Higgins from Cork.

Rosamond Praeger (1867–1954), from Holywood, Co. Down, was a sister of the distinguished Irish botanist, Robert Lloyd Praeger. She studied art at the Belfast Government School of Art before going to the Slade School, where she worked under Alphonse Legros. Later she spent a brief spell in Paris before returning to Holywood, where she settled for the rest of her life. Most of Praeger's best work was

191

Rosamond Praeger
Spring, c.1934
Ulster Museum

done close to the turn of the century. She is remembered for her rather sentimental, but often delightful, figures, of which *The Fairy Fountain*, 1900–1 (cata. no.120), and *The Philosopher*, c. 1920, both of which are in the Ulster Museum, are perhaps the best examples. But sadly more hackneyed pieces, such as innumerable plaster reliefs of the Irish legends, dominated her work from the second decade or so of the century and these are of no consequence to the development of sculpture in Ireland. In the 1930s, however, she produced two relief panels in stone, namely *Spring* (cata. no.121) and *Tug-of-War* (both Uster Museum), which should be noted for the spirited and fluid manner in which she handled compositions crowded with figures in motion.

Frank Wiles
*Dawn of
Womanhood*, 1918
Ulster Museum

Joseph Higgins
Michael Collins
1922

Frank Wiles (1889–1956) was born in Larne in Co. Antrim. He studied at the Belfast College of Art under Seamus Stoupe and from there, in 1909, won a scholarship which enabled him to visit Paris. In 1911 he won another scholarship and went to the Metropolitan School in Dublin where he studied under Oliver Sheppard. In about 1917 he returned to his native Larne and settled there for the rest of his life. Like Rosamond Praeger and many others of his time, Wiles was sentimental in outlook, as his *Dawn of Womanhood*, 1914 (Ulster Museum), which may be his best work, indicates. This piece was made under Sheppard's supervision at the Metropolitan School and in the precise, well delineated modelling of the forms and slightly quixotic concept, it illustrates the influences brought to bear by his teacher. From the 1920s onwards portrait busts, such as that of *Judge J. Creed Meredith*, c.1924, and reliefs were Wiles' principal subject-matter, although his most widely known work is probably the seated lion on the war memorial at Newcastle, Co. Down, executed in about 1928 or 1929.

Morris Harding (1874–1964), an Englishman, came to Belfast in 1925 to do carvings for St. Anne's Cathedral. Harding first made a name for himself as a sculptor of animals, and his *Polar Bear Cubs at Play*, 1909 (Queen's University, Belfast), is a good example of his work in this vein. As a young man he treated such groups expressively and with great fluidity, but later works, such as *The Kill*, 1931 (Royal Ulster Academy), are stiff and lack the ease of his earlier work. Unfortunately a lack of ease also typifies the major work of his career, that is, the series of sculptures on the capitals—representing the Arts, Science and Industry—of the nave arcade of St. Anne's Cathedral which, along with other pieces in the same building, he completed in the late 1920s and early 1930s. Harding is also remembered for a font, carved for St. Peter's Church, Antrim Road, Belfast, in about 1934 or 1935 and for a number of portrait heads, such as that of *J. L. MacQuitty, OBE, QC*, 1946, many of which he exhibited at the Royal Hibernian Academy.

Joseph Higgins (1885–1925) was born in Co. Cork. He studied at Cork School of Art where he specialized in modelling and wood carving. He spent his entire career working and teaching in and around Cork and, even though he exhibited from time to time at the Royal Hibernian Academy, he is less well-known than he deserves to be. Higgins' best work, in the main, was done before 1920 and he is mostly remembered for his *Boy with a Boat*, of about 1910 (Fitzgerald Park, Cork), which, like Praeger and Wiles, verges on the sentimental. Generally, he had a light touch and a fluid, atmospheric style which was suited to works of a domestic scale, as can be seen in his head of *Michael Collins*, 1922, which is almost Expressionist in execution and is unique in Irish sculpture of the time.

* * *

In the mid-1930s Laurence Campbell and Seamus Murphy came on the scene. Neither of them had the technical virtuosity of their predecessors, Sheppard and Power, but they brought a degree of stylization to their work which was new to Irish sculpture and which suggests an affinity for the work of some of their British contemporaries such as Barbara Hepworth, Eric Gill, Dick Reid and also of Ivan Mestrovic, the Yugoslavian sculptor who had a considerable influence in England during the 1930s.

Laurence Campbell (1911–68) was born in Dublin. He learned stone carving with a firm of commercial sculptors while at the same time studying art in the evenings under Oliver Sheppard at the Metropolitan School.[6] In 1935 he won the Taylor Scholarship for a figure of *Lawrence of Arabia* and the following year won the Henry Higgins Travelling Scholarship, which took him to the Royal Academy of Fine Arts in Stockholm. There he studied sculpture under Nils Sjören and painting under Isaac Grünewald, a Swede who had been a pupil of Matisse and who worked in an Expressionist manner.[7] On leaving Stockholm Campbell spent a year in Paris at the Académie Ranson, before returning to Dublin in late 1939 to take up an appointment as acting professor of sculpture at the National College of Art during the absence of Frederich Herkner.

With the passage of time Campbell's work changed little either in style or execution.

Laurence Campbell
Sean Heuston, 1943
Photograph S.B.K.

His subject-matter embraces two distinct areas, namely figure works, including religious pieces and architectural reliefs, and portrait busts. He also made some paintings, such as his *Pont de l'Alma, Paris* (cata. no.100), and occasional etchings, woodcuts and portrait drawings, but the latter are relatively slight.

In general Campbell's figure subjects show an awareness of Modernism, notably in his simplification of forms. On occasions these can be severe, almost Cubist, while again they are rhythmical, with an emphasis on line. These characteristics are clearly evident in his *Mother and Child* of 1933 (cata. no.123). Carved in sandstone, this is one of the most avant-garde pieces of Irish sculpture of its time. Significantly, it was made before Campbell went abroad and we can only assume that the influence

195

behind it came from illustrations seen in journals, although the emphasis on rhythm in it recalls certain works by Mainie Jellett done at about the same time. Campbell's *Mother Eire*, an architectural relief done in about 1938 or 1939, however, is less rigorous, although its stylized forms recall similar works of the same period by a number of English scupltors. *Mother Eire* is the centre piece of a triptych, the side pieces representing a warrior to the left and a female cult figure to the right. The work was commissioned by the architect Michael Scott[8] for the façade of the Theatre Royal, Dublin, but was later removed when the building was demolished. Other architectural reliefs by Campbell executed in these years are *St. Luke, Physician*, 1941 (Kilkenny Hospital), which is also greatly stylized in form, and *Industry*, c. 1940–3, one of two panels made for the Technical School at Marino in Dublin. These latter pieces are worked in a more naturalistic manner and, with a mild suggestion of Social Realism, recall the *Sean Heuston* bust of 1943 which is Campbell's most ambitious work.

The memorial to Sean Heuston, who was executed for his part in the Rising of 1916, is heavily mannered. By drawing attention to the resolution in the sitter's face and to his hands, which are over life size and which are rendered in great detail in comparison to the rest of the work, Campbell has communicated a sense of unwavering determination. The work is carved from a single piece of stone, from which Campbell removed layer after layer to reveal, in a Michelangelesque manner, the figure enclosed within.[9]

Despite the imaginative concept of those works which we have mentioned, Campbell's portraits, on the other hand, were handled in a strictly academic manner which changed little in time. However, he could obtain a good likeness of his sitter and could capture personality, as his studies in plaster of *Melanie le Brocquy*, 1940–1, which shows his skill at modelling, and *Jack B. Yeats*, 1945–6, where the sitter's quiet thoughtfulness renders him as something of an 'elder statesman', demonstrate. His head of *Dick McKee*, 1950 (McKee Barracks, Dublin), shows his ability in bronze but also is unimaginative in execution.

By all accounts, Laurence Campbell was a reclusive individual. He had to relinquish his post at the National College of Art when Frederich Herkner returned there in the late 1940s—he was appointed only in an acting capacity—and this possibly scarred him, for from about that time his work became less rigorous and he seems never to have realized his true potential. In any case, he left Ireland in 1953 and took up a teaching appointment in the United States.

Beside Campbell his contemporary, Seamus Murphy (1907–75), evokes much more pathos. Seamus Murphy was born in Co. Cork. While serving his apprenticeship in a stoneyard in Cork,[10] he studied in the evenings at the Crawford School of Art. In 1931 he was awarded the Gibson Scholarship which enabled him to spend two years in London and Paris, where he studied at the Académie Colorossi, and where he met the Irish-American sculptor Andrew O'Connor. However, neither O'Connor nor Paris seem to have had any influence on his work, which at times is closer to Mestrovic. On returning to Cork he opened his own stoneyard and built up a trade for ecclesiastical and public monuments, although in later years he executed portrait heads of several eminent figures. Elected an associate of the Royal Hibernian Academy in 1944 and a full member in 1954, he rarely exhibited outside the Academy.

Murphy was essentially a stone carver in the tradition of monumental masons. He was at his best when working on a large scale, manipulating bold forms, usually

196

Andrew O'Connor
Christ the King,
1930s
Photograph Bryan Rutledge

with great economy of means. There is a strong linear emphasis even in his earliest works, such as *Prayer*, of 1933 (cata. no.125), or *Dreamline*, 1934, which recalls the rhythms found in Jellett and Campbell, and which in his standing Madonnas he used to emphasize the verticality of the composition. This can be seen, for example, in his *Mother of Sorrows*, 1938 (Ursuline Convent, Waterford), and *Virgin of the Twilight*, 1941–2, the latter not only being one of his best works, but regarded by Oisin Kelly as the most important carving made in Ireland this century.[11] The surface of the work, which is carved in Kilkenny limestone, was originally polished in order to emphasize the linear nature of the composition but, being placed out of doors, weathering has removed the polish so that it now appears more brutal, the expression on the Madonna's face more brooding, than the sculptor intended.[12] By the mid-1940s Murphy's compositions, such as the *Madonna*, of 1945 (Church of the Annunciation, Cork), are still strongly linear and often have a vertical emphasis effected through the fall of drapery, but the figure is now treated in a more naturalistic manner with less of the harshness of his earlier works.

Murphy's portrait heads are strictly representational in treatment and at his best, as in his bust of *Seán O'Faoláin*, 1947 (cata. no.126), which shows vigorous modelling, he could penetrate personality. At other times he was less at ease with his sitter and the resulting work has more of the formality of a commission, as is the case with his portrait of *John Charles McQuaid*, Archbishop of Dublin, 1941 (Blackrock College). His head of *Michael Collins*, 1948 (Fitzgerald Park, Cork), however, is surprisingly spirited for a posthumous work on such a large scale.

During the 1940s Murphy carved a number of low relief panels of which the most successful is the *Annunciation*, 1945, which stands above the main entrance to the Church of the Annunciation, at Blackpool, Cork, a building which he designed and for which he produced several other sculptural works. Here the somewhat austere composition is, as usual, linear and the forms, which are square-cut rather than modelled, are concisely stated, the whole evoking a feeling of reverence and devotion. Other panels from the time are those of the seasons, *Spring*, *Summer* and *Autumn*, all done in 1940 (Fitzgerald Park, Cork)—if a fourth panel for 'Winter' was produced it is unrecorded. Of these last mentioned works, *Summer*, with its boldly succinct composition, strong linear emphasis and square-cut forms, is perhaps the best and reminds us of Murphy's other work as a monumental mason.

Seamus Murphy was sensitive to a tradition in stone carving which reached back to the Middle Ages and beyond. This was his refuge and aesthetic; yet, at the same time, it restricted his horizons and ultimately his expression of the world around him.

In contrast to Campbell and Murphy, both Jerome Connor and Andrew O'Connor worked in the manner of Rodin and had a more emotional appeal. This can be seen in the former's *Lusitania Memorial* at Cobh, which was executed between 1925 and 1943, and the latter's *Christ the King*, 1926 (Dun Laoghaire), a memorial to those who died in the First World War, which takes the form of a triple crucifixion symbolizing the desolation, consolation and final triumph of Christ's passion. Andrew O'Connor (1874–1941) was born in Massachusetts.[13] He had a distinguished career as a sculptor in both the United States and Europe before coming to Ireland in 1932 to work on his figure of *Daniel O'Connell*, which was commissioned by the National Bank of Ireland in Dublin, and which with its fluid modelling powerfully suggests the subject's oratory. O'Connor, however, had little or no influence on the development of sculpture in Ireland.

Jerome Connor (1876–1943) was born in Co. Kerry,[14] but was taken as a child to Massachusetts where he grew up. He trained as a stonecarver and blacksmith before going to Italy in about 1903, but later returned to the United States where he had a distinguished career as a sculptor. In 1925 he returned to Ireland to work on the Lusitania Memorial, a project which was to occupy him for the rest of his life. During the 1930s he also worked on a number of other commissions, some of which he failed to complete—these included the Tralee *Pikeman*, known as the 'Croppy Boy', which in the end Albert Power finished—and because of this eventually he was involved in lawsuits which led to his bankruptcy. Towards the end of his life he made many small portrait heads and studies of figures, which he termed 'little pieces of free work', some of which are among his best works, and it is upon these that his reputation generally is based.

When he arrived in Ireland in 1925 Connor was at the height of his powers and reputation. The evolution of the Lusitania Memorial, which was commissioned by

Jerome Connor
*Lusitania
Memorial*, 1925–43
Photograph Bryan Rutledge

an American committee, was a protracted affair and was still unfinished at the time of his death. In brief, Connor changed his design for the memorial several times and on each occasion the committee in America had to approve the alterations. This led to many delays and much dissatisfaction.

To begin with, Connor seems to have favoured a single female figure representing 'Peace', and a full-scale model for such a figure was made.[15] Later he made at least two variations on this theme, each employing an angel as the central figure,[16] before deciding on the final composition which comprises two groups of figures, namely an Angel of Peace surmounting a stone pedestal in front of which stand two fishermen in mourning. The fishermen were cast in bronze in about 1936, by which time the Angel was also ready for casting,[17] but by then Connor could no longer afford to

Peter Grant
Photograph Charles Collins

have the work done for his American backers had stopped all monetary payments, having lost patience with him because of his slow progress. Moreover, that summer he had been declared bankrupt after court proceedings against him regarding another commission, *Eire*, for a memorial to four Kerry poets for Killarney. Thus the Lusitania Memorial remained unfinished until after his death. However, in 1952 the Hammond Lane foundry in Dublin presented the two fishermen—for which it had never received payment for the casting—to the Friends of the National Collections of Ireland who eventually had them erected in Cobh in accordance with Connor's design and in 1968 the Angel of Peace was cast and united with the rest of the composition.[18]

In some respects the Memorial is unsatisfactory. The two groups of figures relate poorly to each other so that one feels that perhaps a variation on either group by itself would have made a more succinct statement. Also, the whole is over-emotional to the point of piety. No doubt Connor's difficulties with the commission were exacerbated by his financial problems at the time, for he was engaged simultaneously with commissions for the *Pikeman* in Tralee and the Kerry poets memorial, and possibly he simply over stretched himself both intellectually and physically for these other two commissions were fruitless. His design for the former, a young boy posed obediently with a pike suspended at arm's length, was stiff and lifeless[19] and he is known to have been unhappy with it; while the latter, representing *Erin* seated with a harp,[20] is rather hackneyed when compared to his early works like *Emmet*, of 1917 (Washington and St. Stephen's Green, Dublin), which is concisely stated and full of assurance and confidence both in concept and execution.

From about the time of his bankruptcy Connor concentrated on making small studies—his 'little pieces of free work'. Sometimes these pieces are in the form of portraits, but more often they are studies in character. *The Boxer* (cata. no.127), the *Street Singer* (Lane Gallery), and *Peace* (Waterford Art Gallery), all done in the years from about 1936 until 1943, are good examples. In them, Connor was perfectly at ease, modelling briskly, succinctly and omitting all unnecessary details. Also, his study for a *Pikeman* (cata. no.128), done in about 1940, with its rugged modelling, simplicity of pose and defiant expression, contrasts markedly with his abortive effort with the same subject of a decade or so earlier.

* * *

In the early 1940s a number of minor figures, of whom Peter Grant, Peter Brennan and Melanie le Brocquy were at the time the best known, came on the scene, but none of them was influential on the development of sculpture in Ireland.

Peter Grant was born in Co. Tyrone in 1915. In 1935 he won a scholarship to the National College of Art in Dublin where he studied under Keating, Sheppard and Frederick Herkner. Later, during the years 1941 till 1944, he was assistant professor of sculpture at the College. In 1937 he won the Taylor Art Scholarship for his *Moses, The Law Giver*, a somewhat monumental piece. Generally, his early works are academic in concept and execution, but have a feeling for the heroic, as *Eire*, of about 1937, and *Manannan Mac Lir*, 1939 (cata. no.129) show. Occasionally he produced portrait heads somewhat in the manner of his teacher, Herkner. Peter Brennan, too, studied at the National College of Art and while there won the Taylor Scholarship in 1936. His early work, consisting mainly of portrait heads and other figure pieces, is academic in execution although he later made a few more avant-garde pieces. However, since the early 1940s, by which time he was teaching in Kilkenny, he has concentrated his interests on making pottery.[21] Melanie le Brocquy was born in Dublin

Frederick Herkner
Mother Eire, c.1939

Frederick Herkner
W.B. Yeats,
late 1930s

in 1919. She studied art at the National College of Art, the Royal Hibernian Academy School and at the École des Beaux Arts in Geneva. She won the Taylor Scholarship in 1938 and again in 1939 and in the latter year also won the Californian Gold Medal of the Royal Dublin Society. She exhibited regularly at the Royal Hibernian Academy and showed at the Irish Exhibition of Living Art in 1943 and 1944, after which time she seems to have given up sculpture until the mid-1960s.

Also in these years, George MacCann and Elizabeth (Betty) Clements were working

202

in Belfast. They had both studied sculpture at the Belfast College of Art under James (Seamus) Stoupe and at the Royal College of Art in London under Henry Moore. There they developed a semi-Cubist style reminiscent of the work of Jacques Lipchitz but which has little originality. They were both members of the Ulster Unit and exhibited there in December 1934. They were, however, along with F. E. McWilliam, whom we have already mentioned, amongst the few Irish sculptors of their generation to take any cognizance of the Modern Movement.

In the later 1940s Frederich Herkner, Hilary Heron and Oisin Kelly began to exhibit, but each of them belongs really to the 1950s and later. Frederich Herkner (1902–86) was born in Austria. After a distinguished early career, during which time he was a Rome Scholar in sculpture, in 1938 he became professor of sculpture at the National College of Art in Dublin. But a year later, on the outbreak of war, he returned to Germany where he remained until about 1948 when he was again able to take up his old post in Dublin. Thus, his influence both as a teacher and sculptor during our period was less than it might otherwise have been. Herkner's early work, done before he came to Ireland, was in the tradition of Rodin although by the time he arrived in Dublin it had acquired a simplicity of form and emphasis on line which recalls Maillol. This is the character which he retained into the late 1950s and 1960s when much of his best work was done. At times, as in his *Mother Eire* of 1939, done for the Irish Pavilion at the New York World's Fair, his work has a romantic quality, but often, too, it is characterized by a harsh, almost mechanical representation of form as can be seen in his head of *W. B. Yeats*, done in the late 1930s. This severity links him mildly with the more avant-garde developments of the 1950s.

Hilary Heron (1923–77) was the first—and probably the only—holder of the Mainie Jellett Travelling Scholarship, which she won in 1948, and which allowed her to travel to France and Italy a year or so later. In all her work she emphasized the natural qualities of her medium, as is evident, for example, in her study of *James Connolly*, done in 1946 (cata. no.130).

Oisin Kelly (b.1915), too, emphasized the inherent character of his materials, as can be seen in *Stepdancer*, of 1947, a work which also demonstrates the bold simplicity of his handling of form at the time.

It is in part in Laurence Campbell and in Frederich Herkner, but moreso in Hilary Heron and Oisin Kelly—with their emphasis on truth to materials—that we see the beginnings of Modernism in sculpture in the south of Ireland and, with the exception of Campbell, they were among the avant-garde of Irish sculptors until the 1960s.

THOMAS BODKIN,
REPORT ON THE ARTS IN IRELAND

AFTER the general election held in Ireland in February 1948 John A. Costello became Taoiseach at the head of a coalition government. A year later, in July 1949, Costello wrote to his friend Thomas Bodkin, sometime director of the National Gallery of Ireland but since 1935 Barber Professor of Fine Art at the University of Birmingham, commissioning him to examine and report on the state of the arts in Ireland. Bodkin's brief was wide. He was to examine the working of the national institutions, both cultural and educational, relationships between the arts and industry, and to comment on the advisability of establishing an organization to encourage a knowledge of Irish culture in foreign countries. Bodkin's *Report on the Arts in Ireland* was compiled with amazing speed and was published on 30 September 1949.[1] It was severely critical of almost all aspects of the art scene, noting that little or nothing had been done to stimulate the arts since the coming of independence in 1922. 'In the intervening twenty-seven years', said Bodkin,

> We have not merely failed to go forward in policies concerning the Arts, we have, in fact, regressed to arrive, many years ago, at a condition of apathy about them in which it had become justifiable to say of Ireland that no other country of Western Europe cared less, or gave less, for the cultivation of the Arts.[2]

Bodkin's main recommendation was that a department or sub-department of fine art should be established, under the control of the Taoiseach, to correlate and supervise the administration of the existing art institutions and to act in an advisory capacity to such Ministries as might from time to time require its services. This department, he said, should also have responsibility for new National Academies of Music and Painting which he recommended should be created, and he also advised that it should either control or exercise influence over a variety of schemes ranging from art education at school and university level to official publications, patronage, industrial design, town planning and other projects. Indeed, had such a department come into existence, the State would have exercised an almost tyrannical control over all the arts in Ireland. If this scheme should present problems of recruitment and implementation from within the Civil Service, said Bodkin, the Arts might best be served by establishing alongside it another less formal body, which he suggested might be called the Arts Commission, the Board of Arts, the Institute of Arts, or the Arts Council of Ireland, similar in function to the recently established Arts Council of Great Britain. Such a body, he continued, should have its own director or chairman and staff, its own budget and freedom to administer it save for the requirement of presenting an annual report to the Dáil.[3]

Of all the recommendations in his *Report*, this last one was acted upon and it led to the establishment, under the Arts Bill of 1951, of *An Chomhairle Ealaíon*/The Arts Council of Ireland, which came into being shortly before Costello's government went out of office that year.

Bodkin's views as expressed in his *Report* can be traced back to 1913 to an article which he published entitled 'The Present Position of Art in Ireland'.[4] There he lamented the neglect and apathy shown towards the arts as highlighted by a number of issues, including the tardy affair of the Hugh Lane pictures and the Dublin Municipal Gallery; the 'melancholy' state of the Royal Hibernian Academy; the 'parochial' methods of instruction at the Metropolitan School of Art; the National Gallery, which was little patronized; and, finally, the absence of a recognizable school of Irish art. In 1922 Bodkin returned to these issues in a memorandum addressed to the Minister of Education, but received no reply. In 1923 he repeated his criticisms in an essay entitled 'The Condition and Needs of Art in Ireland',[5] and in June 1935, in a lecture entitled 'The Importance of Art to Ireland', delivered at Trinity College, he re-stated his views once again. Thus can be explained the expeditious manner in which he compiled and presented his *Report*.

With the publication of Bodkin's *Report* in 1949, and with the establishment of the Arts Council of Ireland as a consequence of it, we come to the beginning of a new era in the history of the arts in Ireland. Since that time the State itself has grown older and more stable, it has patronized the arts in a manner with which we are now familiar and there has been greater personal affluence than ever before, much of which, witnessed by the proliferation of public and commercial galleries in many towns, has been expended on the arts.

* * *

Looking back on the development of art in Ireland during the first half of the twentieth century we find, overall, a fetish for tradition coloured by a search for a distinct Irish school. Such a school eluded most observers; yet it *did* exist, but in a different guise to that which almost all dreamed of. As for the Modernists it is surprising that, for all their efforts to embrace the avant-garde, at least some of them in the 1920s and 1930s did not turn wholeheartedly to Surrealism, which was the real force of the time. Also, the absence of Constructivism, of artistic manifestoes, or of a body of work with a keen political edge in such a post-revolutionary period is significant, although the latter can be accounted for by the quest for national identity in the fledgling State. Like their counterparts in most European countries, other than France, Germany and Italy, Irish artists merely reacted to Modernism, they did not help to shape its development, other than in regional terms. Yet within the context of events at home, they brought a Modernist viewpoint to play upon the often momentous issues of the times. That is what makes them distinct from their counterparts elsewhere. By the late 1940s, principally through the Living Art exhibitions, the most influential artists in the country came within the embrace of Modernism and this coincided with a time when much of the romance of the previous decades was giving way to a more realistic view of life in the post-war world. Not the least of the achievements of the Irish Modernists was that, unlike their literary contemporaries, they eased the way for this development.

CATALOGUE OF WORKS

The following works are arranged, as far as possible, in the order of their appearing in the main text. Thus the structure of the catalogue reflects that of the text.

In references to exhibitions the number in brackets after the title, venue and dates of the exhibition is the catalogue number in that exhibition of the work referred to.

All measurements are given in centimetres, height before width.

All newspaper references to works have been omitted unless they are substantive.

Thanks are due to all those persons who have lent works from their collections, both public and private, to make this exhibition possible.

Cata. no. 1.
Photograph
Glasgow Art
Gallery.

208

JAMES MacNEILL WHISTLER (1834–1903)

1. Arrangement in Grey and Black, No.2: Portrait of Thomas Carlyle 1872–3

Oil on canvas 170.2 x 142.2.

Signed with a butterfly device at right.

Coll: Glasgow Art Gallery.

Exh: Pall Mall Gallery, London, 1874; Grosvenor Gallery, London, 1877; Loan Exhibition, Scottish National Portraits, Edinburgh, 1884; Paris Salon, 1884; Dublin Sketching Club, 1884 (242, as *Thomas Carlyle*); Royal Glasgow Institute of Fine Arts, 1888; Working Women's College, London, 1891–2; Goupil Gallery, London, 1892; Fine Art Exhibition, Albert Institute, Dundee, 1895; Burns Exhibition, Royal Glasgow Institute, 1896; Aberdeen Artists' Society, 1896; Fine Art Exhibition, Perth, 1898; Guildhall, London, 1900; Walker Art Gallery, Liverpool, 1900; Paisley Art Institute, 1902; Industrial Art Exhibition, Wolverhampton, 1902; Royal Scottish Academy, Edinburgh, 1904; Whistler Memorial Exhibition, International Society of Sculptors, Painters and Gravers, London, 1905; Mappin Art Gallery, Sheffield, 1905; Art Gallery, Leeds, 1909; Walker Art Gallery, Liverpool, 1922; Tate Gallery, London, 1939 and 1946.

Lit: [There is an extensive bibliography relating to this painting, set out in McLaren Young, et al., 1980. Below are listed only the more substantial references]: T.R. Way & G.R. Dennis, *The Art of J. McN. Whistler*, 1903, pp.8, 10, 16, 35, 42, repr., 43; Bryan's *Dictionary of Painters and Engravers*, vol.5, 1905, pp.360–2; 'The International Society's Whistler Exhibition', *Studio*, vol.34, 1905, p.232; Bernhard Sickert, 'The Whistler Exhibition', *Burlington Magazine*, vol.6, 1905, pp.430, 438; F. Wedmore, *Whistler and Others*, 1906; E.R. & J. Pennell, *Life of J. McN. Whistler*, 1908, vol.1, pp.170–2, repr., 313–5 and *passim*, vol.2, pp.114–16 and *passim*; T.R. Way, *Memories of J. McN. Whistler*, 1912, pp.13, 29, 44; E.R. & J. Pennell, *The Whistler Journal*, 1921, p.10 and *passim*; S. Dick, *Our Favourite Painters*, 1923, pp.294, 295, 299; J. Laver, *Whistler*, 1930, pp.204–5 and *passim*; Frank Rutter, *Modern Masterpieces* (n.d.), vol.1, p.110; *Whistler: Arrangements in Grey and Black*, Glasgow Art Gallery, 1951, pp.14–17, 20–22 and *passim*, repr.; Andrew McLaren Young, Margaret MacDonald, Robin Spencer, *The Paintings of James McNeill Whistler*, 1980, vol.1, catalogue number 137, repr., vol.2, pl.99 in colour; Ronald Anderson, 'Whistler in Dublin, 1884', *Irish Arts Review*, vol.3, 1986, pp.46, 48, 50, repr. in colour; S.B. Kennedy, *Irish Art and Modernism 1920–1949*, unpublished Ph.D. dissertation, University of Dublin, 1987, vol.1, pp.6, 7; Bruce Arnold, *The Art Atlas of Britain & Ireland*, 1991, p.312, repr. in colour.

This is one of the great masterpieces of early Modernism in British art. When exhibited at the Dublin Sketching Club in 1884, along with other works by Whistler, it caused a stir among the critics and public. In his art Whistler emphasized the aesthetic side of picture making. To him painting was concerned with something more significant than 'story telling' or the portrayal of morality; it had to do with the manipulation of purely visual things, of colour, line, space, light and pattern. His views on this matter were close to Walter Pater's pronouncement that all art 'constantly aspires towards the condition of Music', and his Nocturnes, Symphonies, Harmonies and Arrangements were the labels which he used to emphasize this conviction. Whistler's reputation had been notorious since 1878, the year of his celebrated court case with Ruskin, and that such a person should have been invited to exhibit at the annual exhibition of a conservative art society, such as the Dublin Sketching Club, seems unusual, to say the least. However, the *Carlyle* and the other accompanying Whistler's were the first avant-garde pictures to be seen in Ireland and the future development of Modernism in this country can be traced back to them. When purchased by the Glasgow Art Gallery in 1891, the *Carlyle* was the first picture by Whistler to enter a public collection, although its companion work, *Arrangement in Grey and Black No. 1: Portrait of the Artist's Mother* (Louvre), was acquired for the Luxembourg Gallery in Paris later that same year. Moves had earlier been made to acquire both of these works for Dublin, but, alas, these came to naught. Thomas Carlyle (1795–1881), the philosopher and historian, is here depicted in old age, ill, but with great pathos.

Exhibited HLMG only.

JOHN BUTLER YEATS (1839–1922)

2. W. G. Fay
Oil on canvas 74.6 x 62.2.
Inscr: 'JB Yeats 1904'.
Coll: Hugh Lane Municipal Gallery of Modern Art.
Prov: Sir Hugh Lane.
Exh: *Jack B. Yeats and his Family*, Sligo Museum, October–November 1971.

William George Fay (1872–1947) was an actor and theatrical producer. Born in Dublin, with his elder brother, Frank, he formed his own small theatrical company, playing in many parts of Ireland. The Fay brothers later joined W.B. Yeats and Lady

211

Gregory in founding the Abbey Theatre. In 1908, however, they broke with the Abbey and went to the USA. In 1914 William went to London where he had a distinguished career on the English stage.

Cata. no. 3.
Photograph
National Gallery,
London.

EDGAR DEGAS (1834–1917)

3. Sur la Plage c.1876–7
Oil on paper on canvas 46 x 81.
Inscr: 'Degas' b.r.
Coll: National Gallery, London.
Prov: Henri Rouart; Sir Hugh Lane 1912; Tate Gallery 1917, transferred to National Gallery, London 1950.
Exh: Third Impressionist Exhibition, Paris, April 1877 (50, as *Bains de Mer; Petite Fille Peignée par sa Bonne*).
Lit: Thomas Bodkin, *Hugh Lane and his Pictures*, 1932, repr. pl.27, and subsequent eds.; John Rothenstein, *One hundred modern Foreign Pictures in the Tate Gallery*, 1947, repr. pl.54; Martin Davies, catalogue of the *French School*, National Gallery, London, 1957, p.68.

Martin Davies (loc. cit.) notes that it is possible that in this picture Degas was influenced by Manet. Ambrose Vollard claims that Degas said that it was painted in the studio, not in the open air. A lithograph of the picture was made by G.W. Thornley in about 1889.

212

Cata. no. 4.
Photograph
National Gallery,
London.

ÉDOUARD MANET (1832–83)

4. Éva Gonzalès 1870
Oil on canvas 191 x 133.
Inscr: 'Manet 1870' b.r.
Coll: National Gallery, London.
Prov: Given by Manet to the sitter; Henri Guérard, the sitter's husband; Durand-Ruel 1899; Sir Hugh Lane 1906; Tate Gallery 1917, transferred to National Gallery, London, 1950.
Exh: Paris Salon, 1870 (1852, as *Portrait de Mlle. E.G.*); Manet Exhibition, Paris, 1884 (56); *Exposition Centennale de L'Art Français*, Paris, 1900 (443); *Internationale Kunstausstellung*, Munich, June–October 1901 (1118a); *Grosse Kunstausstellung*, Dresden, 1904 (2200); *Pictures presented to the City of Dublin to form the nucleus of a Gallery of Modern Art, also Pictures lent by the Executors of the late Mr. J. Staats Forbes and others*, Winter, 1904 (4); Grafton Galleries, London, January–February 1905 (101); MGMA, between 1908 and 1913 (122); *Manet and his Circle*, Tate Gallery, 1954 (10).
Lit: *A Selection from the Pictures*, pl.17, Salon d'Automne, Pairs, October–November 1905, p.191, no.8 of Manet section; Thomas Bodkin, *Hugh Lane and his Pictures*, 1932, repr. pl.41, and subsequent eds.; John Rothenstein, *One hundred modern Foreign Pictures in the Tate Gallery*, 1947, repr. pl.28; Martin Davies, catalogue of the *French School*, National Gallery, London, 1957, pp.140–1; Kenneth McConkey, exhibition catalogue, *Orpen and the Edwardian Era*, Pyms Gallery, London, 1987, pp.82–3, repr.

The painter Éva Gonzalès (1849–83) was Manet's pupil from 1869. She married Henri Guérard, an engraver, in 1879.

Cata. no. 5.
Photograph
National Gallery,
London.

CLAUDE MONET (1840–1926)

5. Vétheuil: Sunshine and Snow 1881
Oil on canvas 59.5 x 81.
Inscr: 'Claude Monet 1881' b.r.
Coll: National Gallery, London.
Prov: Durand-Ruel 1891; Sir Hugh Lane 1905; Tate Gallery 1917, transferred to
National Gallery, London, 1950.
Exh: *Grosse Berliner Kunst-Austellung*, Berlin, 1903 (621); Grafton Galleries,
London, January–February 1905 (119); National Museum of Ireland, 1905 (10);
MGMA, between 1908 and 1913 (109).
Lit: Thomas Bodkin, *Hugh Lane and his Pictures*, 1932, repr. pl.43, and
subsequent eds.; John Rothenstein, *One hundred modern Foreign Pictures in the
Tate Gallery*, 1947, repr. pl.45; Martin Davies, catalogue of the *French School*,
National Gallery, London, 1957, pp.160–1, as *Lavacourt (?), Winter*.

Vétheuil is on the Seine, below Mantes. Although the picture has traditionally been
called *Vétheuil*, Bodkin (op. cit.) claims that the scene is Lavacourt, a village on the
opposite side of the Seine from Vétheuil. In concept and execution this picture is
quintessentially Impressionist.

PAUL HENRY (1876–1958)

6. The Potato Diggers 1910–11
Oil on canvas 71 x 81.
Inscr: 'PAUL HENRY' b.l.
Private collection.
Exh: (?) *Paintings of Irish Life: Mr. & Mrs. Paul Henry*, Pollock's Gallery, Belfast, March 1911 (35); *Pictures of the West of Ireland by Mr. & Mrs. Paul Henry*, Mills' Hall, Dublin, April 1917 (39); (?) *Paintings by Mr. & Mrs. Paul Henry*, Magee's Gallery, Belfast, April 1920 (10); New Irish Salon, Mills' Hall, Dublin, February–March 1926 (2); (?) *Paintings & Charcoals: Paul Henry R.H.A.*, Waddington Galleries, Dublin, February–March 1952 (16); *Irish Painting 1903–1953*, MGMA, April–July 1953 (49); *Some Paintings by Modern Irish Artists*, Crawford School of Art, Cork, April–May 1960 (15, repr. facing p.7); *Paul Henry 1876–1958*, TCD & UM, October 1973–January 1974 (7, repr. p.10).
Lit: Kennedy: 1987, vol.1, pp.34, 37, repr. vol.2 pl.1; 'Paul Henry: An Irish Portrait', *Irish Arts Review, Yearbook 1989–90*, 1989, p.45, repr. p.46; *Irish Times,* 20 December 1989, p.12, repr.; Kenneth McConkey, *A Free Spirit: Irish Art 1860–1960*, 1990, p.159.

Paul Henry's earliest oil paintings date mainly from the beginning of his Achill period and are dominated by figure compositions of peasants working in the fields or, occasionally, at play. The 'potato diggers' was one of his favourite subjects and he made a number of compositions on this theme. This picture was painted shortly after he first visited Achill. The pose of the figures is similar to that in a number of works by Millet, which Henry knew from seeing his paintings in Paris and from Alfred Sensier's *Life of Millet* (1881), which he read as a young man. Another, smaller, version of this composition, with the figures identically posed but with a different background, is reproduced in McConkey, op. cit., p.159.

Exhibited HLMG only.

Cata. no. 7.
Photograph
Ulster Museum.

JOHN (SEÁN) KEATING (1889–1977)

7. Slán leat, a Athair/Goodbye, Father 1935
Oil on canvas 175.9 x 175.
Inscr: 'KEATING' b.l.
Coll: Ulster Museum.
Prov: Haverty Trust, Dublin; to UM 1941.

Exh: RHA, 1936 (82); Haverty Trust, *Second Quinquennial Exhibition,* National College of Art, Dublin, 1940 (35); *A Vision of Ireland: 20th Century Irish Paintings,* Herbert Art Gallery, Coventry, 1989 (14, repr.); *A Room with a View,* UM, October 1990–March 1991 (no numbers).
Lit: *A Concise Catalogue of the Drawings, Paintings & Sculptures in the Ulster Museum,* 1986, p.70; Kennedy: 1987, vol.1, pp.316, 328, 344, 345, repr. vol.2, pl.164; 'Irish landscape painting in a political setting, 1922–48', M. Hill & S. Barber (eds.), *Aspects of Irish Studies,* 1990, p.50; Kenneth McConkey, *A Free Spirit: Irish Art 1860–1960,* 1990, p.67, repr.

Painted on Inisheer, the smallest of the Aran Islands. The composition depicts the departure of a priest from the island to the mainland, and the figures depicted were locals who were well-known to Keating, who had lived on the island periodically from 1914. Keating is seen at his best when portraying a narrative event, such as the subject of this composition.

Cata. no. 8.
Photograph
Ulster Museum.

PAUL HENRY (1876–1958)

8. Dawn, Killary Harbour 1922–3
Oil on canvas 69.1 x 83.3.
Inscr: 'PAUL HENRY' b.l.
Coll: Ulster Museum.
Prov: Magee Gallery, Belfast.
Exh: *Pictures by Mr. & Mrs. Paul Henry,* Magee's Gallery, Belfast, April 1923;

218

Northern Ireland Painters, Art Exhibitions Bureau, London, tour to Harrogate, Reading, Battersea, Gateshead, Guildford, Nottingham, Southgate, Southend, Hartlepool, September 1959–September 1960 (all 23); *100 Years of Ulster Landscapes,* UM, 1967; *Paul Henry 1876–1958,* TCD & UM, October 1973–January 1974 (39); *A Vision of Ireland: 20th Century Irish Painting,* Herbert Art Gallery & Museum, Coventry, 1989 (9); *A Room with a View,* UM, October 1990–March 1991 (no numbers).

Lit: Bruce Arnold: 'Landscape into Art', *Ireland of the Welcomes,* vol.17, May–June 1968, p.28, repr.; *A Concise History of Irish Art,* 1969, p.167, repr. in colour pl.139, revised ed. 1977, p.140, repr. in colour; Patrick Trevor-Roper, *The World Through Blunted Sight,* 1970, revised ed., 1988, repr. in colour; Paul Henry, *Further Reminiscences,* 1973, repr. p.57 and in colour on cover; George Dawson, 'Paul Henry 1876–1958', *Ireland of the Welcomes,* vol.25, March–April 1976, p.25, repr in colour; *A Concise Catalogue of the Drawings, Paintings & Sculptures in the Ulster Museum,* 1986, p.50; *Rhyme & Reason,* 1987, repr. pl.139; Kennedy: 1987, vol.1, p.42, repr. vol.2, pl. 6; 'Paul Henry: An Irish Portrait', *Irish Arts Review, Yearbook 1989–90,* p.50, repr. in colour p.53; *Paul Henry 1876–1958,* 1991, p.9, repr.

In this painting can be seen many of the characteristics of Paul Henry at his best: there is a complete absence of people, yet a redolence of humanity; a strong sense of early morning light and atmosphere; and, in the simple massing of forms and almost monochromatic palette, an emphasis on abstraction underpinning the composition. The latter quality demonstrates the influence of Whistler, which remained with Henry throughout his career but which was particularly strong in his work of the early-mid 1920s. This rendering of Killary Harbour, a fjord-like inlet in Connemara, is one of Henry's finest 'pure' landscapes.

GRACE HENRY (1868–1953)

9. The Top of the Hill c.1910–13
Oil on canvas 61 x 50.5.
Inscr: 'G. Henry' b.r.
Coll: Limerick City Gallery of Art.
Lit: Kennedy, 1987, vol.1, p.51, repr. vol.2, pl.15.

Almost certainly painted shortly after Grace Henry first went to Achill. The treatment of the subject in an almost illustrative manner contrasts with Paul Henry's more *malerisch* rendering of the same theme in a number of compositions of these years.

Cata. no. 10.
Photograph
Bryan Rutledge.

GRACE HENRY (1868–1953)

10. Spring in Winter No.9 c.1920–5
Oil on canvas 50.8 x 61.
Inscr: 'G. Henry' b.r.
Coll: J.G. Cruickshank.
Prov: Sold, James Adams, Dublin, 1982.
Lit: Kennedy, 1987, vol.1, p.51, repr. vol.2, pl.18.

This is a good example of Grace Henry's boldly Expressionist work of the 1920s. The fervour of her brushwork and jarring contrasts of reds and greens are probably the result of her mood at the time, for the 1920s were an unsettled period in her life. Almost certainly painted in the west of Ireland, the picture is quite different in feeling to the more romantic images generally associated with that area.

Cata. no. 11.

E.M.O'R. DICKEY (1894–1977)

11. From the Summit of Errigal 1919–23
Oil on canvas 76.5 x 101.5.
Inscr: 'DICKEY' b.l.; also 'E.M.O'R. DICKEY 1919', and 'Entirely re-painted
1923' on reverse.
Private collection, Bedford.
Prov: By descent from the artist.
Exh: (?) *Paintings of the Sabine Mountains & other Subjects by E.M.O'R. Dickey*,
Leicester Galleries, London, December 1923 (32, as *Lough Altan, County
Donegal, from the summit of Errigal*).
Lit: Kennedy, 1987, vol.1, p.48, repr. vol.2, pl.12.

In this composition Dickey has treated the landscape as a panorama seen from a
height, in a manner which became characteristic of his work in general. His rendering
of the Irish landscape is refreshingly free from the sentimentality associated with
most of his native contemporaries.

12. San Vito, Romano 1923

Oil on canvas 82.1 x 101.9.
Inscr: 'DICKEY' b.l., also 'E.M.O'R. DICKEY 1923' on reverse.
Coll: Ulster Museum.
Exh: Royal Academy, London, 1923 (623).
Lit: *Colour*, summer 1924 (no details); *A Concise Catalogue of the Drawings, Paintings & Sculptures in the Ulster Museum*, 1986, p.31; Kennedy, 1987, vol.1, p.48, repr. vol.2, pl.10.

This is a good example of Dickey's approach to landscape seen as a panorama and viewed from a height. The strong sense of atmospheric heat is also typical of much of his work done near Rome in the early 1920s. The emphasis on the formal structure of the landscape and the block-like shapes of the houses stepped up a hillside recalls Cézanne, but the treatment of the foreground and foliage betrays the influence of Dickey's contemporaries and friends in London, notably Harold Gilman and Robert Bevan. San Vito is a town situated about forty miles east of Rome.

Exhibited UM only.

JACK B. YEATS (1871–1957)

13. Riverside Long Ago 1923

Oil on canvas 61.4 x 91.7.
Inscr: 'JACK B. YEATS' b.l.
Coll: Ulster Museum.
Prov: Artist's studio to Dawson Gallery, Dublin; Ms. Kathleen Fox; Waddington
Gallery, Dublin; to UM 1967.
Exh: *Life in the West of Ireland: Pictures by Jack B. Yeats*, Engineers' Hall,
Dublin, March 1924; *A Vision of Ireland: 20th Century Irish Painting*, Herbert Art
Gallery & Museum, Coventry, 1989 (14, repr.)
Lit: *Connoisseur*, vol.164, January–April 1967, p.185, repr.; Bruce Arnold, *A
Concise History of Irish Art*, 1969, p.162, repr. pl.134, revised ed., 1977, p.138,
repr. pl.135; Hilary Pyle, *Jack B. Yeats*, 1970, p.123 and revised ed. 1989, p.123;
J. Ford Smith, 'Acquisitions of Modern Art by Museums', *Burlington Magazine*,
vol.113, August 1971, p.490 (35), repr. p.491; *A Concise Catalogue of the
Drawings, Paintings & Sculptures in the Ulster Museum*, 1986, p.181.

This picture belongs to what is usually called Yeats' middle period. The setting is
the riverside at Sligo, although the composition was probably made from Yeats'
'pool of memories', drawn from his sketchbooks. Ms. Nora Niland, librarian and
curator of Sligo County Library and Museum told the author (letter of 5 December
1978): 'There is a place in Sligo facing the Garavogue river which is known as "The

Riverside". It is here that boats were hired for the trip to Lough Gill. The place was undoubtedly well known to Jack B. Yeats when he lived with his grandparents, the Pollexfens, in Sligo during his childhood. He came back to Sligo frequently as a young man to relive the early scenes. Sligo was very dear to him and gave him the inspiration for many of his paintings among them being "Riverside long ago" and "Leaving the far point".' Hilary Pyle has noted that the figures of a man and woman in this composition appear also in another work by Yeats, namely *The Waterfall, Glencar, Co. Sligo* of 1924 (catalogue, *Irish Paintings from the 24th Irish Antique Dealers' Fair*, Cynthia O'Connor Gallery, Dublin, August 1989, no.2).

Cata. no. 14.
Photograph
Bryan Rutledge.

LETITIA HAMILTON (1880–1964)

14. Venice 1923–4
Oil on canvas 50 x 57.
Not inscribed.
Private collection.
Prov: By descent.
Exh: Dublin Painters' gallery, February 1924 (no details); (?) RHA, 1933 (9).
Lit: Kennedy, 1987, vol.1, p.89, repr. vol.2, pl.44; exhibition catalogue, *Irish Women Artists*, 1987, p.36, repr.

This work was almost certainly painted in the autumn of 1923 during Letitia Hamilton's first visit to Venice with her sister, Eva. The effect of the strong Italian sunshine evident in the work, was an influence which remained with her for the rest of her career. Her technique of using a heavy impasto, often applied with a palette knife is also evident here.

Exhibited HLMG only.

LETITIA HAMILTON (1880–1964)

15. Donkeys c.1930–2
Oil on board 55.9 x 66.
Inscr: 'LMH' b.l.
Coll: Ulster Museum.
Prov: Haverty Trust, Dublin; to UM 1936.
Exh: RHA, 1932 (94); Haverty Trust, *First Exhibition of Paintings*, Mansion House, Dublin, November 1935 (1).
Lit: *A Concise Catalogue of the Drawings, Paintings & Sculptures in the Ulster Museum*, 1986, p.47.

Letitia Hamilton was well-known for her paintings of market scenes in the midlands of Ireland, of which this is a good example. Usually she worked on the spot, recording events with great spontaneity. Her manner is refreshingly free from the rigidities of academic painting.

Exhibited UM only.

HARRIET KIRKWOOD (1880–1953)

16. House near Clondalkin c.1936
Oil on canvas 61.5 x 74.
Not inscribed.
Private collection.
Prov: By family descent to present owner.
Lit: Kennedy, 1987, vol.1, p.90, repr. vol.2, pl.46.

Although Harriet Kirkwood approached painting in a fairly traditional manner, the feeling for form and structure in this composition nevertheless shows the influence of Cézanne, whom she greatly admired. Much of her work, as here, is strongly lyrical in character, and her style changed little over the years. She was, however, opposed to the narrow outlook of nationalism prevalent in Ireland in her time and felt that if artists were truly to create a worthwhile and distinct school of painting they should endeavour to reflect in their work the spirit of the times and eschew mere symbols of nationality.

Cata. no. 17.
Photograph
Ulster Museum.

CHARLES LAMB (1893–1964)

17. A Lough Neagh Fisherman 1920
Oil on canvas 76 x 50.8.
Inscr: 'C. LAMB 1920' b.r.
Coll: Ulster Museum.
Exh: RHA, 1921 (158); Belfast Art Society, BMAG, October–November 1921
(218); *Charles Lamb R.H.A. 1893–1964*, Memorial Exhibition, MGMA, April
1969 (2).
Lit: *Studio*, vol.88, July–December 1924, p.162, repr.; exhibition catalogue, *Celtic
Splendour*, Pyms Gallery, London, 1985, p.90; Martyn Anglesea, *The Royal
Ulster Academy of Arts*, 1981, pp.62, 65, repr.; *A Concise Catalogue of the
Drawings, Paintings & Sculptures in the Ulster Museum*, 1986, p.71; Kennedy,
1987, vol.1, p.86, repr. vol.2, pl.41; Kenneth McConkey, *A Free Spirit: Irish Art
1860–1960*, 1990, pp.63, 64, repr., 79, 157.

This work shows Lamb at the height of his powers. Painted just before he first visited
the west of Ireland, it demonstrates his ability to represent figures as character 'types'.
A prominent member of the Dublin Painters' Society, Lamb later became one of its
more academic members.

Cata. no. 18.

CHARLES LAMB (1893–1964)

18. Hearing the News c.1920–2
Oil on canvas 63.3 x 53.3.
Inscr: 'C. LAMB' b.r.
Private collection.
Exh: Dublin Painters, autumn exhibition, 1922; *Charles Lamb R.H.A : A Memorial Exhibition*, MGMA, April 1969 (8, repr.)
Lit: Thomas Bodkin (intro.), *Twelve Irish Artists*, 1940, repr.; Kennedy: 1987, vol.1, p.86, repr. vol.2, pl.3; 'Irish landscape painting in a political setting, 1922–48', M. Hill & S. Barber (eds.), *Aspects of Irish Studies*, 1990, p.48.

In its depiction of a reader reading the news to a group of companions, this composition represents a scene common in the west of Ireland in the 1920s and earlier.

230

Cata. no. 19.
Photograph
Bryan Rutledge.

MARY SWANZY (1882–1978)

19. White Tower (San Gimignano) c.1925–7
Oil on canvas 100 x 80.5.
Inscr: 'SWANZY' b.l.
Collection Pat and Antoinette Murphy.
Prov: Bequeathed to the present owner by the artist.
Lit: Kennedy, 1987, vol.1, p.60, repr. vol.2, pl.26.

This is an example of the more formal, semi-Cubist style which Mary Swanzy evolved in the late 1920s. While such works lack the theoretical aspect of Cubism proper, they recall the dynamic movement and energy associated with the Italian Futurists, and *White Tower*, with its upward thrust of a tall building, may have been influenced by the architectural drawings of the well-known Futurist, Antonio Sant'Elia. San Gimignano, a town in Tuscany, is well-known for its tall towers.

Cata. no. 20.
Photograph
Hugh Lane Municipal
Gallery of Modern
Art.

MARY SWANZY (1882–1978)

20. The Message c.1940–5
Oil on panel 45.7 x 53.3.
Coll: Hugh Lane Municipal Gallery of Modern Art.
Prov: Haverty Trust, Dublin; to MGMA 1945.
Exh: *Mary Swanzy*, retrospective exhibition, MGMA, June 1968 (25); *Irish Art 1900–1950*, Cork, December 1975–January 1976 (138, repr.); *Irish Women Artists*, Dublin, 1987 (136, repr.)
Lit: Julian Campbell, *Mary Swanzy HRHA (1882–1978)*, Pyms Gallery, London, 1986, pp.24, 73, repr. p.25.

Dated 1926–40 in the catalogue of the 1968 retrospective exhibition, but stylistically this work almost certainly dates from the early-mid 1940s. Swanzy was profoundly affected by the horror and destruction of the Second World War and in compositions such as this she made use of Symbolism to express her belief in the ultimate triumph of humility over aggression.

Cata. no. 21.
Photograph
Ulster Museum.

MAINIE JELLETT (1897–1944)

21. Seated Female Nude 1921–2
Oil on canvas 56.3 x 46.2.
Not inscribed.
Coll: Ulster Museum.

Prov: Artist's estate; Miss Bay Jellett; Neptune Gallery, Dublin; to UM 1975.
Exh: *Mainie Jellett 1897–1944*, Neptune Gallery, September–October 1974 (21, repr.); *Some Recent Acquisitions*, UM, March–April 1976 (28); *Irish Women Artists*, Dublin, 1987 (116, repr.).
Lit: *A Concise Catalogue of the Drawings, Paintings & Sculptures in the Ulster Museum*, 1986, p.63; Kennedy, 1987, vol.1, p.64, repr. vol.2, pl.28.

Probably painted shortly after Mainie Jellett first began to work in a Cubist manner under André Lhote. Amongst the artist's sketchbooks is one, signed and dated 'March 20th 1922' and inscribed 'Paris', which contains five preliminary drawings for this painting. The highly formalized treatment of the figure, the chair in which she is seated and the background in this composition, all of which combine to suggest a flattening of the picture-plane, are characteristic of early, or 'Analytical', Cubism.

Cata. no. 22.
Photograph
Ulster Museum.

234

MAINIE JELLETT (1897–1944)

22. Abstract 1922
Oil on canvas 91.9 x 72.
Inscr: 'M. JELLETT 1922' b.l.
Coll: Ulster Museum.
Prov: Dr. Eileen MacCarvill; Neptune Gallery, Dublin; to UM, 1975.
Exh: Paris, 1922 (no details); *Mainie Jellett 1897–1944*, Neptune Gallery,
September–October 1974 (26, repr.); *Some Recent Acquisitions*, UM, March–
April 1976 (34); *A Vision of Ireland: 20th Century Irish Painting*, Herbert Art
Gallery & Museum, Coventry, 1989 (17, repr.)
Lit: Bruce Arnold, *A Concise History of Irish Art*, revised ed., 1977, repr. p.147; *A
Concise Catalogue of the Drawings, Paintings & Sculptures in the Ulster
Museum*, 1986, p.63; Kennedy: 1987, vol.1, pp.66–7, repr. vol.2, pl.5; 'Irish
landscape painting in a political setting, 1922–48', M. Hill & S. Barber (eds.),
Aspects of Irish Studies, 1990, p.52.

This is one of Mainie Jellett's first, and finest, abstract paintings. The forms are
concisely resolved and boldly juxtaposed one with another and the colours and
handling of paint are used in a manner complementary to the translation and rotation
technique which Jellett developed with Albert Gleizes, and do not detract from it.
The importance of the work, too, lies in the fact that it is amongst the first one or two
truly abstract paintings to have been produced by any Irish artist.

23. Abstract 1925
Oil on canvas 49 x 74.
Inscr: 'M Jellett 1925' b.r.
Private collection, London.
Lit: Kennedy, 1987, vol.1, p.68, repr. vol.2, pl.29.

This is one of the more elaborate compositions which Mainie Jellett developed in
the mid-late 1920s. Usually such works are characterized by a combination of separate
images, or 'voices' as Bruce Arnold has called them, each evolved through the process
of translation and rotation and related to one another within the overall composition
but with a degree of autonomy in themselves. The use of muted colours and an
emphasis on line are also features of these pictures, which recall some of Picasso's
paintings of the same years, such as *Three Masked Musicians*, 1921, or *The Three
Dancers*, 1925 (Tate Gallery).

EVIE HONE (1894–1955)

24. Composition c.1924–30
Oil on canvas 114.5 x 88.
Inscr: 'E. HONE' b.r.
Coll: National Gallery of Ireland.
Lit: Kennedy, 1987, vol.1, p.73, repr. vol.2, pl.32.

In the early 1920s Evie Hone's approach to composition, using the idea of translation
and rotation, was similar to that of Mainie Jellett, but she was never as fully committed

to Cubism as was Jellett and she seems to have concerned herself hardly at all with its theoretical principles. On the contrary, there is always a strong intuitive element in her work and in the late 1930s this more or less ousted the Cubist influence altogether.

25. Landscape with a Tree 1943
Oil on board 69 x 69.
Inscr: 'E. Hone 1943' b.r.
Coll: National Gallery of Ireland.
Prov: Miss R. Kirkpatrick, by whom bequeathed to the NGI, 1979.
Exh: IELA, 1943 (128); *Irish Women Artists*, Dublin, 1987 (122, repr.)
Lit: NGI, *Illustrated Summary Catalogue of Paintings,* 1981, p.218, repr.;
Kennedy, 1987, vol.1, p.74, repr. vol.2, pl.34.

This is an example of Evie Hone's later, Expressionist work done after she had more or less abandoned Cubism. It shows the influence of Rouault whom she admired at the time. The treatment of the background, however, betrays her earlier Cubist work.

Cata. no. 26.
Photograph
Bryan Rutledge.

CECIL SALKELD (1904–1969)

26. Figure Composition 1922
Watercolour on paper 33.8 x 44.
Inscr: 'C. Salkeld.,22' b.r.
Private collection, Dublin.
Prov: By descent.
Lit: Kennedy: 1987, vol.1, p.80, repr. vol.2, pl.36; 'Irish landscape painting in a political setting, 1922–48', in M. Hill & S. Barber (eds.), *Aspects of Irish Studies*, 1990, p.52.

In the early 1920s Salkeld's work was strongly experimental. While he was greatly influenced by the German *Neue Sachlichkeit* movement at the time, there are also traces in his work of the Italian *Pittura Metafisica* painters, such as Giorgio de Chirico. This composition recalls the latter, notably in the rounded forms and hint of symbolism in the imagery.

27. Cinema c.1922–5
Woodcut on paper 22.5 x 17.
Inscr: 'R. Boyd-Morrison from Cecil ffrench Salkeld 1/1/27'.
Private collection, Belfast.
Prov: R. Boyd Morrison.
Lit: Kennedy, 1987, vol.1, p.80, repr. vol.2, fig.5.

This is one of a few woodcuts which Salkeld made in the early 1920s while under the influence of the German *Neue Sachlichkeit* movement. Probable influences on such works were the painters Lyonel Feininger and Oscar Schlemmer and the printmakers E. Dulberg and Heinrich Campendonck. But unlike his German contemporaries, Salkeld did not concern himself with social criticism in these works which are entirely decorative. The emphasis on line apparent here is characteristic of Salkeld's work in general. In 1927 Salkeld collaborated with the Belfast painter R. Boyd Morrison and George Sheringham on the publication of *Robes of Thespis: Costume Designs by Modern Artists* (London, 1928). This print was clearly inscribed for Morrison as a result of that collaboration.

HARRY KERNOFF (1900–74)

28. Bend in the Road near Richmond, Surrey 1947

Oil on board 68.5 x 99.
Inscr: 'KERNOFF 47' b.r.
Coll: Ulster Museum.
Prov: Godolphin Gallery, Dublin; Elizabeth Guinness, Dublin.
Exh: RHA, 1947 (133); *Harry Kernoff Memorial Exhibition,* HLMG, December
1976–January 1977 (75, repr.)
Lit: Kennedy, 1987, vol.1, p.95.

Unlike his Irish contemporaries, who usually emphasized the mood and atmosphere
of the scene they were painting, Kernoff emphasized the physical nature of the
landscape and often focused attention on aspects such as architectural features. As
here, his landscapes are strongly linear, often with curves thrusting into the
background. The almost naïve charm and gentle mannerism of this composition are
characteristic of many of his later works.

NANO REID (1905–81)

29. Galway Peasant 1929
Oil on canvas 41 x 30.7.
Inscr: 'N. Reid' b.r.
Coll: Ulster Museum.
Prov: Haverty Trust, Dublin; to UM 1936.
Exh: Aonach Tailteann, Exhibition of Irish Art, Metropolitan School of Art,
Dublin, June–July 1932 (17); Haverty Trust, First Quinquennial Exhibition,

240

Mansion House, Dublin, November 1935 (21); *Paintings from Belfast Museum & Art Gallery*, Carnegie Hall, Lurgan, January 1961 (23); *Nano Reid: Retrospective Exhibition*, MGMA and UM, November 1974–February 1975 (both 3).
Lit: *A Concise Catalogue of the Drawings, Paintings & Sculptures in the Ulster Museum*, 1986, p.139; Kennedy, 1987, vol.1, p.257, repr. vol.2, pl.120.

This painting shows the bold simplicity and forceful character of Nano Reid's early work. It also recalls Paul Henry's paintings of Connemara peasants done about twenty years earlier. The artist wrote (letter of 25 March 1977, UM archives) that the picture was painted at Letterfrack, Co. Galway, the sitter being a Mrs. Conboy, in whose cottage she lived for two months.

Exhibited UM only.

Cata. no. 30.
Photograph
Bryan Rutledge.

NORAH McGUINNESS (1903–80)

30. The Thames 1932–4
Gouache on paper 34.7 x 50 (sight).
Inscr: 'Norah McGuinness' b.r.
Private collection, Co. Down.
Prov: Taylor Gallery, Dublin.

Exh: (?) *Norah McGuinness*, Zwemmer Gallery, London, February 1934 (no details); (?) *Norah McGuinness*, Dublin Painters' gallery, Dublin, March 1936 (no details); (?) Opening exhibition, Picture Hire Club, Dublin, March 1941; *Norah McGuinness*, TCD, October–November 1968 (22); *Irish Women Artists*, HLMG, July–August 1987 (no numbers, repr. p.41 and in colour pl.25).
Lit: Kennedy, 1987, vol.1, p.253, repr. vol.2, pl.118.

It seems likely that this work was exhibited in Norah McGuinness' one-woman exhibition at the Zwemmer Gallery in 1934, for reviewing that show *The Times* commented on her organization of space and forms such 'as that of a barge in three-quarters view,' which, it thought, had an 'uncommonly good' sense of values (*The Times*, 26 February 1934). The French Fauvist painter Vlaminck exerted a strong influence on Norah McGuinness in the early 1930s, as can be seen clearly in a group of gouaches done in those years inspired by the river Thames near to where she lived at Hammersmith. These works, of which this is one, are all handled with great bravura and combine brisk brushwork and a lively massing of tones. In them the colours, however, are less strident than one would expect from a Fauvist influence. Arguably, McGuinness never surpassed these paintings, either in concept or execution. The medium, gouache, is perfectly suited to the spontaneity of approach, the dark hues and massing of juxtaposed forms such as barges and warehouses and the areas of contrasting tones ably convey the atmosphere of a great river at work and, although no figures appear, always one senses the bustle of the actual scene which is set down with great simplicity. There is, too, little attempt to suggest recession and, while the imagery is treated in a representational manner, she constantly reminds one of the flatness of the picture-plane, an influence, no doubt, from her earlier Cubist studies. There is a slight melancholy feeling about many of McGuinness' paintings of these years which, in retrospect, may be seen as a metaphor for the times.

HILDA ROBERTS (1901–82)

31. Portrait of George Russell (AE) 1929

Oil on canvas 76.2 x 63.8.

Inscr: 'HILDA ROBERTS. 1929' b.l.

Coll: Ulster Museum.

Prov: Artist's studio.

Exh: *Irish Painters*, Hackett Gallery, New York, February–March 1930; Hilda
Roberts, *Paintings and Drawings*, Dublin Painters' gallery, Dublin, June 1931
(35); *Aonach Tailteann*, Exhibition of Irish Art, Metropolitan School of Art,

Dublin, June–July 1932 (19); RHA, 1933 (289); *Portraits of Great Irish Men and Women*, UM, 1965 (193); *Irish Art 1900–1950*, Crawford Art Gallery, Cork, December 1975–January 1976 (124); *Portraits of Irish Writers*, UM, June–August 1985 (10); *Irish Women Artists*, NGI, 1987 (128, repr).

Lit: *Dublin Magazine*, vol.10, no.4 (new series), 1935, repr.; John Hewitt: 'George William Russell ("AE")', BMAG, *Quarterly Notes*, 53, June 1937, pp.8–10 and repr. as frontispiece; 'The Folded Dream: The Printed Words of AE', *Arts in Ireland,* vol.1, no.3, p.50, repr.; *A Concise Catalogue of the Drawings, Paintings & Sculptures in the Ulster Museum*, 1986, p.140; Kennedy, 1987, vol.1, p.101.

Repr: BMAG, *Report*, 1937, as frontispiece; Henry Summerfield, *That Myriad-Minded Man: a biography of George William Russell "A.E." 1867–1935*, 1975, repr. in colour on cover.

George Russell, better known by his pseudonym 'AE', was a painter, poet, journalist and economist. He was a pivotal figure in the Irish Literary Revival. Born in 1867 in Lurgan, Co. Armagh, he was a contemporary and friend of W.B. Yeats. He became a prominent member of Dublin's Theosophical Society and later was associated with Sir Horace Plunkett's Irish Agricultural Organization Society and edited its journals, the *Irish Homestead* (1905–23) and the *Irish Statesman* (1923–30). Throughout these years he continued to paint, often working during the summer at Marble Hill in Co. Donegal. He also published a number of collections of poems, including his *Collected Poems* (1913), which in time underwent successive editions and enlargements. In 1933 he retired to England and died at Bournemouth in July 1935. Like his poems, AE's paintings deal mainly with spiritual imagery. Often in his work there is an evocation of wistfulness, a seeking for the 'essence' of the countryside. In this composition, which was commissioned by the Hackett Gallery, AE is portrayed as a man of ideas, as if about to surge into action. It well exemplifies Hilda Roberts' work as a portraitist, the genre for which she is best remembered.

LILIAN DAVIDSON (1879–1954)

32. Low Tide, Wicklow c.1934
Oil on canvas 73 x 92.
Inscr: Monogram b.l.
Coll: Ulster Museum.
Prov: Haverty Trust, Dublin, acquired from the RHA exhibition, 1934; to UM 1936.
Exh: RHA, 1934 (38); *First Exhibition of Paintings,* Haverty Trust, Dublin, 1935 (20); *Irish Art 1900–1950*, Crawford Art Gallery, Cork, December 1975–January 1976 (18).
Lit: Hilary Pyle, 'Irish Art 1900–1950', *Introspect,* no.1, December 1975, p.30 repr.; *A Concise Catalogue of the Drawings, Paintings & Sculptures in the Ulster Museum,* 1986, p.30.

Dated c.1934 on the assumption that it was recently painted when exhibited at the Royal Hibernian Academy.

JACK HANLON (1913–68)

33. Maynooth College c.1939
Watercolour on paper 27 x 33.
Inscr: 'J.P.HANLON' b.r.
Coll: St. Patrick's College, Maynooth.
Lit: Kennedy, 1987, vol.1, p.100, repr. vol.2, pl.61.

Much of Hanlon's best work was done in watercolour, in which medium his style was both agile and delightfully economic. As in this composition, he often treated his subject-matter humourously. In general his work is characterized by direct observation of his subject and brisk execution.

Exhibited HLMG only.

Cata. no. 34.
Photograph
Bryan Rutledge.

JACK HANLON (1913–68)

34. Still Life with Figure 1945
Oil on canvas 37 x 54
Inscr: 'J P HANLON 45' b.r.
Coll: St. Patrick's College, Maynooth.
Lit: Kennedy, 1987, vol.1, p.100, repr. vol.2, pl.60.

Although he had a mild flirtation with Cubism, Hanlon developed a style which, as can be seen here, laid emphasis on colour and light.

Exhibited HLMG only.

Cata. no. 35.
Photograph
National Gallery of
Ireland.

247

FRANCES KELLY (fl.1930s)

35. Seán T. O'Kelly 1947–8
Oil on canvas 91.5 x 71.5.
Inscr: 'FRANCES KELLY' b.r.
Coll: National Gallery of Ireland.
Prov: The sitter and by descent to his widow, at whose sale purchased by the NGI, 1984.
Exh: *Cuimhneachán 1916. A Commemorative Exhibition of the Irish Rebellion 1916*, NGI, 1966 (83).
Lit: NGI, *Acquisitions 1984–1986*, pp.16, 17 repr.

Seán T. O'Kelly was born in Dublin in 1882 and was educated at the O'Connell Schools. He was a founder-member of Sinn Féin and subsequently served as its Honorary Secretary. A member of the Irish Volunteers, he fought in the General Post Office, Dublin, during the Easter Rising of 1916. After a career of public service he became President of Ireland in 1945 and served in that office for the maximum of two seven year terms. He died in 1966.

MAY GUINNESS (1863–1955)

36. Still Life 1922–5
Oil on canvas 142 x 76.
Coll: Hugh Lane Municipal Gallery of Modern Art.
Prov: Artist's executors; to MGMA 1956.
Lit: Kennedy, 1987, vol.1, p.55, repr. vol.2, pl.22.

This composition illustrates the influence of André Lhote and Cubism on May Guinness in the early 1920s. Her technique in these years was to apply Cubist stylization to scenes from everyday life in order to make bold patterns but, at the same time, to retain recognizable imagery. This work is notable for its almost monochromatic use of colour.

Cata. no. 36.
Photograph
Hugh Lane Municipal
Gallery of Modern
Art.

37. Mardi Gras 1925–30
Oil on canvas 92 x 73.3.
Inscr: 'M.GUINNESS' b.r.
Coll: Corporation of Drogheda.
Prov: The artist's executors.
Exh: *Irish Art 1900–1950*, Crawford Art Gallery, Cork, December 1975–January 1976 (34).
Lit: Kennedy, 1987, vol.1, p.56, repr. vol.2, pl.24.

From the mid-late 1920s May Guinness returned from Cubism to a more Fauvist manner of painting. Rhythm and movement often invade her compositions in these years, as in this carnival scene with its gentle pastel colours evoking a mood of gay abandon.

Cata. no. 38.

RALPH CUSACK (1912–65)

38. Christmas in My Studio 1943
Oil on canvas 55 x 70.
Inscr: 'Cusack 43' b.l.

Collection Morris Sinclair, Switzerland.
Prov: A gift from the artist to the present owner.
Exh: IELA, 1943 (46); Ralph Cusack, *A Year's Painting,* Dublin Painters' gallery, Dublin, October–November 1943 (3).
Lit: Kennedy, 1987, vol.1, p.98, repr. vol.2, pl.55.

This is a good example of Cusack's involvement with Cubism which preoccupied him in the late 1930s and early 1940s. The juxtaposition of diverse themes—an interior, a still life, landscape—was common in his work at the time.

Cata. no. 39.
Photograph
Bryan Rutledge.

PATRICK HENNESSY (1915–81)

39. Kinsale Harbour 1940
Oil on canvas 50.8 x 38.1.
Inscr: 'Hennessy '40' b.r.; also 'Kinsale Aug. 25th 40' at left.
Coll: Limerick City Gallery of Art.
Exh: *Irish Art 1900–1950*, Craford Art Gallery, Cork, December 1975–January 1976 (42).

This composition illustrates the sense of almost Surrealist mystery and intrigue with which Hennessy could imbue his work. The meaning of the picture is something which we individually, as spectators, must bring to it. The high degree of realism in the treatment of the imagery is characteristic of Hennessy's work in general.

THURLOE CONOLLY (b.1918)

40. Hall's Barn, Rathfarnham 1945
Oil on board 52 x 41.5.
Inscr: 'Thurloe Conolly, Jan., 1945' on reverse.
Coll: Brian and Mary Boydell.
Exh: *Thurloe Conolly,* Dublin Painters' gallery, Dublin, February 1945 (no details); *Irish Art 1943–1973*, Crawford Art Gallery, Cork, August–November 1980 (21).
Lit: Kennedy, 1987, vol.1, p.261, repr. vol.2, pl.126.

This picture, with its emphasis on surface and the tactile nature of the picture-plane, shows the early phase of Conolly's work when he was much influenced by the English painter John Piper.

Cata. no. 40.
Photograph
Bryan Rutledge.

ELIZABETH RIVERS (1903–64)

41. The Ark 1948
Oil on canvas 40.6 x 50.8.
Inscr: 'Rivers' b.r.
Courtesy of the Gorry Gallery, Dublin.
Exh: (?) IELA, Dublin, August–September 1948 (91, as '*And the ark went upon the face of the waters*'); (?) Dublin Painters' gallery, Autumn Exhibition, October 1948 (20, as *The Ark in Storm*); *Elizabeth Rivers, Memorial Exhibition*, MGMA, Dublin, March 1966 (15); *Elizabeth Rivers 1903–1964: A Retrospective View*, Gorry Gallery, Dublin, May–June 1989 (5, repr. in colour on cover).

Despite the lyrical nature of this composition one can see the Cubist influence of André Lhote on Elizabeth Rivers' work of the late 1940s. The bold use of line to define forms, the use of strong colours and a broad brush, the mild Symbolism of the composition are features which remained characteristic of her work. In *The Ark* Rivers attained a degree of completeness which she rarely achieved in her later work. It is also one of the first of a number of works by her which have a strong religious theme.

JOHN LUKE (1906–75)

42. Connswater Bridge 1934

Oil on canvas 71 x 95.
Inscr: 'J.LUKE' b.r.
Coll: The Queen's University of Belfast.
Prov: Presented by the Queen's University Guild.
Exh: *Ulster Unit*, Locksley Hall, Belfast, December 1934 (17); *Ulster Artists Exhibition: The Work of John Luke*, BMAG, September 1946 (18); *John Luke (1906–1975)*, UM, January–March 1978 (25).
Lit: John Hewitt, *John Luke (1906–1975)*, 1978, pp.26, 35; Kennedy, 1987, vol.1, p.132, repr. vol.2, pl.64.

Here, in the use of large masses boldly juxtaposed one with another in a severely stylized manner, we can see the beginnings of the extreme stylization which characterizes Luke's later work and which ultimately stultified his development as an artist. Precise draughtsmanship is a notable feature, too, of his whole *œuvre*. The subject depicted here was a railway bridge in East Belfast. It was demolished in the 1970s.

R.C. TOOGOOD (1902–66)

43. The Backyard 1934
Oil on board 61.2 x 48.6.
Inscr: 'R.C. TOOGOOD 1934' b.r.
Coll: Mr. & Mrs. L. Powell.
Prov: Mrs. Anne Toogood.
Exh: *Ulster Unit*, Locksley Hall, Belfast, December 1934 (14); Ulster Academy of
Arts, Old Museum Building, Belfast, December 1934 (90); *R.C. Toogood 1902–
1966*, Arts Council of Northern Ireland, Belfast, April 1978 (13); *R.C. Toogood*,
Bell Gallery, Belfast, August 1989 (15).
Lit: Kennedy, 1987, vol.1, p.132, repr. vol.2, pl.65.

257

Painted in Dungannon, Co.Tyrone. The mild stylization apparent in this composition became a dominant feature of Toogood's work by the mid-1930s, but thereafter he adopted a more *malerisch* technique.

Cata. no. 44.
Photograph
Bryan Rutledge.

CECIL SALKELD (1904–69)

44. Leda and the Swan c.1943–8
Oil on canvas 59.5 x 49.5.
Inscr: 'Salkeld' b.l.
Private collection, Dublin.
Exh: *Cecil Salkeld: A Selection of His Paintings*, Godolphin Gallery, Dublin, 1980 (19).
Lit: Kennedy, 1987, vol.1, p.84, repr. vol.2, pl.39.

258

The strong stylization, precisely delineated forms and characteristically smooth paint surface of this composition show Salkeld at the height of his powers.

Cata. no. 45.
Photograph
Bryan Rutledge.

PAUL NIETSCHE (1885–1950)

45. Black Eve and Green Apples 1949
Oil on board 61 x 50.
Inscr: 'Paul Nietsche 1949' b.l.
Coll: Mr. & Mrs. A.H.K. Roberts.
Prov: Artist's estate.

Exh: *Exhibition of Recent Work by Paul Nietsche*, CEMA, Belfast, October 1949 (9); *Exhibition of Paintings by the late Paul Nietsche*, Ulster Farmers' Union Hall, Belfast, October–November 1952 (7).

The close attention paid to the form and structure of the objects depicted in this composition illustrate Nietsche's debt to Cézanne and to his teachers, Ladyzhensky and Kostandi, at the Art Academy in Odessa.

CHARLES EDWARD GRIBBON (1898–1939)

46. Ischia c.1934
Oil on canvas 50.3 x 61.
Coll: Mrs. G.H. Bryson.
Prov: Artist's studio.
Lit: Kennedy, 1987, vol.1, p.136, repr. vol.2, pl.69.

Gribbon's landscapes are characterized by the use of strong colours and an emphasis on sunlight which gives to them a distinct Mediterranean character. Here, his semi-Expressionist brushwork is perfectly matched to the rugged scene depicted.

Cata. no. 47.
Photograph
courtesy Eamonn
Mallie.

TOM CARR (b.1909)

47. Ormond Quay 1938
Oil on canvas 63.5 x 76.2.
Inscr: 'T. Carr' b.r.
Private collection, Belfast.
Exh: *Paintings by Thomas Carr*, Leicester Galleries, London, March 1945 (16);
Tom Carr Retrospective, UM and Douglas Hyde Gallery, Dublin, November
1983–January 1984 (12); *Tom Carr HRHA*, RHA, Dublin, November–December
1989 (34, repr. on cover in colour).
Lit: Eamonn Mallie, Tom *Carr,* 1989, p.31, repr.

Almost certainly painted during a visit to Dublin where Carr went to prepare for his
exhibition with the English painter Graham Bell at the Contemporary Picture Galleries
in May 1939. There is a watercolour study of this work in the Ulster Museum. The
emphasis on realism evident in this picture exemplifies all Tom Carr's work and
was reinforced by his association with the Euston Road Group in London in the
1930s.

Exhibited UM only.

BASIL RAKOCZI (1908–79)

48. Dublin Alley 1940
Oil on paper 77 x 97 (sight).
Inscr: 'Rakoczi' b.r.
Private collection.
Exh: *White Stag Group*, 30 Upper Mount Street, Dublin, October 1940 (6).
Lit: Kennedy, 1987, vol.1, p.185, repr. vol.2, pl.87.

The use of pencil to draw into the still wet paint in order to define forms, as has been
done in this picture, characterizes Rakoczi's technique at the time he came to Ireland.
It was a method of working which he developed in the late 1930s. In the early 1940s
Rakoczi drew a lot of inspiration from observing and setting down scenes from
everyday life in Dublin and, on his travels, in the west of Ireland.

Exhibited HLMG only.

BASIL RAKOCZI (1908–79)

49. Galway Market c.1943
Watercolour and ink on paper 48 x 65.
Inscr: 'Rakoczi' b.r.
Private collection, Brussels.
Exh: New English Art Club (no details); Midland Regional Group of Artists &
Designers, Nottingham, November 1950.

This is an excellent example of Rakoczi's representational manner of painting of the
mid-1940s, an approach which he maintained alongside his Subjective works of the
same years. The treatment of the subject-matter here, the handling of the paint and
sense of humour in the composition recall the English artist Edward Burra, whose
work Rakoczi would certainly have been familiar with.

Cata. no. 50.
Photograph
S.B.K.

KENNETH HALL (1913–46)

50. Old Phaleron, Greece 1938

Oil on board 50.5 x 71.1.
Inscr: 'HALL' b.r.; also 'VIEW FROM 79 ODOS TRITONOS, OLD
PHALERON 17/18/19/5/1938' on stretcher.
Private collection, Sussex.
Prov: Mrs. Lucy Wertheim; by descent to her daughter Hilary Hume.
Lit: Kennedy, 1987, vol.1, p.192, repr. vol.2, pl.91.

Painted during a visit to Greece with Basil Rakoczi in 1938. This composition marks
the beginning of the mature phase of Kenneth Hall's art. The treatment of the subject-
matter is, perhaps, the closest Hall ever came to naturalistic painting. The use of a
heavy black line to define forms characterizes his work at the time, and he and
Rakoczi both experimented with this technique. Old Phaleron is a suburb of Athens.
Writing of this work to his friend Lucy Carrington Wertheim (letter of 7 June 1940),
Hall commented, in a manner which illustrates the Expressionist nature of his approach
to art: 'I miss the picture of Athens, it's funny how one can be so terribly bound to
one's creation . . . that one cannot completely relinquish it. . . . I was very unhappy
when it was painted and having in addition a struggle with my work and it was the
only good oil that I did during my three months in Greece, which I loved so much.'

KENNETH HALL (1913–46)

51. Itea 1939
Oil on canvas 15.1 x 20.1.
Inscr: 'HALL' b.r.; also 'ITEA 22.1.39' on stretcher.
From the collection of Jacqueline Robinson, Paris.
Prov: Basil Rakoczi, who gave it to the present owner in the 1960s.
Lit: Kennedy, 1987, vol.1, p.192, repr. vol.2, pl.92.

Despite it small size, the brisk handling of paint and light-hearted treatment of the subject-matter in this painting show Hall at his best. There is a strong Dufyesque quality to the whole which in mood is more relaxed and less self-conscious than in almost any of his other works. Itea is a town by the sea in Greece, north west of Athens.

Cata. no. 52.
Photograph
Bryan Rutledge.

KENNETH HALL (1913–46)

52. Après la guerre 1941
Oil on canvas 28 x 41.2.
Inscr: 'Hall' b.l.; also titled and dated 'September 5th 1941 Hall' on stretcher.
Coll: Patrick Scott.
Prov: Given to the present owner by the artist.
Lit: Kennedy, 1987, vol.1, pp.193, 282, repr. vol.2, pl.97.

This is one of Kenneth Hall's most Expressionist paintings. It is also a *cri de coeur*, representing the depths of despair to which he was at times prone. After more than two years' forced exile in Ireland, with the war at its bleakest and his estrangement from his family almost total, he was utterly forlorn.

KENNETH HALL (1913–46)

53. Little Bird 1941
Oil on canvas 30.2 x 35 (sight).
Inscr: 'Hall' b.r.
Prov: A gift from the artist to the present owner's mother.
Private collection, Dublin.
Lit: Kennedy, 1987, vol.1, p.193, repr. vol.2, pl.96.

Hall was plainly in the depths of despair when he painted this composition. The handling of the paint is strongly gestural and the use of colour, conspicuous brushwork and emphasis on the existential act of painting anticipate post-war Abstract Expressionism. The symbolic image of a bird, which may be a dove, suggests a moral commitment to peace by the artist.

PHYLLIS HAYWARD (1903–85)

54. Still Life with Guitar early 1940s
Crayon and gouache on paper 45.5 x 36.4.
Inscr: 'HAYWARD' b.r.
Coll: Liam O'Leary private collection.
Lit: Kennedy, 1987, vol.1, p.208, repr. vol.2, pl.107.

The emphasis on line, spontaneity of execution, and use of mixed media in this painting characterize Phyllis Hayward's work in general.

Cata. no. 54.
Photograph
S.B.K.

266

BASIL RAKOCZI (1908–79)

55. Three 1943
Oil on canvas 55.3 x 72.3.
Inscr: 'Rakoczi' b.r.; also: 'HEADS WALKING BASIL RAKOCZI' on edge of
canvas.
Private collection, Bath.
Prov: Artist's studio and by descent to present owner.
Exh: *Exhibition of Subjective Art*, Dublin, January 1944 (40).
Lit: H. Ingouville-Williams, *Three Painters*, 1945, repr. pl.3 as *Three*; Kennedy,
1987, vol.1, pp.186, 187, repr. vol.2, pl.75.

This is one of Rakoczi's early Subjective paintings and illustrates his interest in
psychological fantasies and dreamlike images. There is in it a greater emphasis on
texture, surface and the play of one colour with another than is usual in his work.
This picture has also been called 'Heads Walking'.

Cata. no. 56.
Photograph
S.B.K.

BASIL RAKOCZI (1908–79)

56. Prisoner 1944
Oil on canvas 51.5 x 71.2.
Inscr: 'Rakoczi' b.r.
Private collection, Bath.
Prov: Artist's studio and by descent to the present owner.
Lit: H. Ingouville–Williams, *Three Painters*, 1945, repr. in colour as frontispiece;
Kennedy, 1987, vol.1, p.187, repr. vol.2, pl.90.

The imagery in this picture, especially the form of the head on the left, relates to that in a number of Rakoczi's other compositions of the time, such as *Child Flying,* of about late 1943. The theme is almost certainly autobiographical, referring to four years' exile in war-time Ireland. The composition marks the final phase of development in Rakoczi's work before he left Ireland.

KENNETH HALL (1913–46)

57. Sleeping Duck 1944
Oil on canvas 41 x 51.5.
Inscr: 'Hall' b.l.; also: 'SLEEPING DUCK' on stretcher.
Private collection, Co. Down.
Prov: Ms. Elizabeth Ormsby; Basil Rakoczi and by descent to Christopher Rakoczi, Esq.
Exh: *Kenneth Hall 1913–1946: A Retrospective Exhibition,* European Modern Art, Dublin, March 1991 (41).

This is a similar composition to Hall's *Drake Resting* of 1944, which is reproduced in Ingouville-Williams', *Three Painters*, 1945, pl.12. It represents the mature phase of Kenneth Hall's Subjective painting in which animals, in particular birds and fishes, are his principal subject-matter. The composition clearly illustrates his philosophy of Subjectivity and his conditions, laid down in *Three Painters*, governing the use of colour, line and form.

Exhibited UM only.

NICK NICHOLLS (1914–91)

58. Contemplation 1944
Oil on canvas 25 x 29.4.
Inscribed and dated on reverse.
Coll: artist's estate.
Exh: *Nick Nicholls*, White Stag Gallery, Dublin, May 1945 (11, as *Foetus*).
Lit: Kennedy, 1987, vol.1, p.197, repr. vol.2, pl.99.

An example of Nick Nicholls' near-Surrealist work of the mid-1940s. Much of
Nicholls' work has a philosophical and spiritual edge and, as here, is concerned with
ideas of unity, of completeness and personal fulfillment. This picture, which has
also been called *Foetus*, was painted in Nicholls' flat in Upper Mount Street, Dublin.

BRIAN BOYDELL (b.1917)

59. Atlas Approached 1943
Oil on canvas 41.5 x 32.
Ibscr. b.r.
Coll: Brian and Mary Boydell.
Exh: *Exhibition of Subjective Art*, Dublin, January 1944 (30).
Lit: Kennedy, 1987, vol.1, p.173, repr. vol.2, pl.80.

Here Boydell had used, in an idealized manner, trees, worm-like creatures and other organic matter which appear to writhe in order to suggest an imaginary hostile landscape of impassable terrain. As was often the case with his work at this time, colour is less important to the picture than the linear design.

PAUL EGESTORFF

60. Vortex 1949
Gouache on paper 23.7 x 29.2.
Inscr: 'P. Egestorff' b.l.
Owned privately.
Prov: Artist's studio.
Exh: *Paul Egestorff: A Retrospective Exhibition*, European Modern Art, Dublin,
May 1990 (39).
Lit: Kennedy, 1987, vol.1, p.173, repr. vol.2, pl.82.

This composition, which shows Egestorff at his best, also illustrates the influence of
and his debt to his teacher, Mainie Jellett. Egestorff here emphasizes the structural
element in composition, concerning himself with tone and prismatic colour
progression to produce what he calls 'adequate provision of *passage*', which enables
the eye to move freely around the picture.

JOCELYN CHEWETT (1906–79)

61. Head c.1943
Stone, height 18.
Coll: Dr. A.J.H. Reford.
Exh: *Exhibition of Subjective Art,* Dublin, January 1944 (1).
Lit: Kennedy, 1987, vol.1, pp.174, 205, repr. vol.2, pl.83.

While this work is largely Cubist in execution, it also betrays an element of subjectivity in the simplification of the features. It may also owe something to the African and Oriental wooden masks which Chewett would have known from the Trocadéro Museum in Paris and which also influenced Picasso and other Cubists in the early 1900s.

DOREEN VANSTON (1903–88)

62. A Dying Animal c.1943
Oil on canvas 62.7 x 76.1.
Inscr: 'D.VANSTON' t.l.
Coll: Ulster Museum, presented by Louis le Brocquy.
Prov: Artist's studio.
Exh: *Exhibition of Subjective Art*, Dublin, January 1944 (20); *Young Irish Painters*, Arcade Gallery, London, April–May 1945 (17); *Irish Women Artists*, Dublin, 1987 (no number).
Lit: Kennedy, 1987, vol.1, p.209, repr. vol.2, pl.84.

The influence of Picasso, whom Doreen Vanston had admired in Paris, is evident in this composition, one of her most successful pictures of the early-mid 1940s. The colours are bold, the handling of the paint is unobtrusive, it does not interfere with the design, and our attention is directed to the feeling of agony evoked by the death-throes of the animal.

Cata. no. 63.
Photograph
Bryan Rutledge.

PATRICK SCOTT (b.1921)

63. Birds on the Shore 2 1943
Oil on canvas 41 x 49.
Not inscribed.
Private collection, Co. Cork.
Prov: Dr. H.A.C. Ingouville-Williams.
Exh: *Paintings by Patrick Scott*, White Stag Gallery, Dublin, November–
December 1944 (10); *Patrick Scott:* Douglas Hyde Gallery, Dublin; Crawford Art
Gallery, Cork; UM, March–August 1981 (all 2, repr.)

As in this composition, birds and animals appear in almost all of Patrick Scott's
early paintings—'a nursery world', Edward Sheehy once called them. Occasionally
studies for such pictures were made at Dublin Zoo, but frequently his models were
stuffed birds. As usual, the pigment has been applied thinly here and the forms
determined by scraping through to reveal the canvas. These forms are then emphasized
by a peripheral line scored with a sharp instrument and highlights added in paint to
emphasize the heads and tails.

Exhibited HLMG only.

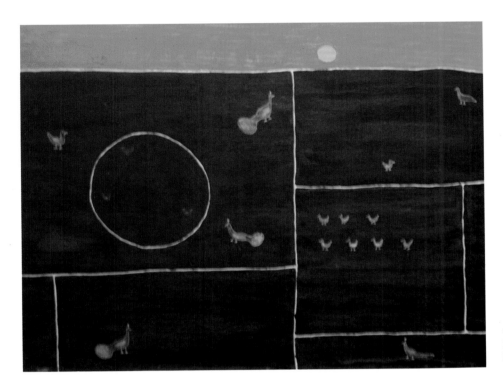

PATRICK SCOTT (b.1921)

64. Evening Landscape 1944
Oil on canvas 70 x 93.
Not inscribed.
Coll: Dorothy Walker.
Prov: Artist's studio.
Exh: Mainie Jellett Memorial Scholarship Exhibition, Dublin, 1948; *Patrick Scott*: Douglas Hyde Gallery, Dublin; Crawford Art Gallery, Cork; UM, March–August 1981 (all 4, repr.)
Lit: Kennedy, 1987, vol.1, p.200.

In this work colour and all other aspects of the composition are of secondary importance to aesthetic considerations to do with the linear divisions of the picture plane. This is one of the last of Scott's paintings of the 1940s done in such a formal geometric manner.

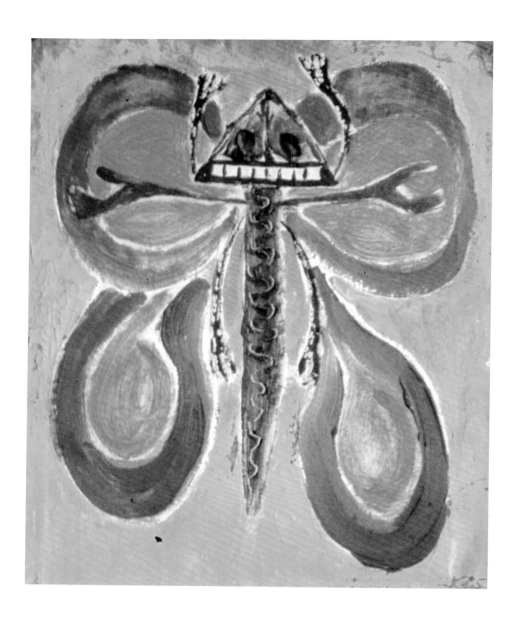

STEPHEN GILBERT (b.1910)

65. Mandala 1944
Oil on canvas 50 x 41.
Inscr: 'S. Gilbert 45' b.r.
Coll: Stephen Gilbert.
Exh: *Stephen Gilbert: Peintures de l'époque COBRA et sculptures/structures en métal 1958–1984*, Galerie 1900–2000, Paris, 1987 (4, repr.)

This is one of Gilbert's so-called 'Cobra-type' paintings, a form of Surrealistic Expressionism which preoccupied him throughout the 1940s and early 1950s. Characteristically, few colours are used and our attention is directed solely to the contorted imagery. For a general reference to Gilbert's work in war-time Dublin see Sarah Wilson, 'Stephen Gilbert in Paris: Spectral Imagery of a Troubled Time', *Art Monthly*, March 1987, p.14.

STEPHEN GILBERT (b.1910)

66. Untitled 1950
Oil on canvas 80.5 x 65.5.
Inscr: 'St Gilbert 50' b.l.
Prov: Sotheby's, London, sale of 'Post War & Contemporary Art', 23 February 1989, lot 430.
Coll: Ulster Museum.
Exh: *Stephen Gilbert: Peintures de l'époque COBRA et sculptures/structures en métal 1958–1984*, Galerie 1900–2000, Paris, February 1987 (18, repr.)

Gilbert's work continued to be Expressionist in manner throughout the late 1940s and early 1950s, that is, the period of his involvement with the European Cobra Group of artists. The anguish and turmoil of the Second World War provided a stimulus for all the Cobra artists.

Exhibited UM only.

NICK NICHOLLS (1914–91)

67. Untitled 1944
Oil on canvas 51 x 40.6.
Inscr: 'Nick Nicholls 44' (indistinctly) at left.
Collection Patrick Scott.
Lit: Kennedy, 1987, vol.1, p.198, repr. vol.2, pl.100.

In this work the image of a bird represents peace, a symbol which often occurred in Nicholls' work until the late 1950s. The patterning of the foliage on the lower part of the composition, which contrasts with the more *malerisch* treatment of the top portion, is also characteristic of his work at the time.

Cata. no. 67.
Photograph
Bryan Rutledge.

LOUIS LE BROCQUY (b.1916)

68. A Picnic 1940

Oil and wax resin on canvas 40.5 x 40.5.

Inscr: 'LE BROCQUY' b.r.

Private collection.

Exh: RHA, 1941 (203); *Irish Contemporary Art*, Limerick, 1941 (no details);
Students' Art Exhibition, Royal Dublin Society, 1942 (no details); *Sculpture by
Melanie le Brocquy: Paintings by Louis le Brocquy*, 13 Merrion Row, Dublin,
December 1942 (6); *Louis le Brocquy: A Retrospective Selection of Oil Paintings
1939–1966*: MGMA and UM, November 1966–January 1967 (both 2, repr.)

Lit: Dorothy Walker, *Louis le Brocquy*, 1981, pp.78, repr. pl.43, 161; Kennedy,
1987, vol.1, p.249.

In this composition, which was influenced by Degas' *Sur la Plage* (catalogue number
3 above), one of the 'Lane' pictures in the Dublin Municipal Gallery, Le Brocquy
has flattened the picture plane in such a way as to suggest a mild abstract quality,
which is emphasized by the sense of isolation, even mystery, of the three individuals.

The artist noted (letter of 20 April 1984) that the figure depicted at the top of this picture was of what he called a 'composite' sitter; while the man in the centre was Arthur Osborne and the woman at the bottom left was Patsy Atkinson Stoney, his first wife's sister. Regarding the element of mystery in the composition he commented, in a manner which reveals the intuitive element in his work at the time: 'I really did not know what was going on, nor why. Even after all this time [40 years] the imagery still seems rather mysterious to me'. The precise linear definition of forms seen here is characteristic of much of le Brocquy's early work. There is a full-size study for this work in a private collection in Amherst, Massachusetts.

Exhibited HLMG only.

LOUIS LE BROCQUY (b.1916)

69. The Spanish Shawl 1941
Oil on silk 98 x 79.5.
Inscr: 'LE BROCQUY' t.r.
Private collection.
Prov: Mrs. Rynne, who acquired it in 1943; by gift to the present owner.
Exh: *Sculpture by Melanie le Brocquy: Paintings by Louis le Brocquy*, 13 Merrion Row, Dublin, December 1942 (11); IELA, 1943 (23); RHA, 1963 (137, as *A study in white*); *Louis le Brocquy: A Retrospective Selection of Oil Paintings 1939–1966:* MGMA and UM, November 1966–January 1967 (both 4, as *The Spanish Shawl, a study in white*).
Lit: A.J. Leventhal, 'The Living Art Exhibition', *Irish Art: A Volume of Articles and Illustrations*, 1944, p.88, repr. p.91; Kennedy, 1987, vol.1, pp.226, 235, 249, repr. vol.2, pl.111; Kenneth McConkey, *A Free Spirit: Irish Art 1860–1960*, 1990, p.82, repr.

The rejection of this picture by the selection committee of the Royal Hibernian Academy in 1942 was one of the events which contributed directly to the foundation of the Irish Exhibition of Living Art a year later. Although depicting a group of figures, le Brocquy's interest in the isolation of the individual is clearly apparent. The figure on the left was the artist's brother Noel; that on the right was his brother-in-law, the late Professor F.S. Stewart; Hazel Malcolm modelled for the main figure. The setting was the morning room at number 51 Kenilworth Square, Dublin (le Brocquy, letter of 20 April 1984). The subtle juxtapositions of colour in the composition echo Manet, whom le Brocquy greatly admired. The artist once commented of the picture: 'At the time I was interested in the analogy between colour and musical cycles or scales. *The Spanish Shawl* was painted in the minor key of vermilion—as I conceived it—red-orange, yellow, blue' (le Brocquy, quoted in the 1966–7 retrospective exhibition catalogue, p.16).

Cata. no. 69.
Photograph
Bryan Rutledge.

LOUIS LE BROCQUY (b.1916)

70. Variety Rehearsal at the Olympia 1942
Oil on pulpboard 52.9 x 65.6.
Inscr: 'Le Brocquy 42' b.r.; also titled and dated on reverse.
Coll: Ulster Museum.
Prov: Haverty Trust, Dublin; to UM 1945.
Exh: '*In Theatre Street*', Contemporary Picture Galleries, Dublin, November–
December 1942 (7); *Sculpture by Melanie le Brocquy: Paintings by Louis le
Brocquy*, 13 Merrion Row, Dublin, December 1942 (12); Haverty Trust, *Third
Quinquennial Exhibition*, MGMA, 1945 (46); *Louis le Brocquy: A Retrospective
Selection of Oil Paintings 1939–1966*: MGMA and UM, November 1966–January
1967 (both 6).
Lit: *A Concise Catalogue of the Drawings, Paintings & Sculptures in the Ulster
Museum*, 1986, p.74; Kennedy, 1987, vol.1, p.250, repr. vol.2, pl.73.

Painted while designing sets for Sybil le Brocquy's translation of Jean Giraudoux's
play *Amphityron 38* at the Olympia Theatre, Dublin. The afternoon auditorium is
draped in white dust-sheets. The artist wrote to the author (letter of 2 July 1975, UM
archives): 'The spatial—and indeed ritual—drama seen from the flies of a theatre,
during a rehearsal in face of an auditorium swathed in white sheets, impressed me
greatly. . . . In '42, influenced by Jack Yeats' articulate and evocative qualities, I
loosened up my work (even using a palette knife; a dangerous weapon). But I
mistrusted Yeats's romantic informalism, much as I admired the poetry of his work'.

Exhibited UM only.

NORAH McGUINNESS (1903–80)

71. Garden Green 1952
Oil on canvas 102 x 71.
Inscr: 'N. McGuinness 52' b.r.
Coll: Hugh Lane Municipal Gallery of Modern Art.
Lit: Bruce Arnold, *The Art Atlas of Britain & Ireland*, 1991, p.311, repr. in colour.
Repr: Michael O'Siadhail, *The Chosen Garden*, 1990, on cover in colour.

The concept and execution of this picture, which is characteristic of Norah
McGuinness's work of the time, betrays the influence on her of Cubism and her time
with André Lhote. The treatment of the table top still life is similar to contemporary
studies of the same subject-matter by William Scott.

Cata. no. 71.
Photograph
Hugh Lane Municipal
Gallery of Modern
Art.

Cata. no. 72.
Photograph
Bryan Rutledge.

COLIN MIDDLETON (1910–83)

72. Our Lady of Bikini 1946
Oil on canvas 63 x 76.
Private collection.
Prov: Artist's studio.
Exh: *Colin Middleton*: UM and MGMA, January–April 1976 (both 21).
Lit: John Hewitt, *Colin Middleton*, 1976, pp.34, 36 repr.; Kennedy: 1987, vol.1,
pp.265, 282; 'Irish landscape painting in a political setting, 1922–48', in M. Hill
& S. Barber (eds.), *Aspects of Irish Studies*, 1990, p.54.

Middleton displayed a strong social conscience in his work of the mid-late 1940s.
The war and its aftermath made a deep impression on him. This dark and menacing
composition, with its Surrealist overtones, was inspired by the atomic tests held at
Bikini atoll in the Pacific.

284

Cata. no. 73.
Photograph
Dermot Dunbar.

COLIN MIDDLETON (1910–83)

73. Jacob Wrestling with the Angel 1948
Oil on canvas 81 x 66.
Inscr: 'Colin M' b.r.
Private collection.
Prov: Z. Lewinter-Frankl.
Exh: *Contemporary Ulster Paintings*, Scottish Arts Council, Edinburgh, 1951
(22); *Colin Middleton*, BMAG, September 1954 (4); *Colin Middleton*: UM and
MGMA, January–April 1976 (both 24, repr.)

Lit: John Hewitt, *Colin Middleton*, 1976, p.34, repr. p.39; Kennedy, 1987, vol.1, p. 265.
Repr: Max Wright, *Told in Gath*, Belfast, 1990, in colour on cover.

In the immediate post-war years Middleton was one of the few Irish artists to concern himself with the plight of refugees in Europe. This composition, with its Symbolism, bold Expressionist brushwork and emotionally evocative colours evokes the troubled character of the times. The title is almost certainly a biblical reference (Genesis, 32:22–32) to the turning point in Jacob's life when, at Peniel, he was humbled by the angel.

COLIN MIDDLETON (1910–83)

74. Untitled 1938
Oil on board 31.7 x 15.
Inscr: 'Colin M. 1938' b.r.
Coll: Ulster Museum.
Prov: John and Roberta Hewitt; to UM 1987.

This is one of Middleton's earliest Surrealist paintings and one of the first such works to have been made by an Irish artist.

NANO REID (1905–81)

75. Edward Sheehy c.1944
Pencil on paper 44.4 x 34.3.
Inscr: 'Nano Reid' b.l.
Coll: Jeanne Sheehy.
Prov: Given by the artist to the present owner in 1974.
Exh: *Nano Reid*, Dublin Painters' gallery, Dublin, April–May 1944 (56); *Nano Reid: A Retrospective Exhibition*: MGMA and UM, November 1974–February 1975 (both 18).
Lit: Kennedy, 1987, vol.1, p.257, repr. vol.2, pl.122.

This is an outstanding example of Nano Reid's draughtsmanship. It displays a boldness of line, great economy of means, and is a penetrating character study. Edward Sheehy was one of the most influential art critics of his time in Ireland, his writing appearing in the *Dublin Magazine*.

Cata. no. 75.
Photograph
S.B.K.

NANO REID (1905–81)

76. Forest Pool 1946
Oil on canvas 50.8 x 60.9.
Inscr: 'NANO REID' b.l.
Coll: The Garden Gallery.
Exh: Irish Pavilion, 25th Biennale, Venice, 1950 (15); *Nano Reid: A Retrospective*

Exhibition: MGMA and UM, November 1974–February 1975 (both 26); *Nano Reid 1900–1981* [sic], Droichead Arts Centre, Drogheda, April–May 1991 (11). Lit: Kennedy, 1987, vol.1, p.258, repr. vol.2, pl.124.

As the 1940s progressed Nano Reid's work became increasingly Expressionistic as this study, with its harsh, angular forms, illustrates. To some extent it recalls the work of the German Brücke painters of the years before the First World War.

Cata. no. 77.
Photograph
Ulster Museum.

GERARD DILLON (1916–71)

77. Yellow Bungalow 1954
Oil on canvas 76.8 x 81.2.
Inscr: 'GERARD DILLON' b.r.
Coll: Ulster Museum.
Prov: Haverty Trust, Dublin; to UM 1956.
Exh: Haverty Trust, *Fifth Quinquennial Exhibition*, MGMA, 1955 (37); *Gerard Dillon 1916–1971: A Retrospective Exhibition*: UM and MGMA, November 1972–February 1973 (both 61, repr.); *Collectors Choice*, Playhouse Gallery, Leeds, September–October 1976 (Gerard Dillon 1); *British and Irish Paintings*

1930–1960, UM, March 1977 (17); *A Vision of Ireland: 20th Century Irish Painting*, Herbert Art Gallery & Museum, Coventry, 1989 (28, repr. in colour on cover).

Lit: Michael Kane, 'Where You're At', *Structure*, vol.1, Dublin, winter 1972–3, p.4, repr.; James Burns, *Leaving Certificate Art History and Appreciation,* 1976, p.50, repr.; *A Concise Catalogue of the Drawings, Paintings & Sculptures in the Ulster Museum*, 1986, p.31; Kennedy, 1987, vol.1, pp.269, 270.

Repr: Colour print, Arts Council of Northern Ireland, 1977; Allied Irish Banks, calendar 1978, at month of December; Dermot Healy, *Banished Misfortune*, London, 1982, in colour on cover.

Although just beyond the date limit of this exhibition, this is one of Dillon's finest works and, in terms of its emphasis on the solitariness of the individual, represents an important stage in his development. The notion of solitariness is present in many of Dillon's works, both of these years and later, and compositions by him such as *Aran Islanders*, c.1946–9, invite comparison with the same qualities found in le Brocquy (cf. the latter's *The Picnic*). The bird's eye view, narrative format and hint of Symbolism present here are also familiar characteristics of his work and almost certainly were influences from Chagall. On the back of the canvas is another painting showing three robed male figures, a child, horse and rider, bird, two dogs and cattle, set in a landscape with cottages and stone walls.

Cata. no. 78.
Photograph
Bryan Rutledge.

289

DOREEN VANSTON (1903–88)

78. El Carruno de San Antonio 1948
Watercolour on paper 27.2 x 36.2 (sight).
Inscr: 'D. Vanston' b.l.
Private collection, Dublin.
Lit: Kennedy, 1987, vol.1, p.209, repr. vol.2, pl.110.

The sensitive use of watercolour washes and juxtapositions of colours and tones in this picture, which was painted in Costa Rica, are typical of Doreen Vanston's work until the late 1960s. Her oils, however, are often more Expressionist in treatment than her watercolours.

Cata. no. 79.
Photograph
Ulster Museum.

GEORGE CAMPBELL (1917–79)

79. Claddagh Duff, Connemara c.1950–1
Oil on board 51.3 x 61.1.
Inscr: 'Campbell' b.r.
Coll: Ulster Museum.
Prov: Haverty Trust, Dublin; to UM 1957.
Exh: (?) *Recent Paintings: George F. Campbell*, Waddington Galleries, Dublin, February–March 1951 (12); Haverty Trust, *Fifth Quinquennial Exhibition*, MGMA, 1955 (4); *Northern Ireland Painters*, Art Exhibitions Bureau, London,

tour to Harrogate, Reading, Battersea, Gateshead, Guildford, Nottingham, Southgate, Southend, Hartlepool, July 1959–September 1960 (all 7); *British and Irish Paintings 1930–1960*, UM, March 1977 (15); *Modern and Contemporary Art from the Ulster Museum*: Wexford Arts Centre, Wexford; Crawford Art Gallery, Cork, October–December 1979 (both 20); *A Vision of Ireland: 20th Century Irish Painting*, Herbert Art Gallery & Museum, Coventry, 1989 (32, repr.).

Lit: Kennedy: 1987, vol.1, pp.278, 279, vol.2, pl.139; 'Irish landscape painting in a political setting, 1922–1948', in M. Hill & S. Barber (eds.), *Aspects of Irish Studies*, Belfast, 1990, p.54; *A Concise Catalogue of the Drawings, Paintings & Sculptures in the Ulster Museum*, 1986, p.21.

Although the artist told the author (undated letter, September 1976) that this picture was painted in about 1947, that date seems unlikely to be correct. Rather, judging from stylistic comparisons of his work, c.1950–1 is more likely to have been the date of execution. Also, other Connemara subjects were exhibited by him at the Living Art exhibitions of 1950 and 1951 so it seems likely that he was painting in that area at the time. Judging by the titles of works which he exhibited in the period 1944–52, Campbell seems to have painted little, if at all, in the west of Ireland before about late 1950. Claddagh Duff is a village situated in the most westerly part of Connemara. Campbell painted this picture, he said (op. cit.), ' . . . because I liked the build-up of textures and shapes; it's difficult to say precisely but the whole thing is a nice unit'. The treatment of the landscape, with bold, vigorous brushwork and an emphasis on surface texture, is Expressionist in quality and ably captures the nature of the rugged terrain. It is refreshingly free from the sentiment common in Paul Henry, J.H. Craig and other painters of the previous generation.

NEVILL JOHNSON (b.1911)

80. The Clown c.1950
Oil on canvas 80 x 54.5.
Inscr: 'Nevill Johnson' b.l.
Coll: Trinity College, Dublin.
Prov: Z. Lewinter-Frankl; to TCD 1963.
Exh: *Contemporary Ulster Paintings*, Scottish Arts Council, Edinburgh, 1951 (17).
Lit: Kennedy, 1987, vol.1, p.283, repr. vol.2, pl.142.

This work illustrates the most advanced stage of the influence of Cubism on Johnson. The relative flattening of the picture-plane, as here, remained a feature of his work until the mid-1950s, as did his dominant use of yellow and tones of grey. The smooth, evenly painted surface of the canvas is characteristic of Johnson's work in general.

NEVILL JOHNSON (b.1911)

81. Landscape Rock Pool c.1950

Oil on canvas 40.6 x 55.8.
Inscr: 'Nevill Johnson' b.l.
Coll: Hugh Lane Municipal Gallery of Modern Art, Dublin.
Lit: Kennedy: 1987, vol.1, p. 283, repr. vol.2, pl 142; 'Irish landscape painting in a political setting, 1922–48', in M. Hill & S. Barber, (eds.), *Aspects of Irish Studies*, Belfast, 1990, p.54.

This composition, dating from about 1950, marks the beginning of the most important period for Johnson's painting, a period in which he questioned the very existence and nature of things around him. The new post-war order, the human plight in the face of the atomic age, these were the issues which stimulated this and similar compositions from these years in which are depicted a desolate wasteland of hopelessness. Johnson first exhibited works like this at the Waddington Galleries, Dublin, in 1947 and reviewing that exhibition the *Irish Tatler & Sketch* (October 1947, p.14) saw them as macabre symbols of the new age. It argued that they marked the end of an epoch in Irish painting and were a foretaste of things to come. From the turn of the century, it commented perceptively, Irish artists had concentrated on painting the landscape and recording its changing moods; but few of the younger generation were now interested in the landscape, they preferred to paint figure compositions. 'The post-war world is allergic to tradition. A chapter is closed', it concluded. Works like this, Middleton's *Our Lady of Bikini* and Yeats' *On Through the Silent Lands*, of 1951 (UM), catch the predicament of the times.

Cata. no. 82.
Photograph
S.B.K.

THURLOE CONOLLY (b.1918)

82. The Juggler 1953
Oil on board 60.5 x 40.
Inscr: 'Thurloe Conolly Summer 1953', with title, on reverse.

Private collection, Essex.
Lit: Kennedy, 1987, vol.1, p.262, repr. vol.2, pl.128.

Although painted just beyond the terminal date for this exhibition, *The Juggler* represents the culmination of a style and phase of Conolly's work which had begun in the late 1940s with compositions such as *Man with a Draughts Board* of 1948 (private collection). It is one of the few semi-figurative works from this last phase of his development, but the concern for surface texture and pattern evident in it is common to all Conolly's work. The graffiti-like imagery in this and similar paintings was the outcome of his growing interest at the time in native Oceanic, American and African art.

Cata. no. 83.
Photograph
Ulster Museum.

DAN O'NEILL (1920–74)

83. Place du Tertre 1949
Oil on canvas 64 x 76.7.
Inscr: 'D O'Neill'b.l.
Coll: Ulster Museum.
Prov: Mrs. S.A. Forbes.
Exh: Daniel O'Neill, *Paintings 1944–1952*, BMAG, March–April 1952 (22);
Recent Acquisitions & Loans, UM, March–April 1974 (29).
Lit: *A Concise Catalogue of the Drawings, Paintings & Sculptures in the Ulster Museum*, 1986, p.127; Kennedy, 1987, vol.1, p.273, repr. vol.2, pl. 135.

Painted during O'Neill's first visit to Paris. There is here a strong influence of the French painters Vlaminck and Utrillo, whose work O'Neill must have seen there. The Place du Tertre is in the Montmartre district of Paris, close to the Basilica of the Sacre-Coeur. O'Neill has captured perfectly the bohemian night-life of the area.

DAN O'NEILL (1920–74)

Cata. no. 84.
Photograph
Ulster Museum.

84. The Blue Skirt 1949
Oil on canvas 60 x 73.
Inscr: 'D. O'Neill' t.r.
Coll: Ulster Museum.
Prov: Haverty Trust, Dublin; to UM 1951.
Exh: IELA, 1949 (17, repr.); Haverty Trust, *Fourth Quinquennial Exhibition*, MGMA, Dublin, 1950 (16); *Daniel O'Neill, Paintings 1944–1952*, BMAG, March–April 1952 (20); *Paintings from Belfast Museum & Art Gallery*, Carnegie Hall, Lurgan, January 1961 (21).
Lit: Sam Hanna Bell et al. (eds.), *The Arts in Ulster: A Symposium*, 1951, repr. facing p.81; Kenneth Jamison, 'Painting and Sculpture', in M. Longley (ed.), *Causeway: The Arts in Ulster*, 1971, p.46; *A Concise Catalogue of the Drawings, Paintings & Sculptures in the Ulster Museum*, 1986, p.127; Kennedy, 1987, vol.1, p.273.

Writing of this picture the critic Kenneth Jamison (op. cit., p.46) described it as being 'a kind of northern odalisque . . . [which] seemed to belong to the great European tradition and yet to be something excitingly new'. Its effect on the younger painters when first exhibited was, he said, 'electrifying'.

Exhibited UM only.

ANNE YEATS (b.1919)

85. One Room c.1954
Oil on canvas 40.6 x 45.6.
Inscr: 'ANNE YEATS' b.r.
Coll: Ulster Museum.
Prov: Haverty Trust, Dublin (purchased 1954); to UM 1957.
Exh: Haverty Trust, *Fifth Quinquennial Exhibition*, MGMA, 1955 (22); *Paintings from Belfast Museum & Art Gallery*, Carnegie Hall, Lurgan, January 1961 (24).
Lit: *A Concise Catalogue of the Drawings, Paintings & Sculptures in the Ulster Museum*, 1986, p.181; Kennedy, 1987, vol.1, p.284, repr. vol.2, pl.143.

In about 1948 or 1949 Anne Yeats turned from watercolours and took up oils as a medium, but her subsequent technique, as can be seen here, often resembles her use of wax, which she had previously combined with watercolour.

Exhibited UM only.

F.E. McWILLIAM (b.1909)

86. Man and Wife 1948
Coloured Portland Stone aggregate, waste mould 91.5 x 34.3 x 33.
Not inscribed.
Coll: Ulster Museum.
Prov: Contemporary Art Society, London; to UM 1949.
Exh: *F.E. McWilliam: Recent Sculpture*, Hanover Gallery, London, October–
November 1949 (3); *International Exhibition: Sculpture*, BMAG, January–

February 1960 (no numbers); Royal Ulster Academy, BMAG, October–November 1961 (61); *F.E. McWilliam: Five Sculptures*, UM, May 1978 (no numbers); *F.E. McWilliam*, a retrospective exhibition, Arts Council of Northern Ireland and An Chomhairle Ealaion: UM; Douglas Hyde Gallery, Dublin; Crawford Art Gallery, Cork, April–August 1981 (all 17, repr. p.25); *British Sculpture in the Twentieth Century Part One: Image and Form 1901–50,* Whitechapel Art Gallery, London, September–November 1981 (no numbers); *Sculpture from the permanent collection*, UM, February 1988 (no numbers); *F.E. McWilliam*, Tate Gallery, London, 1989 (34, repr.)

Lit: *The Museum in Pictures*, illustrated souvenir, BMAG, 1954 and second ed. 1961, p.5, repr. pl.8; Roland Penrose (ed.), *F.E. McWilliam*, 1964, p.7, repr. pl.18; George MacCann, 'Notes on F.E. McWilliam', *Northern Review*, vol.1, 1965, p.73 as 'Man and his Wife'; Bruce Arnold, *A Concise History of Irish Art*, 1969, p.194, repr. pl.169; revised ed. 1977, p.164, repr. pl.166; John Hewitt, *Art in Ulster:1*, 1977, p.134; Christopher Fitz-Simon, *The Arts in Ireland: A Chronology*, 1982, p.219; *A Concise Catalogue of the Drawings, Paintings & Sculptures in the Ulster Museum*, 1986, p.86; Brian Kennedy, *A Catalogue of the Permanent Collection:2—Twentieth Century Sculpture*, UM, 1988, pp.55–7.

This is one of a number of works on a theme which occupied McWilliam for a time immediately after the Second World War. During the 1930s he had begun to make sculptures in which attention was drawn only to certain parts of the body, usually the extremities, and in which the mass of the torso was often, as here, omitted. The work of Picasso was at the time an influence on this approach as was the fact that our knowledge of objects is gained in a fragmentary manner so that we never instantly perceive all that is to be known about an object. Also, while serving in India during the war he had been intrigued by certain aspects of Indian sculpture which compelled one to view figures and objects not as autonomous images but as elements in a general cultural context. Thus after the war in his figure works he decided to omit all unnecessary parts of the body so as to leave the spectator free to fill the empty spaces according to his or her imagination. 'The tension he has created in empty space,' wrote Roland Penrose (op. cit., p.7) of these works, 'is bound to provoke our good-humoured participation and prove to us the simultaneous existence and non-existence of reality'. Paradoxically, these fragmented figures have about them an air of serene completion and the idea of using such fragments has recurred from time to time in McWilliam's career. Other works contemporary with this one were *Kneeling Woman* and *Kneeling Man*, both of 1947, and *Father and Daughter*. A study in terracotta for this work was included in the Hanover Gallery exhibition in 1949 (21), but its whereabouts is unknown to the present writer.

WILLIAM SCOTT (1913–89)

87. The Frying Pan 1946
Oil on canvas 53 x 66.
Inscr: 'W SCOTT' t.r.
Coll: Arts Council. The South Bank Centre, London.
Exh: *William Scott*: UM; Guinness Hop Store, Dublin; Scottish National Gallery
of Modern Art, Edinburgh, June–November 1986 (all 9, repr.)
Lit: *Arts Council Collection*, London: Arts Council of Great Britain, 1979, p.220,
repr.

Even in this early still life one can see Scott's preoccupation with the flatness of the
picture-plane. The various elements in the composition have been reduced to virtual
symbols of their origin, the table top has almost become a vertical plane rather than
a horizontal surface, and the whole composition has begun to assume a feeling of
abstraction. The picture is a precursor of Scott's so-called 'pots and pans' abstract
works of the 1950s.

SIR WILLIAM ORPEN (1878–1931)

88. Homage to Manet 1909.
Oil on canvas 157.5 x 129.5.
Coll: Manchester City Art Gallery.
Exh: New English Art Club, 1909; Birmingham, 1909; Glasgow, 1910.
Lit: *Art Journal*, 1909, repr., an earlier version; Manchester City Art Gallery, *Handbook to the Permanent Collection*, 1910, pp.93–5; Lawrence Hayward, *Illustrated Guide to the Art Collections in the Manchester Corporation Gallery*, 1945, p.94, repr.; P.G. Konody & Sidney Dark, *Sir William Orpen*, 1932, p.210, repr.; Thomas Bodkin, *Hugh Lane and his Pictures*, Dublin, 1956, repr. on cover; Bruce Arnold: *Orpen: Mirror to an Age*, 1981, pp.227ff, repr.; *The Art Atlas of Britain and Ireland*, 1991, p.107, repr. in colour; exhibition catalogue, *Irish Renaissence*, Pyms Gallery, London, 1986, p.72; Kenneth McConkey: 'Sir William Orpen: His Contemporaries, Critics and Biographers', in exhibition catalogue *Orpen and the Edwardian Era*, Pyms Gallery, London, 1987, pp.13, 15, 82–3; *A Free Spirit: Irish Art 1860–1960*, 1990, p.127.
Repr: Sir William Orpen, *Stories of Old Ireland and Myself*, 1924, facing p.62.

This composition pays homage to Manet as a leader of the Modern Movement and is based on Fantin-Latour's *Hommage à Delacroix*, in which a number of artists and writers, including Manet and Whistler, are grouped before a portrait of Delacroix, who, in his day, broke the bonds of tradition. The group represents Orpen's friends, from left to right, George Moore, Wilson Steer, Henry Tonks, Sir Hugh Lane, Walter Sickert and D.S. MacColl, gathered in his home in South Bolton Gardens, London, under Manet's portrait of Éva Gonzalès. In reality the composition is a tribute to Sir Hugh Lane, who at the time had done so much to further the cause of Modernism in Dublin.

JACK B. YEATS (1871–1957)

89. A Race in Hy Brazil 1937
Oil on canvas 71.1 x 91.4.
Coll: Allied Irish Banks.
Prov: H.T. De V. Clifton, 1938; Leger Gallery, 1943; Z. Lewinter-Frankl; J.B. Kearney.
Exh: *Nicholson & Yeats,* London, January 1942 (23); *Exhibition of paintings from the collection of Mr. Zoltan Frankl,* CEMA at BMAG, summer 1944 (34); Jack B. Yeats, *National Loan Exhibition,* National College of Art, Dublin, June–July 1945 (97); JBY, *Loan Exhibition,* Temple Newsam House, Leeds, June–August 1948 (repr.); JBY, *Loan Exhibition,* Arts Council of Great Britain at the Tate Gallery, London, August–September 1948 (24), and subsequent tour to Aberdeen and Edinburgh; JBY, *A first retrospective American exhibition:* Washington, San Francisco, Colorado Springs, Toronto, Detroit, New York, March 1951–1952 (not

in cata.); JBY, *Paintings,* CEMA at BMAG, February–March 1956 (23); *Zoltan Lewinter-Frankl Collection,* BMAG, March 1958 (75); JBY, *Paintings,* York Festival, 1960 (16); *Pictures from Ulster Houses,* BMAG, May–July 1961 (219); JBY, *The Late Paintings:* Bristol, London, The Hague, February–September 1991 (11, repr.).
Lit: *New Knowledge,* 6 April 1966, repr. p.967; Hilary Pyle, *Jack B. Yeats,* 1970, pp.131, 134n, 136 & revised ed., 1989.

Hy Brazil is a mythical island lying in the Atlantic ocean off the west coast of Ireland. It is Tir na n'Og, the 'Land of Youth', and thus to Yeats in this composition it is the symbolic setting for the strand races he knew as a boy. Here the lightness of the brushwork and feeling of transience perfectly capture the spirit of the place.

Cata. no. 89.
Photograph
Allied Irish Banks.

JACK B. YEATS (1871–1957)

90. Tinkers' Encampment: The Blood of Abel 1940
Oil on canvas 91.4 x 121.9.
Private collection, Dublin.
Prov: Artist's studio.

301

Exh: RHA, 1941 (73); *Nicholson & Yeats*, London, January 1942 (ex-catalogue); JBY, *National Loan Exhibition*, National College of Art, Dublin, June–July 1945 (107); *Society of Scottish Artists 52nd Exhibition*, Royal Scottish Academy, Edinburgh, 1946 (155); JBY, *Loan Collection*, Sligo Art Society, Town Hall, Sligo, August 1961 (4); JBY, *Loan Exhibition*, Municipal Gallery, Waterford, June–July 1965 (15); JBY, *A Centenary Exhibition*: Dublin, Belfast, New York, December 1971–June 1972 (all 84).

Lit: Thomas MacGreevy, *Jack B. Yeats*, 1945, pp.35–7, repr.; T.G. Rosenthal, *Yeats*, 1966, repr. pl.9; Hilary Pyle, *Jack B. Yeats*, 1970, pp.132, 134n, 158 & revised ed., 1989; Roger McHugh, 'Jack B. Yeats 1871–1957', *Ireland of the Welcomes*, vol.20, July–August 1971, p.20, repr. in colour p.26.

By the mid-1940s Yeats was indisputably the doyen of Irish artists. He had recorded the dramatic intensity of his time and, in compositions such as this, which was inspired by the horror of the war then raging, set down images redolent of the universality of human experience. The tinkers' encampment of the title of the composition is, in MacGreevy's interpretation (op. cit., p.35) a metaphor for the 'human odyssey', the world being in effect a human encampment, a transient place; while the sub-title, which referrs to the biblical Abel (see *Genesis*, 4:10; *Matthew*, 23:35), innocently slain by his brother Cain, is a metaphor for those innocents caught up in the Second World War.

Cata. no. 90.
Photograph
John Kellett.

302

DERMOD O'BRIEN (1865–1945)

91. The Estuary of the Shannon 1935

Oil on canvas 50.7 x 60.9.
Inscr: 'D. O Brien 1935' b.l.
Coll: Ulster Museum.
Prov: Dr. R.I. Best; Friends of the National Collections of Ireland; to UM 1959.
Exh: RHA, 1939 (87, as *The Estuary of the Shannon at Foynes*); *A Vision of Ireland: 20th Century Irish Painting,* Herbert Art Gallery & Museum, Coventry, 1989 (4, repr.)
Lit: A *Concise Catalogue of the Drawings, Paintings & Sculptures in the Ulster Museum,* 1986, p.126; Kennedy, 1987, vol.1, p.318, repr. vol.2, pl.144.

Painted near Foynes in Co. Limerick. This is a fine example of O'Brien's late landscape work in which the mood and atmosphere of the scene have been rendered with great fidelity. It conveys clearly O'Brien's innate love of pastoral countryside.

DERMOD O'BRIEN (1865–1945)

92. Executive of the Royal Dublin Society 1940
Oil on canvas 152 x 197.5 (sight).
Not inscribed.
Coll: Royal Dublin Society.
Exh: RHA, 1940 (20).
Lit: Kennedy, 1987, vol.1, pp.328, 331, repr. vol 2, pl.151.

This is one of the few group portraits done in Ireland during the period under discussion. It was clearly inspired by Rembrandt's *The Syndics* in the Rijksmuseum, Amsterdam. Unfortunately O'Brien was less at ease with compositions like this than he was with landscapes and the whole has a feeling of stiffness, a lack of cohesion amongst the members of the Board who are treated merely as individuals. The sitters are, from left to right, John Leonard, Hon. W.E. Wylie, Harry Franks (seated), Professor Felix E. Hackett.

Cata. no. 93.
Photograph
Ulster Museum.

SIR JOHN LAVERY (1856–1941)

93. His Eminence Cardinal Logue 1920

Oil on canvas 79.1 x 64.1.

Inscr:'J. Lavery' t.l; also 'H.E. Cardinal Logue By John Lavery. Armagh 1920' on reverse.

Coll: Ulster Museum.

Prov: Artist's studio; to UM 1929.

Exh:RHA, 1921 (32); Glasgow Institute of Fine Art, 1921; Irish Exhibition, Paris, 1922; Royal Scottish Academy, Edinburgh, 1922; *Portraits, Interiors & Landscapes by Sir John Lavery, RA, RSA, LL.D*, Duveen Galleries, New York, November–December 1925 (1); *Portraits & Landscapes by Sir John Lavery, RA,*

Vose Galleries, Boston, December 1925–January 1926 (2); *Portraits, Interiors & Landscapes by Sir John Lavery*, Carnegie Institute, Pittsburg, March–April 1926 (13); *Meisterwerke Englischer Maleri aus Drei Jahrhunderten*, Vienna Secession, 1927 (170, repr.); Palm Beach, Whitehall, 1927; *Exposition d'Art Irlandais*, Musée d'Art Ancien, Brussels, May–June 1930 (71); *Loan Exhibition of Paintings by Sir John Lavery, RA, 1856–1941*, BMAG, May–June 1951 (13); *Great Irish Men and Women*, UM, June–July 1965 (120); Seamus Heaney, *A Personal Selection*, UM, 1982 (8); *Sir John Lavery RA, 1856–1941:* Fine Art Society, Edinburgh & London; UM; NGI, August 1984–March 1985 (all 94, repr.)
Lit: Shane Leslie, 'Sir John Lavery's Masterpiece', *Irish Independent*, 14 October 1920; BMAG, *Sir John Lavery Collection of Paintings*, 1929 & subsequent eds., all pl.4; *Dictionary of National Biography 1922–30*, 1937, pp.516–17; Sir John Lavery, *The Life of a Painter*, 1940, pp.209–10, 254, repr. pl.27; Sam Hanna Bell, et al. (eds.), *The Arts in Ulster*, 1951, p.83; John Hewitt, *Art in Ulster:1*, 1977, p.50, repr. p.51; *A Concise Catalogue of the Drawings, Paintings & Sculptures in the Ulster Museum*, 1986, p.73; Kennedy, 1987, vol.1, p.332; Kenneth McConkey, *A Free Spirit: Irish Art 1860–1960*, 1990, pp.70 repr., 71.

This portrait, a penetrating study in character, was painted in Armagh in October 1920. Technically, it hints at the influence on Lavery of the seventeenth century Spanish painter, Velazquez, notably in the treatment of the hands and the fluid rendering of the lace. The work has a breadth of concept, a spontaneity of execution and freedom from unnecessary detail which distinguishes Lavery from his home-bound Irish contemporaries. Michael Logue (1840–1924), was born at Carrigart, Co. Donegal. Educated at Maynooth, he became Professor of Dogmatic Theology at the Irish College in Paris in 1866, the year in which he was ordained. He became Archbishop of Armagh in 1888 and Cardinal in 1893. He was a keen Irish speaker and supported the Gaelic League. Although he opposed partition, he accepted the Anglo-Irish Treaty of 1921. He died at Armagh in November 1924.

LEO WHELAN (1892–1956)

94. The Rt. Hon. The Earl of Dunraven 1933
Oil on canvas 127 x 102.
Inscr: 'LEO WHELAN 1934'b.l.; also 'Windham Henry 5th Earl of Dunraven & Mount Earl painted by Leo Whelan RHA 1934' on reverse.
Private collection.
Exh: RHA, 1934 (24); Royal Academy, London, 1935 (654).
Lit: *Royal Academy Illustrated*, 1935, p.110; Kennedy, 1987, vol.1, p.336, repr. vol.2, pl.156.

Although dated 1934, this portrait was in fact painted at Adare Manor, Co. Limerick, in 1933. Leo Whelan was, arguably, the leading portrait painter in Dublin during the 1930s and 1940s and this work is possibly his masterpiece. Executed with great dexterity and technical accomplishment, it demonstrates his ability to penetrate outward appearances and to capture character and personality. The pose, with the sitter seen in three-quarters view, is typical of Whelan, as is the smooth film of paint which has been applied with great deliberation. The modelling of the head and hands is masterly and the figure is seated at ease and with great authority. Col. Windham Henry Wyndham-Quin, 5th Earl of Dunraven and Mount-Earl, was born in 1857. He served in the army during the Boer War and later in South Africa and was mentioned in despatches. He was MP for South Glamorganshire 1895–1906 and High Sheriff for Co. Kilkenny 1914. He died in 1952.

Exhibited HLMG only.

Cata. no. 94.
Photograph
Bryan Rutledge.

SEÁN O'SULLIVAN (1906–64)

95. W.B. Yeats 1934
Oil on canvas 127 x 102.
Inscr: 'Sean O'Sullivan, RHA 34' b.r.
Coll: Abbey Theatre, Dublin.
Prov: Haverty Trust, Dublin (purchased RHA, 1934).
Exh: RHA, 1934 (32); Haverty Trust, *First Exhibition of Paintings*, Mansion
House, Dublin, November 1935 (18); *Irish Painting 1903–1953*, MGMA, April–
July 1953 (24).
Lit: Kennedy, 1987, vol.1, p.338, repr. vol.2, pl.158; Benedict Kiely, *Yeats'
Ireland*, 1989, repr. in colour p.115.

This study of the poet W.B. Yeats, done when O'Sullivan was only twenty-eight
years of age, shows him already at the height of his powers as a portraitist. The sitter
is depicted deep in thought, in a pose which appears natural and not contrived. The
painting is executed with bold brushwork and a judicious use of colour which
complements the mood of the sitter. The triangular shaped composition was a device
often employed by O'Sullivan and the emptiness of the background serves to heighten
the feeling of meditation.

SEÁN O'SULLIVAN (1906–64)

96. An Taoiseach, Eamon de Valera 1943
Oil on board 163 x 120 (sight).
Not inscribed.
Coll: Áras An Uachtaráin, Dublin.
Lit: Kennedy, 1987, vol.1, pp.326, 339, repr. vol.2, pl.146.
Repr: *Irish Art: A Volume of Articles and Illustrations,* 1944, p.6.

An Taoiseach, Eamon de Valera, is painted here as a man of action and purpose.
Tonally, the composition, which has great presence, is rather subdued and somewhat
uncharacteristic of O'Sullivan's work in general, but it ably illustrates O'Sullivan's
thesis that a portrait should be a statement of what the artist thinks of his sitter, and
that in a successful portrait the sitter should be regarded 'as dispassionately as a
piece of still life' (O'Sullivan, *Irish Art*, op. cit., p.11).

Cata. no. 96.
Photograph
Bryan Rutledge.

JOHN (SEÁN) KEATING (1889–1977)

97. Men of the West 1916

Oil on canvas 102 x 127.
Inscr: 'KEATING' b.r.
Coll: Hugh Lane Municipal Gallery of Modern Art.
Exh: RHA: 1917 (4); 1978 (85); *Exhibition of Contemporary Irish Art*, North America, 1950 (45); *Irish Painting 1903–53*, MGMA, April–July 1953 (12); *John Keating: Paintings—Drawings*, MGMA, 1963 (1, repr.); *Sean Keating, P.R.H.A. 1889–1977*, RHA, November–December 1989 (31).
Lit: J.J.R. O'Beirne, 'A Coming Irish Artist: The Work of John Keating', *Irish Rosary,* 1917, p.575, repr. as frontispiece; Anne Crookshank & The Knight of Glin, *The Painters of Ireland c.1660–1920*, second ed., 1979, p.273; Brian de Breffny (ed.), *Ireland: A Cultural Encyclopaedia*, 1983, p.124, repr.; exhibition catalogue, *Celtic Splendour*, Pyms Gallery, London, 1985, p.68; Kennedy: 1987, vol.1, pp.344, 345, repr. vol.2, pl.164; 'Irish landscape painting in a political setting 1922–48', in M. Hill & S. Barber (eds.), *Aspects of Irish Studies*, 1990, p.49; Benedict Kiely, *Yeats' Ireland*, 1989, repr. in colour pp.106–7; Kenneth McConkey, *A Free Spirit: Irish Art 1860–1960*, 1990, pp.64, repr., 65, 150.

It was with this early composition that Keating firmly expressed his sympathies for Nationalist politics. A strong element of patriotism characterizes his whole *œuvre* and the romantic visionaries of this composition were later to become realists in his

Men of the South, 1922, and his symbolically rugged compatriots in *The Race of the Gael*, 1939. This composition, perhaps more than any other, symbolizes the rugged fibre of the Irish people in their struggle for political independence. In James White's words, here 'for the first time Ireland is presented not as a romantic landscape but as a vision of men united' (exhibition catalogue, *John Keating*, MGMA, 1963, p.8). The figure to the left of the composition is that of Keating himself and the other two figures are his brother and a friend. The picture was painted for the Irish National Aid Association.

Cata. no. 98.
Photograph courtesy Poetry/Rare Books Collection, SUNY, Buffalo.

PATRICK TUOHY (1894–1930)

98. John Stanislaus Joyce 1923–4
Oil on canvas 99 x 79.
Not inscribed.
Coll: The Poetry/Rare Books Collection/University Libraries, State University of New York at Buffalo.
Prov: Acquired by the present owner in 1950 from Librairie La Hune, Paris; Joyce Paris apartment.
Exh: RHA, 1924 (84).
Lit: Richard Ellmann, *Letters of James Joyce*, vol.3, New York, 1966, pp.96, 101, 107; C.G. Anderson, *James Joyce and his World*, 1967, p.9, repr.; Richard Ellmann, *James Joyce*, revised ed., 1982, pp.12n, 565, 715; Kennedy, 1987, vol.1, p.314; Rosemarie Mulcahy, 'Patrick J. Tuohy 1894–1930', *Irish Arts Review, Yearbook 1989–90*, 1989, pp.114, repr., 115.

This portrait of his father was commissioned by James Joyce. The composition well illustrates Tuohy's powers of characterization, an aspect which was noted by George Russell (AE) when reviewing it in the 1924 RHA exhibition. To Russell, it was the best picture in the show, and his description of it is still enlightening: 'The nervous hunched-up figure with taut hands and puckered face is full of vitality, and it is more remarkable—this fixing of an expression of transient querulous irritability—when we consider the slow elaboration of the method adopted and the artist's determination to be unhurried, whether his sitter was raging or not' (*Irish Statesman*, 19 April 1924, p.166). As Rosemarie Mulcahy has commented (op. cit., p.114), for Tuohy the key to good portraiture lay in observation and that is the success of this work. Shortly after this portrait was completed Tuohy also painted a portrait of James Joyce.

CHRISTOPHER CAMPBELL (1908–72)

99. Self-portrait 1950
Oil on canvas 91.5 x 71.
Inscr: 'CAMPBELL' b.l.
Owned privately.
Exh: *Irish Art 1943–1973*, Crawford Art Gallery, Cork, November–December 1980.
Lit: Kennedy, 1987, vol.1, p.358, repr. vol.2, pl.170.

Campbell's portraits are full of vitality and in concept and execution are distinct from those of his Irish contemporaries. In the 1940s, the boldness of his brushwork and use of heavy impasto gave way to a more precise style, although his use of colour and sense of pose remain distinctive. These attributes can be seen clearly in this painting, a strikingly candid work. Here the juxtaposition of colours is most daring and accomplished and the painting of the face, with soft modulations of flesh tints interspersed with greens and reds, is unequalled by any of his contemporaries.

Cata. no. 99.
Photograph
Bryan Rutledge.

Cata. no. 100.
Photograph
Bryan Rutledge.

LAURENCE CAMPBELL (1911–68)

100. Pont de l'Alma, Paris c.1940
Oil on canvas 50.8 x 61.
Inscr: 'Laurence Campbell R.H.A.' b.r.
Coll: Waterford Corporation.
Prov: Haverty Trust, Dublin.
Lit: Peter Jordan, *Waterford Municipal Art Collection,* Garter Lane Arts Centre,
Waterford, 1987, n.p.; Kennedy, 1987, vol.1, p.402, repr. vol.2, pl.74.

While best known as a sculptor, this is a rare example of Laurence Campbell's work
as a painter. Executed in an Impressionist technique, full of vigour and atmosphere,
it was almost certainly done from sketches made during 1938–9 when he was in
Paris.

Exhibited HLMG only.

Cata. no. 101.
Photograph
Bryan Rutledge.

WILLIAM CONOR (1881–1968)

101. Dr. Douglas Hyde, President of Ireland 1938–9
Oil on canvas 90 x 67.
Inscr: 'CONOR' t.l.
Coll: University College, Dublin.
Exh: RHA, 1939 (176); *William Conor*, BMAG in association with CEMA, 1957
(25).

315

Lit: Mairin Allen, 'Contemporary Irish Artists XIV—William Conor, R.O.I., A.R.H.A.', *Father Mathew Record*, October 1942, p.4; Judith Wilson, *Conor 1881–1968*, 1981, pp.48–9, repr. p.49 in a photograph of the artist at work on the portrait; Kennedy, 1987, vol.1, pp.360–1, repr. vol.2, pl.171.

William Conor is best known for his genre scenes of life in Belfast, but this work, which was commissioned in 1938, probably to mark Douglas Hyde's election as the first President of Ireland, is one of his most successful forays into portraiture. Here he has captured well the personality of his sitter, has used the strong colours of the academic robe to bring vitality to the composition, and his brushwork, which is often obtrusive, is more restrained than usual. Douglas Hyde was born in Co. Roscommon in 1860. Educated at Trinity College, Dublin, he became a noted linguist. He took his LL D in 1888 but devoted his life to literary pursuits and the revival of the Irish language. In 1893 he helped to found the Gaelic League and became its first president. He was appointed the first Professor of Modern Irish at University College, Dublin, in 1909, and held the chair until his retirement in 1932. In 1937, under the new Constitution of that year, he was elected the first President of Ireland and held the office until his term expired in 1945. He died in 1949. Hyde was a central figure in the Irish Literary Revival.

FRANK McKELVEY (1895–1974)

102. William Blair Morton, MA, D.Sc. 1945
Oil on canvas 98 x 83.
Inscr: 'Frank McKelvey 1945' b.r.
Coll: The Queen's University of Belfast.
Lit: Kennedy, 1987, vol.1, p.364, repr. vol.2, pl.174.

Frank McKelvey was one of the most prominent portraitists of his day working in Belfast. His portraits are executed in a strictly academic manner but at their best, as here, are very acomplished and he could achieve a penetrating characterization of his sitter. Educated at the Queen's College, Belfast and St. John's College, Cambridge, William Blair Morton (1868–1949) had a distinguished career at Queen's University as a teacher of natural philosophy.

W. J. LEECH (1881–1968)

103. The Bridge, Regents Park c.1935
Oil on board 34.9 x 45.1.
Inscr: 'LEECH' b.l.
Private collection, Isle of Man.
Exh: RHA, 1935 (4).

This composition, with its strong sunlight percolating through the trees, is characteristic of Leech's work of the 1930s, by which time the Post-Impressionist influence which pervaded his earlier work had given way to a more pastoral treatment.

317

Leech's palette was brighter than that of most of his contemporaries in Ireland and his outlook less introspective. He returned to this particular subject in the 1940s and again in the 1950s.

Cata. no. 103.
Photograph
Denise Ferran.

J. H. CRAIG (1878–1944)

104. Glendun, near Cushendun c. 1930–5
Oil on canvas 54.6 x 74.3.
Inscr: 'J.H.CRAIG' b.l.
Coll: North Down Borough Council.
Prov: Presented to North Down Borough Council by the artist's widow.
Lit: John Hewitt, *Art in Ulster:1*, 1977, p.83 repr.; Kennedy: 1987, vol.1, p.363, repr. vol.2, pl. 172; 'Irish landscape painting in a political setting 1922–48', in M. Hill & S. Barber (eds.), *Aspects of Irish Studies*, 1990, p.48.

Craig reacted directly to the landscape, working quickly in a loose Impressionist manner which was characterized, as John Hewitt noted (loc. cit.), by 'the swift notation of the insistent effect, the momentary flicker, the flash of light, the passing shadow'. His subtle brushwork and feeling for the ever changing mood of the landscape are clearly apparent in this work.

Cata. no. 105.
Photograph
Ulster Museum.

FRANK McKELVEY (1895–1974)

105. Evening, Ballycastle c.1924
Oil on canvas 76.5 x 102.
Inscr: 'FRANK McKELVEY' b.l.
Coll: Ulster Museum.
Exh: Royal Ulster Academy, May 1975 (2).
Lit: John Hewitt, *Art in Ulster:1*, 1977, pp.92 repr., 95; *A Concise Catalogue of the Drawings, Paintings & Sculptures in the Ulster Museum*, 1986, p.84; Kennedy, 1987, vol.1, p.364.

This is a good example of McKelvey's early landscape work in which he concentrated on capturing the essential visual effect of the scene. In appearance, his work is in the tradition of Dermod O'Brien and has less of the romance associated with J.H. Craig and other of his contemporaries. Unfortunately, however, McKelvey failed to make the most imaginative use of his great technical ability. A watercolour study for this work was exhibited at the Gorry Gallery exhibition, *18th, 19th and 20th Century Irish Paintings*, during November–December 1990, catalogue number 32, as *Ballycastle*. The well-known headland seen here in the distance is Fair Head.

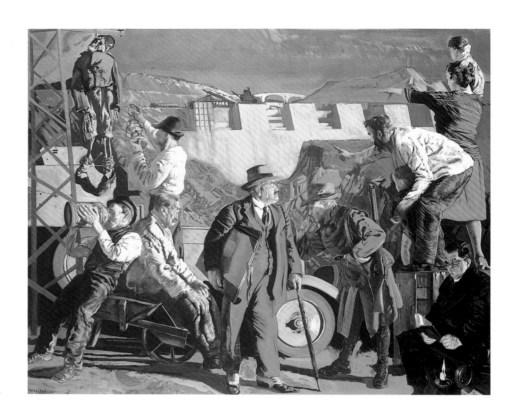

JOHN (SEÁN) KEATING (1889–1977)

106. Night's Candles are Burnt Out 1928–9

Oil on canvas 99.1 x 104.1.
Inscr: 'KEATING' b.l.
Coll: Oldham Art Gallery. Reproduced by arrangement with the Electricity Supply Board, Dublin.
Exh: Royal Academy, London, 1929 (421); *Keating and the ESB*, RHA, July 1985 (20); *Sean Keating and the ESB*, Arts Council Gallery, Belfast, August 1987 (no numbers); *Sean Keating, P.R.H.A. (1889–1977)*, RHA, November–December 1989 (107).
Lit: Exhibition catalogue, *Irish Renascence*, Pyms Gallery, London, 1986, p.78; Kennedy: 1987, vol.1, p.328, repr. vol.2, pl.149; 'Irish landscape painting in a political setting 1922–48', in M. Hill & S. Barber (eds.), *Aspects of Irish Studies*, 1990, pp.49–50.
Repr: *Royal Academy Illustrated*, 1929, p.97; Padric Colum, *Cross Roads in Ireland*, 1930, facing p.366.

Painted during the late 1920s when Keating was recording the construction of the hydro-electric scheme on the river Shannon at Ardnacrusha in Co. Limerick. The composition is an allegory of the new Ireland then emerging after 1922. Literally, we see the advancing power of electricity about to replace the candle and the oil lamp. Groups of figures, who symbolize the changing country, include young parents with

320

their children (top right) who look to the future and various workmen and a contractor, who represent latent entrepreneurial skills. The hanging skeleton at the left repesents the death of the old era and the contractor's contemptuous stare at the gunman to his left is an historical reference to the recently ended civil war of 1922–3.

Cata. no. 107.
Photograph
Hugh Lane Municipal
Gallery of Modern
Art.

MAURICE MacGONIGAL (1900–79)

107. Dockers 1933–4
Oil on canvas 125.4 x 100.
Inscr: 'MacCongail', in Irish script, b.l.
Coll: Hugh Lane Municipal Gallery of Modern Art.
Exh: RHA, 1934 (177); Haverty Trust, *First Exhibition of Paintings*, Mansion House, Dublin, November 1935 (4).
Lit: Mairin Allen, 'Contemporary Irish Artists XVIII—Maurice MacGonigal', *Father Mathew Record*, May 1943, p.6; Kennedy, 1987, vol.1, pp.328, 352, repr. vol.2, pl.150.
Repr: As a post card by the HLMG.

This is one of MacGonigal's most successful subject-pictures, although the composition is somewhat stiff and lacks the freedom of his landscapes. The three dock workers depicted seem to be drawn from the context of a mass meeting, but one is never sure as to what is happening; perhaps the theme is defiance in the face of adversity. Mairin Allen (loc. cit.) referred to this picture as 'a document of our times'.

MAURICE MacGONIGAL (1900–79)

108. 'The Olympia', Dublin 1935–6
Oil on canvas 63.6 x 76.5.
Inscr: 'MacCongail', in Irish script, b.r.
Coll: Ulster Museum.
Prov: Haverty Trust; to UM 1941.
Exh: RHA, 1936 (96); Haverty Trust, *Second Quinquennial Exhibition*, National College of Art, Dublin, 1940 (32); *Paintings from Belfast Museum & Art Gallery*, Carnegie Hall, Lurgan, January 1961 (15).
Lit: *A Concise Catalogue of the Drawings, Paintings & Sculptures in the Ulster Museum*, 1986, p.84; Kennedy, 1987, vol.1, p.352, repr. vol.2, pl. 167.

This composition was made from a number of pencil drawings done during a series of visits to the Olympia Theatre in 1935 and 1936. The figure at the right hand side is the painter Harry Kernoff, a life-long friend of MacGonigal's, who regularly attended the theatre with him (Ciarán MacGonigal, letter of 23 May 1976, quoting the artist, UM archives). The strong theatrical lighting in the picture creates atmosphere and the colour and bold contrasts of tone are put to good effect. As subject-matter, it is in a long tradition stretching back to Sickert, Toulouse-Lautrec, Degas and many others.

LEO WHELAN (1892–1956)

109. Interior of a Kitchen c.1935

Oil on canvas 68.3 x 57.5.

Inscr: 'LEO WHELAN' b.r.; also 'Interior of a Kitchen Leo Whelan RHA' on
reverse.

Coll: Ulster Museum.

Prov: Haverty Trust; to UM 1941.

Exh: Haverty Trust, *Second Quinquennial Exhibition*, National College of Art,
Dublin, 1940 (13); *A Vision of Ireland: 20th Century Irish Painting*, Herbert Art
Gallery & Museum, Coventry, 1989 (15, repr.)

Lit: *A Concise Catalogue of the Drawings, Paintings & Sculptures in the Ulster
Museum*, 1986, p.177; Kennedy, 1987, vol.1, p.328, repr. vol.2, pl.70.

Repr: Catalogue of new books, Blackstaff Press, Belfast, 1986, in colour on cover.

This is a good example of Leo Whelan's genre work and is a *tour de force* in the rendering of the nature of material, texture and surface of the objects depicted. In his approach to compositions such as this, Whelan was influenced by the seventeenth century Dutch artist, Vermeer. The figure at the table was the artist's sister, Frances Whelan, and the setting was the basement kitchen in the artist's home in Eccles Street, Dublin (conversation with Ms. Lena Murnaghan, 30 August 1985).

Cata. no. 110.
Photograph
Bournemouth
Museums Service.

324

JAMES SLEATOR (1885–1950)

110. Interior 1931
Oil on canvas 109.2 x 83.8.
Inscr: 'Sleator 1931' b.l.
Coll: Bournemouth Museums Service.
Exh: (?) RHA, 1932 (173, as *Interior—Orpen's Studio*); A Century of Progress, USA, 1933 (no details); Royal Academy, London, 1936 (527); *Coronation Exhibition of Prominent Living Artists,* (?) London (no details); *James Sinton Sleator P.R.H.A. 1885–1950*: Armagh County Museum, Fermanagh County Museum, RHA, April–July 1989 (all 32, repr.)
Lit: Russell-Cotes Art Gallery & Museum, Bulletin, vol.16, September 1937, pp.30–1 and repr. on cover; Kennedy, 1987, vol.1, p.341.

This work depicts Sir William Orpen painting in his studio in South Bolton Gardens, London. Sleator makes good use of a somewhat dramatic chiaroscuro, yet the overall feeling evoked by the painting is one of tranquillity. The composition is strongly Dutch in feeling, recalling especially the work of Vermeer and de Hooch. It may even have been modelled in part on Vermeer's *The Studio* (Kunsthistorisches Museum, Vienna).

JAMES SLEATOR (1885–1950)

111. Still Life with Flowers 1949
Oil on canvas 76 x 61.
Inscr: 'J. SLEATOR 1949' b.l.
Coll: Mr. & Mrs. Michael Bowles.
Prov: Artist's studio; May Fitzgerald; by bequest to Mrs. Catherine Bowles.
Exh: *James Sinton Sleator P.R.H.A. 1885–1950*: Armagh County Museum, Fermanagh County Museum, RHA, April–July 1989 (all 46, repr. in colour).
Lit: Kennedy, 1987, vol.1, p.342, repr. vol.2, pl.161.

This is one of Sleator's finest flower paintings. In the depiction of surface textures, mastery of brushwork, subtle use of colour and sensitivity for his medium it is unsurpassed by any other painter working in Ireland in the period.

GEORGE COLLIE (1904–75)

112. The Mid-day Meal 1927
Oil on board 69 x 91.
Inscr: 'G. Collie' b.l.
Private collection, Dublin.
Exh: RHA, 1976 (59).
Lit: Kennedy, 1987, vol.1, pp.328, 357, repr. vol.2, pl.148.

A piece of Social-realist painting. Collie won the Taylor Art Scholarship with this composition in 1927. It shows the inmates of the Dublin Union at table.

WILLIAM CONOR (1881–1968)

113. A Sup of Tea c.1940s
Oil on board 59.7 x 49.
Inscr: 'CONOR' b.l.
Coll: Hugh Lane Municipal Gallery of Modern Art.
Prov: Miss Julia M. Egan & The Friends of the National Collections of Ireland; to HLMG 1961.
Exh: RHA: (?) 1961 (60, as *A Cup of Tay*); 1968 (4).
Lit: Judith Wilson, *Conor 1881–1968*, 1981, p.146.

Conor's use of heavy impasto is well employed in this composition. His familiar technique, when painting in watercolours, of using wax to give a broken surface can also be seen to have influenced his handling of the paint. His characterization of the elderly woman and the cottage interior vividly evoke a bygone age.

MARGARET CLARKE (1888–1961)

114. Strindbergian 1927
Oil on canvas 127.5 x 102.
Inscr: 'MARGARET CLARKE 1927' b.l.
Coll: Ulster Museum.
Prov: David Clarke, Esq.

Exh: RHA: 1927 (28); 1962 (68); *Margaret Clarke*, Taylor Galleries, Dublin, 1979 (1); *Irish Women Artists*, NGI, July–August 1987 (101, repr.)
Lit: Kennedy, 1987, vol.1, p.354.

This composition, which is based on Strindberg's *The Ghost Sonata,* is enigmatic and Expressionist in concept. The tall figure with arms outstretched to the right of centre is the playwright Lennox Robinson, and other figures were modelled by friends of the artist.

Exhibited UM only.

Cata. no. 114.
Photograph
Ulster Museum.

Cata. no. 115.

BEATRICE GLENAVY (1883–1968)

115. The Intruder 1932
Oil on canvas 70 x 95.
Inscr: 'BG' by monogram b.r.
Private collection, Dublin.
Prov: Prof. Fearon; passed to his executor and thence by family descent.
Exh: Aonach Tailteann exhibition of *Irish Art*, Dublin, 1932 (133); RHA, 1932
(37); Royal Academy, London, 1933 (12); *Irish Painting 1903–53*, MGMA,
April–July 1953 (21); Waddington Galleries, Dublin, 1955 (no details); *Irish
Women Artists*, NGI, July–August 1987 (112, repr.)
Lit: Beatrice Glenavy, *Today we will only Gossip*, 1964, p.148; Kennedy, 1987,
vol.1, p.355, repr. vol.2, pl.169.

Beatrice Glenavy's imagery is often enigmatic. Here, for example, is a sort of
Thessalyian allegory of desire in which a female centaur, having galloped through
the scene, stops to beckon a young man from a group of figures who are picnicking,
while other pairs of figures (lovers?), clearly disturbed by the event, attend with
mild surprise. In her autobiography (op. cit., p.355) Lady Glenavy said that the
meaning of the picture, 'if any', was that 'the unknown was more interesting than
the known'.

OLIVER SHEPPARD (1865–1941)

116. Pádraig Pearse 1936
Bronze, height 73.
Inscr: 'PADRAIG H. PEARSE BY OLIVER SHEPPARD RHA 1936' on back.
Coll: Dail Eireann.
Exh: RHA, 1937 (423).
Lit: Kennedy, 1987, vol.1, p.393, repr. vol.2, pl.175.

In this posthumous bust by Sheppard the pose, the fine modelling and highly polished surface of the bronze combine to depict Pearse heroically, like an Emperor, and we are left in no doubt as the the significance of his presence. The work shows Sheppard at his very best and confirms that, even in his later years, he could muster all the authority of his previous work, of pieces such as *Inis Fáil* (1906) or *Cuchulain* (1911–12).

330

ALBERT POWER (1883–1945)

117. W. B. Yeats 1939

Bronze, height 53.
Inscr: 'A. POWER RHA 1939'.
Coll: National Gallery of Ireland.
Exh: RHA: 1939 (368, another cast); (?) 1946 (22).
Lit: Michael MacLiammoir & Eavan Bolan, *W.B.Yeats & his World,* 1971, repr.
facing p.127; Kennedy, 1987, vol.1, pp.393, 400, repr. vol.2, pl.177; NGI,
Summary Catalogue of Prints and Sculptures, 1988, pp.582, repr., 584 (the plaster
original).

The fluid modelling and handling of the medium in this work are perfectly matched
with the expression and personality of the sitter. This is one of the very best portrait
studies, executed in any medium, done in Ireland this century. This cast was made in
1968 from the plaster original in the National Gallery of Ireland. There is another
cast in Sandycove Green, Dublin.

ALBERT POWER (1883–1945)

118. The Fall of Icarus c.1940

Marble, height 38.
Not inscribed.
Coll: National Gallery of Ireland.
Prov: Mrs. Judith O'Reilly, Co. Wicklow; to NGI 1950.
Exh: RHA: 1941 (401, as *Icarus, Icarus, Nohina–Dedit Aquis*); 1946 (20).
Lit: Alan Denson, *John Hughes: Sculptor*, 1969, p.475; Kennedy, 1987, vol.1,
p.393; NGI, *Summary Catalogue of Prints and Sculptures*, 1988, p.583, repr.

Power was at his best when working in a domestic scale and free from the restraints
of a commission. Here, in his modelling, he exploits with ease the qualities of fine
grained marble to render surface and texture and his sense of realism is perfectly
suited to the subject. The story of Icarus is best known from Ovid, *Metamorphoses*
8. Icarus was the son of Daedalus who made him wings of feathers and wax so that
they could both escape from Crete. Icarus disobeyed instructions, flew too near the
sun, the wax melted and he was drowned. Daedalus buried his body on the island
afterwards called Icaria.

ALBERT POWER (1883–1945)

119. Leenane, Connemara Trout 1944
Marble, height 48.
Inscr: 'ALBERT POWER 1944'.
Coll: National Gallery of Ireland.
Prov: Miss Kathleen Fox; Mrs. Fox Pym; to NGI 1949.
Exh: RHA, 1946 (29).
Lit: Alan Denson, *John Hughes: Sculptor*, 1969, p.475; Kennedy, 1987, vol.1, pp.393, 401, repr. vol.2, pl.178; NGI, *Summary Catalogue of Prints and Sculptures*, 1988, p.583, repr.

In this work, as in his *Fall of Icarus*, Power's emphasis on naturalism is perfectly matched to the subject-matter, and one can clearly sense the upward thrust of the fish as it leaps against the rush of falling water. The setting for the piece was the river near Leenane, at the head of Killary Bay. Power made a number of variants of this composition (James Power, conversation of 16 January 1986). He seems to have worked on the theme for some time, for although it is dated 1944, Mairin Allen in 'Contemporary Irish artists IX—Albert G. Power, R.H.A.' (*Father Mathew Record*, February 1942, p.4) mentions his 'Trout' (probably the work exhibited at the RHA in 1941 [394]) and gives a description of it which suits this work.

Cata. no. 119.
Photograph
National Gallery
of Ireland.

ROSAMOND PRAEGER (1867–1954)

120. The Fairy Fountain c.1900–01

Marble, carved in high relief, 64.8 x 76.5 x 16.5.

Inscr: 'S.R.Praeger' on both bottom right and lower right hand side.

Coll: Ulster Museum.

Prov: Artist's studio; to UM 1926.

Exh: Royal Academy, London, 1901 (1773); RHA, 1902 (349); Belfast Art
Society, BMAG: postponed annual exhibition 1902, January 1903 (178); October–
November 1923 (280); *Exhibition of Irish Art*, in association with Tailteann
Games, Ballsbridge, Dublin, April 1924 (369); *Exhibition of Works by S.R.
Praeger MBE, MA, HRHA (1867–1954)*, Queen's Hall, Holywood, October 1975
(11); *The Edwardian Era*, Barbican Art Gallery, London, November 1987–
February 1988; *Sculpture from the permanent collection*, UM, February 1988 (no
numbers).

Lit: *Ulster Commentary*, July 1948, repr. pp.4–5; Sam Hanna Bell, et al. (eds.),
The Arts in Ulster: A Symposium, 1951, repr. p.97; John Hewitt, *Art in Ulster:1*,
1977, p.180; Martyn Anglesea, *The Royal Ulster Academy of Arts*, 1981, p.85,
repr.; Eileen Black, 'Of art and artists', *Belfast: The Making of a City 1800–1914*,
1983, p.95, repr.; *A Concise Catalogue of the Drawings, Paintings & Sculptures
in the Ulster Museum*, 1986, p.136; Kennedy: 1987, vol.1, p.393; *Catalogue of the
Permanent Collection:2–Twentieth Century Sculpture*, UM, 1988, pp.77–8.

Dated c.1900–01 on the assumption that it was recently made when exhibited at the
Royal Academy in the latter year. Plaster casts of this work are in the possession of
the Collegiate School, Enniskillen, Sullivan Upper School, Holywood, and a private
collection in Omagh, Co. Tyrone.

ROSAMOND PRAEGER (1867–1954)

121. Spring c.1934

Irish limestone relief 18.5 x 72.5.

Not inscribed.

Coll: Ulster Museum.

Prov: Artist's studio; to UM 1947.

Exh: *Contemporary Ulster Art*, BMAG, June–July 1951 (88); Coleraine Art
Society, Town Hall, Coleraine, November 1967 (no numbers); *Exhibition of
Works by S.R. Praeger MBE, MA HRHA (1867–1954)*, Queen's Hall, Holywood,
October 1975 (28); *Sculpture from the permanent collection*, UM, February 1988
(no numbers).

Lit: *A Concise Catalogue of the Drawings, Paintings & Sculptures in the Ulster
Museum*, 1986, p.136; Kennedy: 1987, vol.1, p.393, repr. vol.2, pl.179; *Catalogue
of the Permanent Collection:2–Twentieth Century Sculpture*, UM, 1988, p.79.

The complexity of this composition and of the action depicted are unusual for Praeger.
Also, she rarely attempted to convey such a feeling of recession in her relief works.

Plaster casts of this work are in the possession of Sullivan Upper School, Holywood, and a private collection in Belfast.

Reproduced p. 192

JOSEPH HIGGINS (1885–1925)

122. An strachaire fir c.1910–24
Bronze, height 42.
Not inscribed.
Coll: Crawford Municipal Art Gallery, Cork.

Prov: Artist's studio; to Crawford Art Gallery 1924.
Exh: *Irish Art 1900–1950*, Crawford Art Gallery, Cork, December 1975–January 1976 (178).

Technically Higgins had a light touch and a fluid, atmospheric style which was well suited to works of a domestic scale. The title of this piece has no direct equivalent in English, but approximates to 'The vigorous man' or 'The Tearaway'. It implies a strong, active, burly personality.

Cata. no. 123.
Photograph
Bryan Rutledge.

LAURENCE CAMPBELL (1911–68)

123. Mother and Child 1933
Stone, height 23.1.
Inscr: 'LAURENCE CAMPBELL Sc 1933' on side.
Coll: Ann Simmons.
Prov: Miss Florence Clarke, Ballybrack.
Exh: *Irish Art 1900–1950*, Crawford Art Gallery, Cork, December 1975–January 1976 (166).
Lit: Kennedy, 1987, vol.1, p.402, repr. vol.2, pl.192.

This is one of the most avant-garde pieces of Irish sculpture of its time. The somewhat severe simplification of square-cut forms suggests a Cubist influence and clearly illustrates Campbell's awareness of Modernism. The sense of rhythm and emphasis on line recall certain works by Mainie Jellett done in about the same years.

LAURENCE CAMPBELL (1911–68)

124. Virgin and Child 1948
Wood, height 121.9.
Inscr: 'LAVRENCE CAMPBELL, RHA 1948' on left hand side.
Coll: Jesuit Residence, Cherryfield Lodge, Dublin 6.
Lit: Kennedy, 1987, vol.1, p.403, repr. vol.2, pl.194.

This work illustrates the way in which, by the late 1940s, Campbell's sculpture became more academic in execution, and he seems to have cast aside the Modernist influence evident in earlier works. He has, however, retained a close awareness for the natural characteristics of the wood.

SÉAMUS MURPHY (1907–75)

125. Prayer 1933
Bronze, height 57.
Inscr: 'S. Murphy '33'.
Private collection.
Exh: RHA: 1937 (428); (?) 1953 (197); *Contemporary Irish Art*, National Library of Wales, Aberystwyth, 1953 (75, repr.); *Irish Art 1900–1950*, Crawford Art Gallery, Cork, December 1975–January 1976 (193).

Essentially a stone carver in the tradition of monumental masons, Murphy was at his best when working on a large scale, manipulating bold forms, usually with great economy of means. Here, as in much of his early work, there is a strong linear emphasis which recalls the rhythms found in Mainie Jellett and Laurence Campbell, and which in his standing Madonnas he used to emphasize the verticality of the composition. Hilary Pyle (catalogue, *Irish Art 1900–1950*, p.81) states that this bust was modelled while Murphy was at Collarossi's in Paris.

Cata. no. 125.

126. Seán O'Faolain 1947
Bronze, height 37.
Inscr: 'SEAN O FAOLAIN S. MURPHY' on reverse.
Coll: University College, Cork.

Murphy's portrait heads are strictly representational in treatment and at his best, as here, a work which shows vigorous modelling, he could capture personality. Seán O'Faolain, short story writer and man of letters, was born in Cork in 1900. After a brief spell teaching in the USA and England he settled in Ireland and pursued his writing full time. His early reputation was based not only on his own writing, but on his editorship of *The Bell*, which he founded in 1940 and edited until 1946, which in its time was one of Ireland's most influential literary magazines and a liberal voice during the years of censorship. Seán O'Faolain died in April 1991.

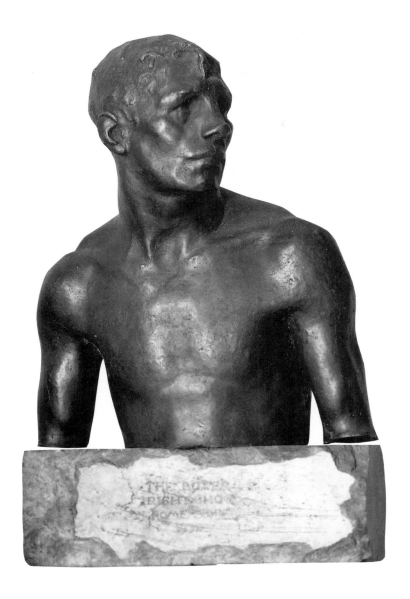

Cata. no. 127.
Photograph
Bryan Rutledge.

JEROME CONNOR (1876–1943)

127. The Boxer 1937
Bronze, height 26.
Not inscribed.
Coll: Myles Digby
Exh: RHA, 1938 (404).
Lit: Kennedy, 1987, vol.1, p.409, repr. vol.2, pl.198.

This is one of Jerome Connor's so-called 'little pieces of free work', done late in his career. Such works by him occasionally take the form of a portrait but more often they are studies in character. Here, free from the constraints of a commission, Connor is perfectly at ease, modelling busily, succinctly and omitting all unnecessary details.

339

JEROME CONNOR (1876–1943)

128. The Pikeman 1940
Bronze, height 83.
Inscr: 'CONNOR' on base.
Private collection.
Prov: By descent from the present owner's father.
Exh: RHA, 1942 (310).
Lit: Kennedy, 1987, vol.1, p.409.

The rugged modelling, simplicity of pose and defiant expression of the figure in this work contrast markedly with Connor's abortive efforts with the same subject—the *Pikeman* in Tralee—of a decade or so earlier.

Cata. no. 129.
Photograph
Bryan Rutledge.

PETER GRANT (b.1915)

129. Manannan MacLir 1939

Bronze 90 x 69 x 42.
Inscr: 'PETER GRANT' on base.
Coll: Helen O'Malley Roelofs.
Exh: RHA, 1944 (333); Irish Sculpture Section, International Exhibition, Royal
Hospital, Kilmainham, Dublin, 1988.
Lit: Kennedy, 1987, vol.1, p.396, repr. vol.2, pl.185.

Generally, Grant's early works are academic in concept and execution, but
nevertheless, as in this piece, they often have a feeling for the heroic. Manannan
MacLir was the God of the Sea in the Irish sagas. He would drive over the ocean
regardless of the state of the seas. He ruled Tir Tairngire ('the Land of Promise').
This piece was modelled in plaster in 1939 and cast in bronze in 1980.

HILARY HERON (1923–77)

130. James Connolly 1946

Wood, height 60.
Inscr: 'HH [monogram] 1946' b.r.
Coll: Bakery & Food Workers' Amalgamated Union, Dublin.
Lit: Kennedy, 1987, vol.1, p.398, repr. vol.2, pl.188.

Here, as in all her work, Hilary Heron emphasizes the natural qualities of her medium,
in this case making good use of the grain of the wood which is as important to our

reading of the work as the identity of the sitter. James Connolly (1868–1916), the socialist and revolutionary, is here seen wearing the uniform of the Irish Citizen Army, which he established in 1913.

Cata. no. 130.
Photograph
S.B.K.

Cata. no. 131.

RALPH CUSACK (1912–65)

131. Fishing Boats, Loughshinney 1940
Oil on canvas 55 x 65.
Inscr: 'Cusack 40' t.r.
Private collection, France.
Exh: *Ralph Cusack Paintings*, Dublin Painters' gallery, Dublin, October 1940 (1).
Lit: Kennedy, 1987, vol.1, p.97, repr. vol.2, pl.54, as *Boats*.

The clarity of expression, emphasis on line and pattern evident in this work are
characteristic of Cusack's painting until the mid-1940s.

Cata. no. 132.

RALPH CUSACK (1912–65)

132. The Way to the World 1945
Oil on canvas 100 x 81.
Inscr: 'Cusack 45' b.l.; also signed and titled on reverse.
Private collection, France.
Exh: IELA, 1945 (82).
Lit: Kennedy, 1987, vol.1, pp.99, 240, repr. vol.2, pl.57.

From about the mid-1940s Cusack seems to have been influenced by the English painter Paul Nash whose gentle Surrealism and metaphysical Symbolism he much admired. This composition, with its symbolic architectural forms and metaphysical treatment of the landscape is clearly 'Nashian'. The theatrical nature of the composition may also be linked to his stage sets done with Anne Yeats for the Olympia and Gaiety theatres in Dublin.

NOTES

Chapter 1

1 Ronald Anderson, 'Whistler in Dublin, 1884', *Irish Arts Review*, vol. 3, 1986, pp. 45–51 gives a detailed discussion of Whistler's involvement in this exhibition. For a note of John B. Yeats' likely involvement see W.B. Yeats, *Autobiographies: Reveries over Childhood and Youth* (London: MacMillan, 1926), p.102.

2 The Rt. Hon. Jonathan Hogg of Dublin tried at the time to purchase both of these paintings but Whistler would not sell them. It is interesting to think that had he purchased them they might one day have found their way into an Irish public collection.

3 'The Dublin Sketching Club', *Irish Times*, 1 December 1884, p.2.

4 E.R. & J. Pennell, *The Life of James McNeill Whistler*, 2 vols. (London: William Heinemann, 1908), vol. 2, p. 36.

5 Whistler set-down his aesthetic creed in *Ten O'Clock*, a lecture which he prepared throughout the autumn and early winter of 1884–5. It was first delivered at Prince's Hall, London, on 20 February 1885 at 10.0pm, the hour thus providing its title (Pennell, op. cit., vol. 2, pp. 36–7).

6 The organization of the exhibition resulted from a meeting held on 8 December 1898, under the chairmanship of Lord Powerscourt, at the Metropolitan School of Art. The executive committee then elected included, amongst others, Walter Armstrong, (Director, National Gallery of Ireland), Walter Osborne, Sarah Purser, George Russell (AE) and W.G. Strickland (Registrar, National Gallery of Ireland).

7 The works by Degas were *Ballet Girls* and *Harlequin* (both pastels); the Monet was *River in Autumn*. They were all lent by Edward Martyn and are now in the National Gallery of Ireland (nos. 2740, 2741 and 852 respectively). Edward Martyn (1859–1924), a playwright, was associated with George Moore and W.B. Yeats in founding the Irish Literary Theatre that same year (1899).

8 'Art Loan Exhibition', *Irish Times*, 1 April 1899, p.6.

9 Thomas MacGreevy, 'Fifty Years of Irish Painting 1900–1950', *Capuchin Annual*, 1949, p. 497. The full title of the exhibition was: *A Loan Collection of Pictures by Nathaniel Hone, R.H.A. and John Butler Yeats, R.H.A.* In this article MacGreevy was sympathetic to the idea of 'Art for Art's Sake' which creed, derived from Théophile Gautier and the Symbolists in France, influenced Whistler in England. It was Whistler who, as we have seen, first showed its fruits in Ireland.

10 The background to this exhibition is set down in detail in William M. Murphy, *Prodigal Father: The Life of John Butler Yeats (1839–1922)*, (Ithaca & London, 1978), pp. 225–34.

11 At £300 this amount had remained unchanged since 1831 (W. G. Strickland, *A Dictionary of Irish Artists* [Dublin, 1913], p. 612.).

12 Little came of this and other attempts by Drew to invigorate the Academy. Yeats always suspected that Drew's primary interest in such matters was his own advancement (Murphy, op. cit., p. 250). Several reports and counter-reports on the institution's future were issued by various parties during the following years, culminating in the 1906 report of the Treasury committee appointed to enquire into the work of the RHA and the Metropolitan School of Art. As the Treasury committee could not agree on its recommendations, however, it issued two reports, the so-called 'Majority' and 'Minority' reports. The former was not favourable to the Academy, recommending a new charter to remedy the defects in its constitution, the amalgamation of its life school with that in the Metropolitan School of Art, and that it should remain in its Abbey Street premises. But as the Metropolitan School of art was primarily concerned to give instruction in the applied arts this report effectively ignored the distinction between an academy of art and a school of applied art. The latter, Minority, report suggested that the Academy and its school should be maintained, fostered and encouraged. It also favoured its transfer to a better site. The result of these two reports, so far as the Academy was concerned, was that no change was made. For a time the academicians agitated for the recommendations of the Minority report to be implemented, but nothing ever came of the matter. (Strickland, op. cit., pp. 619-20 gives a full history of these events).

13 For a brief history of Yeats' old studio see chapter 2 below.

14 'Loan Exhibition of Paintings By Mr. Hone, R.H.A., and Mr. Yeats, R.H.A.', *Irish Times*, 21 October 1901, p.4; Dublin *Daily Express*, 21 October 1901. Yeats' portrait of O'Leary is now in the National Gallery of Ireland (no. 595).

15 Reprinted in George Russell (AE), *Imaginations and Reveries*, (Dublin: Maunsell & Co., 1915), p. 72.

16 George Moore, *Modern Painting* (London: Walter Scott), 1893, enlarged ed. 1898.

17 Bruce Arnold, *Orpen: Mirror to an Age* (London: Jonathan Cape, 1981), p. 140 relates Lane's scheming in this matter. With the exception of the Healy portrait, and those by Yeats, these are all now in the Hugh Lane Municipal Gallery.

18 Murphy, op. cit., p. 584, n. 44 lists a number of these portraits.

19 These works are all listed and reproduced in Thomas Bodkin, *Hugh Lane and his Pictures* (Dublin: Stationery Office), 1932.

20 Although Roosevelt was a veteran Irish enthusiast his support for Lane's project was probably enlisted by John Quinn who, at the time, was closely involved with the Irish Literary circle.

21 A similar proposal was made by Sir Robert Witt in 1938 (letter to *The Times*, 17 May) but it was then unacceptable to the Irish who wanted full ownership of the pictures.

22 *Northern Whig*, 9 January 1905.

23 S. Shannon Millin, *Art in Belfast* (Belfast: Northern Whig), 1903.

24 Maurice Joy, 'Art in Ireland', *Northern Whig*, 24 December 1904.

25 For a brief discussion of the formation of the Joint Committee see Patrick Shea, *A History of the Ulster Arts Club* (Belfast, 1971), pp. 7-8.

26 Hugh Lane, preface to the exhibition catalogue, p. vii.

27 'Modern Art in Belfast', *Northern Whig*, 20 April 1906, p.9.

28 Ibid.

29 Sir Robert Lloyd Patterson (1836-1906), a Belfast linen merchant, bequeathed to the Belfast Museum & Art Gallery his collection of nineteenth century art and the sum of £6,000 to provide adequate accomodation to house it. But the bequest was not to be effectual until the death of his wife, which occurred in 1926. In 1927, however, having taken professional advice on the matter, the authorities of the Museum & Art Gallery decided that, as most of the works were of poorer quality than originally thought, they would sell the bulk of the collection and use the proceeds along with the endowed money to form a new 'Lloyd Patterson Collection' of contemporary art. They obtained the necessary legal powers to do this and carried out the scheme and, with advice from the Contemporary Art Society, London, formed a collection of modern British painting covering the years 1900–1937.

Patterson's bequest was almost certainly prompted by the earlier discussions of Messrs Shannon Millin and Maurice Joy on the state of art in Belfast. For a detailed history of the Lloyd Patterson bequest, see Brian Kennedy, *British Art 1900–1937: Sir Robert Lloyd Patterson Collection*, (Belfast: Ulster Museum), 1982.

30 Hugh Lane, correspondence columns, *Northern Whig* and *Belfast News-Letter*, 28 April 1906.

31 'The Exhibition of Modern Paintings', *Northern Whig*, 25 April 1906, p. 12.

32 For a discussion of the criticism surrounding the two last-mentioned exhibitions see J.B. Bullen (ed.), *Post-Impressionists in England* (London: Routledge), 1988.

33 Patrick Shea, op. cit., p. 10.

34 The Cézanne, for example, was entitled *Baigneurs*, but as Cézanne made a number of paintings of this title and subject-matter this particular picture cannot be singled out. Gauguin's *Enfants* (cata. no.1) or, more probably, *Maori Women* (cata. no.5) may have been the picture now known as *Tahitian Women with Mango Blossoms*, Metropolitan Museum of Art, New York.

35 George Russell (AE), 'The Post-Impressionists: Art and Barbarism', *Irish Times*, 26 January 1911, p. 5.

36 Thomas Bodkin, ' "Post Impressionists" in Dublin,' *Freeman's Journal*, 26 January 1911, p. 8.

37 Monet, for example, was represented by a portrait of *Mlle. Lemonnier*, but as he painted at least four studies of this sitter one cannot identify that which was exhibited in Belfast.

38 Picasso's portrait of *Clovis Sagot*, exhibited in Dublin the previous year, was, of course, an example of Analytical Cubism in an embyronic state. The *Irish Times* review of this exhibition, however, records that it included 'four or five' Cubist works ('Post Impressionists and Cubeists [sic]', *Irish Times*, 29 March 1912, p. 7) as did Ellen Duncan herself ('Modern French Pictures at the United Arts Club', *Irish Review*, vol. 11, May 1912, pp. 164–6).

39 *Irish Times*, 29 March 1912, p. 7.

40 Paul Henry, *Further Reminiscences* (Belfast: Blackstaff Press, 1973), p. 70. Although not published until 1973, Henry drafted this text in the 1950s.

41 Henry, op. cit., p. 73.

Chapter 2

1 Paul Henry, *Further Reminiscences*, p.67.

2 Paul Henry, *An Irish Portrait* (London: Batsford, 1951), p.48.

3   In an advance notice of their exhibition *Paintings of Irish Life*, held at Pollock's Gallery, Belfast, in March 1911, the *Northern Whig* noted that Paul and Grace Henry had recently been on Achill 'For close on a year . . . living amongst the people and getting to know them' ('Pictures of Irish Life', *Northern Whig*, 11 March 1911, p.10). In his autobiography, *An Irish Portrait*, op. cit., p.48, Henry stated that he first went to Achill in 1912, but that is incorrect.

4   Henry, *Further Reminiscences*, pp.65, 68.

5   On the subject of Irish artists working abroad see Julian Campbell, *The Irish Impressionists: Irish Artists in France and Belgium 1850–1914*, exhibition catalogue, National Gallery of Ireland, 1984.

6   These names are given in an advertisement for the Society's first exhibition, *Irish Times*, 6 August 1920 and are mentioned also in reviews of that exhibition published in the *Freeman's Journal* and the *Irish Independent* of the same date. As the Society's records have not survived one must rely solely on exhibition catalogues and press reports for information about the membership.

7   For a discussion of this point, and of Sleator's career in general, see Brian Kennedy, *James Sinton Sleator P.R.H.A. 1885–1950*, exhibition catalogue, Armagh County Museum, Armagh, 1989.

8   Moore (b.1857) was an amateur painter. A botanist by profession, he was sometime President of the Royal Zoological Society of Ireland and Keeper of the Royal Botanic Gardens, Glasnevin, Dublin.

9   Mainie Jellett may have been the first president, but in the absence of records one cannot be certain of this. Paul Henry, however, was the first secretary. Harriet Kirkwood was secretary from 1930–6 and president 1936–40s; Eva Hamilton was president in 1948. The names of the other officers in those early years are unknown.

10 The lease on the premises was completed on 31 March 1921 when it was signed, for the Society, by Clare Marsh, Jack B. Yeats and Paul Henry. Initially the lease was for a period of three years, back dated to 1 June 1920, at an annual rent of £45. The rooms, which were in the return part of the building, were to be used solely as studios and for art exhibitions (certified copy of the 'Memo of Agreement' between Edward Weber Smyth, landlord, and the representatives of the 'Society of Dublin Painters', Paul Henry papers, TCD, MS 7434/2).

11 Yeats continued to pay rent on the studio even after his move to New York in 1907. Katherine Tynan gives a vivid description of the studio during Yeats' occupancy in her *Twenty-five Years: Reminiscences* (London: Smith, Elder & Co., 1913), p.187.

12 'The Dublin Painters' Exhibition', *Irish Times*, 6 August 1920, p.4.

13 *Irish Statesman*, 20 June 1925.

14 Count Plunkett, 'President's Address', *Journal*, Academy of Christian Art, vol. 1 (n.d., but c.1937), p.7.

15 Bruce Arnold, *A Concise History of Irish Art*, revised ed. (London: Thames & Hudson, 1977), p.139.

16 'Dublin Painters: New Society's Successful Opening Exhibition', *Freeman's Journal*, 6 August 1920, p.3.

17 The present whereabouts of this painting is unknown but it was illustrated in colour in the magazine *Colour*, October 1921, p.50.

18 Quentin Bell, *Virginia Woolf: A Biography*, vol.1, 1882–1912 (London: Triad/Paladin, 1976), p.105 n. The Friday Club was formed by Virginia Woolf's sister, Vanessa Bell (née Stephens) in 1905 and existed until the early 1920s. The members met informally at the Stephens' house in Gordon Square, London. They held meetings, lectures and annual exhibitions. Its membership sometimes overlapped with that of the Fitzroy Street Group although on the whole it incorporated artists of different temperament and ideals. For a history of the Friday Club see Richard Shone, 'The Friday Club', *Burlington Magazine*, vol.117, May 1975, pp.279–84.

19 'A Modern Painter', *Irish Times*, 3 February 1922, p.4.

20 He was represented by four paintings, *Rojate* (7), *Soho* (8), *Le Pont de Robert Stephenson* (9) and *Helvellyn* (10) at the prestigious *Exposition d'Art Irlandais*, held at the Musée d'Art Ancien, Brussels during May–June 1930.

21 Yeats to Quinn, letter of 16 September 1907 (John Quinn Memorial Collection, Rare Books and Manuscripts Division, The New York Public Library, Astor, Lennox and Tilden Foundations.)

22 See especially: Thomas MacGreevy, *Jack B. Yeats: An Appreciation and an Interpretation* (Dublin: Waddington Publications), 1945. This essay, originally written in about 1937–8, has been the basis of all subsequent research into Yeats' career and the interpretation of his subject-matter. Essentially MacGreevy saw Yeats as being the champion, in the visual arts, of Irish nationalism and dismissed the possibility of his being concerned with Modernism in general. This view has been sustained by subsequent authors, includ-

ing Hilary Pyle, *Jack B. Yeats: A Biography* (London: Routledge & Kegan Paul, 1970)–the standard work on the artist—and James White in his introduction to the exhibition catalogue *Jack B. Yeats 1871–1957: A Centenary Exhibition* (Dublin, Belfast, New York), 1971–2. A refreshing and, to contemporary eyes, more persuasive view of Yeats' engagement with Modernism is that of Dymphna Halpin in *The Breaker-Out: Jack B. Yeats (1871–1957): A Study of his Change in Style* (unpublished M.Litt. thesis, University of Dublin), 1984, in which she convincingly documents the influence of Modernism on Yeats' career and accounts for his political views in a more catholic manner than previous writers.

23 Letter of 14 June 1913, John Quinn Memorial Collection, Rare Books and Manuscripts Division, The New York Public Library, Astor, Lennox and Tilden Foundations. The Armory exhibition, held at the Sixty-ninth Regiment Armory, New York, was arranged by the Association of American Painters and Sculptors in order to promote an interest in modern painting, in particular Post-Impressionism, in the United States. Yeats at this time might also have had in mind works seen in Ellen Duncan's Dublin exhibition, *Modern French Pictures*, of March 1912.

24 'Distinguished Irishmen, 23: Jack B. Yeats and his art', *Daily Express*, Dublin, 12 October 1929.

25 Halpin, op. cit., discusses in detail these and other influences on Yeats.

26 'The Dublin Painters: Varied Autumn Show', *Irish Times*, 1 November 1921, p.4.

27 Quidnunc, 'An Irishman's Diary', *Irish Times*, 14 September 1948, p.3, in conversation with the artist.

28 'Good Portraiture. Miss Eva Hamilton's Exhibition', *Irish Times*, 8 May 1925, p.6.

29 'Modern Artists: Exhibition at Stephen's Green Gallery', *Freeman's Journal*, 20 October 1923, p.6.

30 Harriet Kirkwood, quoted in 'Influence of Nationalism in Art', *Sunday Independent*, 18 February 1940.

31 Bruce Arnold, *Concise History of Irish Art*, pp.139–40.

32 'Picture Exhibition: The Late Miss Clare Marsh's Art', *Irish Times*, 4 October 1923, p.6.

33 'Belfast Folk', *Irish Statesman*, vol.2, 3 May 1924, p.242.

34 For a comprehensive discussion of Irish artists in France and other European centres during the late nineteenth century see Campbell, *Irish Impressionists*, National Gallery of Ireland, Dublin, 1984.

35 In recent years studies of Cubism have focused mainly on questions of terminology, especially with regard to the term 'synthetic', and some Irish critics (see, for example, Bruce Arnold, 'Mainie Jellett and Modernism', in the exhibition catalogue *Irish Women Artists*, Dublin, National Gallery of Ireland & Douglas Hyde Gallery, 1987, pp.30–3; Peter Brooke, in the journal *Cubism: Recovery of a Tradition*, published in Belfast since 1983, *passim*) have come to regard Synthetic Cubism, especially in the work of Albert Gleizes, as being more fully developed and thus a more consequential form of Cubism than was Analytical Cubism and they regard Picasso, Braque and Gris as having failed to explore the possibilities for development inherent in their own work. This argument has much cogency but ignores, for example, the development of Picasso's late Cubism in works such as his *Three Dancers*, 1925 (Tate Gallery), a painting much indebted to his own decorative form of Synthetic Cubism which he practised during the years from about 1917 until 1925. Moreover, having freed themselves from the obligation of painting representational imagery Picasso, Braque and Gris did not feel compelled to exhaust all the possibilities of the new style; rather they branched into what they no doubt considered to be more fruitful art forms than the potentially arid field of applied theory. However, despite recent studies, the basic division of the movement into Analytical and Synthetic still enjoys wide support amongst art historians (see, for example, Mark Roskill, *The Interpretation of Cubism* [London: Associated University Presses, 1985], pp.161–2 for a view on the current usefulness of these two terms). There exists an extensive bibliography relating to Cubism, but the four most important studies of the movement (all written in English) are: John Golding, *Cubism: A History and an Analysis 1907–1914* (London: Faber & Faber), 1959, revised ed. 1968; Robert Rosenblum, *Cubism & Twentieth Century Art* (New York: Abrahams), 1960, revised eds. 1966, 1977; Edward Fry, *Cubism* (London: Thames & Hudson), 1966; and the most recent, Roskill, op. cit.

36 'Miss Swanzy's Pictures: Arresting Paintings that Challenge the Critic', undated cutting from the *Freeman's Journal*, April 1919, in the artist's scrapbook.

37 'Exhibition of Pictures by Mary Swanzy', *Evening Mail*, April 1919, undated press cutting in the aritst's scrapbook.

38 *Drawings and Paintings by Clare Marsh and Mary Swanzy*, Dublin Painters' gallery, closed 6 November 1920.

39 See 'Unconventional Art: Miss Swanzy's Pictures', *Irish Times*, 31 May 1922, p.7; 'Miss Mary Swanzy's Exhibition of Pictures', *Freeman's Journal*, 31 May 1922 and 'Miss Swanzy's Pictures', *Evening Mail*, 3 June 1922.

40 Her reputation, however, was clearly established for six of her pictures, namely *Maison dans la forêt* (134), *Sous mer* (135), *Nature morte* (137), *La joie des hélices* (137), *Paysage* (138) and *Allegro* (139), were included in the exhibition of Irish art, Brussels, 1930.

41 Gleizes described their time with him as being somewhat like a journey of joint discovery rather than that of a strict master/pupil relationship (Albert Gleizes, 'Hommage à Mainie Jellett', in Eileen MacCarvill (ed.), *Mainie Jellett: The Artist's Vision: Lectures and Essays on Art* [Dundalk: Dundalgan Press, 1958], p.30).

42 Any writer on Mainie Jellett must be indebted to the scholarly work of Bruce Arnold in the exhibition catalogue *Mainie Jellett 1897–1944* (Dublin: Neptune Gallery), 1974, which necessarily must form the basis for future research into the artist's career. This catalogue contains detailed notes on the development of and influences on her work, but it is written from the standpoint of the pre-eminence of Synthetic over Analytical Cubism, a view not shared by the present writer.

43 Mainie Jellett, 'An Approach to Painting', *Irish Art Handbook* (Dublin: Cahill & Co., 1943), pp.17–18.

44 Albert Gleizes & Jean Metzinger, *Du Cubisme* (Paris), 1912, English translation (London), 1913.

45 Jellett, 'Approach to Painting', p.18.

46 See Gleizes, 'Hommage à Mainie Jellett', p.31.

47 Ibid.

48 Jellett, 'Approach to Painting', p.18 (my italics).

49 *Du Cubisme*, unabridged reprint in R.L.Herbert (ed.), *Modern Artists on Art* (New Jersey: Prentice-Hall, 1964), pp.3, 13.

50 For a development of this argument see J.M.Martin, 'The Nature of Cubism: A study of conflicting explanations', *Art History*, vol.3, December 1980, pp.435–47.

51 For an illustrated discussion of the principles of translation and rotation see Peter Brooke (ed.), 'Space Time Rythm/Gleizes: Laws of Painting', in *Cubism: Recovery of a Tradition*, no.3, winter 1983–4, pp.1ff.

52 'The Dublin Painters', *Irish Statesman*, 27 October 1923, p.206. Marian Burleigh has noted that before 1922 AE's American patron and collector, John Quinn, had prodded him towards recognizing the merits of artists like Cézanne, Seurat, Matisse, Picasso and other Modernists whom Quinn was then buying. But, Burleigh continued, no doubt referring to the works by Jellett now on show at the Dublin Painters' gallery: 'In 1923 . . . he [AE] returned to the attack, partly, one suspects, in a typically Irish spirit of keeping up one's side in an argument, and told Quinn that the artists he [Quinn] admired were "spiced art for jaded palates"' (Marian Burleigh, *George Russell (AE)— The Painter of the Irish Renaissance*, Ph.D. thesis, University of New York, 1978, p.235).

53 Thomas McGreevy, 'Picasso, Mamie [sic] Jellett & Dublin Criticism', *The Klaxon*, winter 1923-4, pp.23-7.

54 In the absence of the exhibition catalogue we cannot know the identity of the other work which she exhibited on this occasion. Moreover, as it most likely bore a title such as 'Abstract' or 'Painting' its identity is probably lost for ever.

55 Exhibition catalogue, *Mainie Jellett: Abstracts*, Neptune Gallery, Dublin, 1980 (n.p. but inside front cover).

56 'The Cubist School: Miss M.H.Jellett's Paintings', *Irish Times*, 12 June 1928, p.4. MacCarvill, op. cit., pp.56–7 illustrates a number of drawings showing her translation and rotation of this composition.

57 'Exhibition of Paintings by Miss Jellett', *Irish Statesman*, 16 June 1928, p.292. Russell's change of opinion towards these paintings may have been the result of a visit he made to Paris with C.P.Curran in 1926 when, for the first time, he would have seen the breadth of Cubist painting in France.

58 *Irish Times*, 11 June 1924, p.4; *Irish Statesman*, 28 June 1924, p.495 respectively.

59 This Society, composed mainly of young artists, was in outlook during the inter-war years complementary to the London Group. Its name was derived from an initial intention that the membership should consist of seven painters and five sculptors. Hone exhibited with the Society only in 1926 and 1927. Jellett, who was not a member, also exhibited with them in 1926 (Charles Harrison, *English Art & Modernism 1900–1939* [London: Allen Lane, 1981], pp.345–7).

60 Mary Chamot, Denis Farr & Martin Butlin (eds.), Tate Gallery catalogue, *The modern British paintings, drawings and sculptures*, vol.1, (London: Oldbourne Press, 1964), p.298. The group was founded in 1931 by Georges Vantonger-

loo, Auguste Herbin and Jean Hélion (G.H.Hamilton, *Painting & Sculpture in Europe 1880-1940* [Harmondsworth: Penguin Books, paperback ed., 1967], p.349). I am grateful to Bruce Arnold for informing me that Mainie Jellett too was a founder-member of this group.

61 Information from a curriculum vitae prepared by the artist in about 1953.

62 Anna Sheehy gives 1921 as the year of his departure for Germany in 'Cecil Ffrench Salkeld', the *Bell*, vol.2, June 1941, pp.48–51. As the records of the Kasseler Kunstakademie were destroyed during the Second World War this information cannot be confirmed.

63 This Union comprised a group of like-minded individuals but they had no commonly agreed manifesto. I am grateful to Frau Scarlett Pfau of the Kunstmuseum Dusseldorf (letter of 17 October 1985) for drawing my attention to this information.

64 Exhibition catalogue, *I, Internationale Kunstausstellung Dusseldorf*, 1922.

65 Founded in 1919 at Weimar by the architect Walter Gropius, the Bauhaus is the most famous school of architecture, design and craftsmanship of modern times. It has had an inestimable influence on art school training all over the world. In 1925 the school moved to Dessau and then to Berlin where, in 1933, it was closed by the Nazis. Essentially its teaching emphasized the interdependence of all the arts and drew attention to the necessity of designing for machine production in the modern age.

66 He was the founder and director of the Irish National Ballet School which he ran from his home at number 43 Morehampton Road, Dublin. The Classes were held at number 19 Ely Place (information from the artist's papers).

67 'Post-Cubism: Pictures at 7 St. Stephen's Green', *Irish Statesman*, 25 October 1924, p:212.

68 Register of students, Metropolitan School of Art (now National College of Art & Design), Dublin.

69 Salkeld, 'The Principles of Painting', *To-Morrow*, August 1924, p.3.

70 *To-Morrow*, September 1924, p.5.

71 Salkeld, 'The Progress of a Painter', the *Bell*, vol.14, p.69. The italics are Salkeld's.

72 'New Irish Salon', *Irish Times*, 5 February 1924, p.4; 'Mr. Cecil Salkeld's Pictures', *Irish Times*, 15 October 1924, p.6 respectively.

73 For example, he once told a newspaper reporter who suggested that his work was in the tradition of Kandinsky, Picasso, Léger and others that he 'would rather be damned as a realist painter than glorified with the whole lot of them' (undated cutting from 'An Irishman's Diary', *Irish Times*, Kernoff papers, National Library of Ireland, MS 20,918[ii]).

74 Harry Kernoff, 'Myself and Painting', *Commentary*, vol.1, February 1942, p.1 records his studentship in these two cities. Unfortunately he gave neither the dates of nor the venues for his studies.

75 Kernoff papers, National Library of Ireland, MS 20,918 (i).

76 Kernoff published an explanation of the symbolism in this composition, which he exhibited at the RHA in 1929 (221), in the *Irish Statesman*, 20 April 1929.

77 The picture and its symbolism are discussed in the Amalgamated Engineering Union, *Monthly Journal*, October 1931, pp.49–51.

78 Máirín Allen, 'Contemporary Irish Artists—XIX: Harry A. Kernoff, R.H.A.', *Father Mathew Record*, September 1943, p.5.

79 Georg Kaiser (1878–1945), a German dramatist, usually regarded as the first Expressionist playwright. His *Gas* trilogy (*Die Koralle*, 1917; *Gas I*, 1918; *Gas II*, 1920) explored utopian attitudes towards Capitalism. Presumably Kernoff's sets were for a Dublin production of the play.

80 Kernoff papers, National Library of Ireland, MS 20,918 (i). Ernst Toller (1893–1939), a German dramatist noted for the strong feelings of pathos in his work. In 1927 the radical German theatre director Erwin Piscator (1893–1966) produced *Hoppla, wir leben!* in Potsdam, the play being a satirical calendar of the materialism and chauvinism of the Weimar republic.

Chapter 3

1 'A Confraternity of Twelve', *Irish Times*, 1 February 1932, p.6; *Irish Times*, 5 February 1935, p.5.

2 'The Dublin Painters', *Irish Times*, 3 February 1933, p.6.

3 *Irish Times*, 5 February 1935, p.5.

4 *Exposition d'Art Irlandais*, Musée d'Art Ancien, Brussels, 10 May–8 June 1930.

5 The murals were commissioned by Thomas Derrig, Minister of Education and Sean Lemass, Minister of Industry and Commerce (Thomas MacGreevy, a memoir of Mainie Jellett, MacGreevy papers, TCD, MS 8002–7). The works, each ten feet high, were placed on the upper part of the walls in the main hall of the pavilion and ran its entire length (Official Guide, Irish Pavilion, p.143). The

whereabouts of these murals—if they survive—is unknown to the present writer, but studies for them are in the National Gallery of Ireland, nos. 18,154–18,175). Judging by these studies, the works were representational in concept although the forms were often stylized and were linked by linear rhythms in the manner then characteristic of Jellett's painting. For a note on the murals see MacCarvill, *The Artist's Vision*, pp.19–21.

6 'Art Sacred & Secular', *Leader*, 6 December 1941, pp.446–7.

7 See especially Mainie Jellett, 'Approach to Painting', op. cit., pp.17–20 and 'A Word on Irish Art', MacCarvill, op. cit., pp.103–6. Of other writers, Eileen MacCarvill, foreword; Albert Gleizes, 'Homage à Mainie Jellett'; Evie Hone, 'Mainie Jellett—Cubist Paintings', all in MacCarvill, op. cit.; and Stella Frost (ed.), *A Tribute to Evie Hone and Mainie Jellett* (Dublin: Browne and Nolan, 1957), are the most notable.

8 Jellett, 'Approach to Painting', p.20.

9 The scholarship was first announced in the catalogue of the *Irish Exhibition of Living Art*, 1944. Funded by public subscriptions, it was to be awarded every second year to an Irish artist under thirty years of age to enable him or her to study contemporary art outside Ireland or Britain. The first, and only, holder during our period of the scholarship, valued at £250, was the sculptor Hilary Heron.

10 The latter phrase comes from Máirín Allen ('Contemporary Irish Artists XV—Grace Henry', *Father Mathew Record*, November 1942, p.4) in conversation with the artist.

11 Ibid.

12 Quoted in 'Personalities: Harry Kernoff', *Irish Tatler & Sketch*, vol.58, no.2, November 1948.

13 For a list of many of these works see the exhibition catalogue, *Dubliners: portraits by Harry Kernoff R.H.A.*, Godolphin Gallery, Dublin, 1975. Many others are reproduced in National Gallery of Ireland, *Summary Catalogue of Drawings, Watercolours and Miniatures* (Dublin: National Gallery of Ireland, 1983), pp.449–67.

14 Conversation with Ms. Lena Kernoff, the artist's sister, 1 Nov. 1984. See, too, Kernoff papers, National Library of Ireland, MS 20,923.

15 Brian Fallon, reviewing the exhibition, *Harry Kernoff: a selection of Dublin paintings* (Godolphin Gallery, Dublin), *Irish Times*, 24 May 1974.

16 Little is known of the Radical Painters' Group. At least some of the members seem to have been associated with the Metropolitan School of Art, for they gave that as their address in a letter of 7 May 1926 to the *Irish Statesman* (published 8 May 1926, p.240) in reply to the *Statesman's* review of their exhibition—called the 'Radical Club'—then showing at Daniel Egan's Salon in St. Stephen's Green. That exhibition included works by Cecil Salkeld, Ewald Dulberg (a woodcut, doubtless lent by Salkeld), Margaret Clarke, Seán O'Sullivan, Patrick Tuohy, Jack B. Yeats, Leo Whelan, Seán Keating, Charles Lamb, Paul Henry, J. Crampton Walker, Thomas Kain and Michael Farrell. Quidnunc, 'A Promising Artist', *Irish Times*, 18 January 1929, notes that MacGonigal had been a founder-member of the Radical Painters' Group and had helped to organize the 1926 exhibition. Other members included P. M. Trench and H.A. Kenney.

17 Details of Norah McGuinness' illustrative work may be found in: Thomas Bodkin, 'The Art of Miss Norah McGuinness', *Studio*, September 1925, pp.168–71; exhibition catalogue, *Norah McGuinness*, TCD, 1968; Marianne Hartigan, 'The Commercial Design Career of Norah McGuinness', *Irish Arts Review*, vol.3, autumn 1986, pp.23–25.

18 The artist, in conversation with the author, 30 October 1980.

19 She also shied from abstraction in general, preferring to paint 'things seen'. 'Pure abstraction would be an empty field for me', she said (conversation with the author, 30 October 1980).

20 Conversation with the author, 30 October 1980.

21 The *Irish Times*, 15 May 1928, records her exhibition.

22 William Holden, who knew Beatrice Glenavy for a number of years, recalled that she considered herself to be strictly an academic painter (letter of 20 May 1985). Holden also said that from time to time she altered her pictures 'as the mood took her'.

23 Cyril Barrett, 'Jack P. Hanlon', exhibition catalogue *Irish art 1943–1973*, ROSC, Crawford Municipal Art Gallery, Cork, 1980, p.30.

24 The *Irish Times*, 9 November 1934, records her winning the Higgins Scholarship which was administered by the Royal Dublin Society. Valued at £150 per year for a period of three years, the scholarship was for study abroad. (For a note of the general conditions attached to the scholarship see 'Royal Dublin Society', *Irish Art Handbook* [Dublin: Cahill & Co., 1943], pp.139–40).

25 Léopold Survage (1879–1968) had exhibited in the Cubist section of the *Salon
des Indépendants* of 1911 and, in 1919,
along with Albert Gleizes and Alexander
Archipenko, he reorganized the *Salon de
la Section d'Or*.

26 This composition (National Gallery of
Ireland, no. 1339) is also known by the
title *A religious procession in Brittany*.

27 She first exhibited at the Royal Hibernian
Academy in 1897 (*Royal Hibernian
Academy, Exhibitors*, vol.1, p.313).

28 She exhibited at the *Salon des
Indépendants* in 1922 and held one-
woman exhibitions in Paris in 1925 and
1930.

29 *May Guinness Memorial Exhibition*,
Dawson Hall, Dublin, 4–13 April 1956.

30 The former composition was bequeathed
to the Lane Gallery by Edward Martyn in
1923.

31 Sold in Christie's sale, 'Fine Irish Paintings and Drawings', Belfast, 31 May 1989
(lot 488), as *A Guinness Barge on the
Liffey*, this latter composition is almost
certainly her *Tugboat on the Seine*, which
Guinness exhibited at the Dublin Painters' gallery in May 1922 (catalogue no.
8). In any case it clearly illustrates the influence on her of French Fauvist painting.

32 Hilary Pyle, in the exhibition catalogue
Irish art 1900–1950, Crawford Gallery,
Cork, 1975, p.31, cites these as the years
of her association with Lhote but does not
quote the source of the information. That
may, however, have been an article on
May Guinness in *Sphere* magazine, 17
October 1925. The present writer has been
unable to trace this article.

33 In *Sphere* (op. cit., and quoted in Pyle,
Irish art, p.31) she said that she had been
'through all the phases, and had now settled down to "stylisation" . . . the flat and
rhythmic arrangements of line and colour'.

34 *Irish Tatler & Sketch*, June 1937, p.10.

35 'Echoes of the Town', *Irish Times*, 27
January 1939, p.4; *Irish Tatler & Sketch*,
March 1939, p.7.

36 'Echoes of the Town', *Irish Times*, 27
January 1939, p.4.

37 *Leader*, 21 February 1942, pp.86, 88.

38 Stephen Rynne, 'Ralph Cusack—A
Square Peg', *Leader*, 12 October 1940.

39 Herbert Read, *Paul Nash*
(Harmondsworth: Penguin Books), 1944.
It is unknown if Cusack had any direct
contact with either Nash or Read but the
apparent influence of the former on his
work is self-evident. Also, in January 1944
he was involved, as was Read, with the
exhibition of Subjective Art held in
Dublin, so it is likely he would have read
Read's recent publication on Nash.

40 Cusack was renowned for his not infre-
quent outbursts of quick temper, as has
been recorded in a brief memoir of him
by Anthony Cronin (Cronin, *Dead as
Doornails* [Swords: Poolbeg Press], 1980,
chapter 2). Cronin here suggests that
Cusack did not rate his painting highly, a
view corroborated by Charles Acton who
knew the artist well (Acton, conversation
with the author, 24 February 1981).

41 Nothing seems to be recorded about
Cicely Peel. In this exhibition she showed
oils, watercolours and pen and ink drawings of landscapes, portraits and still lifes.

42 For a detailed discussion of Elizabeth
Rivers' life and career see Brian Kennedy,
*Elizabeth Rivers 1903–1964: A Retro-
spective View* (Dublin: Gorry Gallery),
1989.

43 The Society, however, continued to oper-
ate much as we have described it until its
premises were taken over for
re-development in about the spring of
1969 (*Eire-Ireland*, Spring 1969, p.114).
The Society's last exhibition was held at
the Royal Hibernian Academy, Ely Place,
Dublin, in June 1968 (*Irish Times*, 15 June
1968, p.15).

Chapter 4

1 The dates of the six exhibitions, so far as
is known were as follows:-
    1923 From 4 March
    1924 4 February–1 March
    1925 2–27 February
    1926 8 February–6 March
    1927 1 February–12 March
    1928 1 February–3 March
    (source: press reviews)

2 The New English Art Club (NEAC) was
founded in 1886 by a group of artists who
disliked the reactionary stance of the
Royal Academy. Many of its founders,
including George Clausen, Wilson Steer,
Stanhope Forbes, J.S. Sargent, H.H. La
Thangue and Frederick Browne, had
worked in France and had been influenced
by the *plein airists* and Bastien-Lepage.
Later, several members of the NEAC
joined the Newlyn Group of painters in
Cornwall, while others drifted into the
Academy and still others, including Sir
John Lavery, broke away and formed the
Glasgow School, becoming better known
as the 'Glasgow Boys'. In 1889 the Club
came under the control of a group led by
Sickert and in 1911 these formed the
Camden Town Group. Many of the Irish
artists who were to exhibit at Crampton
Walker's Salon had, as can be seen from
the previous chapters, a background

similar to their contemporaries in the New
English Art Club.

3 'New Irish Salon: Work of Modern School
of Irish Artists', *Irish Times*, 5 March
1923, p.4.

4 *Studio*, vol.87, January–June 1924, p.169.

5 See chapter 2 above.

6 'The New Irish Salon', *Irish Statesman*, 16
February 1924, p.719.

7 'The New Irish Salon: Remarkable Display of Pictures', *Irish Times*, 2 February
1925, p.8; *Studio*, vol.90, July–December
1925, p.56. Amongst the few works which
can be identified from this exhibition are
E.M.O'R. Dickey's *March Sunshine*,
Grace Henry's *Girl in White* (now
HLMG) and Harry Kernoff's *A Nude
Reflection*.

8 *Irish Statesman*, 12 February 1927, p.552.

9 'Accent on Art', *Irish Times*, 14 June
1940, p.4, quotes a letter from Crampton
Walker on the subject of exhibitions which
he had arranged in Dublin and stating the
amount of sales in various instances.

10 For a comprehensive list of the public exhibitions in Ireland and elsewhere in
which works by Leech have been included, plus comments by several critics
on Leech, see Alan Denson, *An Irish
Artist: W.J. Leech R.H.A. (1881–1968)*,
(Kendal, 1968), pp.21–48.

11 For an up-to-date assessment of Lavery's
work see Kenneth McConkey, *Sir John
Lavery R.A. 1856–1941*, an exhibition
catalogue, Ulster Museum; Fine Art Society, Edinburgh & London; National
Gallery of Ireland, 1984–5.

12 Ibid., p.7. Jules Bastien-Lepage (1848–
84), French portraitist and landscape
painter, best known for his scenes of
peasants painted in the manner of Millet.
He advocated painting out of doors with
absolute fidelity to nature. (For a discussion of Bastien-Lepage's influence on
Irish artists, see Campbell, *Irish Impressionists*, pp.92–3.)

13 Letter of 23 January 1984 from Miss
Eileen Ayrton, a committee member of the
Society.

14 Information from Edward L. Mansfield
(letter of 21 February 1984), a founder-
member of the Guild, who attended its inaugural meeting in Hunter's house in
Belfast.

15 Nash's fellow-members of Unit One were:
Henry Moore and Barbara Hepworth
(sculptors); John Armstrong, John Bigge,
Edward Burra, Frances Hodgkins, Ben
Nicholson and Edward Wadsworth
(painters); and Wells Coates and Colin
Lucas (architects). Frances Hodgkins resigned soon after the foundation of the
group and was replaced by Tristram

Hillier (Charles Harrison, *English Art &
Modernism 1900–1939*, [London: Allen
Lane, 1981], p.240).

16 For a note on the Lloyd Patterson Collec-
tion see Chapter 1, n. 29 above. By the
time the Ulster Unit was founded, the
Collection included works by, amongst
others, Vanessa Bell, Roger Fry, Mark
Gertler, Spencer Gore, Duncan Grant,
Augustus John, Paul Nash, Lucien
Pissarro, William Roberts, W.R. Sickert,
Sir Matthew Smith, Wilson Steer, Edward
Wadsworth and Edward Wolfe.

17 Herbert Read (ed.), *Unit 1: The Modern
Movement in English Architecture,
Painting and Sculpture*, (London: Cassell
& Co., 1934), p.12. Nash's letter to *The
Times* was reprinted here at pp.10–11.

18 'Present Day Art: Opening of the Ulster
Unit's Exhibition', *Northern Whig*, 18
December 1934, p.8.

19 'Deirdre McDonagh' was the pseudonym
of Moira Pilkington (1897–1970) of
Tyrelspass, Co. Westmeath. Educated in
France, it was probably there that she first
acquired an interest in modern painting.
In 1920 she married T.H. Hinkson, eldest
son of the writer Kathleen Tynan Hinkson
(1861–1931), and together they settled in
Kenya. In 1929, however, her marriage
failed and she returned to Dublin. She was
an amateur painter and also played in minor roles at Dublin's Gate Theatre (conversation with A. Hinkson, Esq., Deirdre
McDonagh's son, 4 May 1982).

20 John Manning (Jack) Longford was born
in Dublin in 1911. He read medicine at
Trinity College and in Edinburgh but discontinued his studies in favour of literary
and artistic pursuits. He died, after a fall,
in September 1944 (obituary, *Irish Times*,
8 September, 1944).

21 'Contemporary [Picture] Galleries', *Irish
Art Handbook*, (Dublin: 1943), p.149.

22 This view was endorsed by the late Cecil
King (1921–86), conversation of 1 No-
vember 1980, and Tom Nisbet, letter of 3
May 1982.

23 Stephen Rynne, 'Tea with Jack B. Yeats
1940', *Eire-Ireland*, vol.7, 1972, p.106.

24 Sir John Rothenstein, *New English Review*, no.1, July 1946, pp.42–4 and quoted
in Pyle, *Biography*, p.159.

25 'Jack B. Yeats' New Pictures', *Irish
Times*, 28 October 1941, p.4.

26 Stephen Rynne, *Leader*, 23 September
1944, p.12.

27 Kenneth Hall, letter of 19 April 1940 to
Lucy Carrington Wertheim.

28 The subject-matter of the mural is noted
in Anna Sheehy, 'Cecil Ffrench Salkeld',
the *Bell*, vol.2, June 1941, p.48. Salkeld
had been commissioned by Mr. Davy

Byrne to paint the mural in 1938. Although Byrne died later that year, the commission was honoured by his successor, M.J. Doran, who took over the bar in 1941 (conversation with M.J. Doran, 16 May 1985).

29 Those represented are, amongst others: the actor Micheál MacLiammóir, extreme right; George Bernard Shaw, seated centre right under a tree; Davy Byrne, seated centre left under a tree; and Myles naGopaleen (Brian O'Nolan), to the left of Byrne.

30 For a biographical note on Paul Nietsche and a discussion of his development as a painter see Brian Kennedy, 'Paul Nietsche (1885–1950): A Russian Painter in Belfast', in *Irish Slavonic Studies*, no.5 (Belfast: Queen's University, 1984), pp.115–23.

31 Nietsche studied painting at the Odessa Academy of Arts under Gennadiy Ladyzhensky and Kiriak Kostandi, both members of the Society of South-Russian Artists, a group who modelled themselves on the more influential Society of Travelling Artistic Exhibitions, better known as the Peredvizhniki or 'The Wanderers'. It was the ideals of this group which were imbued upon the young Nietsche. Essentially the Peredvizhniki wanted to popularise art and to do so they arranged travelling exhibitions throughout the countryside. To them art had the practical role of elucidating reality as opposed to the widely held contemporary idea of 'art for art's sake' which had a purely aesthetic import. Consequently they emphasized pictorial technique and the observation of nature in a manner similar to the *plein airism* of the French Barbizon painters. The Peredvizhniki were at their most influential during the thirty years or so after 1890, that is, at the time when Nietsche was a student in Odessa.

32 For a complete list of one-man and group exhibitions which included works by Nietsche see Brian Kennedy, *Paul Nietsche 1885–1950*, exhibition catalogue, Arts Council of Northern Ireland, Belfast, 1984. This catalogue also contains a note relating to sources relating to Nietsche's career and art and a bibliography.

33 Information kindly supplied by the artist's son (letter of 29 August 1980).

34 For example, the annual purchase grant of £1,000 to the National Gallery of Ireland, remained unchanged from 1866 until 1937, when it was increased to £2,000. This grant was cut during the years of the 'Emergency' (1939–45), but was reinstated at £2,000 in 1946. However, during these years some monies were avail-able to the Gallery from the Lane Fund, which had been established as a consequence of Sir Hugh Lane's will (National Gallery of Ireland, *Summary Catalogue*, pp.xvii–xxxvi). The Hugh Lane Municipal Gallery of Modern Art had no purchase grant at all until 1972; the Belfast Museum & Art Gallery had a modest purchase grant (specific figures are no longer available but the museum's annual reports list acquisitions by purchase, along with grants from outside sources such as the Victoria & Albert Museum, London); the Crawford Art Gallery, Cork, had no purchase grant at all and relied entirely on the Gibson Bequest for its acquisitions.

35 Crawford Municipal School of Art, Minutes Book 1922–6.

36 Thomas Haverty, last will and testament, 1911 (Dublin, Public Record Office). Although Haverty died in 1916, certain provisions in his will were subject to the life-interest of his sister-in-law, Mrs. Caroline Haverty, who lived until 1929. Sir Francis Chantrey, RA (1781–1841), by his will of December 1840, which became effective after the death of his wife in 1876, left a sum of money to the Royal Academy, London, to be used for the purchase of paintings and sculptures either by British artists or by artists resident in Britain. His will also envisaged the establishment of a separate national collection of British art, a vision which was later encouraged by other bequests, including the Turner Bequest to the National Gallery, London, in 1856. Eventually these endeavours culminated in the opening of the Tate Gallery in July 1897. (For a brief note on the Chantrey, Turner and other bequests see Dennis Farr, *English Art 1870–1940* [Oxford: Clarendon Press, 1978], pp.340–2). Thomas Bodkin, in a speech given at the Belfast Museum & Art Gallery in 1934, said that Thomas Haverty had first confided his scheme for the furtherance of art in Ireland to Dermod O'Brien whose 'wise counsels' helped to shape the provisions of Haverty's will (Bodkin papers, Trinity College, Dublin, MS 6918:34).

37 Filed 21 October 1929, Saorstat Eireann High Court of Justice (1928, No.5169). The appointed trustees were the President of the Royal Hibernian Academy, the Director of the National Gallery of Ireland and the Lord Mayor of Dublin, each for the time being. The endowment, named the 'Haverty Trust', was set up in memory of Colonel J.G. Haverty and Thomas Haverty himself. The scheme for administering the endowment provided for a selection committee consisting of the trustees, the Lord Mayor of Belfast, the

Curator of the Belfast Museum & Art Gallery and three other representatives from the National Gallery and the Royal Hibernian Academy who alone had power to acquire pictures which, as the will directed, were to be by painters of Irish birth who lived in Ireland and preference was to be given to historical or 'fancy subjects'. No landscapes were to be purchased 'except perhaps an occasional one of a very high order'. All works purchased under the scheme were to be given to public galleries or institutions as decided by the selection committee and one-fourth of the works purchased were to go to institutions in Northern Ireland. The scheme also directed that if at any time the capital value of the endowment fell below £10,000 purchasing was to be suspended until dividends from the fund restored it to that figure. The scheme was amended, with Court approval, in 1936 so that 'historical' works could be understood to include portraits or studies of types or conditions of life that were distinctively Irish and at the same time the trustees were empowered to give works purchased under the scheme to Irish legations and Colleges at home and abroad and to other public buildings of a similar kind.

38 Haverty's will did not stipulate that the works acquired should be contemporary but that in effect was to be the case (see catalogues of the Trust's quinquennial exhibitions held in 1935, 1940, 1945 and 1950).

39 John Hewitt, curator of art at the Belfast Museum & Art Gallery, commented that this work by Jellett was the first abstract painting to be acquired by the museum (J. Hewitt, 'Belfast Gets a New Picture Collection', *Belfast Telegraph*, 15 January 1941).

40 For a brief outline of the history of this collection see chapter 1 above.

41 Sarah Purser's involvement with the Friends is detailed in O'Grady, *Sarah Henrietta Purser*, unpublished Ph.D. dissertation, University College, Dublin, 1974, pp.189–91 and *passim*. The National Art Collections Fund was founded in 1903 to buy works of art for British public collections with funds raised by individual subscription. Its members hoped to restrain the export of Old Master paintings emanating from private collections in Britain. (For a note on the history and purpose of the NACF see Dennis Farr, op. cit., pp.351f).

42 Friends of the National Collections of Ireland, item number 2 of constitution, reprinted in the Society's *Report*, 1951–2, p.2.

43 Friends of the National Collections of Ireland, annual reports, 1924–50.

44 Ibid.

45 A cumulative list of acquisitions and their eventual recipients is regularly published in the Society's annual reports.

46 Friends of the National Collections of Ireland, annual report, 1931, n.p.

47 Ibid., 1937, n.p.

48 Letter of 21 November 1942 from the President of the College to the Friends of the National Collections.

49 Terence de Vere White, *A Fretful Midge* (London: Routledge & Kegan Paul, 1957), pp.125–7 recounts these events. For comparison, we might note that the Tate Gallery declined to accept Rouault's *Têtes à Massacre (La Mariée)* and Matisse's *Liseuse à l'Ombrelle* in 1932 when they were offered as gifts by the Contemporary Art Society. But both works were eventually accepted by the Gallery in 1935 and 1938 respectively (Farr, op. cit., p.350).

50 'The New Art Patronage', *Irish Times*, 18 August 1944.

51 'Continental Art', *Irish Times*, 28 August 1944, p.3.

52 In Bodkin, *Hugh Lane and his Pictures*, pp.62–8.

53 Friends of the National Collections of Ireland, annual report, 1927, n.p.

54 Bodkin, op. cit., p.67. Sarah Purser's role in the acquisition of Charlemont House is fully documented in O'Grady, op. cit., pp.196–201. An outline of the building work involved in the conversion is given in the souvenir booklet, *Municipal Gallery of Modern Art & Civic Museum* (Dublin), 1933.

55 John Dowling, 'Poor Wine, but a lovely Bottle', *Ireland To-Day*, vol.1, October 1936, pp.51–2.

56 Terence de Vere White, op. cit., pp.124–5.

Chapter 5

1 F.S.L. Lyons, *Ireland Since the Famine* (London: Fontana, revised ed. 1973), p.553. Two or three hundred of the IRA fought for the republican side in Spain and some seven hundred 'Blueshirts' fought for Franco.

2 Lyons, op. cit., p.550.

3 For a discussion of war-time espionage in Ireland see Enno Stephan, *Spies in Ireland* (London, 1963). Stephan is principally concerned with relations between Abwehr, the German Intelligence organization, and the IRA, but much information is given about the attitude of the Irish government to espionage.

4   Karin Stephen (née Costelloe), was the wife of Adrian Stephen, brother of Vanessa Bell and Virginia Woolf (Kenneth Hall, autobiography, unpublished typescript, c.1942–3, p.27). Hall here gives a detailed history of the Society for Creative Psychology from its foundation.

5   Many artists over the years had worked at this address. Whistler and Sickert each had a studio there (Robert Emmons, *The Life & Opinions of Walter Sickert* [London, 1941], p.183) as had Augustus John, Henry Lamb and F.J. Porter. Vanessa Bell and Duncan Grant were both in residence at the same time as Rakoczi (Richard Shone, *Bloomsbury Portraits: Vanessa Bell, Duncan Grant and their Circle* [London: Phaidon, 1976], p.210 and *passim*).

6   Rex MacGall, 'Basil Rakoczi Interviewed', *Commentary*, March 1946, p.4; Jacqueline Robinson, *Basil Ivan Rakoczi: Monographie et Catalogue Provisoir* (Paris: published privately, 1971), p.3.

7   The term 'psychological analysis' is Rakoczi's and is a differentiation from the Freudian technique of psychoanalysis. The study of psychology remained a life-long interest for Rakoczi, and the teachings of Freud formed the basis of his method, which also incorporated the discoveries of Adler, Jung and his own researches (Elizabeth Ormsby, *An Introduction to Psychological Analysis* [Creative psychology pamphlet, no.2, White Stag Press, London, 1937], n.p.)

8   This point has been emphasized by a number of those associated with them, including Bobby Dawson (letter of 24 November 1980), Phyllis Hayward (letter of 17 November 1980), Victor Meally (letter of 19 November 1980) and Patrick Scott (interview of 28 October 1980).

9   Hall, op. cit., p.54.

10 These titles are taken from the printed invitation card to the lectures. Such invitations suggest that the proceedings were conducted with a certain amount of formality.

11 Paul Egestorff, interview of 28 October 1980.

12 White Stag Group, exhibition catalogues, 1940–6.

13 Shelah Richards, letter of 14 December 1980. 'Peter Warlock' was the pseudonym of Philip Heseltine (1894–1930), a composer of delicate songs and chamber music.

14 Victor Meally, conversation of 9 December 1980.

15 Vaughan Biscoe, letter of 25 May 1984. Biscoe, like Stephen Gilbert and his wife too, occupied a flat in the same building in Lower Baggot Street.

16 '"White Stag Group": Exhibition at Lower Baggot Street', *Irish Times*, 16 April 1940, p.6.

17 'Exhibition of Pictures: White Stag Group's Work', *Irish Times*, 10 October 1940, p.6.

18 Hall, autobiography, pp.47–8. Hall thought Rakoczi did not produce his best work in this manner. 'His best work was done more solid and static', he wrote (op. cit., p.47). The German Expressionist painter Helmut Kolle (1899–1931), like Rakoczi and Hall, also exhibited during the 1930s at the Wertheim Gallery, London.

19 Hall, autobiography, p.62.

20 I am grateful to Nick Nicholls for supplying these biographical details on Georgette Rondel (Nicholls, interview of 24 June 1984).

21 Many of these works were lent by Evie Hone, who also lent Gleizes' *Abstract* and Marchand's *Houses* to the exhibition in February 1941. The former may have been Gleizes' *Painting*, 1923 (now NGI), and the latter Marchand's *Paris Roofs*, also NGI, both of which were acquired through the Evie Hone bequest in 1955.

22 'Mr. Basil Rakoczi's Paintings', *Irish Times*, 23 November 1940, p.4.

23 We shall discuss this term, as used by Rakoczi and his friends, later on.

24 His difficulties at the time were largely financial.

25 He often stayed with Mrs. Thea Boyd (a sister of Dorothy Blackham) who owned the Amethyst Hotel at Keel, Achill, and with Alec Wallace, also a hotelier, nearby at Louisburg (conversation with Mrs. Boyd and Mr. Wallace, 19 April 1981). His voluminous correspondence with Lucy Wertheim corroborates their statements and documents his visits there. On one occasion (3 September 1940) he wrote to Mrs. Wertheim, from Achill: 'Oh Lucy! This is such a heavenly place . . . the sadness and mystery of the Irish countryside are so over-powering one sinks into a quiet passive state of mind where nothing seems really to matter'.

26 Painted in Paris in January 1939 from sketches made in Greece during April–May 1938 (Hall, autobiography, p.40).

27 I am not the moon
    I am not of wood
    Without my soul
    I wish to escape
    And I want to climb [the] trees
    To look for Beauty there.
    Cf. Baudelaire's 'Hymne à la Beauté', from *Les Fleurs du Mal*. I am grateful to Alison Kennedy for drawing my attention to this association of ideas.

28 In his autobiography (pp.59–60) Hall said

that by 1941 his work had become increasingly Subjective and that in *La tête grecque*, *Après le guerre*, *Little Bird* and *Square man* he had expressed his feelings better than ever before. *La tête grecque* and *Square man* have not been traced by the present writer.

29 Hall confided to Scott that he had begun to paint birds and animals under the latter's influence. Scott, however, influenced only Hall's subject-matter and not his technique (Patrick Scott, interview of 9 June 1981).

30 Scott, quoted in *Three Painters*, intro. by Herbrand Ingouville-Williams, (Dublin: Three Candles, 1945), p.24.

31 Patrick Scott, interview of 28 October 1980.

32 Scott has always preferred to use transparent or translucent pigments (Scott, interview of 9 June 1981). As many oil-bound pigments are opaque, even when mixed with a medium normally used with transparent glazes, this preference to some extent limited his choice and range of colours.

33 She showed along with Bobby Dawson and Cicely Peel in the exhibition, *Three New Dublin Painters*, Contemporary Picture Galleries, 11–22 November 1941.

34 Phyllis Hayward, tape recorded conversation with Liam O'Leary, Esq., 20 July 1977.

35 Doreen Vanston, letter of 1 December 1980.

36 Kether was the Head figure in the Cabal, the theosophical interpretation of the Hebrew scriptures.

37 The secretary, Slade School of Fine Art, letter of 18 June 1981.

38 I am grateful to Stephen Gilbert (interview of 24 May 1981) for this outline of Jocelyn Chewett's career.

39 Cf. her remarks quoted at n.52 below.

40 Such an emphasis on using so-called 'pure' forms, or Purism, stemmed from Synthetic Cubism and was widespread in Europe during the inter-war years. Its best-known protagonists were the painter Amedée Ozenfant and the architect Le Corbusier. The Purists aimed to free art from any representational relation to natural objects by using only abstract elements. In this way they hoped to achieve an entirely spiritual expression of the universal. (Cf. the abstract compositions of Mainie Jellett who had a similar aim.)

41 Jocelyn Chewett, quoted in the exhibition catalogue *Jocelyn Chewett sculpteur: son oeuvre abstraite 1949–1979*, Centre Culturel Canadien, Paris, 1981, p.2. The original date of the quotation is unknown.

42 Gilbert, quoted in the exhibition catalogue, *Stephen Gilbert: Cobra Paintings 1940–1950*, Court Gallery, Copenhagen, October 1971 (n.p.) In late 1945 Gilbert and his wife left Ireland and, after a short stay in England, returned to Paris where they settled permanently. In 1948 Gilbert exhibited in the Salon des Surindépendants where the Danish painter Asger Jorn admired his work and asked him to join the recently founded Cobra Group. Other members of Cobra were: Pierre Alchinsky, Karel Appel, Constant, Corneille, Dotremont, Egill Jacobsen, Edouard Jaguer, Lucebert, Karl H. Pedersen and Wemaere. The group, which existed from 1948 until 1951, was an international association of artists and writers interested in an experimental art, sympathetic to Expressionism and Surrealism but opposed to geometric art. Their work resembled the canvases of the American Abstract Expressionists. The name 'Cobra' was derived from the initial letters of the three cities where the key members lived, namely COpenhagen, BRussels and Amsterdam. A Cobra review was published in Denmark from 1948 until 1951. (For a history of the Group see Jean-Clarence Lambert, *Cobra* [London: Sotheby Publications], 1983.) At the Group's second exhibition, *La Fin et les Moyens*, held at the Palais des Beaux-Arts, Brussels, in March 1949, Gilbert showed works based on insects, fantastic creatures and vegetation which he had painted in Ireland (Lambert, op. cit., pp.110–11).

43 Patrick Scott, interview of 9 June 1981.

44 Scott's reported comment that the Japanese flag was the strongest influence on his work (Doroty Walker, *Patrick Scott*, exhibition catalogue, Douglas Hyde Gallery, TCD, 1981, p.27) was more metaphorical than real (Scott, interview of 20 October 1981).

45 *Three Painters*, op. cit., p.24.

46 In his autobiography (p.61) Kenneth Hall wrote that from 1942 Rakoczi's paintings were like 'something out of a dream a world new for somebody to see . . . .'

47 Nick Nicholls, Letter of 1 September 1982 and interview of 24 June 1984. Unless stated otherwise, these are the source of information here.

48 Letter of 17 April 1981 from Noel Moffett. The Moffetts had met Herbert Read in London. It was their idea to invite him to Dublin.

49 Hall and Rakoczi selected the exhibits in conjunction with each artist (Margot Moffett, letter of 1 December 1943 to Patrick Scott). Colin Middleton was in-

vited to exhibit but was prevented from doing so by customs restrictions arising from war-time regulations.

50 Programme of events as set out in a letter of 28 December 1943 from Margot Moffett to Patrick Scott.

51 Why he was unable to come to Ireland is unknown, but permission to travel was almost certainly withheld either by the Irish or by the British authorities. Read himself wrote, rather euphemistically, in an article entitled 'Art and Crisis' (*Horizon*, May 1944, p.336): 'A short time ago I was invited to give a lecture in Dublin, but owing to certain circumstances connected with the war, that lecture was never delivered'. Writing about the exhibition in a letter to the *Irish Times* (7 May 1944), Dr. Ingouville-Williams said: 'It was most unfortunate that Mr. Read was unable to cross the Channel, but in the present emergency we are naturally only too willing to bow to the decision of the authorities'.

52 Statement accompanying the article 'On Subjective Art', the *Bell*, February 1944, p.429. This article was a reprint of Herbert Read's introduction to the catalogue of the exhibition of Subjective Art. Statements by Jocelyn Chewett (referred to as 'Hewitt') and Thurloe Conolly were also printed.

53 Bobby Dawson, interview of 9 December 1980.

54 Paul Egestorff, interview of 28 October 1980.

55 See n.52 above.

56 This was a view shared by the artist (letter of 1 December 1980).

57 See n.52 above.

58 Herbert Read, introduction to the catalogue, Exhibition of Subjective Art, 1944, n.p. Read had seen only photographs of the works exhibited before writing his introduction.

59 'Subjective Art', *Irish Times*, 5 January 1944, p.3.

60 *Irish Independent*, 5 January 1944.

61 *Irish Press*, 5 January 1944.

62 *Evening Mail*, 14 January 1944.

63 Ibid., 15 January 1944.

64 Theodore Goodman, 'Subjective Art', *Commentary*, February 1944, p.3.

65 Edward Sheehy, 'Subjective and Objective', *Dublin Magazine*, April–June 1944, p.53.

66 The *Bell*, vol.7, February 1944, pp.424-49.

67 *Horizon: A Review of Literature and Art*, May 1944, pp.336-50.

68 Read, op. cit., pp.342, 349. In an essay entitled 'The Modern Epoch in Art', written in about 1948–51 (pub. H. Read, *The Philosophy of Modern Art: collected essays by Herbert Read* [London: Faber & Faber, 1964], pp.17–43), Read described subjectivism as a mental climate with its roots in Kierkegaard and Hegel in the nineteenth century.

69 *Horizon*, April 1945, pp.261-7.

70 Dr. H.A.C. Ingouville-Williams was born in London in 1896. Educated at Eton and the Royal Military College, Camberwell, he served in the First World War and was mentioned in dispatches. He was wounded while on service and was awarded the MC. He entered Jesus College, Cambridge, in 1919 and took his BA degree in 1921 and MA in 1927. During the early 1920s he spent a brief period in the Foreign Office before returning to Cambridge to read medicine (Eton College Register; Records, Jesus College, Cambridge). In 1927 he married Zenia Poushkine, an émigrée Russian princess, but the marriage broke-up in the early 1930s. He came to Ireland in 1939, became a licentiate of the Royal College of Physicians of Ireland in 1940 (secretary, RCPI, letter of 9 March 1981), and worked at Grangegorman Mental Hospital, Dublin, while living at number 40 Fitzwilliam Square, where he also had consulting rooms. He died in Dublin on 9 March 1945 (obituary, *Irish Times*, 12 March, 1945). Ingouville-Williams often took part in the activities of the White Stag Group and provided financial backing for Rakoczi and Hall. He was a subscriber to the Exhibition of Subjective Art. The material for his book, *Three Painters*, was collected in 1944, but published posthumously.

71 Herbert Read, preface, *Three Painters*, p.6. Sigmund Freud was, of course, the founder of psychoanalysis.

72 Herbrand Ingouville-Williams, introduction, *Three Painters*, pp.11, 14.

73 Ibid., pp.15–16.

74 Ibid., p.22.

75 John Russell, 'Dufy and Others', *Listener*, 10 May 1945, p.524.

76 Edward Sheehy, 'Art Notes', *Dublin Magazine*, April–June 1945, p.47.

77 Patrick Scott, interview of 9 June 1981.

78 Kenneth Hall, quoted in *Three Painters*, pp.23–4.

79 Nick Nicholls, interview of 24 June 1984.

80 Rakoczi, quoted in *Three Painters*, p.23.

81 Rex MacGall, 'Basil Rakoczi Interviewed', *Commentary*, March 1946, pp.3–4, 8.

82 Phyllis Hayward, letter of 17 November 1980.

83 Edward Sheehy, 'Art Notes', *Dublin Magazine*, July–September 1945, p.45.

Chapter 6

1 See chapter 2 above. The RHA was not alone at the time in attracting criticism. Its sister-institution at Burlington House in London was also the object of scorn for broadly similar reasons as, for example, in April 1938 when Augustus John resigned his membership in protest at the rejection by the selection committee of Wyndham Lewis's portrait of the poet T.S. Eliot. Lewis, criticising the Academy for rejecting his picture, said that Mr. John's resignation would be 'a mortal blow to the Royal Academy—if it is possible to use the expression "mortal blow" with reference to a corpse' (Lewis, quoted in an *Irish Times* editorial on the matter, 26 April 1938, p.6). Throughout the 1930s the Royal Academy had been widely criticised for its mediocrity.

2 Louis le Brocquy, letter of 2 May 1982.

3 His rejection may even have promoted the writing of this article, for its author and he were close friends, but there is no way of being certain about this. It is, however, important to remember that at the time le Brocquy had not yet acquired the celebrity of his later career.

4 Mainie Jellett, 'The R.H.A. and Youth', *Commentary*, May 1942, pp.5,7.

5 O'Faoláin, 'The Stuffed-Shirts', the *Bell*, June 1943, p.339 and quoted in Terence Brown, *Ireland: A Social and Cultural History 1922–1979* (London: Fontana, 1981), p.202.

6 Brigid Ganly, 'Mainie Jellett and the R.H.A.: a reply to the article the R.H.A. and Youth', *Commentary*, June 1942, p.3 (my italics).

7 T. MacS., 'A Provincial Views the R.H.A. 1942', *Commentary*, July 1942, pp.3,5.

8 *Leader*, 25 April 1942, pp.302-3.

9 As the minutes of the Academy meetings are privy only to its members it has not been possible to confirm this point.

10 '"Moderns" Not Wanted', *Irish Times*, 3 April 1943, p.3 and *Irish Times*, 19 April 1943, p.5 respectively.

11 Stephen Rynne, 'The Royal Hibernian Academy', *Leader*, 1 May 1943, pp.236–7.

12 Brigid Ganly, 'The R.H.A., 1943', *Commentary*, 2 May 1943, pp.5–6.

13 A.J. Leventhal, 'Royal Hibernian Academy of Arts Exhibition, 1943', *Dublin Magazine*, July-September 1943, pp.69–70.

14 Irish Exhibition of Living Art (IELA), minutes book, first meeting of committee, 12 May 1943, para.2.

15 I am grateful to Louis le Brocquy for this information and, unless stated otherwise, for the outline of events which follows.

The source of this chronology is a diary kept by him at the time (Louis le Brocquy, letter of 16 November 1980).

16 For a complete list of patrons and guarantors of the Living Art exhibitions in the 1940s see Appendix 3 below.

17 IELA, first recorded minutes of committee, meeting at 13 Merrion Row, Dublin, 12 May 1943, para.1. The title of the exhibition had been suggested by Sybil le Brocquy (Louis le Brocquy, letter of 16 November 1980).

18 Louis le Brocquy, letter of 2 May 1982.

19 IELA, minutes of committee, 12 May 1943, paras.3,5,6 respectively. Jellett was proposed as chairman by Norah McGuinness and seconded by Louis le Brocquy.

20 Ibid.: 21 June 1943, paras.1,2,3; 15 July 1943, para.1.

21 IELA, entry form for the 1943 exhibition.

22 At a meeting of the Committee held on 15 July, Mainie Jellett proposed, and it was agreed, that the selection of works should be made by the whole organizing committee and 28 August was fixed for this purpose, although the date was later changed to 30 August. The meeting of 15 July turned out to be the last meeting of the Committee which Mainie Jellett attended for soon after it she became ill and went into hospital. The next recorded meeting of the Committee was held on 11 October 1943 in Louis le Brocquy's studio and Norah McGuinness was by then chairman. The date of her election as chairman is not recorded in the committee's minutes, but it may have taken place on or about 30 August when the selection of works was made and by which time Mainie was probably already in hospital. Norah McGuinness was chairman, and later president of the Living Art committee until 1972.

23 George Russell (AE), 'Two Irish Artists', *Imaginations and Reveries* (Dublin: Maunsell & Co., 1915), p.72.

24 IELA, minutes of committee, 11 October 1943. These sales represented about one third of the works offered for sale. Visits by school parties from the fifth and sixth standards upwards were arranged in association with the Department of Education and to encourage such visits the organizing committee offered a prize of one guinea for the best criticism of the exhibition written by a child.

25 'Living Art—A New Departure', *Irish Times*, 16 September 1943, p.3.

26 'A Stimulating Display', *Irish Independent*, 10 September 1943, p.2.

27 'The Exhibition of Living Art', the *Bell*, October 1943, p.78.

28 Máirín Allen, 'Irish Post-Impressionism',

Father Mathew Record, November 1943, p.10.

29 A.J. Leventhal, 'The Living Art Exhibition', *Irish Art: A Volume of Articles and Illustrations* (Dublin: Parkside Press, 1944), pp.92–3.

30 *Leader*, 25 September 1943, pp.136–7.

31 *Irish Times*, 1 October 1943, p.3.

32 See especially: exhibition catalogue, *Louis le Brocquy: A Retrospective Selection of Oil Paintings 1939–1966*, HLMG and UM, 1966–7; Dorothy Walker, *Louis le Brocquy* (Dublin: Ward River Press), 1981. The latter work also contains an introduction by John Russell, notes on different aspects of le Brocquy's art by various writers, a list of the artist's principal one-man exhibitions and extensive bibliographic sources.

33 Le Brocquy, letter of 16 November 1980. Unless stated otherwise this letter is the source of information below.

34 Le Brocquy, letter of 20 April 1984.

35 Le Brocquy, letter of 2 July 1975, UM archives.

36 A.J. Leventhal, op. cit., p.84.

37 Lucy Carrington Wertheim, *Adventure in Art* (London: Nicholson & Watson, 1947), p.48 lists 'past and present' members of the Twenties Group. Formed in 1930, the Group comprised artists all aged between twenty and thirty.

38 Anne Crookshank, introduction to the catalogue of the retrospective exhibition of Norah McGuinness' work, TCD, 1968, p.6.

39 Conversation with the author, 30 October 1980. She also said on this occasion that she thought abstraction became too arid for Evie Hone.

40 Thurloe Conolly, letter of 4 February 1981.

41 I am grateful to Ms. Yvonne Boydell for suggesting the following evolution of Conolly's style. The artist, however, later approved it (letter of 4 Feb. 1981).

42 Leventhal, op. cit., pp.88,90.

43 *Irish Times*, 16 September 1943, p.3; *Father Mathew Record*, November 1943, p.10.

44 Allen, op. cit., p.10.

45 Leventhal, op. cit., p.92; Rynne, *Leader*, 25 September 1943, pp.136–7.

46 Louis le Brocquy, letter of 2 May 1982.

47 IELA, minutes of committee, 6 February 1944. The proposal to include non-Irish artists came from Louis le Brocquy and was seconded by Ralph Cusack.

48 The works by these artists were sent from England by the Pilgrim Trust, but the minutes are unclear as to how the loan was initiated (IELA, minutes of committee, 31 May 1944).

49 IELA, minutes of committee, 15 November 1945.

50 *Irish Independent*, 14 September 1944, p.2; *Leader*, 23 September 1944, p.12.

51 'Exhibition of Living Art', *Irish Press*, 14 September 1944.

52 Stephen Rynne, *Leader*, 23 September 1944, p.7; Edward Sheehy, 'Living and Partly Living', *Dublin Magazine*, January–March 1945, p.40.

53 Siegfried Sassoon, *The Heart's Journey XII*.

54 *Commentary*, October 1944, p.11; *Irish Times*, 14 September 1944, p.3.

55 The French artists were: Yves Aix, Jean Cavailles, Cornelis Van Dongen, André Lhote, Jean Lurçat, Frans Masereel, Edouard Pignon and Charles Walch. The English were: Edward Ardizzone, Vanessa Bell, Edward Burra, William Coldstream, Laurence Gowing, Duncan Grant, Ivon Hitchens, Frances Hodgkins, Henry Moore, Paul Nash, Victor Pasmore, Ruskin Spear, Matthew Smith and Graham Sutherland.

56 IELA, minutes of committee, 15 November 1945. This figure for sales is especially significant as there were no Haverty Trust purchases from the exhibition that year compared with £101 worth purchased by the Trust the previous year. The period was also a high point in sales for the RHA.

57 Edward Sheehy, 'Art Notes', *Dublin Magazine*, October–December 1945, p.41.

58 Stephen Rynne, *Leader*, 1 September 1945, p.13.

59 'Variety Keynote at One-Man Art Show', *Northern Whig*, 8 September 1943, p.2.

60 'Colin Middleton Exhibition', *Irish Times*, 25 February 1949, p.3.

61 Michael Longley, 'Colin Middleton', *Dublin Magazine*, autumn/winter 1967, p.42.

62 Colin Middleton, in the film *The Trace of a Thorn*, commissioned by the Arts Council of Northern Ireland, 1983.

63 John Hewitt, 'Colin Middleton', the *Bell*, August 1942, p.338 and Hewitt, *Colin Middleton* (Belfast: Arts Council of Northern Ireland & An Chomhairle Ealaíon, 1976), p.30.

64 Edward Sheehy, 'Contemporary Irish Painters (5): Colin Middleton', *Envoy*, April 1950, p.34.

65 John Hewitt, referred to in Pat Murphy, 'Arts & Studies: Ireland's Greatest Surrealist', *Irish Times*, 31 December 1980, p.8.

66 'Gerard Dillon Exhibition', *Irish Times*, 24 February 1942, p.2.

67 John Hewitt, 'Under Forty: some Ulster

Artists', *Now in Ulster* (Belfast: published privately, 1944), p.34.

68 J.M. Synge, *The Playboy of the Western World*, illustrated by Seán Keating, 1927.

69 Gerard Dillon, 'The Artist Speaks', *Envoy*, February 1951, p.39. The Chagall paintings in the Tate Gallery, for example, were not acquired until the 1940s, so they could not have influenced Dillon's decision to take up painting. He may, of course, have seen them later.

70 John Hewitt, in the foreword to the catalogue of Dillon's joint exhibition held with Allen Adams at the CEMA gallery, Belfast, in December 1949, noted that 'In seeking to extend his range' over his Aran subject-matter, Dillon had 'more recently sought further devices and motifs in the relief-sculptures of the High Crosses of this land' (n.p.)

71 Sidney Smith (1912–82) was born in Belfast and studied art briefly at Belfast College of Art and privately under R. Boyd Morrison (1896–1969). In 1948 he went to live in London where he made a reputation as a painter of murals.

72 Cecil Salkeld, 'Daniel O'Neill: A Critical Appreciation', *Envoy*, December 1949, p.32.

73 IELA, minutes of committee, 27 November 1946, 29 August 1947 and 23 March 1948 respectively.

74 James White, *Standard*, 15 August 1947.

75 Edward Sheehy, 'Art Notes', *Dublin Magazine*, October–December 1948, p.51.

76 Arland Ussher papers, TCD, MS9088.

77 Jeanne Sheehy, exhibition catalogue, *Nano Reid* (An Chomhairle Ealaíon & the Arts Council of Northern Ireland, 1974), p.5.

78 Describing her method of composition she said, late in life: 'I work only when the spirit moves . . . .I never draw before I do a painting, never make a note. Things come quickly or not at all . . . . It either comes off or it doesn't' ('Harriet Cooke talks to the painter Nano Reid', *Irish Times*, 6 July 1973, p.10).

79 The artist, quoted in James White (ed.), *George Campbell* (Dublin, n.d., but c.1964), p.4.

80 For a note on the Progressive Painters Group and the Northern Ireland branch of the Artists International Asociation see chapter 7 below.

81 Arthur Campbell, conversation of 14 January 1986. See, too, 'An Irishman's Diary', *Irish Times*, 18 August 1949, p.5.

82 The year of his first Spanish visit is recorded in 'Passion for Spain made this Exhibition', *Irish News*, 14 February 1952, a review of Campbell's one-man show then in progress at the CEMA gallery.

83 See especially: 'This Artist has a Social Conscience', *Unity*, 26 February 1944; 'Belfast Art Show', *News-Letter*, 29 February 1944.

84 The artist told the present writer (undated letter of September 1976) that this was one of the first six or seven oil paintings he ever did. Smithfield was a variety market near to the centre of Belfast. It was destroyed by fire in about 1972.

85 Theodore Goodman, 'Here is an Irish Artist', *Commentary*, April 1946, n.p.

86 'Paintings by George Campbell', *Irish Times*, 1 April 1946.

87 Conversation with the artist, 30 September 1980. Unless stated otherwise this is the source of information below.

88 Nevill Johnson, letter of 14 October 1980. The exhibition of Surrealist paintings may have been the *International Surrealist Exhibition*, held at the New Burlington Galleries, London, in June 1936, which they could have seen on their way through London to Paris.

89 The short-lived MacGaffin Gallery was situated at number 12 Pottinger's Entry, off High Street, Belfast. It was run by Frederick Fitz-Currie Trench, a southerner who had been living in Northern Ireland since the early 1940s. The gallery opened in about 1945 or early 1946 (Nevill Johnson and John Hewitt, conversations of 30 September and 11 November 1980 respectively).

90 Nevill Johnson, autobiography, *The Other Side of Six* (Dublin: Academy Press, 1983), p.22.

91 'Art in Ireland', *Irish Tatler & Sketch*, February 1948, p.16.

92 Johnson, *The Other Side of Six*, p.50.

93 H.R.F. Keating, 'The Art of Nevill Johnson', *Icarus* (Dublin: TCD), May 1952, p.89.

94 Noelle Brissac, 'Contemporary Irish Painters (3): Thurloe Conolly', *Envoy*, February 1950, p.33.

95 Yvonne Boydell, letter of 17 August 1982.

96 Brian Fallon, 'Irish painting in the fifties', *Arts in Ireland*, vol.3, no.1 (n.d.), p.30.

97 Kenneth Jamison, 'Painting and Sculpture', in M. Longley (ed.), *Causeway: The Arts in Ulster* (Belfast: Arts Council of Northern Ireland, 1971), p.46.

98 H.J.P. Bomford, Aldbourne, Wiltshire, an English private collector.

99 The latter paper was reprinted in Herbert Read, *The Philosophy of Modern Art* (London: Faber & Faber, 1964), pp.44-57.

100 That is, the Friends of the National Collections of Ireland.

101 Louis le Brocquy, letter of 21 January

1949 to Norah McGuinness. The original letter does not seem to have survived but the text as quoted here is taken from an exact copy of the original among the papers of the late Margaret Clarke. Le Brocquy's resignation from the committee is noted in the minutes of its meeting of 16 March 1949.

102 IELA, minutes of committee, 16 March 1949.

103 IELA, minutes of committee, 17 May 1949. The French pictures selected were all by relatively unknown artists.

104 Information from the artist, interview of 19 January 1982.

105 'Vitality at Art Exhibition', *Irish Times*, 16 August 1949, p.5.

106 *Irish Tatler & Sketch*, September 1949, p.19.

107 Edward Sheehy, 'Art Notes', *Dublin Magazine*, October-December 1949, p.36.

108 Brian Fallon, 'Irish painting in the fifties', op. cit., p.28.

Chapter 7

1 Seán O'Faoláin, 'The Price of Peace', the *Bell*, July 1945, p.288 and quoted in Terence Brown, *Ireland: A Social and Cultural History*, p.211.

2 The gallery was opened by James Joseph Gorry and his son James A. Gorry. The latter had been a contemporary of Seán O'Sullivan at the Metropolitan School of Art. He later studied at the Slade School, London, before returning to Dublin in about 1938–9 (James Gorry, James A. Gorry's son, conversation of 17 January 1984).

3 Letter of 6 August 1982 from Tom Nisbet, Esq., who ran the gallery.

4 I am grateful to Mr. Sean Dorman for providing me with information on the Picture Hire Club (letters of 18 and 22 November and 3 and 18 December 1982). For a brief history of the Club see Sean Dorman, 'Suicide Among the Artists', in *Writing*, summer 1980, republished in the same author's *Limelight over the Liffey* (Fowey: Raffeen Press, 1983), p.95 and *passim*. As relatively few exhibitions were held at the Picture Hire Club during its brief existence the following list, which is complete, records the Club's activities and indicates the kind of art which it supported (sources: Dorman correspondence, exhibition catalogues and notes in *Commentary*):-

Paintings by Stephen Gilbert, 5–17 May 1941 (opened by Mainie Jellett)
Basil Rakoczi, *Landscape and Flower*

Paintings, 4–17 June 1941 (opened by Lennox Robinson)
F.A. Ross, *Irish Watercolours*, 19 June–2 July 1941
Paintings by Joan Cavers, 24 October–6 November 1941
New Works by Dermod O'Brien, 10–20 Nov. 1941 (opened by Hilton Edwards)
Noel Moffett, *Photographs of Donegal and Mayo*, 26 November–8 December 1941 (opened by Eoin O'Mahony)
Richard Pearsall, paintings in oils, 11–24 December 1941 (opened by Dermod O'Brien)
Paintings by Maurice MacGonigal, R.H.A., 15 December 1941–14 January 1942.

5 Michael Grace, 'Profile: Victor Waddington', unidentified press cutting dated April 1956, in Norah McGuinness' papers.

6 Victor Waddington, letter of 24 November 1980.

7 Michael Grace, op. cit.

8 A brief history of the gallery is given in the catalogue of the exhibition, *School of London*, held at the Waddington Galleries during March–April 1947.

9 In February 1939 he took to New York 270 works by Douglas Alexander, Moyra Barry, C.W. Bion, Michael Burke, Jerome Connor, William Conor, J.H. Craig, C.M. Doran, Frank Eggington, Eva and Letitia Hamilton, Grace Henry, Seán Keating, Harry Kernoff, Charles Lamb, Maurice MacGonigal, Seán O'Sullivan, Grace Trench and Maurice Wilks. His intention was not to exhibit these as a group, but to arrange with different art dealers throughout the United States to show a selection of them ('Irish Art for America', *Irish Times*, 13 February 1939, p.8).

10 'New Art Gallery Opened', *Irish Times*, 28 March 1947, p.6.

11 'French Picture Exhibition Disappoints', *Irish Times*, 3 May 1947, p.5.

12 Thomas Bodkin, introduction, *Twelve Irish Artists*, pp.5–7.

13 Pyle, *Yeats: A biography*, p.206.

14 In passing we might note that Waddington opened a gallery in Cork Street, London, in February 1958. There he remained until his retirement in the late 1970s. Victor Waddington died in 1981.

15 Victor Waddington, letter of 24 November 1980.

16 'Ulster Painting: An Attractive Exhibition', *Belfast Telegraph*, 21 August 1944.

17 For a note on the development of the AIA see Charles Harrison, *English Art & Modernism 1900–1939* (London: Allen Lane, 1981), pp.251–2 and *passim*.

18 Exhibition catalogue, *Belfast Commentary*, BMAG, 29 March–28 April 1945.

19 '"Belfast Commentary" in paint', *Irish News*, 5 April 1945.

20 Information from Arthur Campbell, Esq., conversation of 14 January 1986. See, too, '"Belfast Commentary" in paint', *Northern Whig*, 30 March 1945 which confirms Miss Loewenthal's role in organizing the Belfast branch.

21 The origins of CEMA, Northern Ireland, along with a note on its aims and policy, are set out in its first Annual Report, 1943–4, p.2. A detailed note on the Council and its early development is given in its fifth Annual Report, 1947–8, pp.5–13.

22 'Czech Art Exhibition Opened', *Irish Times*, 4 July 1947, p.3.

Chapter 8

1 The Academy was reorganized under a new charter in 1861. Later, in 1940, the government of the Irish Free State, under the 'Royal Hibernian Academy (Adoption of Charter) Order', essentially re-affirmed the 1861 charter but now vested those powers originally held by the Lord Lieutenant and, after 1922, the Governor General, in the Taoiseach ('Statutory Rules & Orders, 1940, No.331', Stationery Office, Dublin). A meeting of the Academy's general assembly, held on 18 April 1944, agreed to change its by-laws in order to bring them into line with the provisions of the Adoption of Charter Order by stating that those powers previously held by the Lord Lieutenant, namely that the election of a president and secretary each year should be dependent upon his approval, should now reside with the Taoiseach. This action was agreed by the Dáil and subsequently became law (government minutes, 11 May 1944, NAI, G3/9, p.227).

2 Although it did not occupy the Ely Place premises until July 1939, the resolution to purchase the house was passed at the Academy's annual general meeting in October 1937 (RHA, Annual Report 1937–8, n.p.)

3 Beatrice Glenavy, *Today we will only Gossip* (London: Constable, 1964), p.156.

4 Thomas Bodkin, 'The Royal Hibernian Academy', *Report on the Arts in Ireland* (Dublin: Stationery Office, 1953 ed.), p.29.

5 Strickland, *A Dictionary of Irish Artist*s (Dublin: Maunsell & Co., 1913), p.612, gives 1831 as the year when the Academy first received financial help from the state. The amount, £300, remained unchanged until 1941 when it was withdrawn. That year acceptance of the grant was conditional upon government inspection of the work of students in the Academy's school, a practice which had not regularly taken place hitherto. To this the Academy objected on the grounds that the right of inspection was not incorporated in its charter and that its autonomy would thus be eroded. There the matter rested. One senses, however, that the Academy's objection was influenced by the fact that the inspection would probably have been carried out by an official of the National College of Art—formerly the Metropolitan School of Art—to which it did not wish to appear deferential ('Why R.H.A. Rejects £300 Grant', *Irish Times*, 8 April 1943; 'R.H.A. To Return Grant: Minister on "Misleading Report", ' *Irish Press*, 9 April 1943).

6 Money was also in hand from the compensation of £8,000 paid by the British Government after the Academy House fire. Also, the site in Abbey Street was subsequently sold and the proceeds of the sale invested. By 1949 the Academy's investments amounted to about £22,000 (Bodkin, *Report*, p.29).

7 For an up-to-date assessment of Orpen, see Bruce Arnold, *Orpen*, 1981.

8 Terence de Vere White, *A Fretful Midge*, p.111.

9 Bodkin, *Irish Builder*, April 1913, pp.84, 87.

10 Bodkin, *Studio*, vol.87, January-June 1924, p.284.

11 George Russell (AE), writing as 'Y.O.', *Irish Statesman*, 24 April 1926, p.178.

12 'Modern Irish Art', *Saorstát Éireann: Irish Free State: Official Handbook* (Dublin: Talbot Press, 1932), p.240.

13 This was true of so-called criticism of all the arts and not just of the visual arts in Ireland at the time. See Terence Brown, *Ireland: A Social and Cultural History*, pp.204–5.

14 George Russell (AE), writing as 'Y.O.', 'The Hibernian Academy', *Irish Statesman*, vol.2, 19 April 1924, p.166.

15 'Royal Hibernian Academy', *Irish Times*, 7 May 1932, p.4.

16 Seán Keating, letter of 8 July 1975, Ulster Museum archives.

17 *Irish Times*, 9 April 1934, p.6.

18 *Irish Times*, 1 May 1934, p.4. The new Academy consisted of sixteen full academicians and eight associates. The names of the office bearers are given in a review of the Academy's 1938 exhibition in the *Leader*, 7 May 1938, p.207. Along with those of its forerunner the Academy held the following exhibitions in Dublin during its brief existence:-

Associated Irish Artists' Society:
1931 from 27 April: Mansion House
1932 from 9 May: Egan's Gallery,
  37 St. Stephen's Green
1933 from 1 May: Angus Gallery,
  36 St. Stephen's Green
1934 from 4 May: Egan's Gallery

Academy of Irish Art:
1935 from 8 April: Angus Gallery
1936 from 20 April: Angus Gallery
1937 from 3 May: Egan's Gallery
1938 2–14 May: Academy of Christian
  Art, 42 Upper Mount St.
1939 from 9 November: Mills' Hall,
  Merrion Row

(Source: press reviews of the above exhibitions, in each case published in the *Irish Times* for the day immediately after the opening of the exhibition).

19 'Echoes of the Town', *Irish Times*, 29 April 1938, p.4.

20 'At the Royal Hibernian Academy', *Leader*, 30 April 1938, pp.186–7. L.S. Gogan was keeper of the Art and Industry section at the National Museum, Dublin.

21 George Nobel, Count Plunkett, 'President's Address', *Journal*, Academy of Christian Art, vol.1 (n.d., but c.1937), p.7. The constitution of the Academy provided for a council of twelve members, including the president, vice-president, honorary treasurer and three honorary secretaries (Academy of Christian Art, constitution, in minutes book of meetings held). The first committee of the Academy, elected in 1929, comprised the following persons: Count Plunkett, president; Professor Arthur Clery, vice-president; Constantine Curran, honorary treasurer; G. Plunkett, secretary (Gaelic & English); Professor F.P. Stockley, secretary (modern languages); E. Enright, secretary (Latin & Greek); and six members, namely Messrs Byrne, Darley, Gogan, O'Kelly, Geoghegan and a Miss Gleeson (minutes book of meetings held). Meetings of the Academy were held monthly, when members and invited guests would present papers on a range of topics. From time to time exhibitions of paintings were held at various venues in Dublin and, from October 1934, in the Academy's rooms at number 42 Upper Mount Street. The Academy also maintained a collection of several hundred photographs and other illustrations of paintings and sculptures of religious subjects, which could be consulted by its members and which were used for educational purposes.

22 Stephen Rynne, *Leader*, 28 April 1945, pp.10–12.

23 Stephen Rynne, *Leader*, 11 May 1946, p.14.

24 'The Battle of the Critics', *Dublin Magazine*, July–September 1946, p.42.

25 Edward Sheehy, 'Art Notes', *Dublin Magazine*, July–October 1948, pp.47-9.

26 Stephen Rynne, *Leader*, 28 April 1945, pp.10–12.

27 Two points should be noted here which belie the development of the Academy as we have outlined it, namely, the number of visitors to it and the revenue derived from sales of pictures at its exhibitions in our period. During the 1920s and early 1930s both the numbers of visitors attending the exhibitions and the amount of sales generated were fairly consistent, and they increased only gradually in the late 1930s. But after the outbreak of war in 1939, both visitors and sales increased greatly only to settle back somewhat in the post-war period. However, this was a phenomenon common to nearly all art exhibitions held in Dublin during the war-years and should not be taken as a reflection of growing public interest in the Academy. For the number of visitors attending its annual exhibitions and the amount of sales thereat see RHA annual reports. Regarding the increase in numbers of works of art sold in Dublin during the war-years see 'Ireland's Increased interest in Art', *Irish Times*, 11 December 1944, p.1.

28 Stephen Rynne, *Leader*, 22 April 1939, pp.161–2.

29 'Studio Talk', *Studio*, vol.51, 1910–11, p.63.

30 Charles Michel Maria Verlat (1824-90), Belgian painter of historical subjects, hunting scenes and portraits.

31 For a full biography of Dermod O'Brien see Lennox Robinson, *Palette and Plough* (Dublin: Browne & Nolan), 1948.

32 Robinson, op. cit., p.132.

33 'Royal Hibernain Academy Exhibition', *Irish Times*, 30 March 1942, p.3.

34 Leo Whelan in 'What is a Portrait?', *Irish Art: A Volume of Articles & Illustrations*, p.16.

35 Purser, quoted in Kenneth C. Bailey, *A History of Trinity College Dublin 1892-1945* (Dublin: University Press, 1947), p.70.

36 He is said to have studied under Gerald Spencer Pryse at the Central School of Art, London, and under Henri Morriset and Angel Zarrago, a Mexican painter, in Paris (*Capuchin Annual*, 1936, p.317). A brief pen portrait of O'Sullivan is recorded in John Ryan, *Remembering How We Stood* (Dublin: Gill & Macmillan, 1975), pp.45-7.

37 These, and many others, are now in the National Gallery of Ireland.

38 Anne Crookshank, 'Portraits of Irish Medicine', in Eoin O'Brien, Anne Crookshank, Sir Gordon Wolstenholme, *A Portrait of Irish Medicine* (Dublin: Ward River Press, 1984), p.45.

39 Seán O'Sullivan, 'What is a Portrait?', in *Irish Art: A Volume of Articles & Illustrations*, p.11.

40 The *Irish Times*, 19 October 1945, notes his election which took place the previous day.

41 For a detailed discussion of Sleator's career see Brian Kennedy, *James Sinton Sleator P.R.H.A.*, 1989.

42 Bruyere, 'Some Irish Artists: XV—Mr. James Sleator', *Irish Times*, 7 July 1923, p.10.

43 The theme is noted in 'The Problem Picture: End of the Stage Irishman', a discussion of Keating's *Night's Candles are Burnt Out*, *Irish Times*, 6 May 1929, p.6.

44 In the former composition, for example, the figure to the left is a self-portrait; the models for the other two figures were the artist's brother and a friend (J.J.R. O'Brien, 'A Coming Irish Artist: The Work of John Keating', *Irish Rosary*, vol.21, 1917, p.575).

45 Quidnunc, *Irish Times*, 25 August 1933, p.4, states that O'Hickey was the sitter here.

46 Keating once said that in portraiture he endeavoured to penetrate visual appearances, to reach beneath the surface 'where character and intellect are eternal' (Sean Keating, 'What is a Portrait?', in *Irish Art: A Volume of Articles & Illustrations*, p.20).

47 'The Hibernian Academy', *Irish Statesman*, vol.11, 10 April 1920, p.359.

48 For an up-to-date assessment of Patrick Tuohy's career see Rosemarie Mulcahy, 'Patrick J. Tuohy 1894-1930', *Irish Arts Review*, Yearbook 1989–90, pp.107–18.

49 David Clarke, conversation with the author, 23 February 1982.

50 For a full biography of Conor, see Judith Wilson, *Conor 1881–1968: The life and work of an Ulster artist* (Belfast: Blackstaff Press), 1981.

51 Stephen Rynne, *Leader*, 1 May 1943, p.236.

52 Stephen Rynne, *Leader*, 28 April 1945, pp.10–12; 11 May 1946, pp.13–14.

53 Hewitt, *Art in Ulster:1*, p.83.

54 Ibid., p.95.

55 Robert Sydney Rendle Wood was born in Plymouth in 1894. He studied art in Plymouth and Edinburgh before going to Belfast probably in the early 1920s. Later he settled in St. Austell, Cornwall. He was a close friend of the painter Paul Nietsche.

Theo Gracey was prolific as a watercolourist. Mainly a landscapist his principal sources were counties Antrim and Donegal and Connemara. James Stanley Prosser was born in Manchester in 1887. Later he came to Belfast where he studied at the College of Art after which he became best known for his landscapes, genre and still life works. He married a sister of J.H. Craig.

56 'Royal Hibernian Academy', *Irish Times*, 6 April 1925, p.6.

57 Ciarán MacGonigal, the artist's son, conversation with the author, 28 October 1980. Unless stated otherwise this is the source of information below.

58 Máirín Allen, 'Contemporary Irish Artists XVIII—Maurice MacGonigal', *Father Mathew Record*, vol.37, May 1943, p.6.

59 MacGonigal, quoted in Geraldine Coster, 'With Our Artists-No.5: Mr. Maurice MacGonagle [sic], R.H.A', *Personality Parade*, September 1946, p.16.

60 'Royal Hibernian Academy', *Irish Times*, 11 April 1927, p.8.

61 Crookshank & Glin, *The Painters of Ireland*, p.273.

62 Seán Keating, letter of 26 January 1974, to Mons. John Hanly, Irish College in Rome. I am grateful to Mons. Hanly for drawing my attention to this letter. The artistic lineage which Keating here outlines was: J.A.D. Ingres (1780-1867), who influenced Alphonse Legros (1837-1911), who came to England from France to teach at Kensington School of Fine Art and the Slade School, who in turn influenced Henry Tonks (1862-1937), who was a friend of Orpen.

63 Keating, interviewed, *Belfast News-Letter*, 1 May 1965.

64 *Irish Times*, 4 December 1933.

65 Ciarán MacGonigal, conversation of 28 October 1980.

66 His sister was the model for many of these works and the setting in most cases was the basement kitchen in Whelan's house in Eccles Street, Dublin (Ms. Lena Murnaghan, the artist's neice, conversation of 3 August 1985).

67 Lady Glenavy published her autobiography as *Today we will only Gossip* (London: Constable), 1964. Also, a detailed biographical note on her, along with a list of the numerous prizes and awards which she won, is given in Alan Denson, *John Hughes: Sculptor* (Kendal: published privately, 1969), pp.438–40.

68 Her election to constituent membership took place on 18 October 1934 (RHA, Annual Report 1934–5, n.p.) Some sources incorrectly cite 1933 as the year of her election.

69 William Holden, who knew Lady Glenavy
for a number of years, said she considered herself strictly an academic painter
(letter of 20 May 1985). Holden also said
that from time to time she altered her pictures 'as the mood took her'.

70 Beatrice Glenavy, *Today we will only
Gossip*, p.148.

71 For a detailed history of these bodies see
Martyn Anglesea, *The Royal Ulster
Academy of Arts*, (Belfast: Royal Ulster
Academy of Arts), 1981. The Ulster
Academy of Arts obtained its Royal
charter in 1950.

72 *Leader*, vol.82, 17 May 1941, pp.371-2.

73 'Sketching Club Exhibition. Memories of
the Past: Renewed Appeal for Support',
Irish Times, 2 October 1937, p.5.

74 A brief history of the Oireachtas art exhibitions, from the time they were first held
in 1905, is given in the catalogue of the
1977 exhibition.

75 The members of the selection committee,
as far as is recorded, in these years were:-
1941: Seán Keating, Seán O'Sullivan,
Maurice MacGonigal, Senator Joseph
Brennan and Liam Gogan; 1942: probably
as for the previous year; 1943: Keating,
O'Sullivan, Brennan; 1944: Dermod
O'Brien, James Sleator, Leo Whelan, Jack
B. Yeats, Arthur Power; 1945: Sleator,
Keating, Laurence Campbell, Brigid
Ganly; 1946: Sleator, O'Sullivan, Cecil
Galbally, Seamus Murphy; 1947:
O'Sullivan, Fergus O'Ryan, Oisin Kelly
(I am grateful to Mr. Donnchadh
O'Súilleabáin [letter of 1 February 1983],
retired secretary of An tOireachtas, for this
information).

Chapter 9

1 For a detailed discussion of the background to these works see John Turpin,
'Oliver Sheppard's 1798 Memorials',
Irish Arts Review, Yearbook 1990–91,
pp.71–80.

2 Section 12: Literature and Art, 'Irish Free
State 1921–1931', supplement to the *Irish
Times*, January 1932.

3 Máirín Allen, 'Contemporary Irish Artists
IX. Albert G. Power, R.H.A.', *Father
Mathew Record*, February 1942, p.3. Most
sources do not mention his studentship
under Hughes at the Metropolitan School,
but 'Some Irish Artists: XXIII–Mr. Albert
Power', *Irish Times*, 1 September 1923,
p.9, records him as having studied under
Hughes. Also, Hughes taught at the Metropolitan School from 1894–1901 and, as
Power probably attended evening classes
there from about 1896, he would have
been Hughes' pupil. For a detailed discussion of Power's work see Sighle
Bhreathnach-Lynch, 'Albert Power,
RHA', *Irish Arts Review*, Yearbook 1990–
91,pp.111–14. Bhreathnach-Lynch notes
Hughes as being amongst Power's teachers.

4 The architects responsible for the new
cathedral building were M/s W.H. Byrne
& Son of Dublin. Ralph Byrne recommended Power for the sculptures (Mark
Leonard, Esq., M/s W.H. Byrne & Son,
the late Ralph Byrne's office manager,
conversation of 25 September 1986).

5 Rev. John Brady, *A Short History of the
Parishes of Mullingar and Navan* (Navan:
Meath Chronicle, 1936), p.78. The agreement, dated 27 September 1934, between
Power and Dr. Mulvany for the commission stipulated that the figures in this last
mentioned group should be portraits.

6 Metropolitan School of Art, Register of
Students. Campbell was a student there
from 1927 until 1936.

7 The Registrar, Kungl. Akademien Für De
Fria Konsterna, Stockholm, letter of 18
September 1985. Campbell was a student
in Stockholm during 1936–8.

8 Information from Richard Guy, architect
(conversation of 15 January 1986). Guy
later acquired these works and built them
into the façade of his house.

9 For a series of photographs which vividly
illustrate the method of working, see 'A
Contemporary Irish Master: Laurence
Campbell R.H.A., at work on his statue
of Seán Heuston', *Capuchin Annual*,
1945–6, pp.337–52.

10 He recorded his time at the stoneyard,
which was run by John Aloysius
O'Connor, in his book, *Stone Mad* (London: Routledge & Kegan Paul, 1966).
Delightfully written, it is, however, largely
anecdotal.

11 Oisin Kelly, 'Allegorical Figures and
Madonnas', exhibition catalogue, *Séamus
Murphy 1907–1975*, Dublin and Cork,
1983, p.20.

12 The work is reproduced in its original state
in *Séamus Murphy 1907–1975*, op. cit.,
p.14, where, as can be seen, the polished
stone softens the overall effect of the
piece.

13 For a chronology of O'Conor's life see
Homan Potterton, *Andrew O'Connor*,
exhibition catalogue, Trinity College,
Dublin, 1974, pp.11, 13–14. This work
also contains a discussion of the sculptor's
career, numerous illustrations of his work
and a list of bibliographical sources.

14 Mairin Allen, in three articles on Connor,
namely: 'Jerome Connor—one'; 'Jerome
Connor—two'; and 'Jerome Connor—

three', *Capuchin Annual*, 1963, 1964, 1965 respectively, discusses Connor's life and career in detail. In the first of these articles (p.354) she divides his career into four distinct periods, thus: formative years, 1889–1903; early period, 1904–12, culminating in his Archbishop Carroll Memorial (Georgetown Catholic University); middle period, 1913–24, culminating in his Nuns' Memorial, Washington; late or 'Irish' period, 1925–43, dominated by the Lusitania Memorial. We are here, of course, only concerned with this last period.

15 The design for this figure is known from a photograph reproduced in the *Irish Times* of 30 November 1929.

16 These works are reproduced in Mairin Allen, 'Jerome Connor—three', pp.378–9.

17 A photograph of a maquette for the Angel, as it was eventually cast, was reproduced in the *Irish Times*, 18 September 1936, p.5. Allen, 'Jerome Connor—three', p.382, implies that this model was not completed until 1938 but that is not so.

18 'Angel of Peace Comes Home To Complete 50-Year Memorial', *Irish Times*, 11 May 1968, p.5.

19 It is illustrated in the *Irish Times*, 25 September 1931, p.4.

20 This work was begun in 1931 and was to have been completed in time for the Eucharistic Congress planned for Dublin the following year. When Connor failed to complete the commission, the committee who were financing it sued him for breach of contract and his bankruptcy followed as a result of the case ('An Unfinished Memorial: Sculptor Sued for Breach of Contract', *Irish Press*, 9 July 1936, p.3.) The work was eventually cast in bronze in about 1973 and was placed in Merrion Square, Dublin, in 1976.

21 Information from the artist, conversation of 19 December 1985.

Postscript

1 For an up-to-date assessment of Bodkin's *Report* and a full discussion of the background to it see Brian P. Kennedy, *Dreams and Responsibilities: The State and The Arts in Independent Ireland* (Dublin: Arts Council), 1990.

2 Bodkin, *Report on the Arts in Ireland,* 1953 ed., p. 8.

3 Ibid., p. 59.

4 Bodkin, 'The Present Position of Art in Ireland,' *Ireland To-day,* (London: 1913), pp. 113–20.

5 Bodkin, 'The Condition and Needs of Art in Ireland,' in W. G. Fitz-Gerald (ed.), *The Voice of Ireland* (Dublin: 1923), pp. 492–7.

APPENDIX 1

Society of Dublin Painters

Provisional list of members 1920–1950
(Sources: exhibition catalogues and press reviews)

Name	Years of Membership*
Paul Henry[1,2,3]	1920–post 1938 (Secretary 1920)
Grace Henry[1,2,3]	1920–c. 1950s
Jack B. Yeats[1]	1920–c. 1923
Harry Clarke (d. 1931)[1]	1920–31
Letitia Hamilton[1,2,3]	1920–1950s (President late 1950s)
Mainie Jellett (d. 1944)[1,2,3]	1920–44 (President 1920?)
Clare Marsh (d. 1923)[1]	1920–3
Mary Swanzy[1]	1920–c. 1922
E.M. O'R. Dickey[1]	1920–4
Countess Soumarokow Elston	1920 (possibly not a full member)
Sir Frederick Moore	1920 (possibly not a full member)
James Sleator	1920 (possibly not a full member)
James M. Willcox	1920 (possibly not a full member)
Charles Lamb[1,2,3]	1922–c. 1950s
William Conor	1922–
Eva Hamilton[2,3]	1922–1950s (President 1948–)
Harriet Kirkwoood[2,3]	1922–c. 1950s (Hon. Sec. 1930–6; President 1936–48)
Evie Hone[2,3]	1922–c. 1950
Harry Kernoff[2]	1927–c. 1950s
Cecil Salkeld	1927–
Maurice Mac Gonigal[2]	(1929)–1950s
W.E. Horsbrugh Porter[2,3]	(1930)–c. 1950s
Hilda Roberts[2]	(1931)–c. 1950s
Joan Jameson[3]	(1934)–c. 1950s
Nora G. Hamilton[3]	(1934)–c. 1950s
Lady Beatrice Glenavy[3]	(1934)–1950s
Moyra Barry[3]	(1934)–c. 1950
Bridgid O'Brien (Ganly)[3]	(1934)–c. 1950
Nano Reid[3]	(1934)–c. 1950
Lilian Davidson[3]	(1935)–1950s
Stella Frost[3]	(1935)–c. 1950
Norah McGuinnness	1936–c. 1950
Dorothy Blackham	1936–c. 1950
Fr. J.P. Hanlon	1936–c. 1950
Kitty Wilmer O'Brien	1936–1950s
Lady Mabel Annesley	1937–
Margaret Clarke	1937–c. 1950
Sylvia Cooke-Collis	1937–1950s
Frances Kelly	1937–c. 1950
Phyllis Godfrey	(1937)–c. 1950
Mrs Lennox (Dolly) Robinson	1938–c. 1950s
E.A. McGuire	1938–c. 1950
Richard Finney	(1938)–
May Guinness	(1938)–c. 1950

Brenda Gogarty	1939–c. 1950
Ralph Cusack	1940–c. 1950
Patrick Hennessy	(1940)–1950s (President 1954)
Patricia Griffith (Wallace)	1941–c. 1950
Gerard Dillon	1943–
Thurloe Conolly	(1945)–c. 1950
Phoebe Kirkwood	(1945)–
Robert Burke	(1947)–1950s
Anne Yeats	(1947)–1950s
Eugene Judge	(1948)–1950s
Elizabeth Rivers	(1948)– c. 1950
Phyllis Hayward	(1948)–1950–1

* The first year listed is the year in which the person appears to have become a member. The use of parentheses indicates that they are known to have been a member from that year and possibly earlier.

1 In 1920 membership confined to ten persons, marked thus.

2 In 1932 membership confined to twelve persons, marked thus.

3 In about 1934 membership raised to eighteen persons, marked thus, although only seventeen are known for certain.

APPENDIX 2

White Stag Group

Chronology of events 1940–1946

(*)   Denotes exhibitions in which the artist took part.
(§)   L.Bg.St. = Lower Baggot Street, Dublin; Up.Mt.St. = Upper Mount Street, Dublin

1940

	(1) Group Show 15–20 April 34 L.Bg.St. §	(2) Group Show 9–15 Oct 30 Up.Mt.St.	(3) One-man 22 Nov–3 Dec 30 Up.Mt.St.	(4) One-man 26 June 30 L.Bg.St.	(5) Group Show 10–21 Dec 30 Up.Mt.St.
Barbara Bayley	*				
Dorothy Blackham		*			*
Jocelyn Chewett		*			*
Bobby Dawson		*			
Paul Egestorff		*			
Stephen Gilbert		*			*
Kenneth Hall	*	*			*
Evie Hone					*
Mainie Jellett	*	*			*
Eugene Judge		*			
Nick Nicholls	*	*		*	
Elizabeth Ormsby	*	*			
Anthony Rakoczi	*				
Basil Rakoczi	*	*	*		*
Anthony Reford	*	*			
Georgette Rondel	*	*			
Endre Roszda	*				
Patricia Wallace	*	*			

(2)   Sixty-nine works shown, including some by the German artist Helmut Kolle. Exhibition opened by Mainie Jellet, 9 October. Also 9 October, Basil Rakoczi lecture, 'Since Picasso', at 8.15 pm.

(3)   Opened by Lennox Robinson on 21 November at 8.15 pm. Mainie Jellet lectured (title unknown) that same evening. Nearly forty works shown.

(5)   Included works by twenty-two artists ('Dublin Picture Show', *Irish Times*, 12 December 1940, p. 4) but only these seven, apart from those noted as being on loan, have been identified. Opened by Basil Rakoczi, who spoke of the Group's work and its aims.

Other events in 1940

Society for Creative Psychology: lectures during April and May at 25 Lower Baggot Street and during October at 34 Lower Baggot Street.

15 November, Mainie Jellett lecture (title unknown).

20 December, Henri Silvy of the French Legation lecture, 'Legacy of Cubism', at 30 Upper Mount Street.

1941

	(1) Group Show 13–22 Feb 30 Up.Mt.St.	(2) One-man 7–18 Oct 30 Up.Mt.St.	(3) Group Show 6–15 Nov 30 Up.Mt.St.
Lesley Birks			*
Dorothy Blackham	*		*
Jocelyn Chewett	*		*
Ralph Cusack	*		
Bobby Dawson	*		*
Paul Egerstorff			*
H. Gilbert			*
Stephen Gilbert	*		
May Guinness			*
Kenneth Hall	*	*	*
Phyllis Hayward			*
Evie Hone	*		*
Mainie Jellett	*		*
Eugene Judge	*		
E. A. McGuire	*		
Noel Moffett			*
Nick Nicholls	*		
Elizabeth Ormsby			*
Conor Padilla			*
Cicely Peel	*		
Nelson Pollard			*
Anthony Rakoczi			*
Basil Rakoczi	*		*
Anthony Reford	*		*
Nano Reid	*		*
Georgette Rondel	*		
Patrick Scott	*		*
Henri Silvy			*
Donald Teale			*
Martin Teale			*
Doreen Vanston			*
Patricia Wallace	*		

(1) Exhibition opened by Mme. Jammet, 12 February at 8.30 pm. Fifty-one works shown including some on loan by Albert Gleizes, Max Peckstein, Jean Marchand.

(2) Exhibition opened by Jocelyn Chewett. Fifty-one works shown.

(3) Exhibition opened by Phyllis Eason on 6 November at 3.30pm. Sixty-six paintings and four sculptures shown including works on loan by Alfred Wallace.

Other events in 1941

9 May, Jocelyn Chewett lecture, 'Sculpture', at 30 Upper Mount Street.

May, Mainie Jellett lecture, 'The Spiritual Force in Art'.

Society for Creative Psychology: meetings during September and October at 30 Upper Mount Street.

17 October, Basil Rakoczi lecture, 'Subjective Painting', probably at 30 Upper Mount Street.

October, Mainie Jellet lecture, 'Celtic and Abstract Art Compared'.

November, life classes every Monday at 8.10 pm; lecture every Friday at 8.15 pm, all events at 30 Upper Mount Street.

December, Mainie Jellett lecture, 'Georges Rouault'.

1942

	(1) Group Show 3 Feb 6 L.Bg.St.	(2) One-man 6–16 May 6 L.Bg.St.	(3) One-man 30 Sept–10 Oct 6 L.Bg.St.	(4) One-man 9–19 Dec 6 L.Bg.St.
Jocelyn Chewett	*			
Stephen Gilbert	*			
Kenneth Hall	*		*	
Basil Rakoczi	*	*		*
Patrick Scott	*			

(2)   Exhibition of 20 watercolours, opened by Mainie Jellett, 6 May at 3.30 pm.

(4)   Exhibition of 16 watercolours of the Aran Islands. Opened by Miss Isabel Douglas, 9 December.

Other events in 1942

New gallery at 6 Lower Baggot Street opened late January; Basil Rakoczi gave instruction in 'modern art methods'; lectures and life classes continued in evenings as from February.

10 April, lecture, 'The Problem of Communication'; 17 April, poetry reading; 24 April, recital of grammophone records. All events held at 6 Lower Baggot Street.

May, Nick Nicholls published a book of poems from 3 Hatch Street. Edition of 200, each copy with an original drawing by Nicholls on the cover.

November (?)1942 or 1943, four talks on art by Basil Rakoczi, namely: 'Primitive Art and Art Today', 5 November; 'The Sensual Factor in Art', 12 November; 'Art, War and Social Evils', 19 November; 'The Artist and the New Direction in Art', 26 November. All events at 6 Lower Baggot Street.

6 June, Noel Moffett lecture, 'Architecture, Painting and Sculpture: in search of a common grammar', 7.30 pm; recital of grammophone records arranged by Ralph Cusack. Both events at 6 Lower Baggot Street.

December (?)1942 or 1943, two lectures, H.F. Norman, 'AE's Psychology of Vision and Song', 3 December and Dr. H.A.C. Ingouville-Williams, 'Modern Psychotherapeutic Methods', 10 December.

1943

	(1) Group Show 3–10 April 6 L.Bg.St.	(2) Group Show 17–24 April 6 L.Bg.St.	(3) One-man 4–17 May 6 L.Bg.St.
Stephen Gilbert		*	
Kenneth Hall	*	*	
Phyllis Hayward	*		
Nick Nicholls			*
Basil Rakoczi	*	*	
Patrick Scott	*	*	
Doreen Vanston		*	

(1)   Opened by Carl Bonn. 16 watercolours on show.

(2)   16 oils on show

(3)   Exhibition opened by Ralph Cusack, 4 May at 3.30 pm.

1944

	(1) Group Show 4–22 Jan (Subjective Art) 6 L.Bg.St.	(2) One-man 22 Nov–2 Dec 6 L.Bg.St.	(3) One-man 7–16 Dec 6 L.Bg.St.
Brian Boydell	*		
Jocelyn Chewett	*		
Thurloe Conolly	*		
Ralph Cusack	*		
Bobby Dawson	*		
Paul Egestorff	*		
Stephen Gilbert	*		
Kenneth Hall	*		
Phyllis Hayward	*		
Nick Nicholls	*		*
Basil Rakoczi	*	*	
Patrick Scott	*		
Doreen Vanston	*		

(1)   7 January, paper by Herbert Read, 'The Nature of Subjective Art', read in his absence; 17 January, John Hewitt lecture, 'The Adventure of Subjectivity'.

(3)   16 works on show. Exhibition opened by Victor Bewley 3.30 pm on 7 December.

Other events in 1944

From 16 November, exhibition of *Paintings of the Aran Islands* by Hall and Rakoczi, Mid-Day Studio, 96 Mosley Street, Manchester.

1945

	(1) One-man early 1945 6 L.Bg.St.	(2) One-man 25 Jan–3 Feb 6 L.Bg.St.	(3) Group Show 20 Feb	(4) One-man 26 Feb–10 Mar 6 L.Bg.St.	(5) Two-man 21–28 May 6 L.Bg.St.	(6) One-man 17–27 Oct 6 L.Bg.St.
Stephen Gilbert	*					
Kenneth Hall		*				
Ann Miller					*	
Nick Nicholls					*	
Basil Rakoczi				*		*

(3)   Title, *You met them in Paris.* Included works by Hall, Kolle, Rakoczi and Wood. Venue unknown.

(4)   *Exhibition of Landscape and Figure Paintings.* Opened by Erina Brady. 22 works shown.

(6)   *Paintings of Kerry and Louth.* Opened by Miss Isobel Douglas.

Other events in 1945

16 January, exhibition of children's art arranged by the White Stag Group at Contemporary Picture Galleries. Basil Rakoczi lecture, 'Children as Real Artists', to the Parents National Education Union, Dublin Branch.

January, *Picasso Again*, exhibition of sixteen reproductions of works by Picasso, Phelan Gibb, Kolle, Banting, Melville, Rakoczi, and Hall, held at the Mid-Day Studio, 96 Mosley Street, Manchester.

20 April–12 May, exhibition *Young Irish Painters*, Arcade Gallery, Old Bond Street, London, included works by Jocelyn Chewett, Ralph Cusack, Bobby Dawson, Stephen Gilbert, Kenneth Hall, Phyllis Hayward, Nick Nicholls, Basil Rakoczi, Patrick Scott, Doreen Vanston.

May, George Colman's play *The Jealous Wife* presented by Lord Longford at the Gate Theatre, Dublin, with sets by Rakoczi.

Publication of H.A.C. Ingouville-Williams, *Three Painters* (Dublin: Three Candles).

1946

May, Hertha Phyllis Eason, exhibition of paintings at the White Stag Gallery, Merrion Row.

APPENDIX 3

Irish Exhibition of Living Art

Patrons, members of organizing committee, guarantors 1943–1950
(Source: *Irish Exhibition of Living Art,* catalogues of exhibitions 1943–50)

Patrons

Provost, Trinity College, Dublin	1943–50
President, University College, Dublin	1943–50
Director, National Gallery of Ireland	1943–50
President, Royal Hibernian Academy	1943–50

Organizing Committee

Laurence Campbell	1943
Margaret Clarke	1943–50
Elizabeth Curran	1943
Ralph Cusack	1943–50
Evie Hone	1943–50
Mainie Jellett (Chairman)	1943
Louis le Brocquy	1943–8
Norah McGuinness (Chairman late 1943–8, President thereafter)	1943–50
Rev. Jack P. Hanlon	1943–50
Thurloe Conolly	1947–50
Michael Scott	1947–50
Anne Yeats	1947–50
R.R. Figgis	1949–50

Guarantors

Hubert Briscoe	1943–50
Victor Waddington	1943–50
Edward McGuire	1943–50
Terence Gray	1943–50
Mrs. E. MacCarvill	1943–50
R.R. Figgis	1944–8
Major Kirkwood	1949–50
Lord Moyne	1949–50
The Earl of Rosse	1949–50

BIBLIOGRAPHY

The bibliography is divided into primary and secondary sources. The former category is sub-divided into two parts, namely (i) MSS, Private Papers, Letters and Oral Evidence; (ii) Contemporary Exhibition Catalogues; and the second category is sub-divided into four parts, namely (i) List of Newspapers, Periodicals and Journals; (ii) Articles in Periodicals and Journals; (iii) General Works; (iv) Works of Reference. For the sake of brevity bibliographic references to specific works of art in the catalogue section, unless also referred to in the main text, are cited only in the appropriate catalogue entry.

PRIMARY SOURCES
(i) MSS, Private Papers, Letters and Oral Evidence

(Unless stated otherwise all letters were addressed to the author):-

Academy of Christian Art. General papers and minutes book of meetings 1929–51.

Acton, Charles. Interview of 24 February 1981 regarding Thurloe Conolly.

Agreement of contract between Dr. Thomas Mulvany, Bishop of Meath, and Albert Power, dated 27 September 1934, regarding the tympanum sculptures for Mullingar Cathedral.

Archives de France, Série AJ52, AJ53, F21 regarding the École des Beaux-Arts, Paris.

Arnold, Bruce. Interviews of 6 April 1982 and 2 January 1985 regarding Mainie Jellett.

Behan, Mrs. Beatrice. Interviews of 16 May and 30 August 1985 regarding her father, Cecil ffrench Salkeld.

Bodkin, Thomas. Private papers, the library, TCD, MSS 6918:34, 6941:343.

Bourke, Ann. Interview of 13 April 1982 regarding her mother, Margaret Clarke.

Boydell, Dr. Brian. Interviews of 30 September and 18 October 1980 regarding the White Stag Group.

Boydell, Yvonne. Letter of 17 August 1982; interview of 23 June 1984 regarding her husband, Thurloe Conolly.

Brennan, Peter. Interview of 19 December 1985.

Bridle, Kathleen. Interview of 9 June 1980.

Campbell, Arthur. Interviews of 30 April 1982 and 14 January 1986 regarding his brother, George Campbell.

Carrick, Desmond. Letter of 9 October 1976 (UM archives) regarding the RHA.

Charterhouse School, register of pupils.

Clarke, David. Interview of 23 February 1982 regarding his mother, Margaret Clarke.

Clarke, Margaret. Private papers.

Collie, Mrs. G. Interviews of 19 July and 30 August 1985 regarding her husband, George Collie.

Conolly, Thurloe. Letter of 4 February 1981.

Crawford Art Gallery, Cork. Gibson Bequest—Register of Purchases, 1920–80; Minutes Book 1922–6 of Gibson Bequest purchases.

Crichton, Alec. Interview of 31 January 1984 regarding Harriet Kirkwood.

Crowley, Guida. Interview of 26 May 1981 regarding Nevill Johnson.

Cusack, Ralph. Private papers.

Dawson, Bobby. Interview of 9 December 1980; letter of 24 December 1980.

De Buitléar, Lailli. Interview of 16 October 1984 regarding her father, Charles Lamb.

Dickey, Mr. & Mrs. D. Interview of 17 April 1986 regarding E.M.O'R. Dickey.

Digby, Dr. L.D. Interview of 28 November 1985 regarding Jerome Connor.

Dillon, G. Interview of 23 January 1986 regarding his uncle, Gerard Dillon.

Doran, M.J. Interview of 16 May 1985 regarding Cecil ffrench Salkeld.

Dorman, Sean. Letters of 18 and 22 November and 3 and 18 December 1982; private papers regarding the Picture Hire Club.

Dragon School, Oxford. Register of pupils.

Dublin Sketching Club. Archives.

Egestorff, Paul. Interview of 28 October 1980.

Eton College. Register of pupils.

Friends of the National Collections of Ireland. Archives.

Gilbert, Stephen. Letter of 8 December 1980; interview of 24 May 1981.

Glenavy, Lady Beatrice. Private papers.

Gorry, James. Letter of 30 September 1982 regarding the Gorry Gallery.

Grant, Peter. Letter of 23 November 1985; interview of 6 March 1986.

Gribbon, Dr. Philip. Letter of 29 August 1980; interview of 27 January 1981 regarding his father, C.E. Gribbon.

Gribbon, Herbert. Interview of 16 July 1980 regarding his brother, C.E. Gribbon.

Guinness, Charles. Interview of 3 January 1985 regarding May Guinness.

Guinness, Elizabeth. Interviews of 3 January and 19 July 1985 regarding May Guinness.

Hall, Kenneth. Letters to Mrs. Lucy Carrington Wertheim: 16 May, 10 September, 11 December 1939; 12 and 30 March, 19 April, 3 September 1940; 25 February, 24 March 1945.

———. Autobiography, unpublished typescript, c.1942.

Hamilton, Major C.R.F. Interview of 14 February 1984 regarding Letitia and Eva Hamilton.

Hamilton, Eva & Letitia. Private papers.

Haverty, Thomas. Last will and testament, 1911. Dublin, Public Records Office.

Henry, Grace. Private papers, the library, TCD, MS 7438A.

Henry, Paul. Private papers, the library, TCD, MSS 7434/2; 7434/20A.

———. 'As I See It'. Script of a radio broadcast, BBC Northern Ireland, 29 March 1938.

———. 'Painting in Ireland'. Script of a radio broadcast, BBC Northern Ireland Home Service, 7 January 1941.

Herkner, Professor F. Private papers; undated letter of September 1985; interview of 28 November 1985.

Hewitt, John. Interviews of 16 October and 11 November 1980.

Hinkson, Alec. Interview of 4 May 1982 regarding his mother, Deirdre McDonagh.

Holden, William. Letter of 20 May 1985; interview of 9 October 1985 regarding Lady Beatrice Glenavy.

Hugh Lane Municipal Gallery of Modern Art/Municipal Gallery of Modern Art, Dublin, archives.

Hume, Mrs. Hilary. Interview of 27 May 1981 regarding her mother, Lucy Carrington Wertheim.

Irish Exhibition of Living Art. Minutes books of committee meetings; general papers 1943–9.

Irish Free State. Statutory Rules & Orders. *Royal Hibernian Academy (Adoption of Charter) Order, 1940, No.331.* Dublin: Stationery Office, 1940.

Irish Free State. State Paper Office (file S 4 296 A), Government Minutes: 11 May 1944, NAI, G3/9, p. 227.

Johnson, Nevill. Interview of 30 September 1980; letter of 14 October 1980.

Keating, John. Letter of 2 May 1932 to Minister of Education, Irish Free State. State Paper Office, file S 3458.

———. Letter of 8 July 1975 (UM archives).

Kernoff, Harry. Private papers, NLI, MSS 19,402, 20,918(ii); NGI, MS.

Kernoff, Miss Lina. Interview of 1 November 1984 regarding her brother, Harry Kernoff.

Kilkenny Technical College. Letter of 13 May 1986 from the principal regarding Christopher Campbell.

King, Cecil. Interview of 1 November 1980.

Knee, Mrs. Eileen. Letter of 26 February 1982; interview of 8 March 1983 regarding Dublin Sketching Club.

Kungl. Akademien Für De Fria Konsterna, Stockholm. Letter of 18 September 1985 from the registrar regarding Laurence Campbell.

Lancing College, Sussex. Register of pupils, 1927.

Le Brocquy, Louis. Letters of 2 July 1975 (UM archives), 16 November 1980, 2 May 1982, 20 April 1984.

Leonard, Mark. Interview of 25 September 1986 regarding Albert Power.

MacCann, Mrs. Mercy. Interview of 30 May 1980 regarding her husband, George MacCann.

McCord, Mrs. J.D. (née Elizabeth Clements). Interview of 17 June 1980.

MacGonigal, Ciarán. Interviews of 28 October 1980 and 2 October 1982 regarding his father, Maurice MacGonigal.

MacGreevy, Thomas. Private papers, the library, TCD, MSS 8002–7.

McGuinness, Norah. Interview of 30 October 1980.

McMillan, Mrs. P. Interview of 13 June 1985 regarding her uncle, James Sleator.

Mansfield, Edward L. Letter of 21 February 1984.

Meally, Victor. Letter of 19 November 1980; interviews of 9 December 1980 and 10 February 1981 regarding the White Stag Group.

Metropolitan School of Art, Dublin. Register of students.

Mitchell, Mrs. Heloise. Interview of 31 March 1981 regarding Doreen Vanston.

Moffet, Margot. Letters of 22 June and 28 December 1943 to Patrick Scott.

Murnaghan, Miss Lena. Interviews of 19 July and 30 August 1985 regarding her uncle, Leo Whelan.

Murphy, Mrs. Maighread. Interview of 29 October 1985 regarding her husband, Séamus Murphy, and her father, Joseph Higgins.

Nicholls, Nick. Letter of 1 September 1982; interview of 23 June 1984.

Nicholson, Miss. Interview of 23 January 1986 regarding her uncle, J.H. Craig.

O'Brien, Dr. Brendan. Interviews of 15 November and 13 December 1983 regarding his father, Dermod O'Brien.

O'Leary, Liam. Interviews of 10 February and 9 June 1981 regarding Phyllis Teale (née Hayward).

O'Súilleabháin, Donal. Interview of 17 January 1984 regarding John Keating and the Electricity Supply Board.

Potter, Mrs. Dorothy Berry. Letter of 12 April 1976 regarding Emily Grace Henry (UM archives).

Power, May and James. Interview of 16 January 1986 regarding their father, Albert Power.

Purser, Mrs. Betty H. Interview of 2 February 1982 regarding her sister, Mainie Jellett.

Purser, Sarah. Private papers, NLI, MS 10,201.

Quinn, John. John Quinn Memorial Collection, Rare Books and Manuscripts Division, The New York Public Library, Astor, Lennox and Tilden Foundations.

Rakoczi, Basil. Private papers.

Robinson, Jacqueline. Interviews of 25 May 1981, July 1984 and 6 June 1985 regarding Basil Rakoczi.

Royal College of Physicians of Ireland. Letter of 9 March 1981 regarding Dr. H.A.C. Ingouville-Williams.

Royal Dublin Society. Records, Taylor Art Scholarships, 1920–49.

Royal Hibernian Academy of Arts. *Charter, Statutes & Bye-Laws.* Dublin, 1873.

————. Letter of 10 October 1939 to Department of the Taoiseach. Dublin, State Paper Office, file S9 913.

Salkeld, Cecil ffrench. Private papers.

Scott, Dr. Michael. Interview of 30 October 1980.

Scott, Patrick. Interviews of 28 October 1980, 9 June and 20 October 1981.

Sheehy, Mrs. A. and Sheehy, Ms. Jeanne. Interview of 13 April 1982.

Sheppard, Miss Cathleen. Interview of 16 October 1984 regarding her father, Oliver Sheppard.

Slator, C.J. Interview of 20 May 1985 regarding James Sleator.

Stewart, Mrs. Melanie. Interview of 27 September 1985.

Teale, Phyllis. Letters of 17 November and 22 December 1980; 27 December 1981.

————. Tape recorded interview with Liam O'Leary, Esq., 20 July 1977.

Thomas Haverty Trust. Scheme for the administration of the Thomas Haverty Trust, Saorstát Éireann, High Court of Justice, 1928—No.5169, filed 21 October 1929 and later amended 29 June 1936 and 12 June 1950.

Trench, C.E.F. Interviews of 1 December 1981 and 19 January 1982 regarding his wife, Bea Orpen.

Turner, John. Interview of 10 June 1980.

Ulster Museum archives.

University of Cambridge. College Archives; Records, Jesus College.

Ussher, Arland. Private papers, the library, TCD, MS 9088.

Ussher, Mrs. Margaret. Interview of 2 February 1982 regarding her husband, Arland Ussher.

Vanston, Doreen. Letter of 1 December 1980; interview of 1 December 1981.

Walker, Mrs. Dorothy. Interview of 9 June 1981.

Wallace, Alec. Interview of 18 April 1981 regarding the White Stag Group.

Watercolour Society of Ireland. Minutes of meetings of committee, 1920–50; archives.

Wertheim, Mrs. Lucy Carrington. Private papers.

White, Dr. James. Interviews of 20 October 1981, 29 March and 19 April 1983.

————. Evie Hone. Unpublished MS, c.1980–2.

Yeats, Anne. Interviews of 19 January and 6 April 1982.

(ii) Contemporary Exhibition Catalogues

(Chronological listing. All venues were in Dublin unless stated otherwise):-

Dublin Sketching Club, *Catalogue of the First Public Exhibition of Sketches & Studies held in aid of The Artists' General Benevolent Institution.* Leinster Hall, April 1876.

A Loan Collection of Modern Paintings. Leinster Hall, April 1899.

A Loan Collection of Pictures by Nathaniel Hone, R.H.A. and John Butler Yeats, R.H.A. 6 St. Stephen's Green, October–November 1901.

Exhibition of Pictures presented to the City of Dublin to form the nucleus of a Gallery of Modern Art, also pictures lent by the executors of the late Mr. J. Staats Forbes and others. RHA, November 1904.

Exhibition of Modern Paintings. BMAG, April–May 1906.

Works by Post-Impressionist Painters. United Arts Club, 44 St. Stephen's Green, January–February 1911.

Manet and the Post-Impressionists. Grafton Galleries, London. November 1910– January 1911.

Loan Exhibition of Modern Paintings & Early British Water Colours. BMAG, August–September 1911.

Modern French Pictures. United Arts Club, March 1912.

Irish Art. Whitechapel Art Gallery, London, May–June 1913.

Dublin Sketching Club. Catalogues of annual exhibitions 1920–50.

RHA. Catalogues of annual exhibitions 1920–50.

Ulster Academy of Arts. Catalogues of annual exhibitions 1920–50.

Watercolour Society of Ireland. Catalogues of annual exhibitions 1920–50.

I, Internationale Kunstausstellung Dusseldorf. Dusseldorf, 1922.

Exhibition of Paintings & Drawings by Evie S. Hone and Mainie H. Jellett. 7 St. Stephen's Green, June 1924.

Exposition d'Art Irlandais, Musée d'Art Ancien, Brussels, May–June 1930.

Landscapes, Flowers, Drawings by C. Edward Gribbon. Daniel Egan's Gallery, 38 St. Stephen's Green, January 1932.

Ulster Unit: Exhibition of Contemporary Art. Locksley Hall, the Carlton, Belfast, December 1934.

Grace Henry, Doreen Vanston de Padilla, Cecil Salkeld, C. Edward Gribbon. Daniel Egan's Gallery, 38 St. Stephen's Green, February–March 1935.

Thomas Haverty Trust. Catalogues of quinquennial exhibitions, 1935–50.

Loan and Cross-section Exhibition of contemporary Paintings. Contemporary Picture Galleries, 5 South Leinster Street, October 1939.

White Stag Group. Exhibition. 30 Upper Mount Street, October 1940.

————. *Exhibition of Paintings.* 30 Upper Mount Street, February 1941.

————. *Exhibition.* 30 Upper Mount Street, November 1941.

In Theatre Street. Contemporary Picture Galleries, 133 Lower Baggot Street, November–December 1942.

White Stag Group. *Exhibition of Watercolours.* 6 Lower Baggot Street, April 1943.

————. *Stephen Gilbert, Kenneth Hall, Basil Rakoczi, Patrick Scott, Doreen Vanston.* 6 Lower Baggot Street, April 1943.

————. *Nick Nicholls.* 6 Lower Baggot Street, May 1943.

Irish Exhibition of Living Art. Catalogues of exhibitions, 1943–50.

Oils & Watercolours by Gerard Dillon & Daniel O'Neill. Contemporary Picture Galleries, December 1943.

Works of Living Irish Artists (Series I). CEMA, Northern Ireland, touring exhibition, 1943–4.

White Stag Group. *Exhibition of Subjective Art.* 6 Lower Baggot Street. January 1944.

George Campbell, *Exhibition of Paintings & Drawings.* Mol's Gallery, Belfast, February–March 1944.

White Stag Group. *Paintings by Patrick Scott.* 6 Lower Baggot Street, November–December 1944.

————. *Paintings of Birds and Fishes by Kenneth Hall.* 6 Lower Baggot Street, January–February 1945.

Belfast Commentary. Artist's International Association, Northern Ireland Affiliated Group, BMAG, March 1945.

White Stag Group. *Young Irish Painters.* Arcade Gallery, 15 Royal Arcade, Old Bond Street, London, April–May 1945.

————. *Nick Nicholls, Ann Miller.* 6 Lower Baggot Street, May 1945.

Jack B. Yeats. National Loan Exhibition, National College of Art, June–July 1945.

Paintings by George F. Campbell. Waddington Galleries, March–April 1946.

Thomas Davis and the Young Ireland Movement: Exhibition of Pictures of Irish Historical Interest. National College of Art, August 1946.

School of London. Waddington Galleries, March–April 1947.

French Exhibition. Waddington Galleries, May 1947.

Four Ulster Painters. Heal's Mansard Gallery, London, May–June 1948.

Exhibition of Paintings by Allen Adams and Gerard Dillon. CEMA, Belfast, December 1949.

Contemporary Irish Paintings. Providence, Rhode Island; Boston, Massachusetts; Ottawa, March–June 1950.

May Guinness Memorial Exhibition. Dawson Hall, April 1956.

SECONDARY SOURCES
(i) List of Newspapers, Periodicals and Journals

(Short articles and reviews from these sources, which are given in detail in the notes to each chapter, are omitted here):–

Art History
The Bell
Commentary
Daily Express
Eire-Ireland
Evening Mail
Freeman's Journal
Icarus
Irish Arts Review
Irish Independent
Irish Press
Irish Rosary
Irish Times
The Klaxon

The Leader
Magazine of Art
News Letter
The Observer
The Standard
The Studio
The Times
Unity
Writing.

Belfast Telegraph
Capuchin Annual
Cubism: Recovery of a Tradition
Dublin Magazine
Envoy
Father Mathew Record
Horizon
Ireland To-Day
Irish Builder
Irish News
Irish Review and Annual
Irish Tatler & Sketch
Irish Statesman
Journal, Co. Kildare
Archaeological Society
The Listener
New Coterie
Northern Whig
Personality Parade
Studies
Sunday Independent
To-Morrow
University Review

(ii) Articles in Periodicals and Journals

'A Contemporary Irish Master: Laurence Campbell R.H.A. at work on his statue of Seán Heuston',
Capuchin Annual, 1945–6, pp.337–52.

Allen, Mairin. 'Contemporary Irish Artists IX—Albert G. Power, R.H.A.', Father Mathew Record,
February 1942, pp.3–4, 6.

———. 'Contemporary Irish Artists XV—Grace Henry', Father Mathew Record, November
1942, p.4.

———. 'Contemporary Irish Artists XVIII—Maurice MacGonigal', Father Mathew Record,
May 1943, p.6.

———. 'Irish Post-Impressionism', Father Mathew Record, November 1943, p.10.

———. 'Jerome Connor—one', Capuchin Annual, 1963, pp.347–68.

———. 'Jerome Connor—two', Capuchin Annual, 1964, pp.353–69.

———. 'Jerome Connor—three', Capuchin Annual, 1965, pp.365–87.

Anderson, Ronald. 'Whistler in Dublin, 1884', Irish Arts Review, vol.3, autumn 1986, pp.45–51.

Barrett, Cyril. 'Irish Nationalism and Art', Studies, winter 1975, pp.393–409.

Bodkin, Thomas. 'The Art of Miss Norah McGuinness', Studio, September 1925, pp.168–71.

Brissac, Noelle. 'Contemporary Irish Painters (3): Thurloe Conolly', Envoy, vol.1. February 1950,
pp.32–6.

Brooke, Peter. 'Space Time Rhythms/Gleizes: Laws of Painting', Cubism: Recovery of a Tradition,
winter 1983–4, pp.1ff.

Collins, Patrick. 'George Campbell', Envoy, January 1950, pp.44–50.

Coster, Geraldine. 'With Our Artists—No.5: Mr. Maurice MacGonagle [sic], R.H.A.', Personality
Parade, September 1946, p.16.

Denson, Alan. 'W.J. Leech, R.H.A.: A Great Irish Artist (1881–1968)', Capuchin Annual, 1974,
pp.119–27.

Dillon, Gerard. 'The Artist Speaks', Envoy, February 1951, pp.39–40.

Dorman, Sean. 'Suicide Among the Artists', Writing, summer 1980.

Dowling, John. 'Poor Wine, but a Lovely Bottle', Ireland To-Day, vol.1, October 1936, pp.51–3.

Duncan, Ellen. 'Modern French Pictures at the United Arts Club', Irish Review, vol.11, May 1912,
pp.164–6.

Ethelston, John. 'Joseph Higgins Sculptor 1885–1925', Capuchin Annual, 1952, pp.148–57.

Fallon, Brian. 'Irish painting in the fifties', Arts in Ireland, vol.3, n.d., pp.24–36.

Goldsmith, Maurice. 'Design Research Unit: An English Design Co-Operative', Graphis, vol.4,
1948, pp.258–61, 301–2.

Hartigan, Marianne. 'The Commercial Design Career of Norah McGuinness', Irish Arts Review,
vol.3, autumn 1986, pp.23–5.

Hewitt, John. 'Colin Middleton', *The Bell*, vol.4, August 1942, pp.338–9.

Jellett, Mainie. 'The R.H.A. and Youth', *Commentary*, May 1942, pp.5,7.

Keating, H.R.F. 'The Art of Nevill Johnson', *Icarus*, vol.2, May 1952, pp.88–92.

Kernoff, Harry. 'Myself and Painting', *Commentary*, vol.1, February 1942, pp.1–2.

Le Brocquy, Louis. 'Music in Painting', *Dublin Magazine*, October–December 1941, pp.63–6.

Longley, Michael. 'Colin Middleton', *Dublin Magazine*, vol.6, autumn/winter 1967, pp.40–3.

MacGall, Rex. 'Basil Rakoczi Interviewed', *Commentary*, March 1946. pp.3–4, 8.

MacGreevy, Thomas. 'Picasso, Mamie [sic] Jellett & Dublin Criticism', *The Klaxon*, winter 1923–4, pp.23–7.

————. 'Fifty Years of Irish Painting 1900–1950', *Capuchin Annual*, 1949, pp.497–512.

Moffett, Margot. 'Young Irish Painters', *Horizon*, April 1945, pp.261–7.

Nash, J.M. 'The Nature of Cubism: A study of conflicting explanations', *Art History*, vol.3, December 1980, pp.435–47.

O'Beirne, J.J.R. 'A Coming Irish Artist: The Work of John Keating', *Irish Rosary*, vol.21, 1917, pp.571–7.

O'Doherty, Brian. 'Paul Henry—The Early Years', *University Review*, II, 1960, pp.25–32.

O'Grady, John M. 'Sarah Purser 1848–1943', *Capuchin Annual*, 1977, pp.89–104.

Read, Herbert. 'On Subjective Art', *The Bell*, February 1944.

————. 'Art and Crisis', *Horizon*, May 1944, pp.336–50.

Rynne, Stephen. 'Tea with Jack B. Yeats 1940', *Eire-Ireland*, vol.7, 1972.

Salkeld, Cecil. 'The Principles of Painting', *To-Morrow*, vol.1, August-September 1924, pp.3, 5.

————. 'Daniel O'Neill: A Critical Appreciation', *Envoy*, vol.1, December 1949, pp.31–43.

————. 'The Progress of a Painter', *The Bell*, vol.14, no.6, pp.69–72.

Sheehy, Anna. 'Cecil Ffrench Salkeld', *The Bell*, vol.2, June 1941, pp.48–51.

Sheehy, Edward. 'Contemporary Irish Painters (5): Colin Middleton', *Envoy*, vol.2, April 1950, pp.32–40.

Wynne, Michael. 'The Irish Archaeological Inspiration of Evie Hone', *Journal of the County Kildare Archaeological Society*, vol.14, 1964–70, pp.247–53.

(iii) General Works

A Concise Catalogue of the Drawings, Paintings & Sculptures in the Ulster Museum. Belfast: UM, 1986.

Academy of Christian Art. *Journal*, vol.1, n.d. [c.1937].

Alley, Ronald. *Catalogue of the Tate Gallery's Collection of Modern Art other than works by British Artists*. London: Tate Gallery & Sotheby Parke Bernet, 1981.

————. 'William Scott', in the exhibition catalogue, *William Scott*, Arts Council of Northern Ireland and An Chomhairle Ealaíon, UM and subsequent tour to Dublin and Edinburgh, June–November 1986.

Am Anfang: Das Junge Rheinland. Exhibition catalogue, Dusseldorf, 1985.

Anglesea, Martyn. *The Royal Ulster Academy of Arts*. Belfast: Royal Ulster Academy of Arts, 1981.

An Tóstal, *Irish Painting 1903–1953: An Anthology Drawn from the Municipal Gallery & from Private Collections in the City of Dublin*. Exhibition catalogue, MGMA, April–July 1953.

Arnold, Bruce. *Mainie Jellett 1897–1944*. Exhibition catalogue, Dublin, Neptune Gallery, 1974.

————. *A Concise History of Irish Art*. London: Thames & Hudson, revised ed., 1977.

————. *Christopher Campbell 1908–1972*. Exhibition catalogue, Dublin, Neptune Gallery, 1977.

————. *Orpen: Mirror to an Age*. London: Jonathan Cape, 1981.

Bailey, Kenneth C. *A History of Trinity College, Dublin 1892–1945*. Dublin: University Press, 1947.

Baron, Wendy. *Sickert*. London: Phaidon, 1973.

————. *The Camden Town Group*. London: Scolar Press, 1979.

Barrett, Cyril. *Irish Art 1943–1973*. Exhibition catalogue, Cork, ROSC Teoranta, Crawford Art Gallery, 1980.

————. 'Visual Arts & Society 1900–70', first draft for chapter on art in Ireland, *A New History of Ireland*, publication pending.

Basset's Guide to Tipperary. 1889.

Behan, Beatrice. *My Life with Brendan*. London: Leslie Frewin, 1973.

Bell, Quentin. *Virginia Woolf: A Biography*, vol.1, 1882–1912. London: Triad/Paladin, 1976.

Bell, Sam Hanna; Robb, Nesca; Hewitt, John (eds.) *The Arts in Ulster: A Symposium*. London: Harrap, 1951.

Bertram, Anthony. *Paul Nash: The Portrait of an Artist*. London: Faber & Faber, 1955.

Bevan, R.A. *Robert Bevan 1865–1925: A Memoir by his Son*. London: Studio Vista, 1965.

Black, Eileen. *Paintings, Sculptures and Bronzes in the Collection of The Belfast Harbour Commissioners*. Belfast, 1983.

Bodkin, Thomas. 'The Present Position of Art in Ireland', *Ireland To-Day*. London, 1913, pp.113–20.

————. 'The Condition and Needs of Art in Ireland', W.G. Fitz-Gerald (ed.), *The Voice of Ireland. Dublin,* 1923, pp.492–7.

————. *Hugh Lane and his Pictures.* Dublin: Stationery Office, 1932 and later eds.

————. 'Modern Irish Art', *Saorstát Eireann: Irish Free State: Official Handbook.* Dublin: Talbot Press, 1932.

————, (introduction by). *Twelve Irish Artists.* Dublin: Waddington Publications, 1940.

————. *Report on the Arts in Ireland.* Dublin: Stationery Office, 1949; 2nd ed. 1953.

Brady, Rev. John. A *Short History of the Parishes of Mullingar and Navan.* Navan: Meath Chronicle, 1936.

Brown, Terence. *Ireland: A Social and Cultural History 1922–79.* London: Fontana, 1981.

Bullen, J.B. (ed.) *Post-Impressionists in England.* London: Routledge, 1988.

Burke's Irish Family Records. London: Burke's Peerage, 1976.

Burleigh, Marian. *George Russell (AE)—The Painter of the Irish Renaissance.* Ph.D. dissertation, New York University, 1978.

Campbell, Julian. *Irish Artists in France and Belgium 1850–1914.* Unpublished Ph.D. dissertation, University of Dublin, 1980.

————. *The Irish Impressionists: Irish Artists in France and Belgium 1850–1914.* Exhibition catalogue, Dublin: NGI, 1984.

————. *Mary Swanzy HRHA (1882–1978).* Exhibition catalogue, Pyms Gallery, London, 1986.

Campbell College Register, 1894–1954. Belfast.

Causey, Andrew. *Paul Nash.* Oxford: Clarendon Press, 1980.

Celtic Splendour. Exhibition catalogue, Pyms Gallery, London, April–May 1985.

CEMA, Belfast. Annual Reports, 1943–50.

Chamot, Mary; Farr, Dennis; Butlin, Martin (eds.) Tate Gallery catalogue, *The modern British paintings, drawings and sculpture.* 2 vols. London: Oldbourne Press, 1964.

Charles Lamb R.H.A. 1893–1964. Memorial exhibition catalogue, Dublin, MGMA, April 1969.

Citroën, Bernard. *Rakoczi Le Multiple.* Paris: published privately, 1953.

Clarke, Kenneth. *The Other Half: A Self-Portrait.* London: John Murray, 1977.

Colin Middleton, R.H.A. Sale catalogue, Christie's, London, 4 October 1985.

Cronin, Anthony. *Dead as Doornails.* Swords: Poolbeg Press, 1980.

Crookshank, Anne. *Norah McGuinness.* A retrospective exhibition catalogue, TCD, 1968.

————. *Irish Sculpture from 1600.* Dublin: Department of Foreign Affairs, 1984.

————. 'Portraits of Irish Medicine', O'Brien, Eoin; Crookshank, Anne; Wolstenholme, Gordon, *A Portrait of Irish Medicine.* Dublin: Ward River Press, 1984, pp.1–52.

Crookshank, Anne & Glin, The Knight of. *The Painters of Ireland c.1660–1920.* London: Barrie & Jenkins, 1979.

Dawson, George. *Paul Henry 1876–1958.* Exhibition catalogue, Dublin, TCD, 1973.

De Breffny, Brian (ed.) *Ireland: A Cultural Encyclopaedia.* London: Thames & Hudson, 1983.

Denson, Alan. *An Irish Artist: W.J. Leech R.H.A. (1881–1968).* Kendal: published privately, 1968.

————. *John Hughes: Sculptor.* Kendal: published privately, 1969.

Dodgson, C. *Contemporary English Woodcuts.* London: Duckworth, 1922.

Dorman, Sean. *Limelight over the Liffey.* Fowey, Cornwall: Raffeen Press, 1983.

Dubliners: portraits by Harry Kernoff R.H.A. Exhibition catalogue, Dublin, Godolphin Gallery, 1975.

Dunlop, Ian & Orienti, Sandra. *The Complete Paintings of Cézanne.* London: Penguin Books, 1985.

Eates, Margot. *Paul Nash: The Master of an Image 1889–1946.* London: John Murray, 1973.

Ecclesiastical Records 1909. London, India Office Library.

Emmons, Robert. *The Life and Opinions of Walter Richard Sickert.* London: Faber & Faber, 1941.

Farr, Dennis. *English Art 1870–1940.* Oxford: Clarendon Press, 1978.

Friends of the National Collections of Ireland. Annual Reports, 1924–52.

Frost, Stella (ed.) *A Tribute to Evie Hone and Mainie Jellett.* Dublin: 1957.

Fry, Edward. *Cubism.* London: Thames & Hudson, 1966.

German Woodcut in the 20th Century. Exhibition catalogue (Institute for Foreign Cultural Ralations, Stuttgart), UM, 1986.

Gleizes, Albert. 'Hommage à Mainie Jellett', MacCarvill, Eileen (ed.) *Mainie Jellett: The Artist's Vision.* Dundalk: Dundalgan Press, 1958.

Gleizes, Albert & Metzinger, Jean. *Du Cubisme.* Paris, 1912. English translation in Herbert, R.L. (ed.), *Modern Artists on Art.* New Jersey: Prentice-Hall, 1964, pp.1–18.

Glenavy, Beatrice, Lady. *Today we will only Gossip.* London: Constable, 1964.

Golding, John. *Cubism: A History and an Analysis 1907–1914.* London: Faber & Faber, 1959, revised ed. 1968.

Grafik des deutschen Expressionismus. Exhibition catalogue (Institute for Foreign Cultural Relations, Stuttgart), UM, 1985.

Gregory, (Augusta) Lady. *Hugh Lane's Life & Achievement with some Account of the Dublin Galleries*. London: John Murray, 1921.

Haftmann, Werner. *Painting in the Twentieth Century*. 2 vols. London: Lund Humphries, 1965.

Halpin, Dymphna. *The Breaker-Out: Jack B. Yeats (1871–1957): A Study of his change in Style*. Unpublished M.Litt. dissertation, University of Dublin, 1984.

Hamilton, G.H. *Painting and Sculpture in Europe 1880–1940*. Harmondsworth: Penguin Books, 1972.

Harbison, Peter; Potterton, Homan; Sheehy, Jeanne. *Irish art and architecture from prehistory to the present*. London: Thames & Hudson, 1978.

Harrison, Charles. *English Art and Modernism 1900–1939*. London: Allen Lane, 1981.

Harry Kernoff: a selection of Dublin paintings. Exhibition catalogue, Dublin, Godolphin Gallery, 1974.

Henry, Paul. *An Irish Portrait*. London: Batsford, 1951.

—————. *Further Reminiscences*. Edited by Edward Hickey. Belfast: Blackstaff Press, 1973.

Hewitt, John. 'Under forty: some Ulster Artists', *Now in Ulster*, Belfast: published privately, 1944, pp.13–35.

—————. *Colin Middleton*. Belfast: Arts Council of Northern Ireland & An Chomhairle Ealaion, 1976.

—————. *Art in Ulster: 1*. Belfast: Blackstaff Press, 1977.

Illustrated Summary Catalogue of Paintings. Dublin: NGI, 1981.

Ingouville-Williams, Herbrand (introduction by). *Three Painters*. Dublin: Three Candles, 1945.

Irish Art Handbook. Dublin: Cahill & Co., 1943.

Irish Renascence. Exhibition catalogue, London, Pyms Gallery, 1986.

Jamison, Kenneth. 'Painting and Sculpture', Longley, M. (ed.), *Causeway: The Arts in Ulster*. Belfast: Arts Council of Northern Ireland, 1971, pp.43–70.

Jellett, Mainie. 'An Approach to Painting', *Irish Art Handbook*. Dublin: Cahill & Co., 1943, pp.17–20.

—————. 'A Word on Irish Art', MacCarvill, Eileen (ed.), *Mainie Jellett: The Artist's Vision*. Dundalk: Dundalgan Press, 1958, pp.103–6.

Jocelyn Chewett sculpteur: son œuvre abstraite 1949–1979. Exhibition catalogue, Paris, Centre Culturel Canadien, April–May 1981.

Johnson, Nevill. *The Other Side of Six*. Dublin: Academy Press, 1983.

Keating, John. 'What is a Portrait?', *Irish Art: A Volume of Articles & Illustrations*. Dublin: Parkside Press, 1944, pp.18–20.

Keating and the ESB. Exhibition catalogue, Dublin, Electricity Supply Board at the RHA, July 1985.

Kennedy, Brian. *Ulster Museum, A Catalogue of the Permanent Collection:1—British Art 1900–1937 including nineteenth century Irish paintings and other objects from the Sir Robert Lloyd Patterson Collection*. Belfast: UM, 1982.

—————. *Paul Nietsche 1885–1950*. Exhibition catalogue, Arts Council of Northern Ireland, 1984.

—————. 'Paul Nietsche (1885–1950): a Russian painter in Belfast', *Irish Slavonic Studies*, no.5, Belfast The Queen's University, 1984, pp.115–23.

—————. *A Catalogue of the Permanent Collection:2—Twentieth Century Sculpture*. Belfast: UM, 1988.

—————. *James Sinton Sleator P.R.H.A. 1885–1950*. Exhibition catalogue, Armagh County Museum, 1989.

—————. *Elizabeth Rivers 1903–1964: A Retrospective View*. Exhibition catalogue, Gorry Gallery Dublin, 1989.

—————. 'Irish landscape painting in a political setting, 1922–48', M. Hill & S. Barber (eds.), *Aspects of Irish Studies*. Belfast: Institute of Irish Studies, The Queen's University of Belfast, 1990.

Kennedy, Brian P. *Dreams and Responsibilities: The Arts in Independent Ireland*. Dublin: Arts Council, 1990.

Kennedy, S. B. *Irish Art and Modernism 1920–1949*. Unpublished Ph.D.dissertation. 2 vols. University of Dublin, 1987.

Lambert, Jean-Clarence. *Cobra*. London: Sotheby Publications, 1983.

Le Harivel, Adrian (ed.) *Illustrated Summary Catalogue of Drawings, Watercolours and Miniatures*. Dublin: NGI, 1983.

Leventhal, A.J. 'The Living Art Exhibition', *Irish Art: A Volume of Articles & Illustrations*. Dublin: Parkside Press, 1944, pp.82–93.

Lilly, Marjorie. *Sickert: The Painter and his Circle*. London, *1971*.

Louis le Brocquy: A Retrospective Selection of Oil Paintings 1939–1966. Exhibition catalogue, Dublin, MGMA and Belfast, UM, November 1966–January 1967.

Lyons, F.S.L. *Ireland Since the Famine.* London: Fontana, revised ed. 1973.

Mainie Jellett 1897–1944. Exhibition catalogue, Neptune Gallery, Dublin, September–October 1974.

MacCarvill, Eileen (ed.) *Mainie Jellett: The Artist's Vision.* Dundalk: Dundalgan Press, 1958.

McConkey, Kenneth. *Sir John Lavery R.A. 1856–1941.* Exhibition catalogue, Edinburgh & London, Fine Art Society; Belfast, UM; Dublin, NGI, August 1984–March 1985.

————. A *Free Spirit: Irish Art 1860–1960.* London: Antique Collectors' Club & Pyms Gallery, 1990.

MacGreevy, Thomas. *Jack B. Yeats: An Appreciation and an Interpretation.* Dublin: Waddington Publications, 1945.

MacLiammóir, Michael & Boland, Eavan. *W.B. Yeats & his World.* London: Thames & Hudson, 1971.

Marle, Judy. 'Fragments of an Appriciation of the work of F.E. McWilliam', exhibition catalogue, *F.E. McWilliam,* Belfast, Arts Council of Northern Ireland and An Chomhairle Ealaíon at the UM, and subsequent tour to Dublin and Cork, April–August 1981.

M.C.B. Register. (Methodist College). Belfast, 1985.

Meyer, F. *Marc Chagall: Life & Work.* London: 1964.

Middleton, Colin. Soundtrack from the film, *The Trace of a Thorn.* Arts Council of Northern Ireland, 1983.

Millin, S. Shannon. *Art in Belfast.* Belfast: Northern Whig, 1903.

Moore, George. *Modern Painting.* London: Walter Scott, 1893, enlarged ed. 1898.

Municipal Art Gallery, Dublin: Illustrated Catalogue. Dublin: Dublin Corporation, 1908.

Municipal Gallery of Modern Art & Civic Museum. Dublin, 1933.

MGMA. *Illustrated Catalogue.* Dublin: Dublin Corporation, 1958.

Murphy, Seamus. *Stone Mad.* London: Routledge & Kegan Paul, 1966.

Murphy, William M. *Prodical Father: The Life of John Butler Yeats (1839–1922).* Ithaca & London: Cornell University Press, 1978.

NGI, *Acquisitions 1982–83.* Dublin: NGI, 1984.

————. *Acquisitions 1984–86.* Dublin: NGI, 1986.

Obituaries from The Times 1971–75. Reading: Newspaper Archive Developments, 1978.

O'Connor, Frank. *My Father's Son.* London: Pan Books, 1971.

O'Connor, Ulick. *Brendan Behan.* London: Black Swan, 1985.

O'Grady, J. *Sarah Henrietta Purser.* Unpublished Ph.D. dissertation, University College, Dublin, 1974.

O'Neill, Daniel. *Loan Exhibition of Paintings 1944–1952.* BMAG, March–April 1952.

Oireachtas art exhibition. Exhibition catalogue 1977

Ormsby, Elizabeth. *An Introduction .to Psychological Analysis.* London: published privately, c.1938.

O'Sullivan, Seán. 'What is a Portrait?', *Irish Art: A Volume of Articles & Illustrations.* Dublin: Parkside Press, 1944, pp.9–11.

Patrick Scott. Exhibition catalogue, Dublin, Douglas Hyde Gallery; Belfast, UM; Cork, Crawford Art Gallery, March–August 1981.

Pennell, E.R. & J. *The Life of James McNeill Whistler.* 2 vols. London: William Heinemann, 1908.

Pevsner, Nikolaus. *Pioneers of Modern Design.* Harmondsworth: Penguin Books, 1974.

Poole, Phoebe & Orienti, Sandra. *The Complete Paintings of Manet.* Harmondsworth: Penguin Books, 1985.

Potterton, Homan. *Andrew O'Connor.* Exhibition catalogue, Dublin, TCD, 1974.

———— (introduction by). NGI, *Illustrated Summary Catalogue of Paintings.* Dublin: Gill & Macmillan, 1981.

Pyle, Hilary. *Jack B. Yeats: A Biography.* London: Routledge & Kegan Paul, 1970.

————. *Irish Art 1900–1950.* Exhibition catalogue, Cork, ROSC Teoranta, Carwford Art Gallery, December 1975–January 1976.

Read, Herbert (ed.) *Unit 1: The Modern Movement in English Architecture, Painting and Sculpture.* London: Cassell & Co., 1934.

Read, Herbert. *Paul Nash.* Harmondsworth: Penguin Books, 1944.

————. *The Philosophy of Modern Art: Collected essays by Herbert Read.* London: Faber & Faber, 1964.

Report of the Committee of Inquiry into the Work carried on by the Royal Hibernain Academy, and the Metropolitan School of Art, Dublin. Dublin & London: HMSO, Cmd. 3256, 1906.

Reynolds, John (ed.) *Statement of the Claim for the Return to Dublin of the 39 Lane Bequest Pictures now at the Tate Gallery, London.* Dublin: Dublin Corporation, 1932.

Rice, Noreen. *Gerard Dillon 1916–71*. A retrospective exhibition catalogue, Belfast, UM and Arts Council of Northern Ireland and Dublin, MGMA, November 1972–February 1973.

Robinson, Jacqueline. *Basil Ivan Rakoczi: Monographie et Catalogue Provisoir*. Paris: published privately, 1971.

Robinson, Lennox. *Palette and Plough: A pen-and-ink drawing of Dermod O'Brien, P.R.H.A.* Dublin: Browne & Nolan, 1948.

Rosenblum, Robert. *Cubism & Twentieth Century Art*. New York: Abrams, 1960, revised eds. 1966, 1977.

Roskill, Mark. *The Interpretation of Cubism*. London: Associated University Presses, 1985.

Roters, Eberhard. *Painters of the Bauhaus*. London: Zwemmer, 1969.

Royal Academy Illustrated. London, published for the Royal Academy, 1920–50.

Royal Hibernian Academy of Arts. Annual Reports, 1920–50.

Russell, George (AE). *Imaginations and Reveries*. Dublin: Maunsell & Co., 1915.

Ryan, Thomas. *Remembering How We Stood*. Dublin: Gill & Macmillan, 1975.

Sculpture in Britain Between the Wars. Exhibition catalogue, London, Fine Art Society, 1986.

Seamus Murphy 1907–1975. Exhibition catalogue, Dublin, Douglas Hyde Gallery; Cork, Crawford Art Gallery, 1983.

Shea, Patrick. *A History of the Ulster Arts Club*. Belfast: Ulster Arts Club, 1971.

Sheehy, Jeanne. *Walter Osborne*. Ballycotton, 1974.

————. *Nano Reid*. A retrospective exhibition catalogue, Dublin, MGMA and Belfast, UM, November 1974–February 1975.

————. *The Rediscovery of Ireland's Past: the Celtic Revival 1830–1930*. London: Thames & Hudson, 1980.

————. *Walter Osborne*. Exhibition catalogue, Dublin, NGI and Belfast, UM, November 1983–February 1984.

Sheringham, G. & Morrison, R. Boyd (eds.) *The Robes of Thespis: Costume Designs by Modern Artists*. London: Benn, 1928.

Shone, Richard. 'The Friday Club', *Burlington Magazine*, vol.117, May 1975, pp.279–84.

————. *Bloomsbury Portraits: Vanessa Bell, Duncan Grant and their Circle*. London: Phaidon Press, 1976.

————. *The Century of Change*. London: Phaidon Press, 1977.

Stanley Spencer R.A. Exhibition catalogue, Royal Academy, London, September–December 1980.

Stephan, Enno. *Spies in Ireland*. London, 1963.

Stephen Gilbert: Cobra Paintings 1940–1950. Exhibition catlaogue, Copenhagen, Court Gallery, October 1971.

Summary Catalogue of Prints and Sculptures. Dublin: NGI, 1988.

Thomas Haverty Trust. *Report of the Proceedings of the Thomas Haverty Trust*, Dublin, 1930–50.

Tynan, Katherine. *Twenty-five Years: Reminiscences*. London: Smith, Elder & Co., 1913.

Ulster Academy of Arts. Catalogues of exhibitions, 1930–50.

Walker, Dorothy. 'Oisin Kelly', exhibition catalogue, *The Work of Oisin Kelly Sculptor*. Arts Councils of Ireland, Belfast, UM; Dublin, Douglas Hyde Gallery; Cork, Crawford Art Gallery, March–June 1978.

————. *Louis le Brocquy*. Dublin: Ward River Press, 1981.

————. *Patrick Scott*. Exhibition catalogue, Dublin, Douglas Hyde Gallery; Belfast, UM; Cork, Crawford Art Gallery, 1981.

Walker, J. Crampton. *Irish Life & Landscape*. Dublin: n.d. [1925].

Wall, Mervyn. 'A Memoir of Arland Ussher', *The Juggler: Selection from the Journal of Arland Ussher*. Dublin: Dolmen Press, 1982, pp.9–10.

Wertheim, Lucy Carrington. *Adventure in Art*. London: Nicholson & Watson, 1947.

Whelan, Leo. 'What is a Portrait?', *Irish Art: A Volume of Articles & Illustrations*. Dublin: Parkside Press, 1944, pp.16–18.

White, James. 'Independent Painters', *Irish Art Handbook*. Dublin: Cahill & Co., 1943.

———— (ed.) *George Campbell*, Dublin, n.d. [c.1964].

————. *Jack B. Yeats 1871–1957: A Centenary Exhibition*. Exhibition catalogue, Dublin, Belfast, New York, September 1971–June 1972.

White, Terence de Vere. *A Fretful Midge*. London: Routledge & Kegan Paul, 1957.

Wildenstein, Georges. *Gauguin*. Paris: Éditions Les Beaux-Arts, 1964.

Willett, John. *The New Sobriety 1917–1933: Art and Politics in the Weimar Period*. London: Thames & Hudson, 1978.

Wilson, Judith C. *Conor 1881–1968: The life and work of an Ulster artist*. Belfast: Blackstaff Press, 1981.

Wingler, Hans-Maria. *The Bauhaus*. Cambridge, Mass.: M.I.T. Press, 1969.

Yeats, W.B. *Autobiographies: Reveries over Childhood and Youth*. London: MacMillan, 1926.
Young, A. McLaren; MacDonald, Margaret; Spencer, Robin. *The Paintings of James McNeill Whistler*. New Haven & London: Yale University Press, 1980.

(iv) Works of Reference

Bénézit, E. *Dictionnaire critique et documentaire des Peintres, Sculpteurs, Dessinateurs et Graveurs*. 8 vols. Paris: Librairie Gründ, 1960 and revised ed., 1976.
Boylan, H. *A Dictionary of Irish Biography*. Dublin: Gill & Macmillan, 1978.
Bullock, A. & Stallybrass, O. (eds.) *The Fontana Dictionary of Modern Thought*. London: Fontana, 1977.
Bullock, A. & Woodings, R.B. (eds.) *The Fontana Biographical Companion to Modern Thought*. London: Fontana, 1983.
Fitz-Simon, Christopher. *The Arts in Ireland: A Chronology*. Dublin: Gill & Macmillan, 1982.
Fleming, John; Honour, Hugh; Pevsner, Nikolaus (eds) *The Penguin Dictionary of Architecture*. Harmondsworth: Penguin Books, 1972,
Murray, Peter & Linda. *Dictionary of Art and Artists*. Harmondsworth: Penguin Books, 1960 and London: Thames & Hudson, 1965.
Osborne, Harold.(ed.) *The Oxford Companion to Art*. Oxford: Clarendon Press, 1970.
Royal Academy Exhibitors 1905–1970. 6 vols. East Ardsley: EP Publishing, 1973–82.
Scholes, Percy A. *The Oxford Companion to Music*. 10 ed. London: Oxford University Press, 1970.
Stapleton, M. (ed.) *Cambridge Guide to English Literature*. London, 1983.
Stewart, Ann. *Royal Hibernian Academy of Arts: Index of Exhibitors and their Works 1826–1979*. 2 vols. Dublin: Manton Publishing, 1985–6.
Stewart, Ann (ed.) & Kennedy, S.B. (introduction by). *Irish Art Loan Exhibitions 1765–1927*. vol.1, Dublin: Manton Publishing, 1990.
Strickland, W.G. *A Dictionary of Irish Artists*. 2 vols. Dublin: Maunsell & Co., 1913.
Thieme U. & Becker, F. *Allgemeines Lexikon der Bildenden Künstler*. 37 vols. Leipzig: E.A. Seeman.
Waters, Grant, M. *Dictionary of British Artists Working 1900–1950*. Eastbourne: Eastbourne Fine Art, 1975.

INDEX

Titles of paintings, sculptures and other works mentioned in the text are in italics; those in **bold** are reproduced

392